The Seven Deadly Sins volume 33 is a work of fiction. Names, characters, places, and incidents are the products of the author's imagination or are used fictitiously. Any resemblance to actual events, locales, or persons, living or dead, is entirely coincidental.

A Kodansha Comics Trade Paperback Original.

Published in the United States by Kodansha Comics, an imprint of Kodansha USA Publishing, LLC, New York.

Publication rights for this English edition arranged through Kodansha Ltd., Tokyo.

First published in Japan in 2018 by Kodansha Ltd., Tokyo.

ISBN 978-1-63236-797-6

Printed in the United States of America.

www.kodanshacomics.com

9 8 7 6 5 4 3 2 1

Translation: Christine Dashiell
Lettering: James Dashiell
Kodansha Comics edition cover design: Phil Balsman

A beautifully-drawn new action manga from Haruko Ichikawa, winner of the Osamu Tezuka Cultural Prize!

LAND
OF THE
LUSTROUS

In a world inhabited by crystalline life-forms called The Lustrous, every gem must fight for their life against the threat of Lunarians who would turn them into decorations. Phosphophyllite, the most fragile and brittle of gems, longs to join the battle, so when Phos is instead assigned to complete a natural history of their world, it sounds like a dull and pointless task. But this new job brings Phos into contact with Cinnabar, a gem forced to live in isolation. Can Phos's seemingly mundane assignment lead both Phos and Cinnabar to the fulfillment they desire?

THE SEVEN DEADLY SINS

nakaba suzuki presents

33

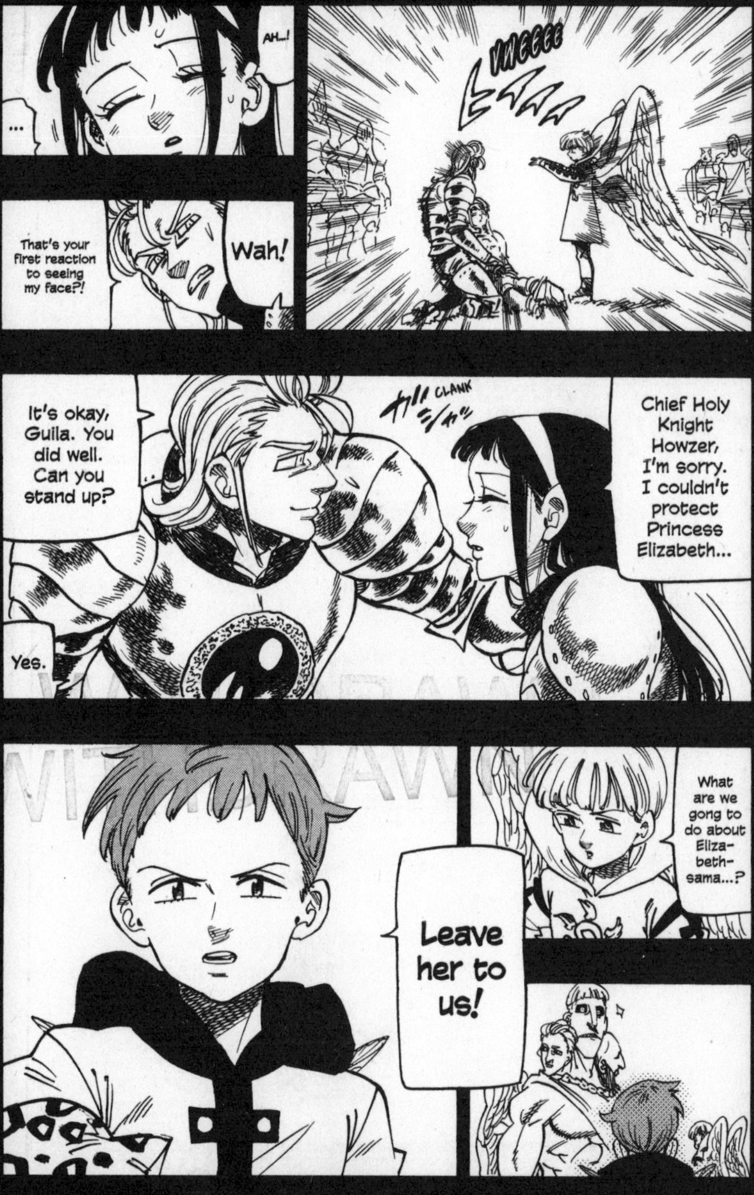

VWEEEE
AH...!
...
Wah!
That's your first reaction to seeing my face?!
Chief Holy Knight Howzer, I'm sorry. I couldn't protect Princess Elizabeth...
CLANK
It's okay, Guila. You did well. Can you stand up?
Yes.
What are we gong to do about Eliza-beth-sama...?
Leave her to us!

CONTENTS

BOAR HAT

The Seven Deadly Sins

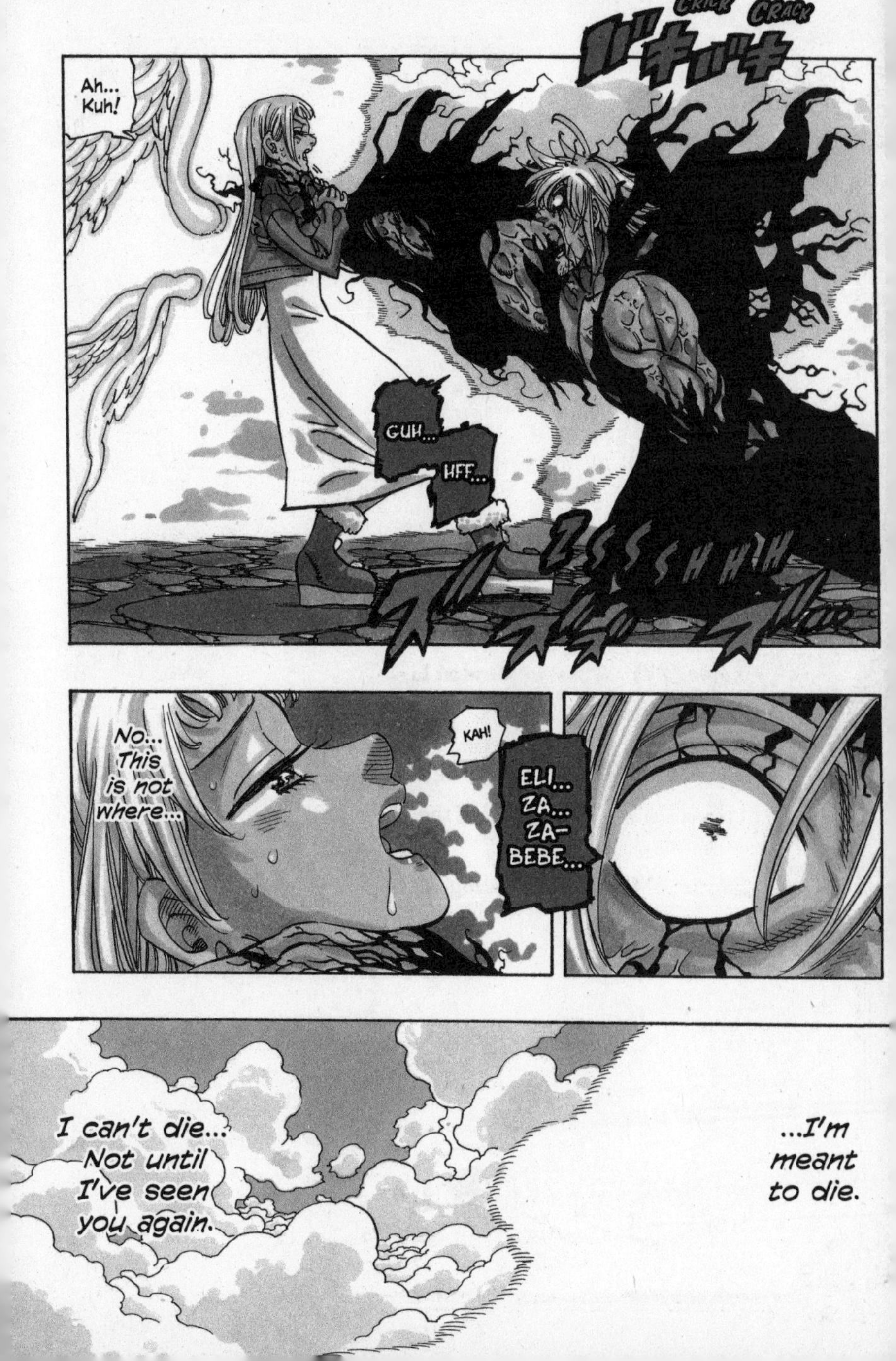
バキバキ
CRICK CRACK
ZSSSHHH
GUH... HFF...
Ah... Kuh!
ELI... ZA... ZA-BEBE...
KAH!
No... This is not where...
...I'm meant to die.
I can't die... Not until I've seen you again.

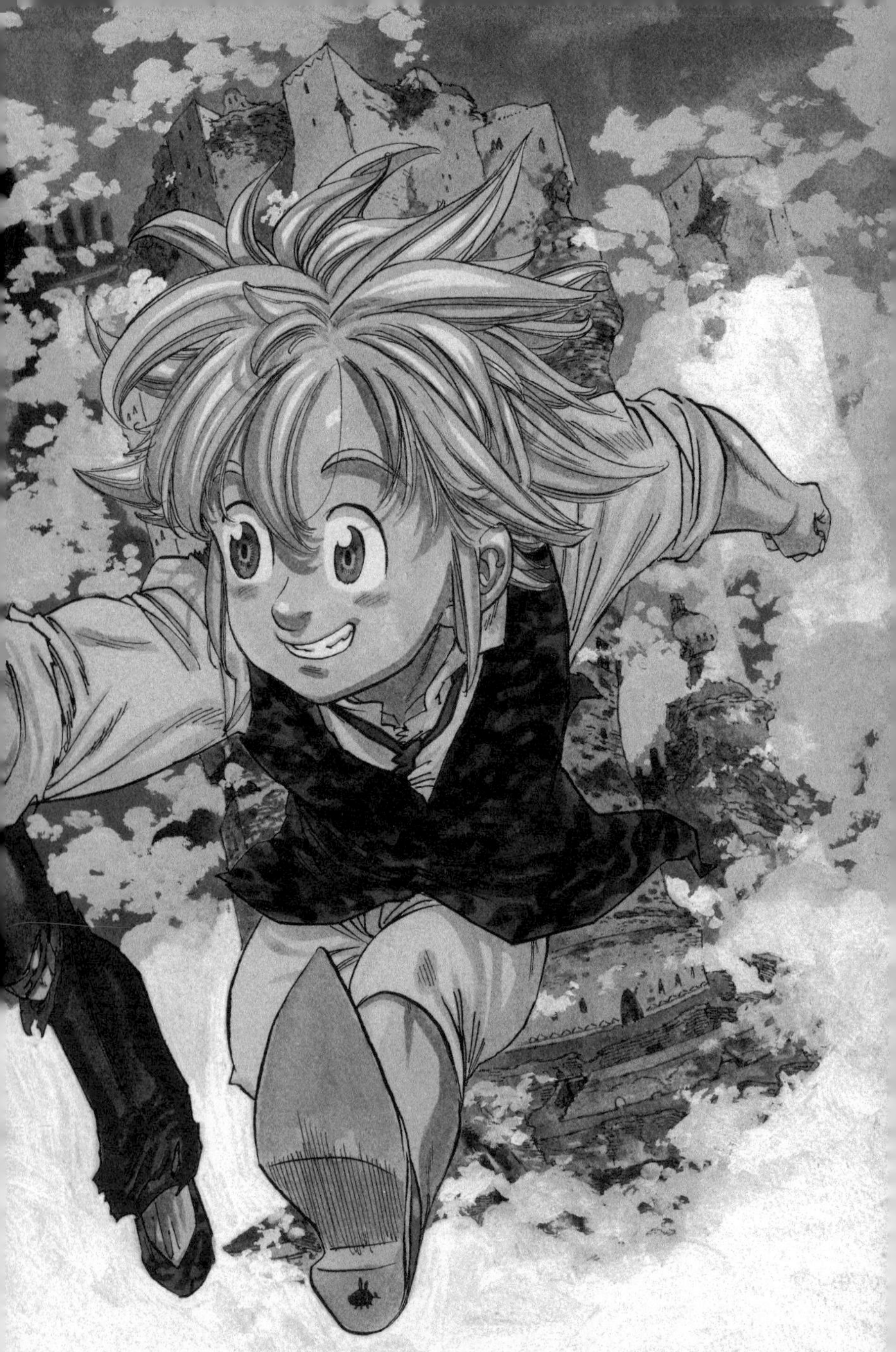

Chapter 267 - From the Skies

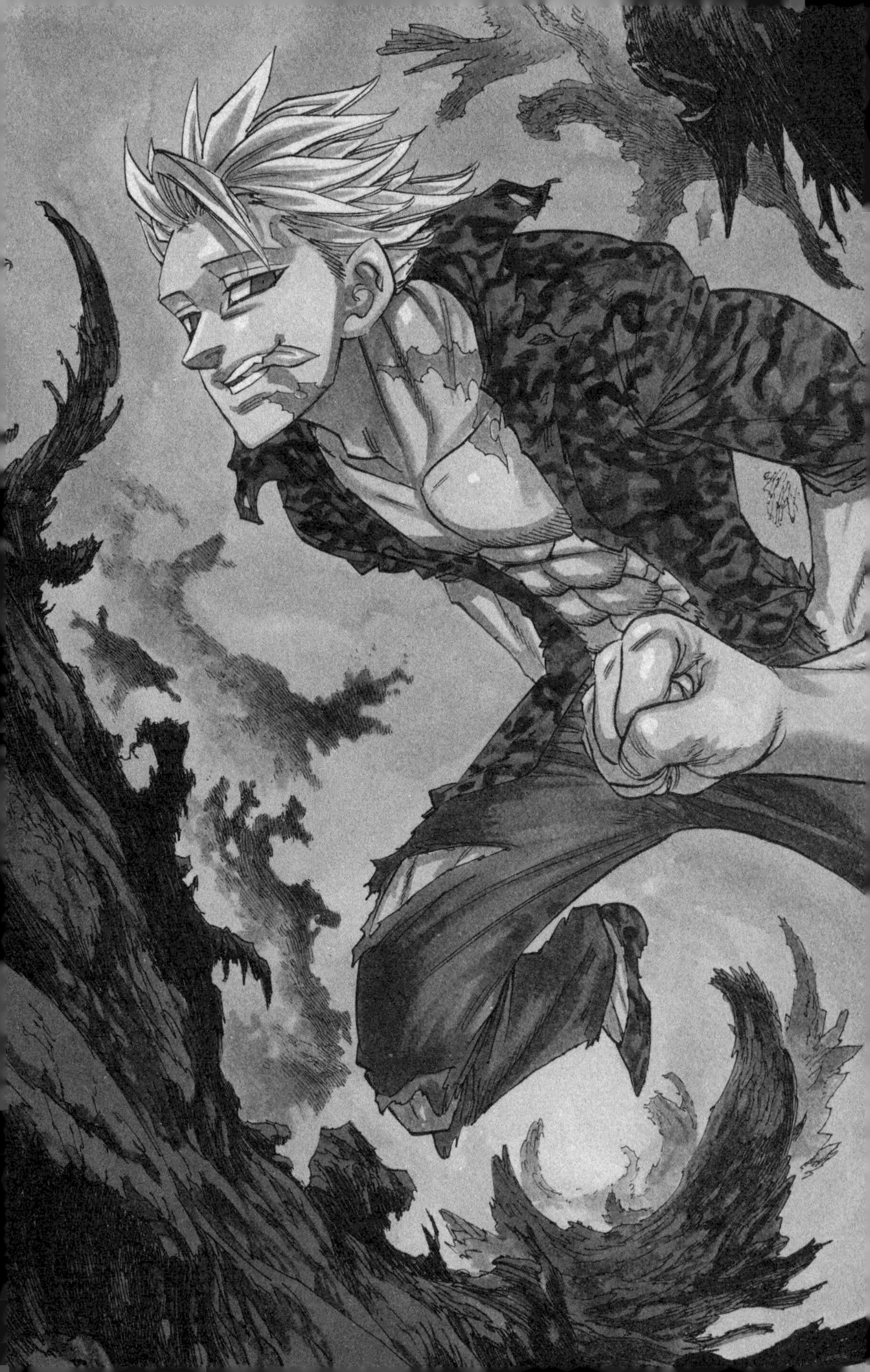

In a sky world of countless floating islands that had once been built to prosperity by the Goddess race, winged beings called Celestials now cling to a meager existence. They are descendants of Goddesses who escaped from the Holy War, but their wings have shrunken, and their magical powers have weakened considerably. Below is the prototype for a character in the movie named "Solaad." He's a young Celestial boy who wears glasses. Initially, I'd created a lazy son of the Celestials' leader to act as his rival(?).
His design ended up being repurposed for "Bellion," the leader of the "Six Knights of Black." Also, the setting was changed so that instead of countless clouds, most of the action was kept to just the one location of the "Sky Palace."

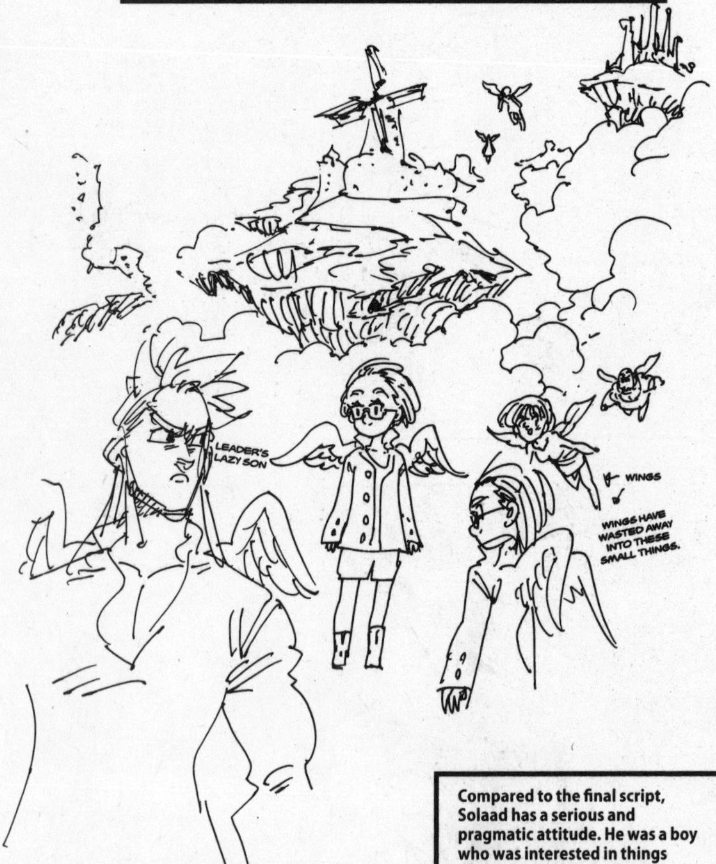
LEADER'S LAZY SON
WINGS
WINGS HAVE WASTED AWAY INTO THESE SMALL THINGS.

Compared to the final script, Solaad has a serious and pragmatic attitude. He was a boy who was interested in things about the land down below.

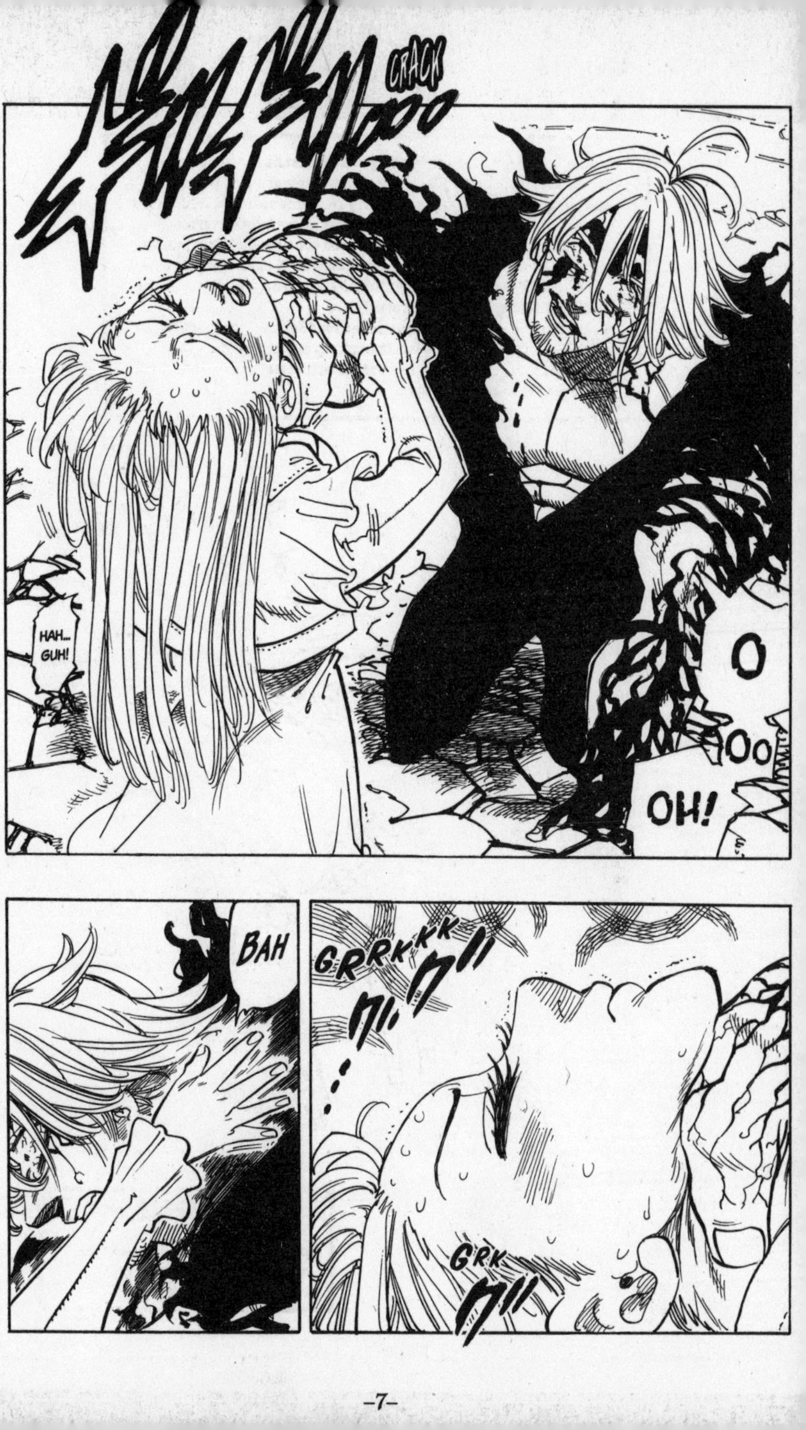
CRACK
O
OO
OH!
HAH... GUH!
GRRKKK
GRK
BAH

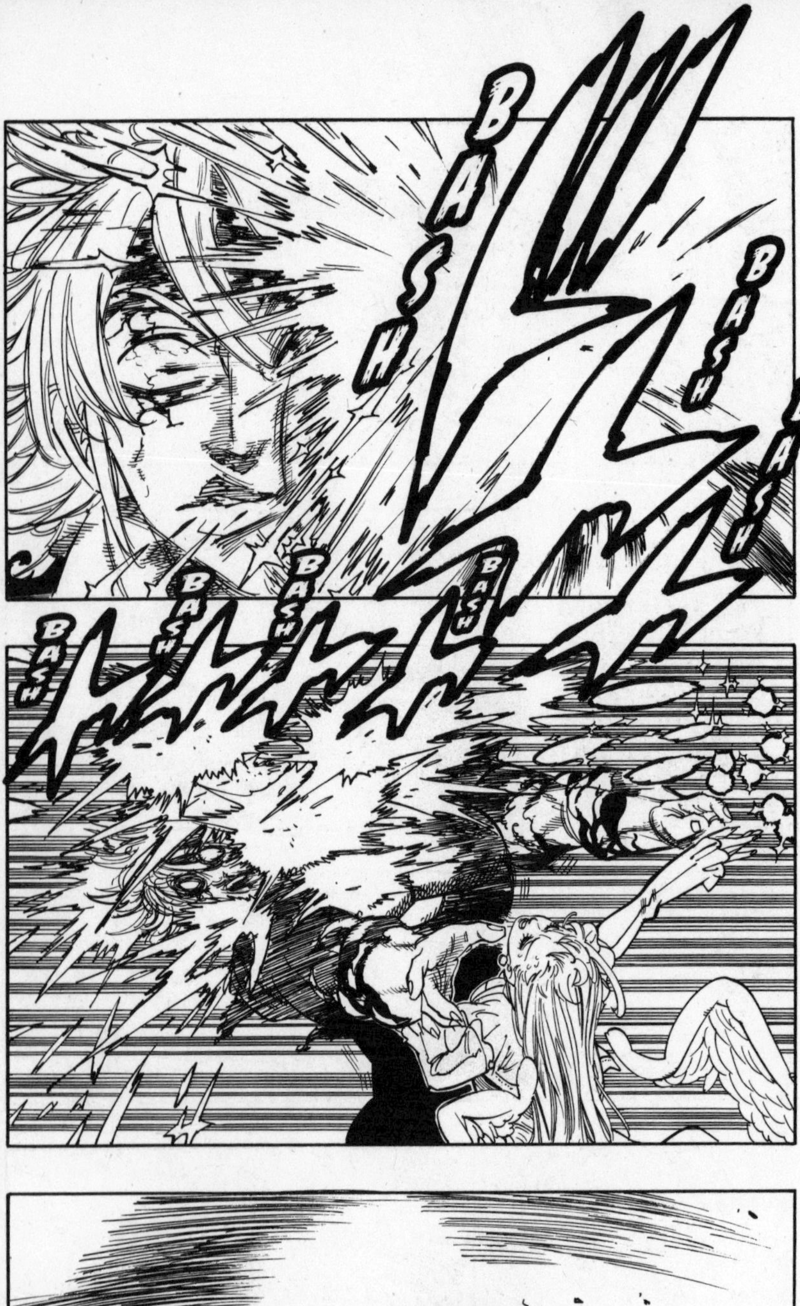
BASH
BASH
BASH
BASH
BASH
BASH
BASH

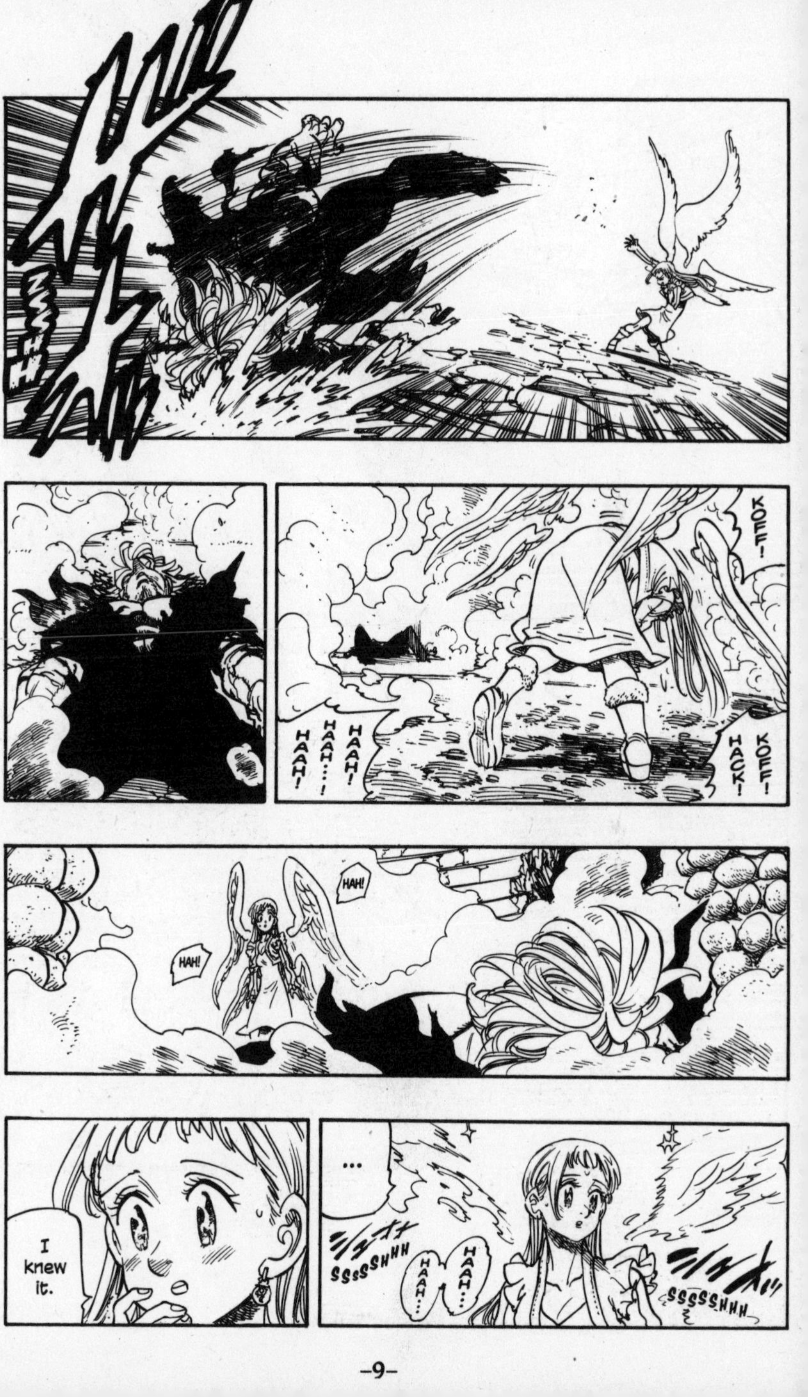
ZSSHH
KOFF!
KOFF!
HACK!
HAAAH!
HAAAH...!
HAAH!
HAH!
HAH!
...
SSSSSHHH
HAAH...
HAAH...
SSsSSHHH
I knew it.

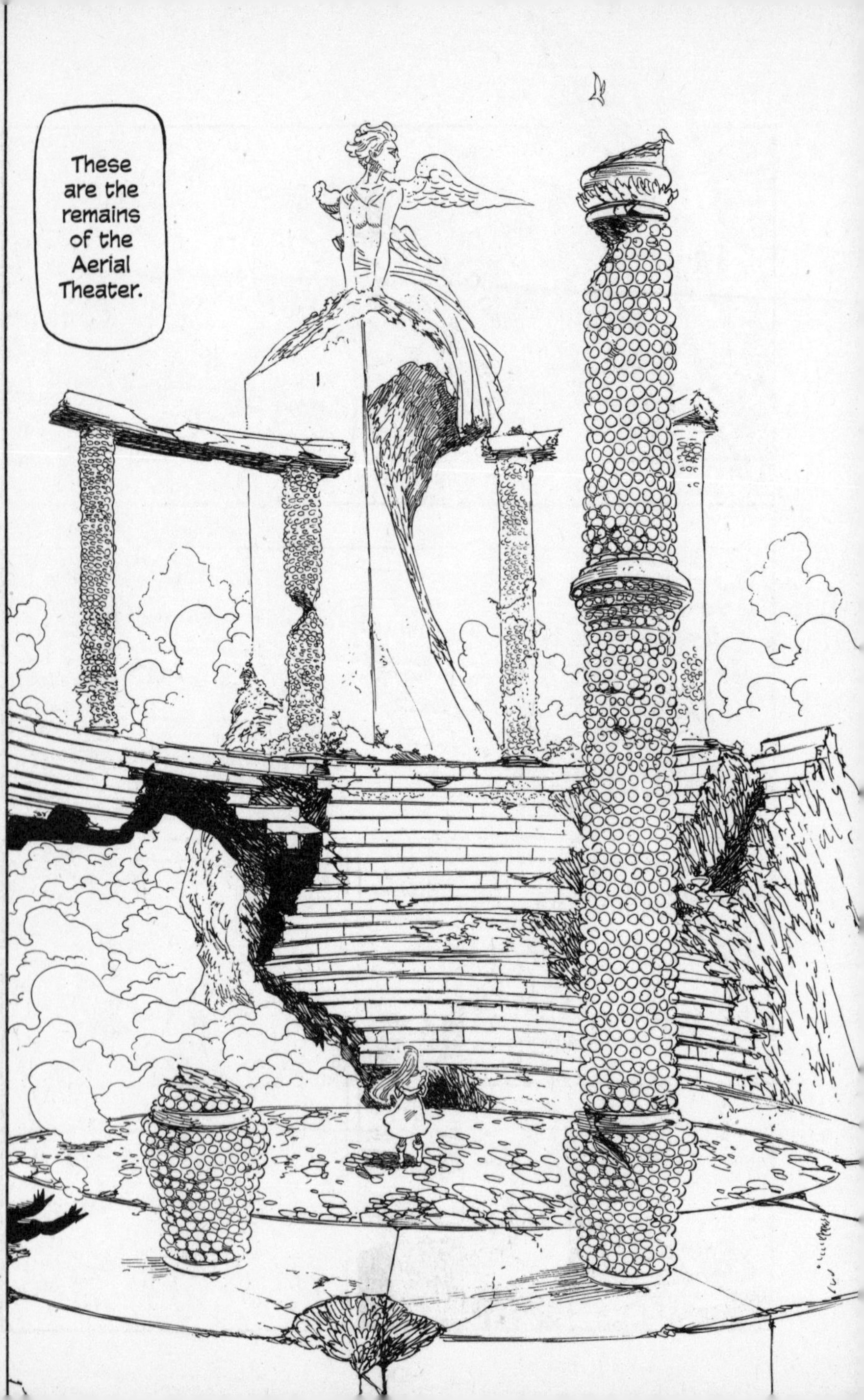
These are the remains of the Aerial Theater.

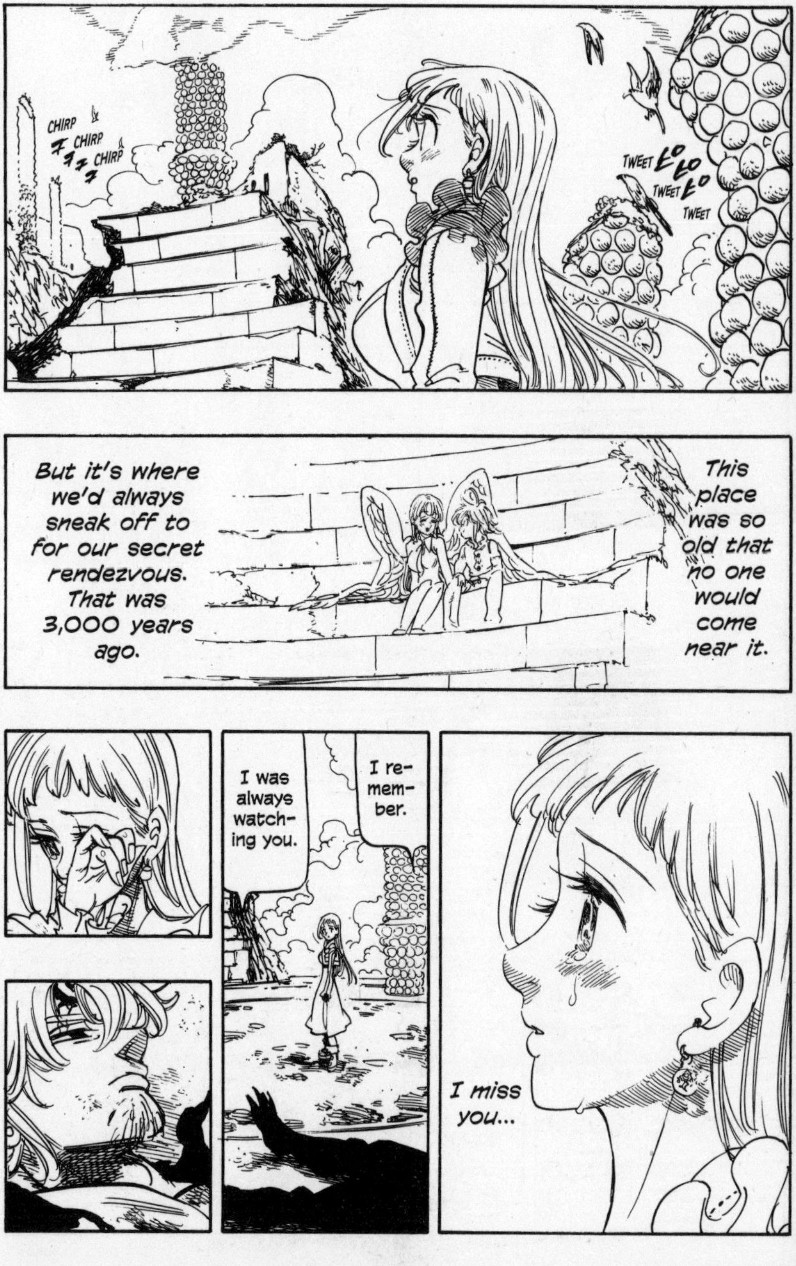
TWEET TWEET TWEET
CHIRP CHIRP CHIRP
This place was so old that no one would come near it.
But it's where we'd always sneak off to for our secret rendezvous. That was 3,000 years ago.
I miss you...
I re-mem-ber.
I was always watch-ing you.

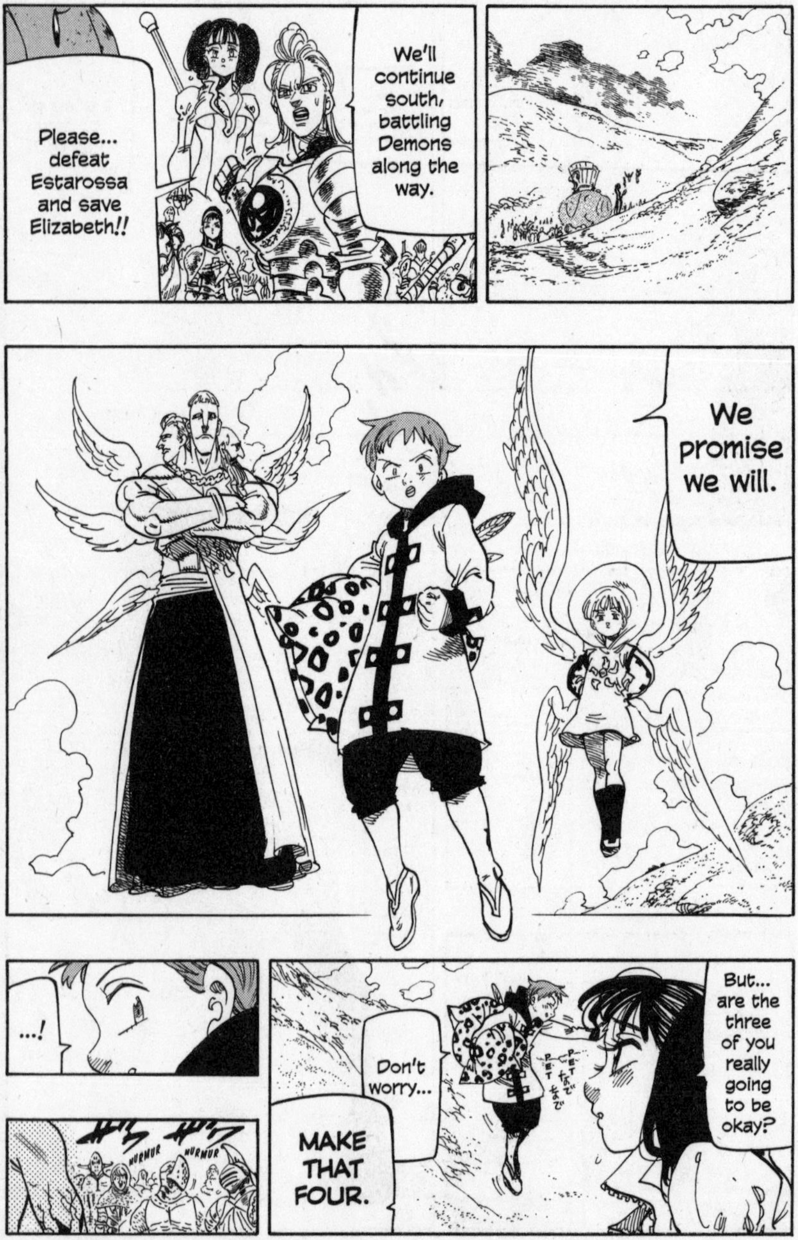
We'll continue south, battling Demons along the way.
Please... defeat Estarossa and save Elizabeth!!
We promise we will.
But... are the three of you really going to be okay?
PET PET
なで なで
Don't worry...
MAKE THAT FOUR.
...!
MURMUR MURMUR

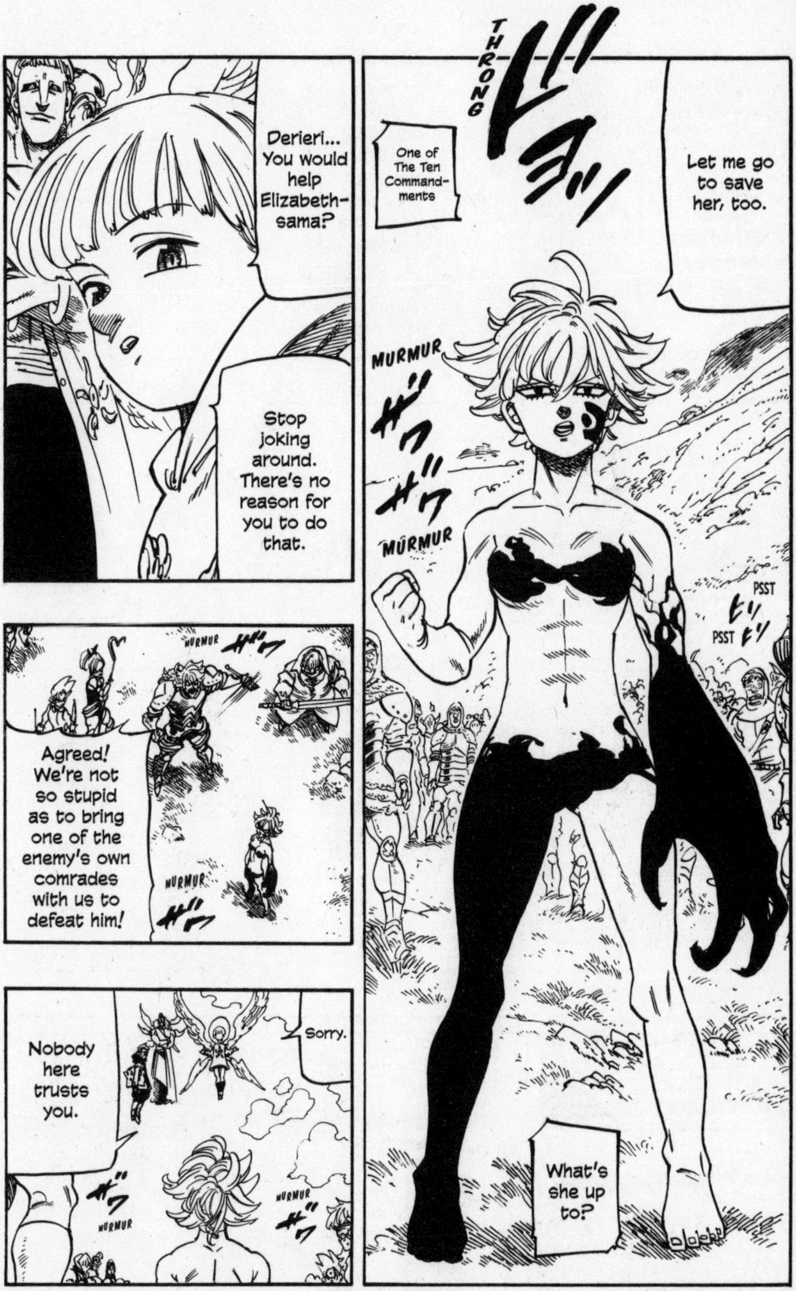
THRONG
One of The Ten Commandments
Let me go to save her, too.
MURMUR
MURMUR
PSST
PSST
What's she up to?
Derieri... You would help Elizabeth-sama?
Stop joking around. There's no reason for you to do that.
MURMUR
Agreed! We're not so stupid as to bring one of the enemy's own comrades with us to defeat him!
MURMUR
Sorry.
Nobody here trusts you.
MURMUR
MURMUR

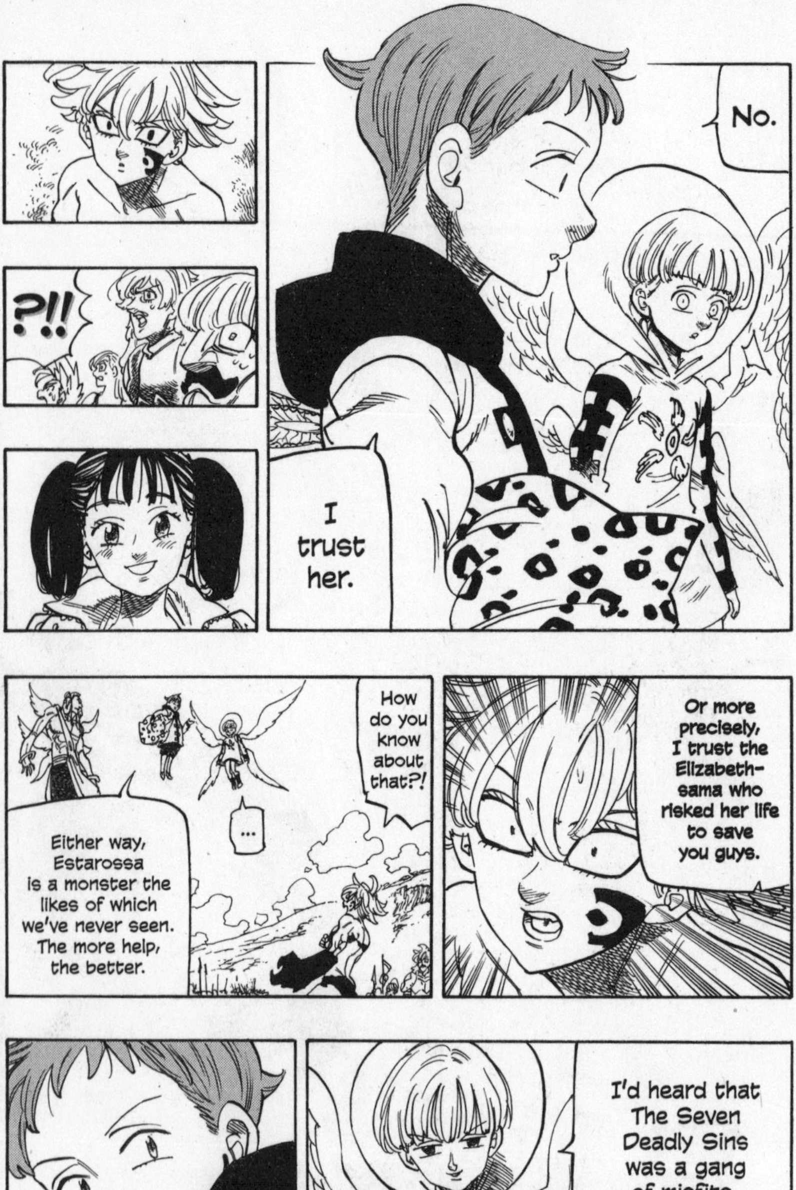
No.
I trust her.
?!!
Or more precisely, I trust the Elizabeth-sama who risked her life to save you guys.
How do you know about that?!
...
Either way, Estarossa is a monster the likes of which we've never seen. The more help, the better.
I'd heard that The Seven Deadly Sins was a gang of misfits. It seems that it's true.
HEH.

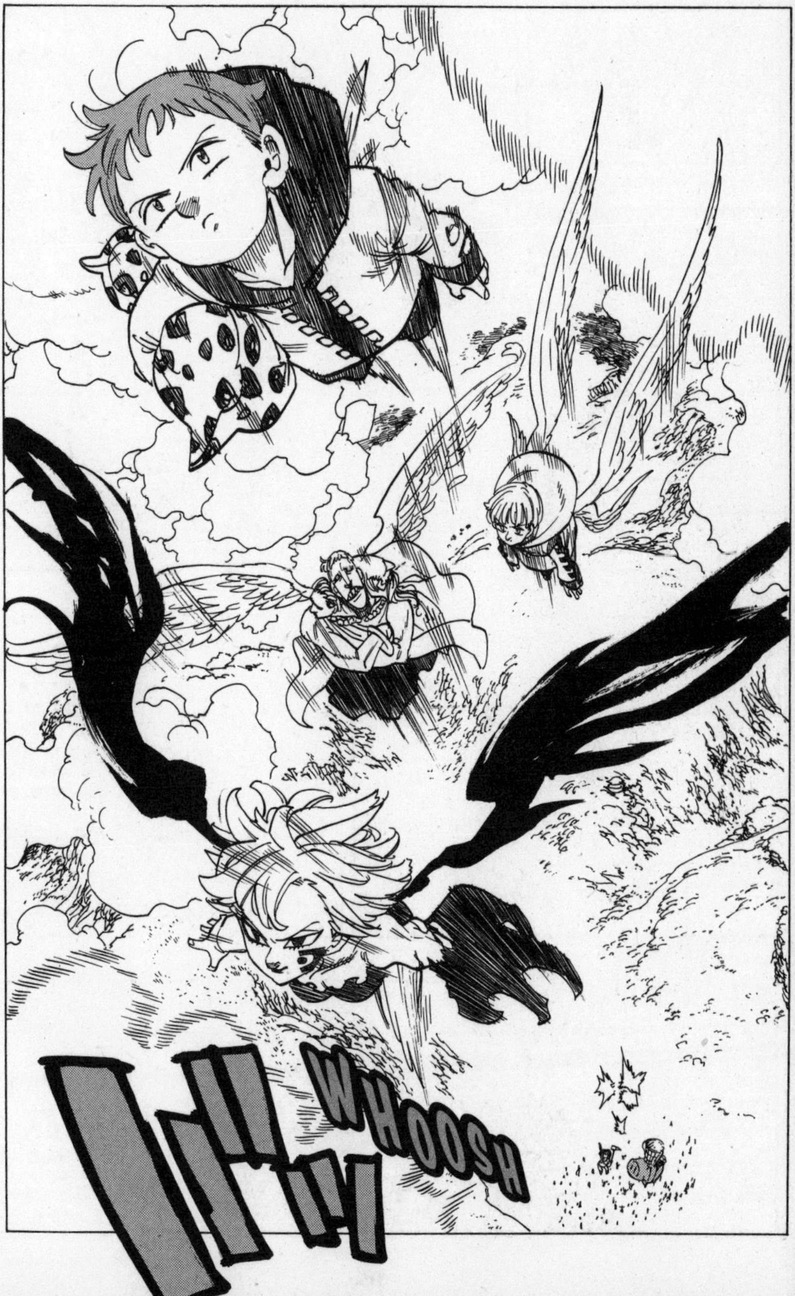
WHOOSH

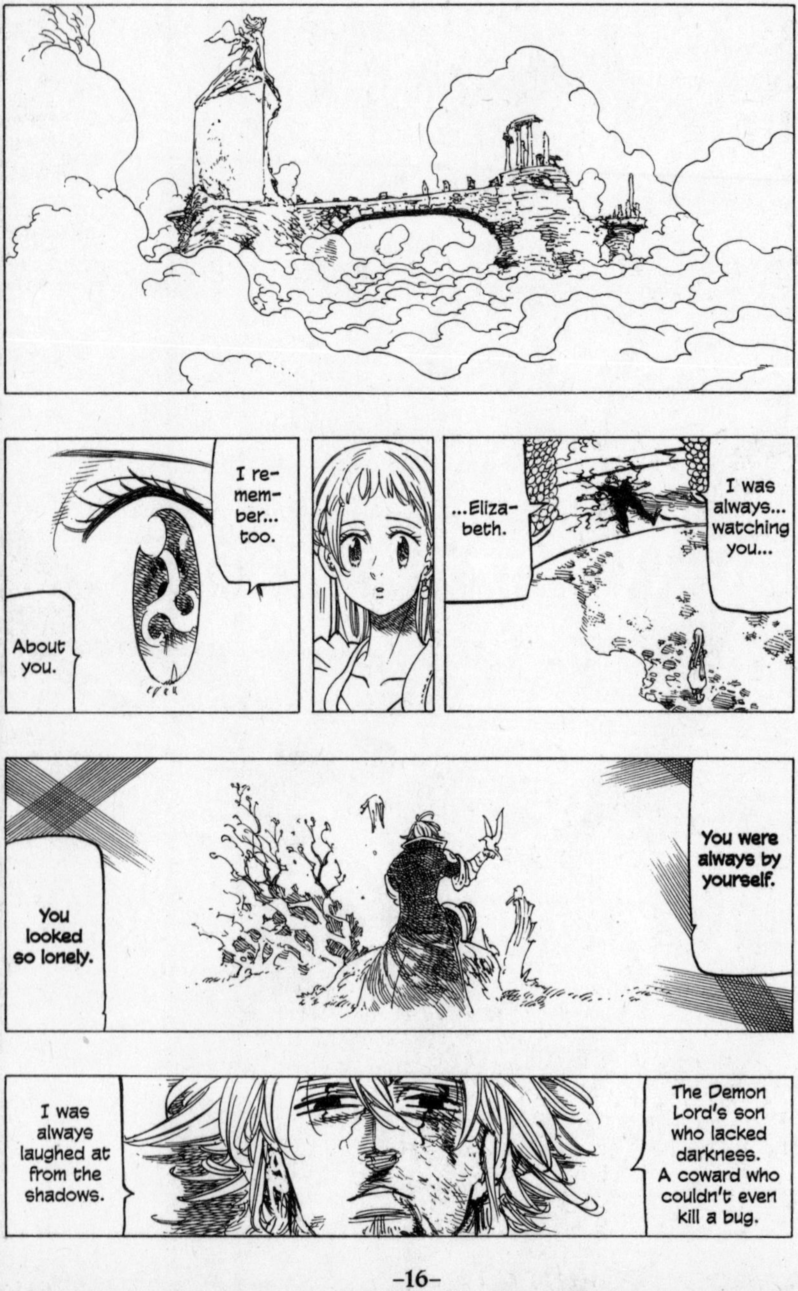
I was always... watching you...
...Elizabeth.
I remember... too.
About you.
You were always by yourself.
You looked so lonely.
The Demon Lord's son who lacked darkness. A coward who couldn't even kill a bug.
I was always laughed at from the shadows.

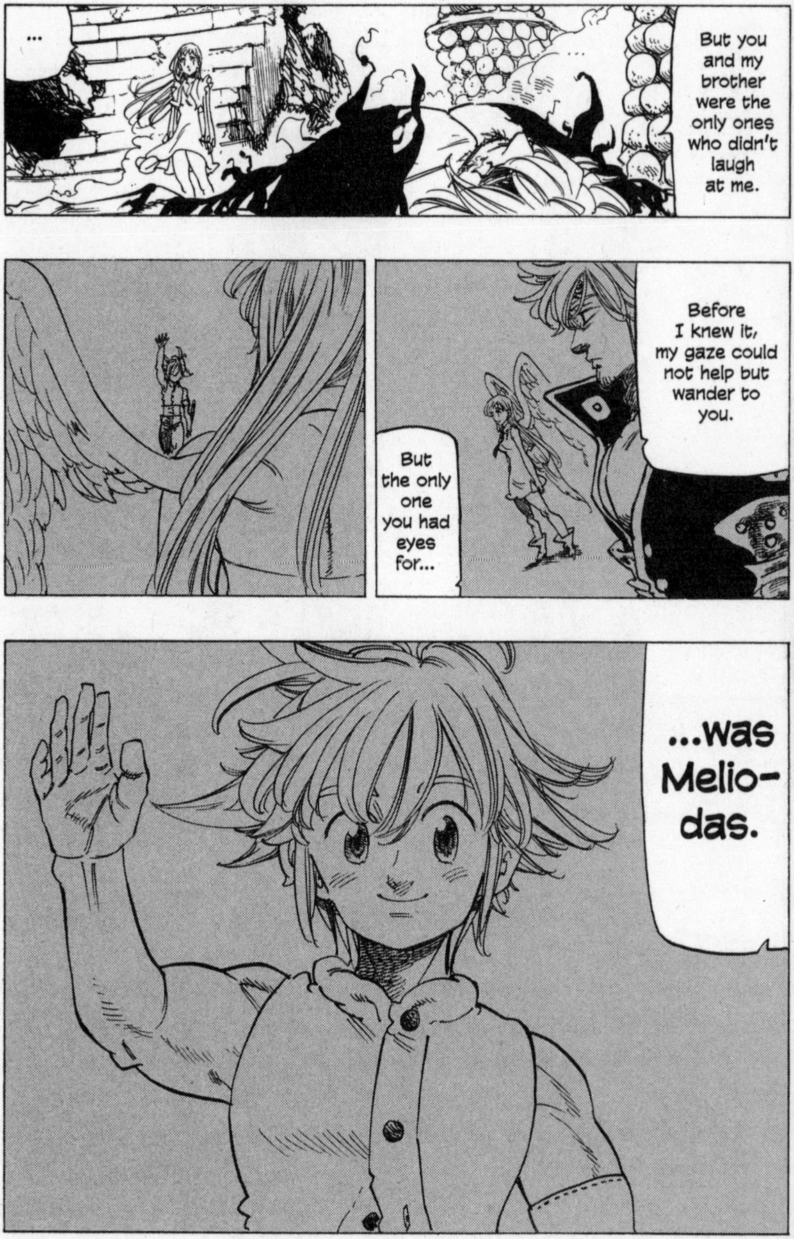

But you and my brother were the only ones who didn't laugh at me.
...
...
Before I knew it, my gaze could not help but wander to you.
But the only one you had eyes for...
...was Melio-das.

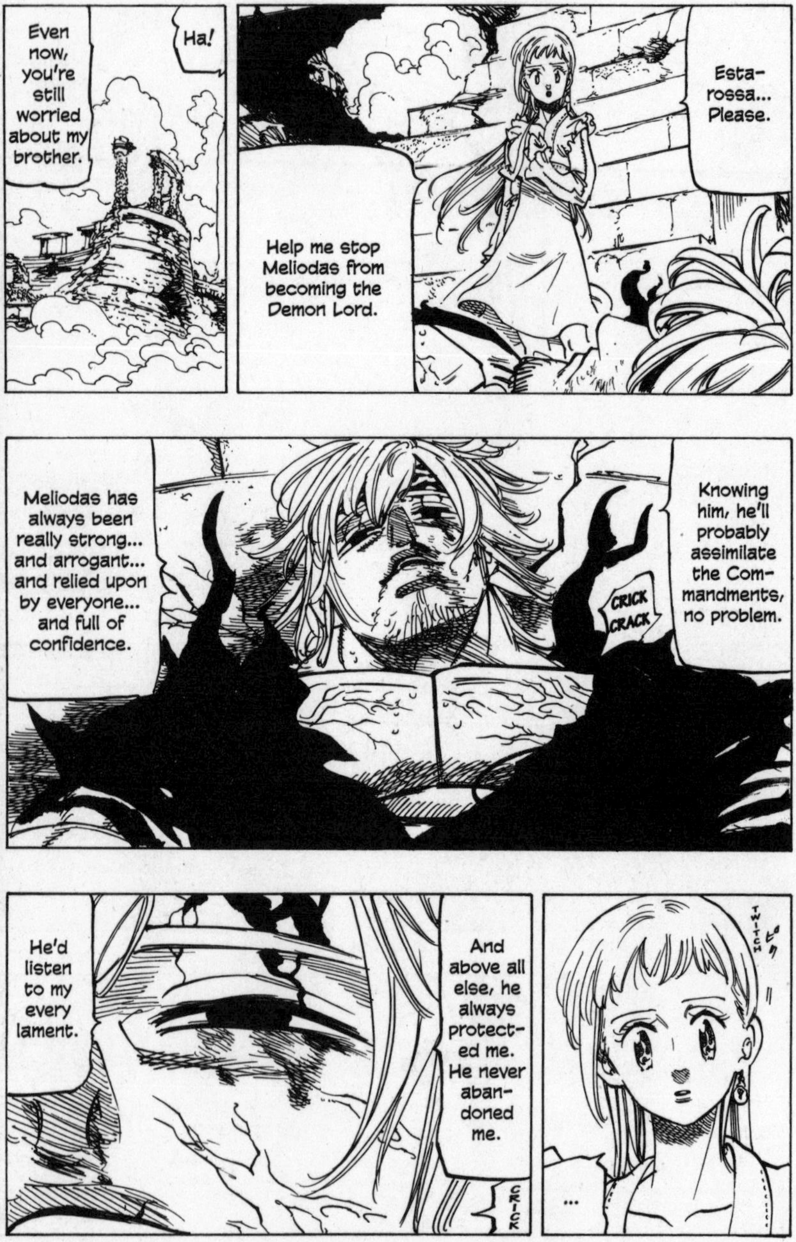
Esta-rossa... Please.
Help me stop Meliodas from becoming the Demon Lord.
Ha!
Even now, you're still worried about my brother.
Knowing him, he'll probably assimilate the Commandments, no problem.
CRICK CRACK
Meliodas has always been really strong... and arrogant... and relied upon by everyone... and full of confidence.
TWITCH
...
And above all else, he always protected me. He never abandoned me.
CRICK
He'd listen to my every lament.

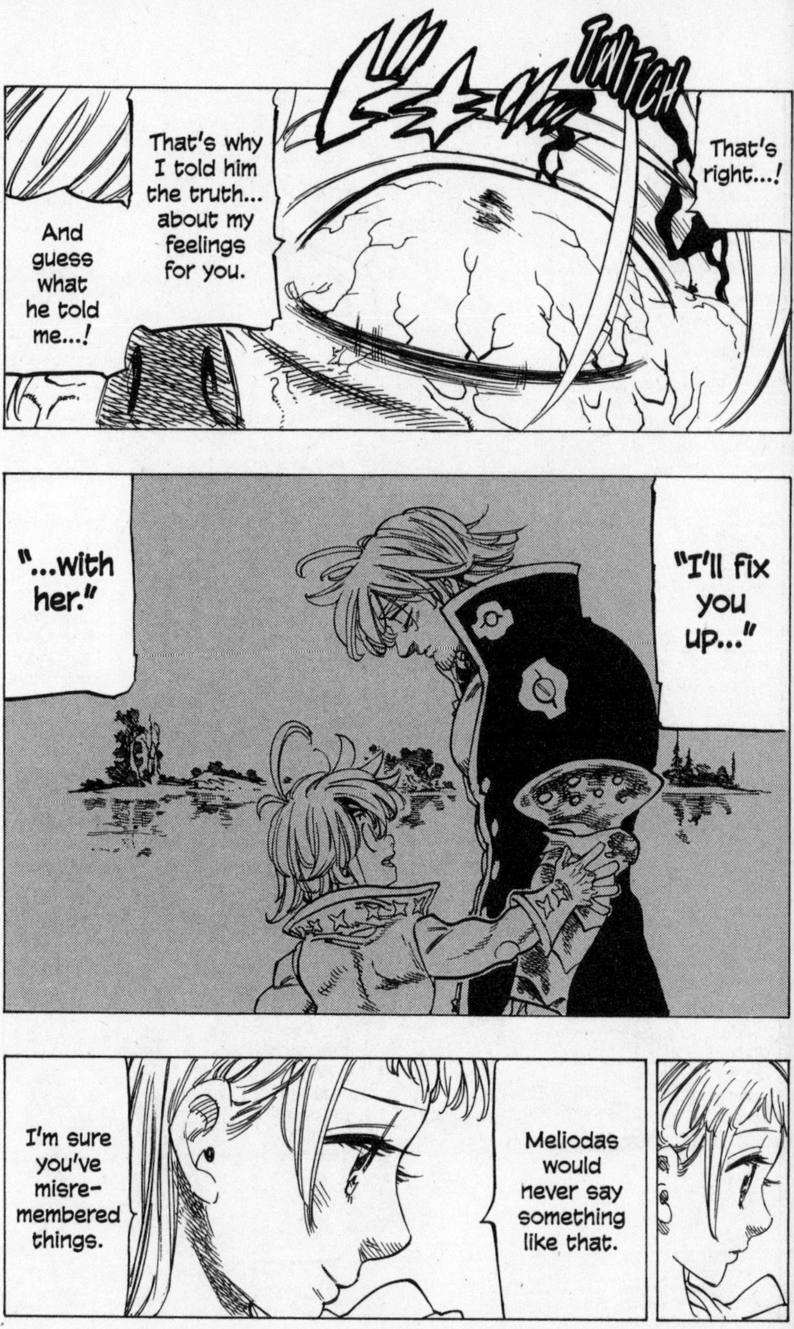
TWITCH
That's right...!
That's why I told him the truth... about my feelings for you.
And guess what he told me...!
"I'll fix you up..."
"...with her."
Meliodas would never say something like that.
I'm sure you've misre-membered things.

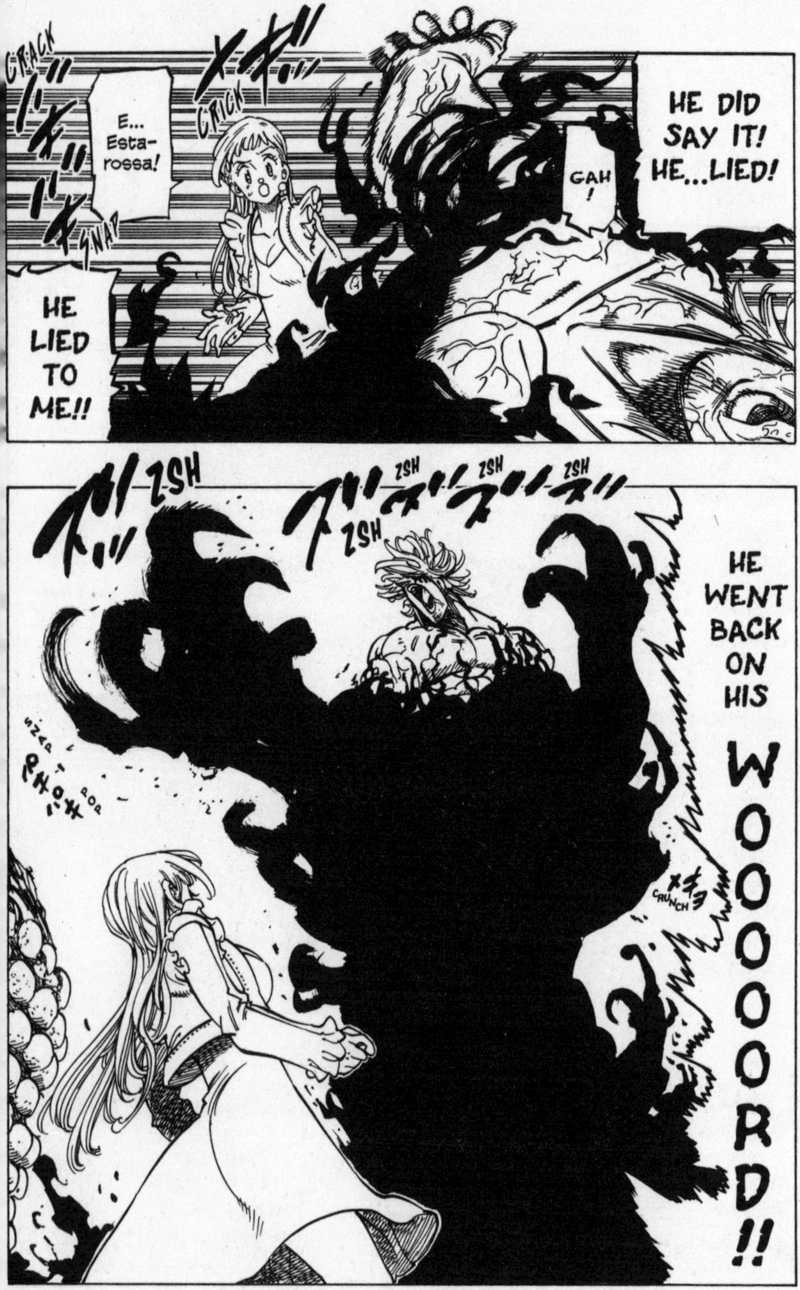
HE DID SAY IT! HE...LIED!
GAH!
CRICK
E... Esta-rossa!
CRACK
SNAP
HE LIED TO ME!!
ZSH
ZSH
ZSH
ZSH
ZSH
HE WENT BACK ON HIS WOOOOORD!!
CRUNCH
POP

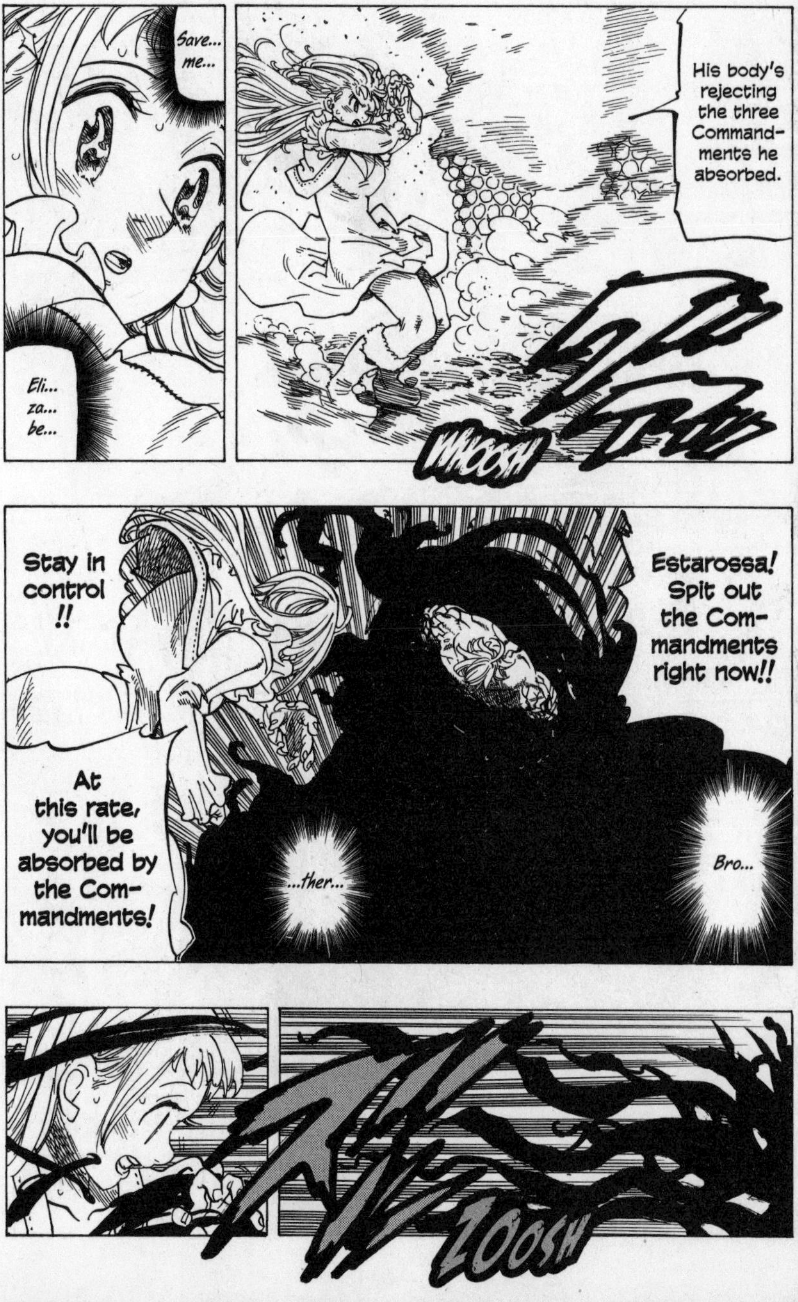
His body's rejecting the three Command-ments he absorbed.
WHOOSH
Save... me...
Eli... za... be...
Estarossa! Spit out the Com-mandments right now!!
Stay in control !!
Bro...
...ther...
At this rate, you'll be absorbed by the Com-mandments!
ZOOSH

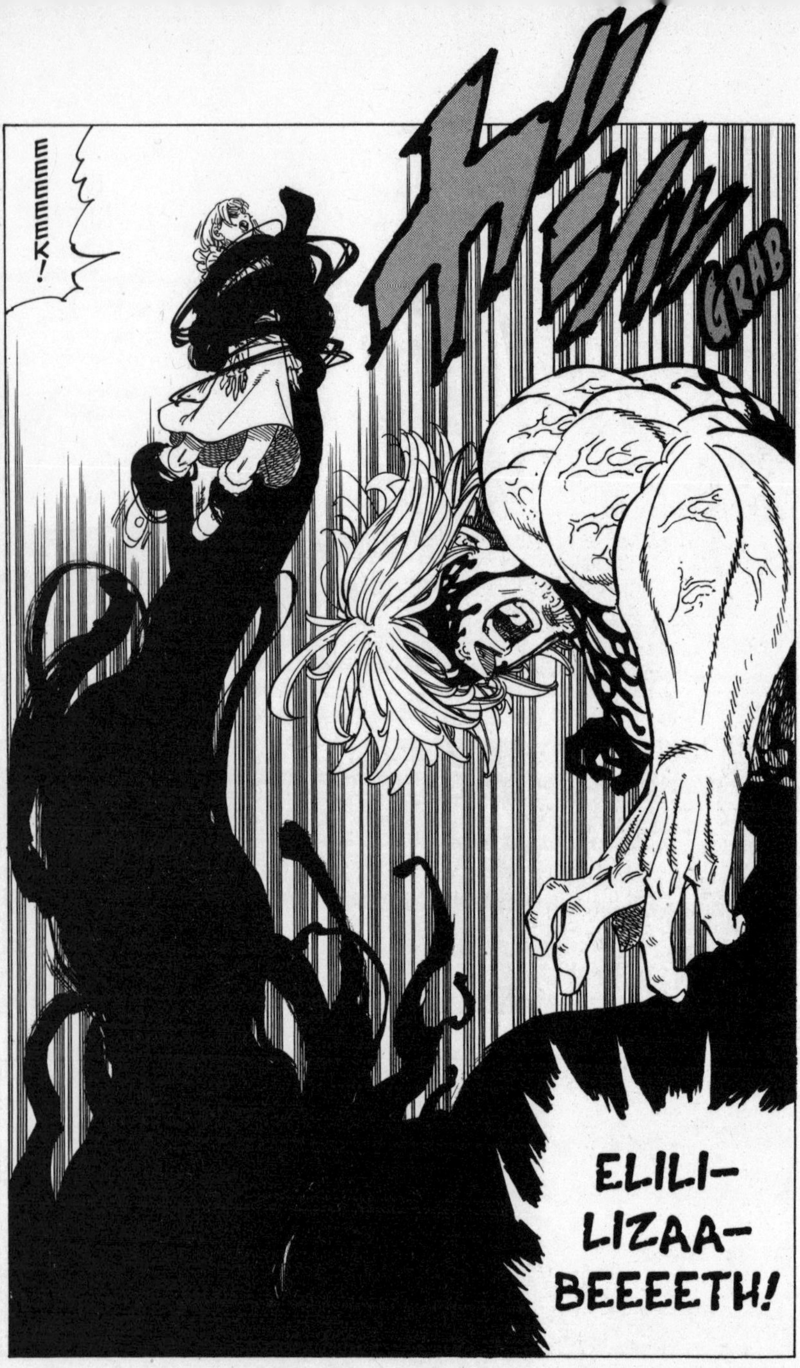
GRAB
EEEEEK!
ELILI-LIZAA-BEEEETH!

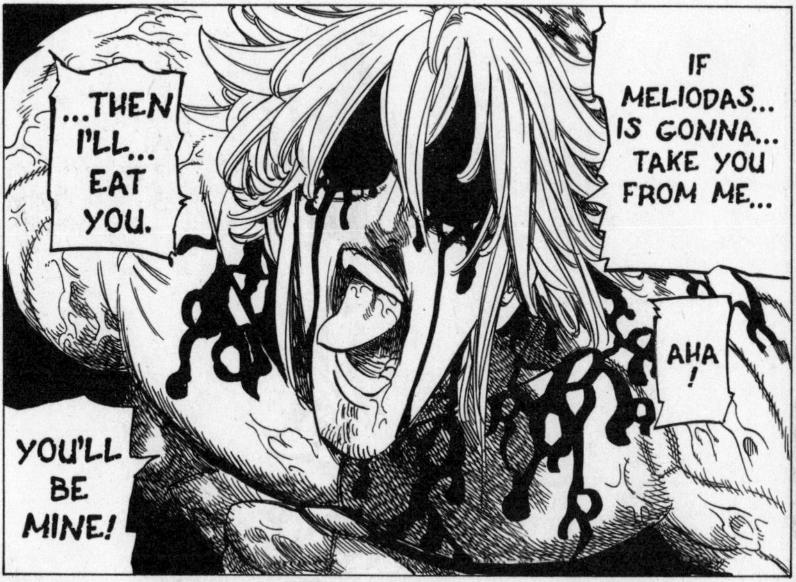
IF MELIODAS... IS GONNA... TAKE YOU FROM ME...
...THEN I'LL... EAT YOU.
AHA!
YOU'LL BE MINE!

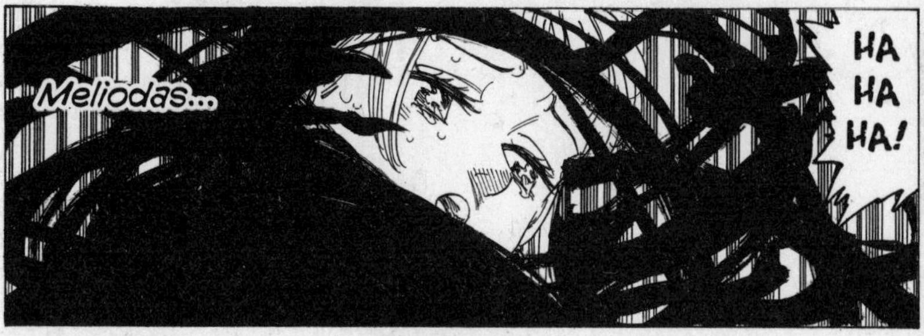
HA HA HA!
Meliodas...

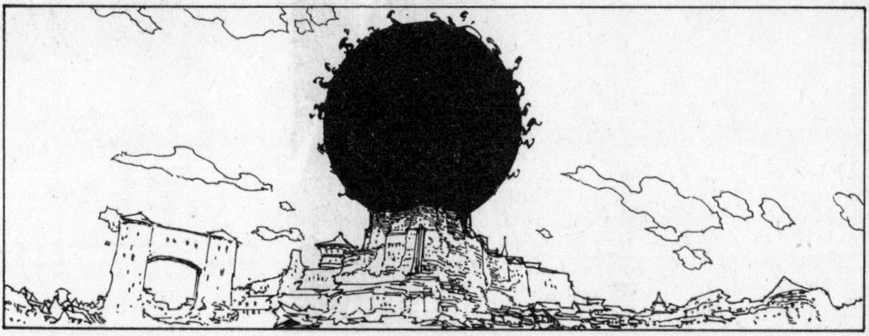

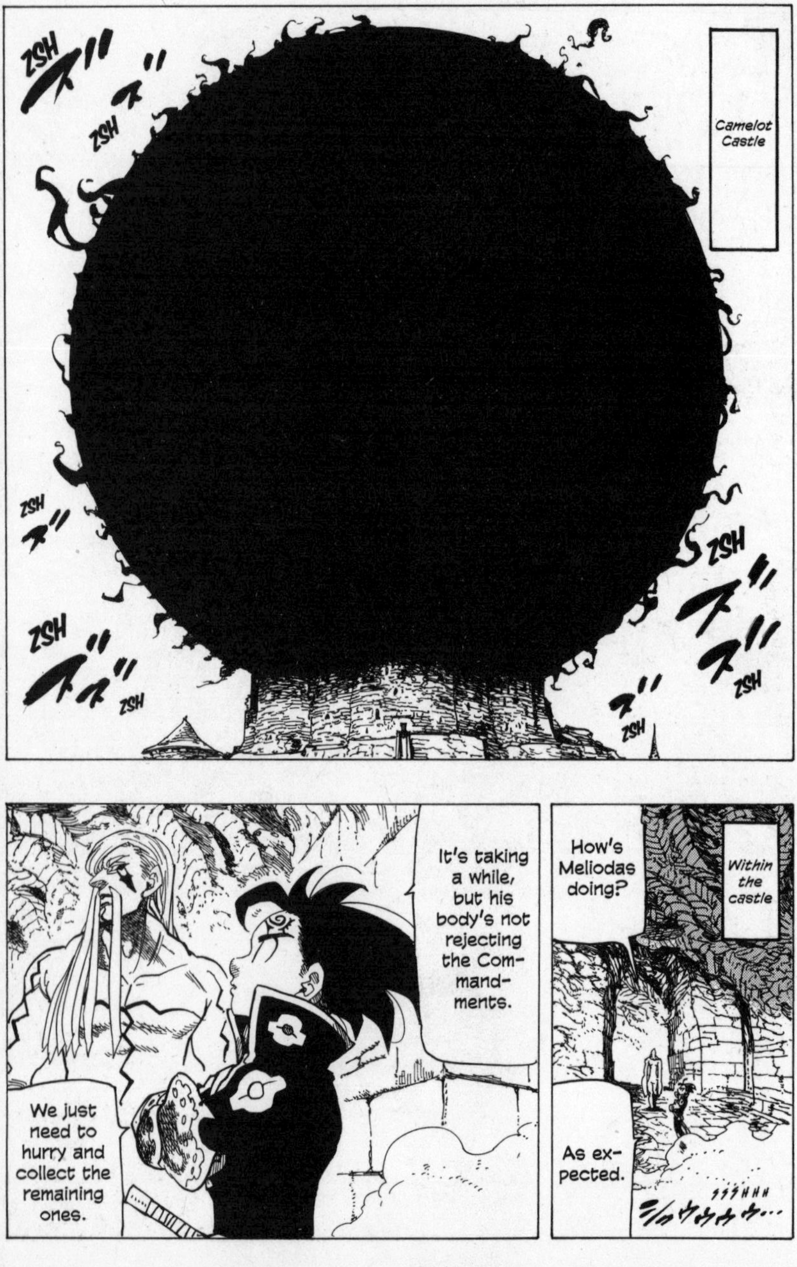
Camelot Castle
ZSH
ZSH
ZSH
ZSH
ZSH
ZSH
ZSH
ZSH
Within the castle
How's Meliodas doing?
As expected.
SSSHHH
It's taking a while, but his body's not rejecting the Commandments.
We just need to hurry and collect the remaining ones.

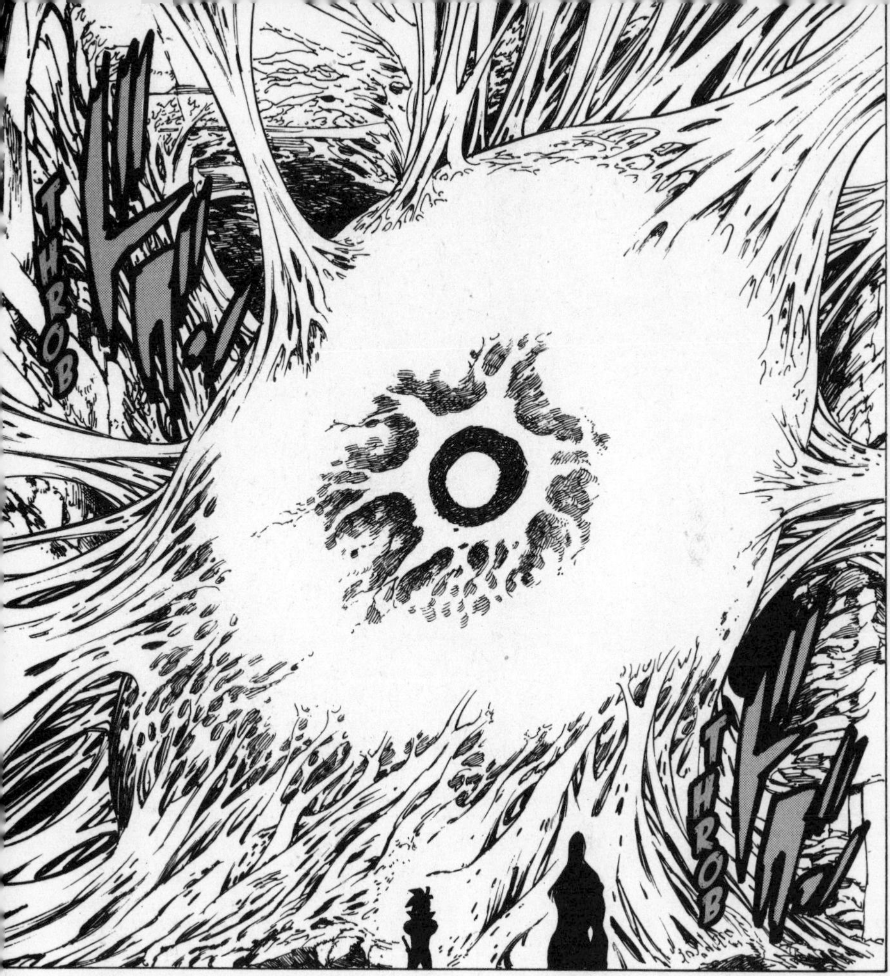
THROB
THROB
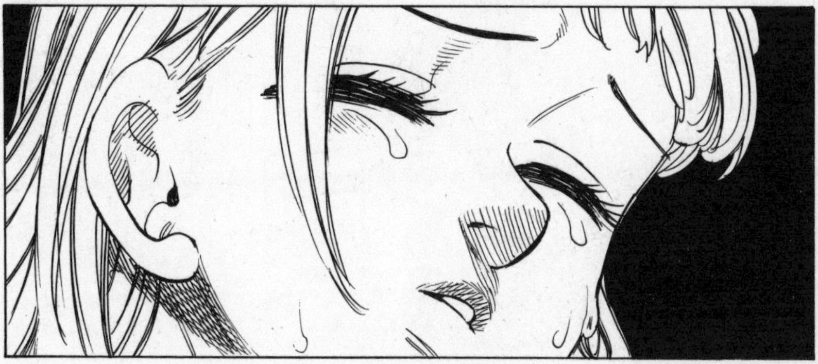

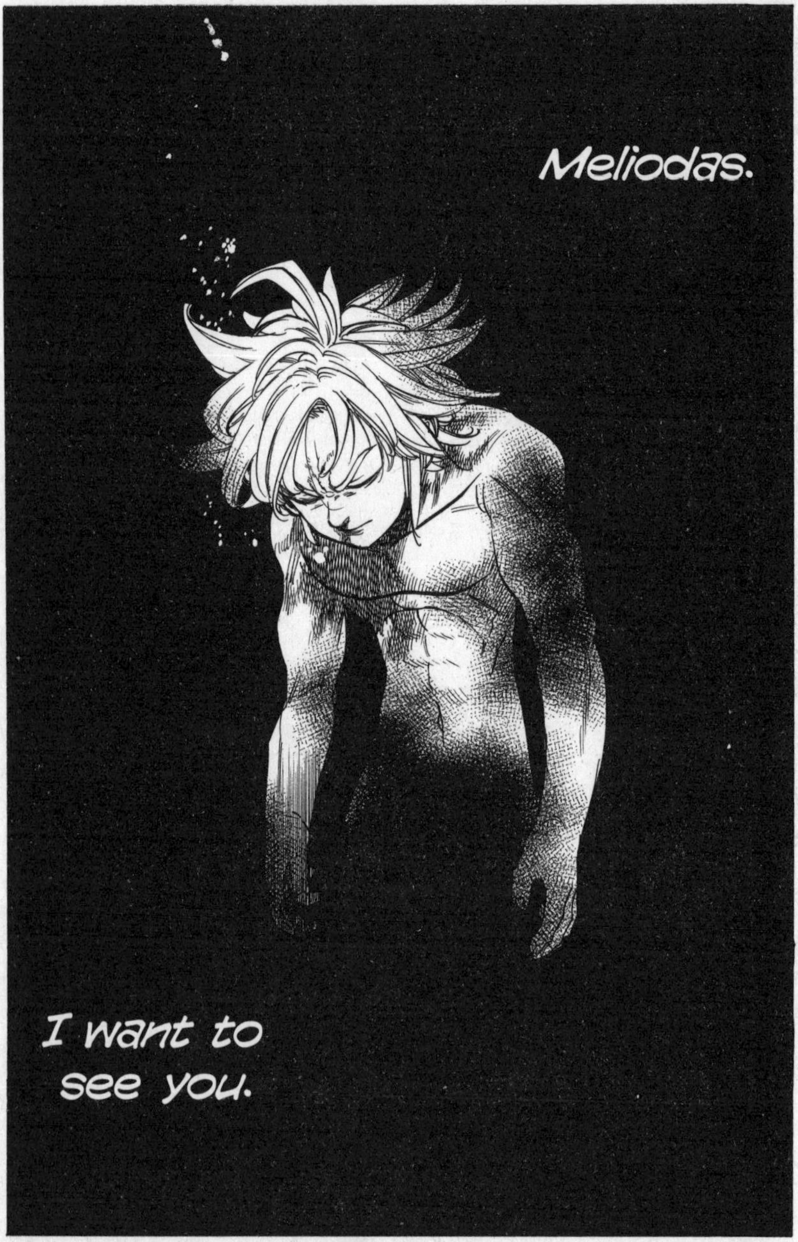
Meliodas.
I want to see you.

Chapter 268 - From Purgatory

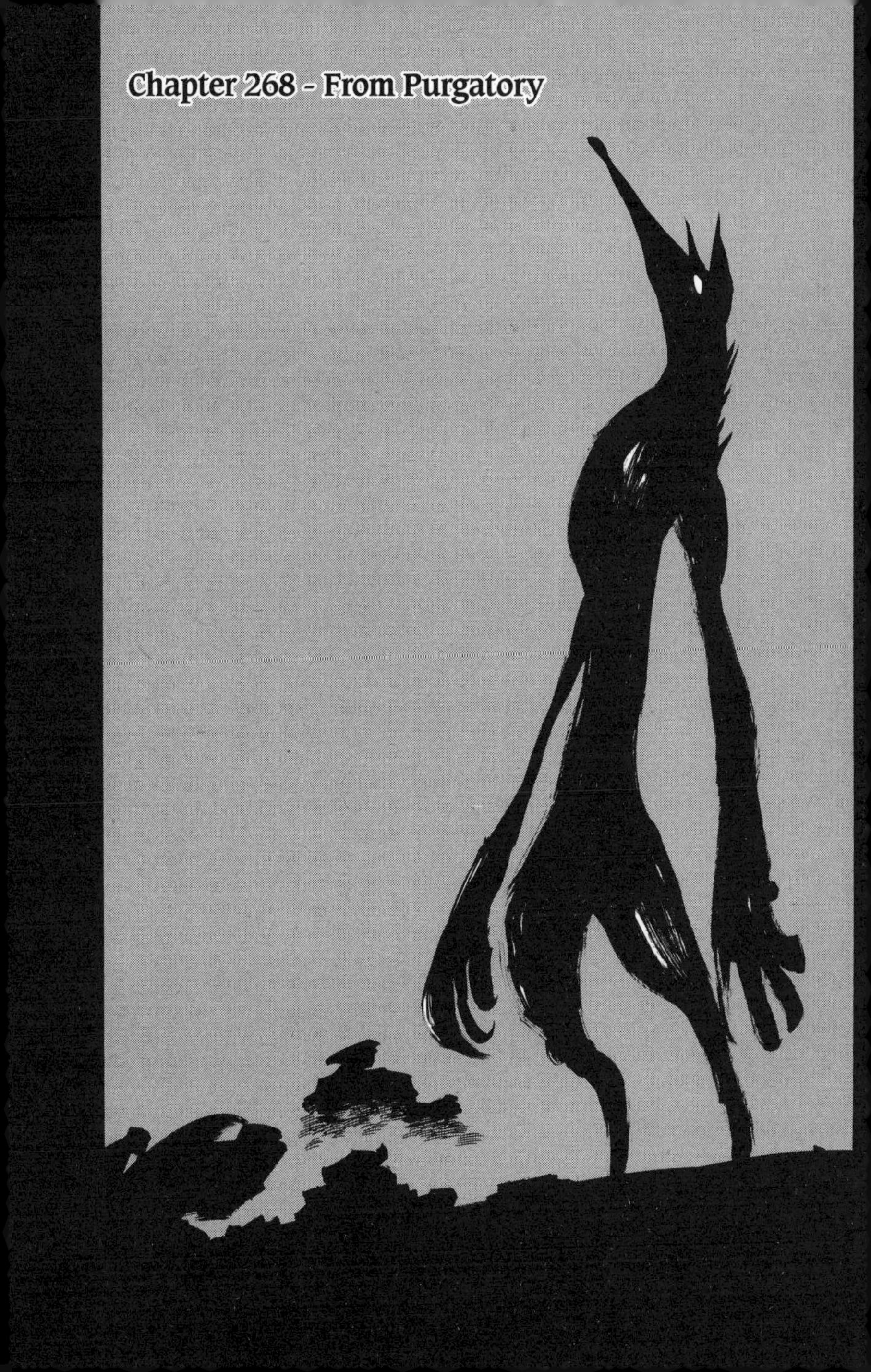

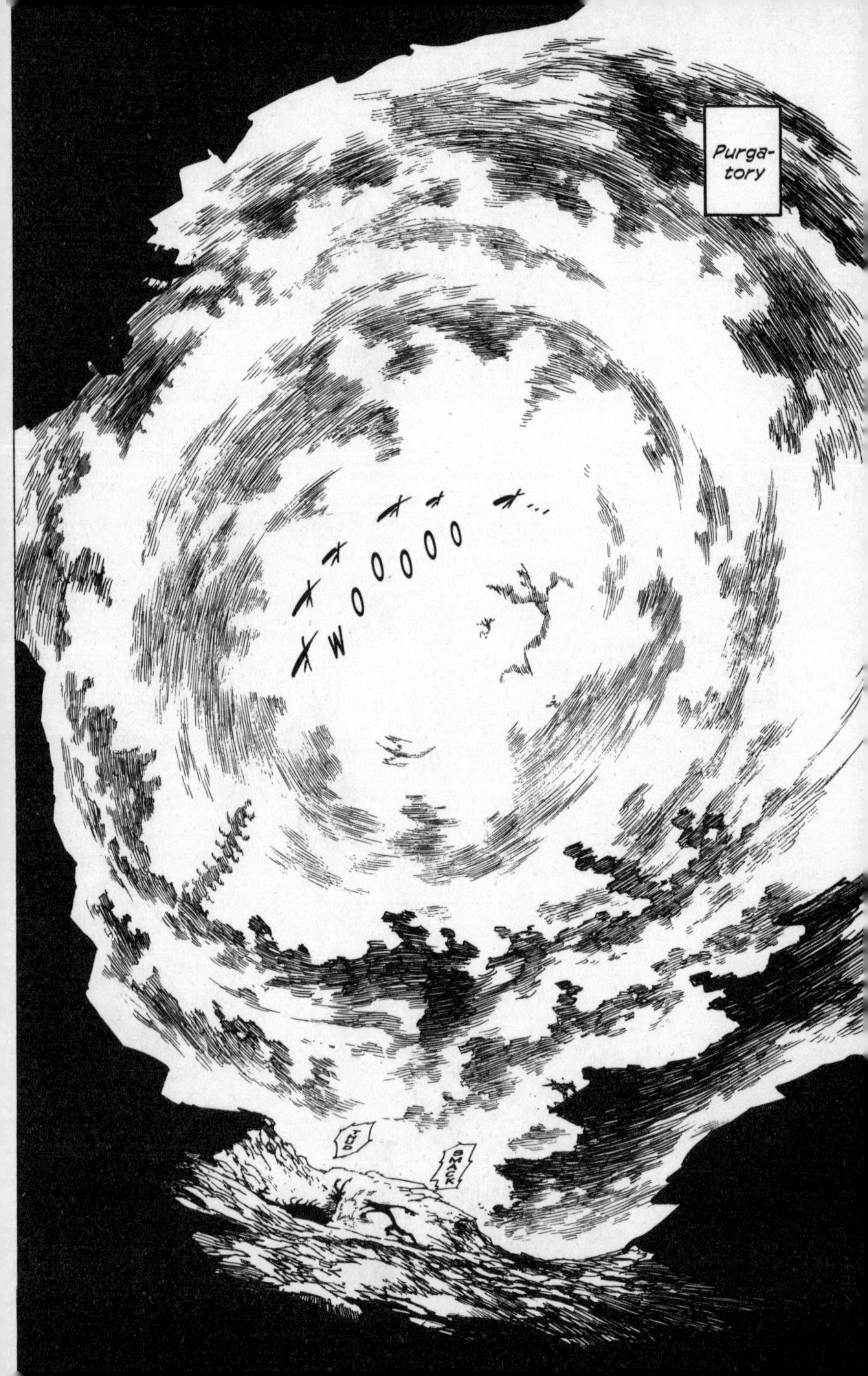
Purga-
tory
WOOOOO
THUD
SMACK

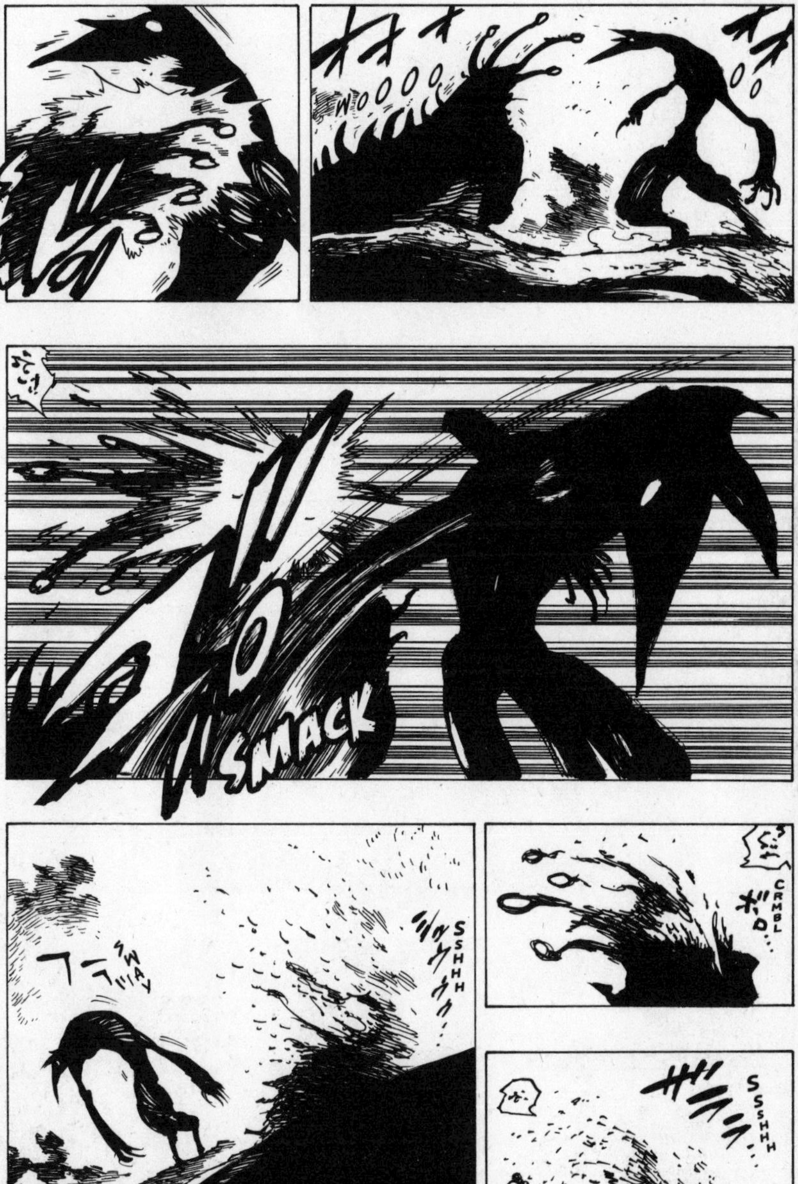

WOOOO
SLAM
SMACK
CRMBL
SSSHHH
SSHHH
SWAY

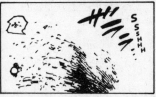

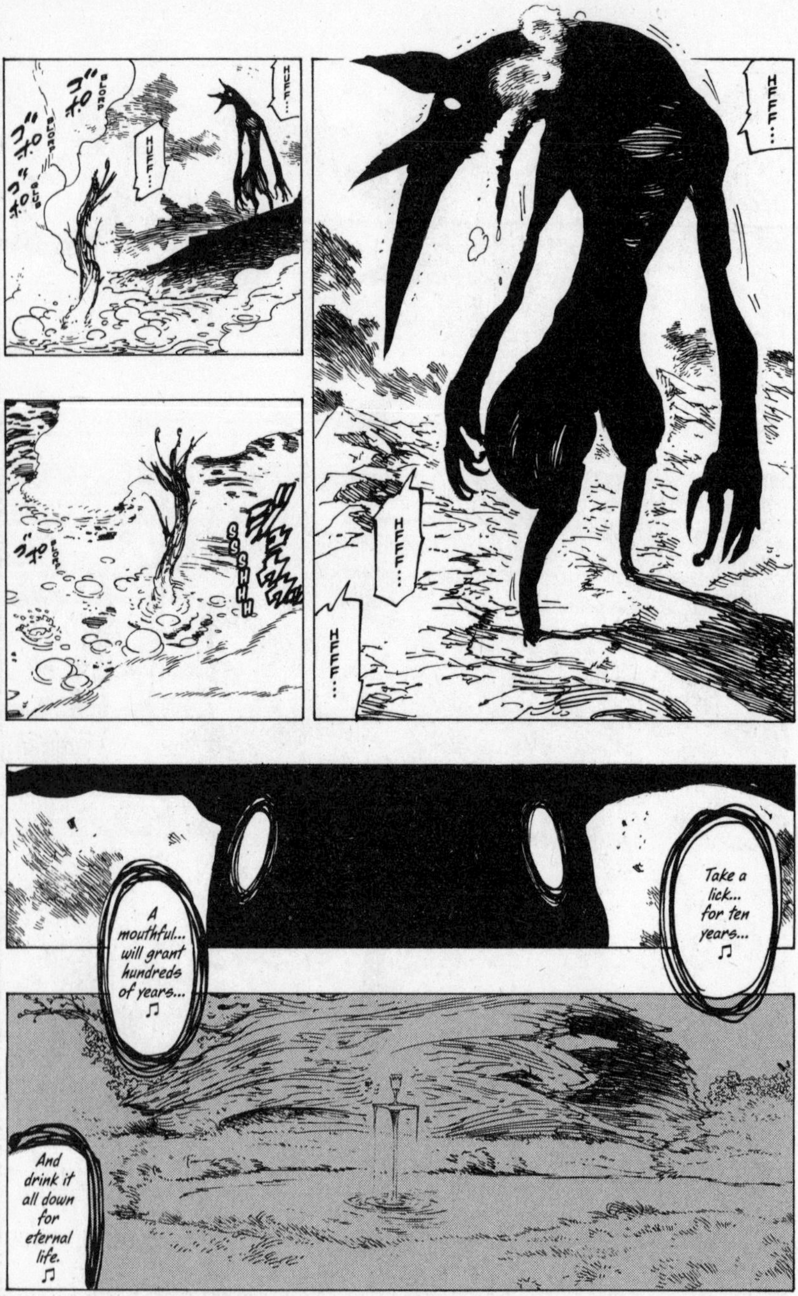
HFFF...
HFFF...
HFFF...
HUFF...
HUFF...
BLORP
BLORP
GLUB
SSSHHH
BLORP
Take a lick... for ten years... ♫
A mouthful... will grant hundreds of years... ♫
And drink it all down for eternal life. ♫

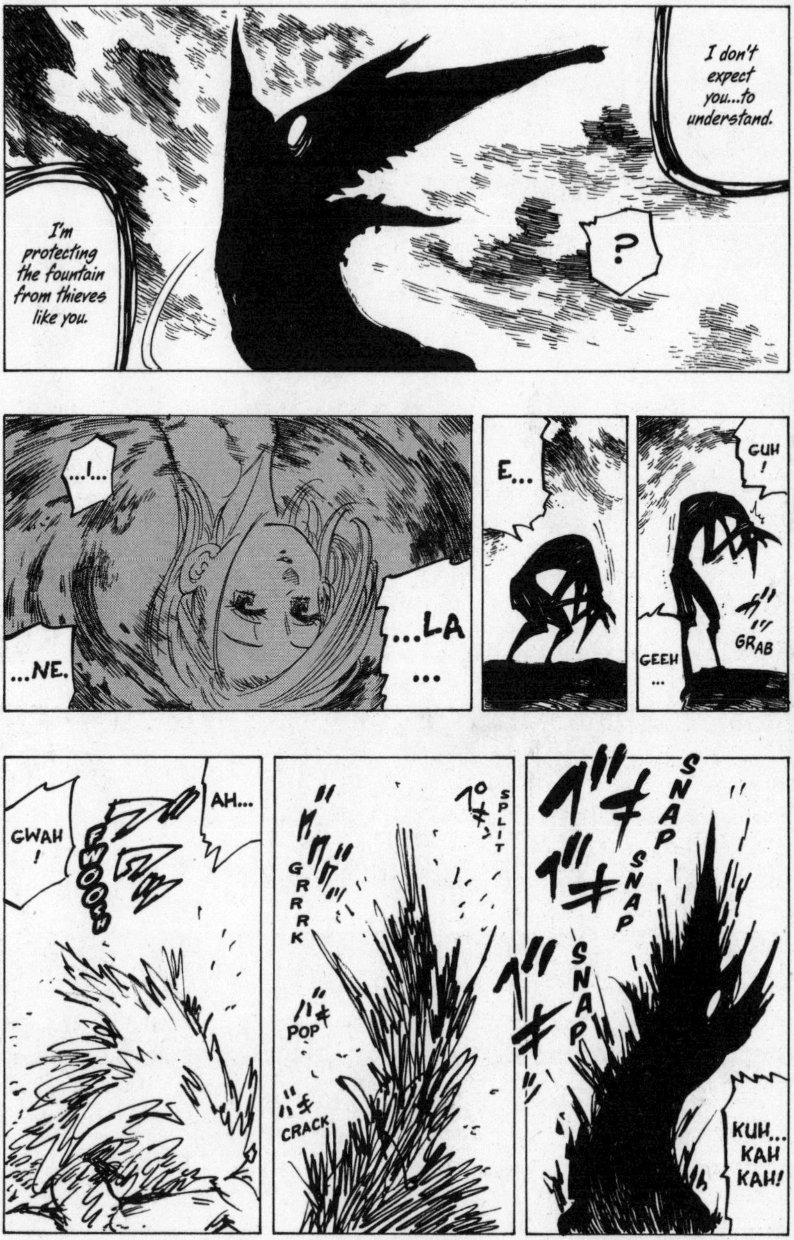

I don't expect you...to understand.
?
I'm protecting the fountain from thieves like you.
GUH!
GRAB
GEEH...
E...
...I...
...LA...
...NE.
SNAP
SNAP
SNAP
KUH... KAH KAH!
SPLIT
GRRRK
POP
CRACK
AH...
FWOOOSH
GWAH!

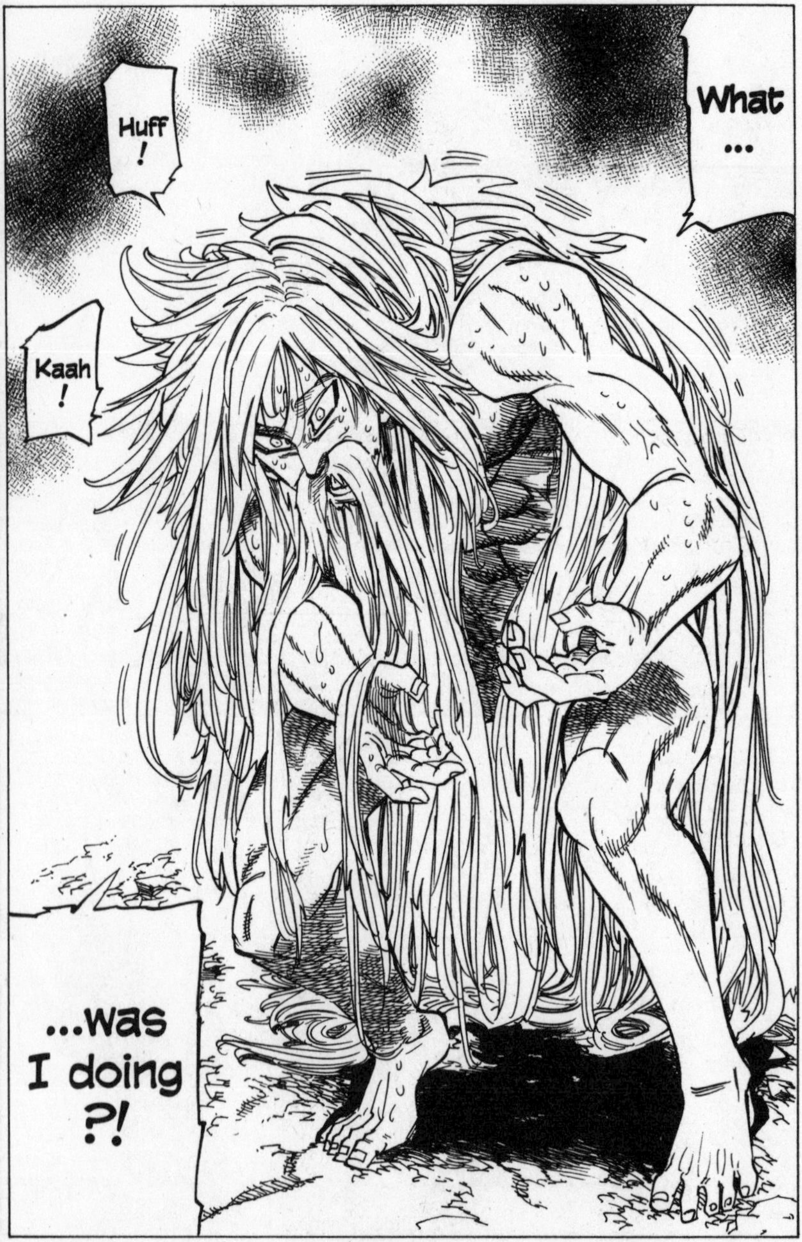
What ...
Huff!
Kaah!
...was I doing?!

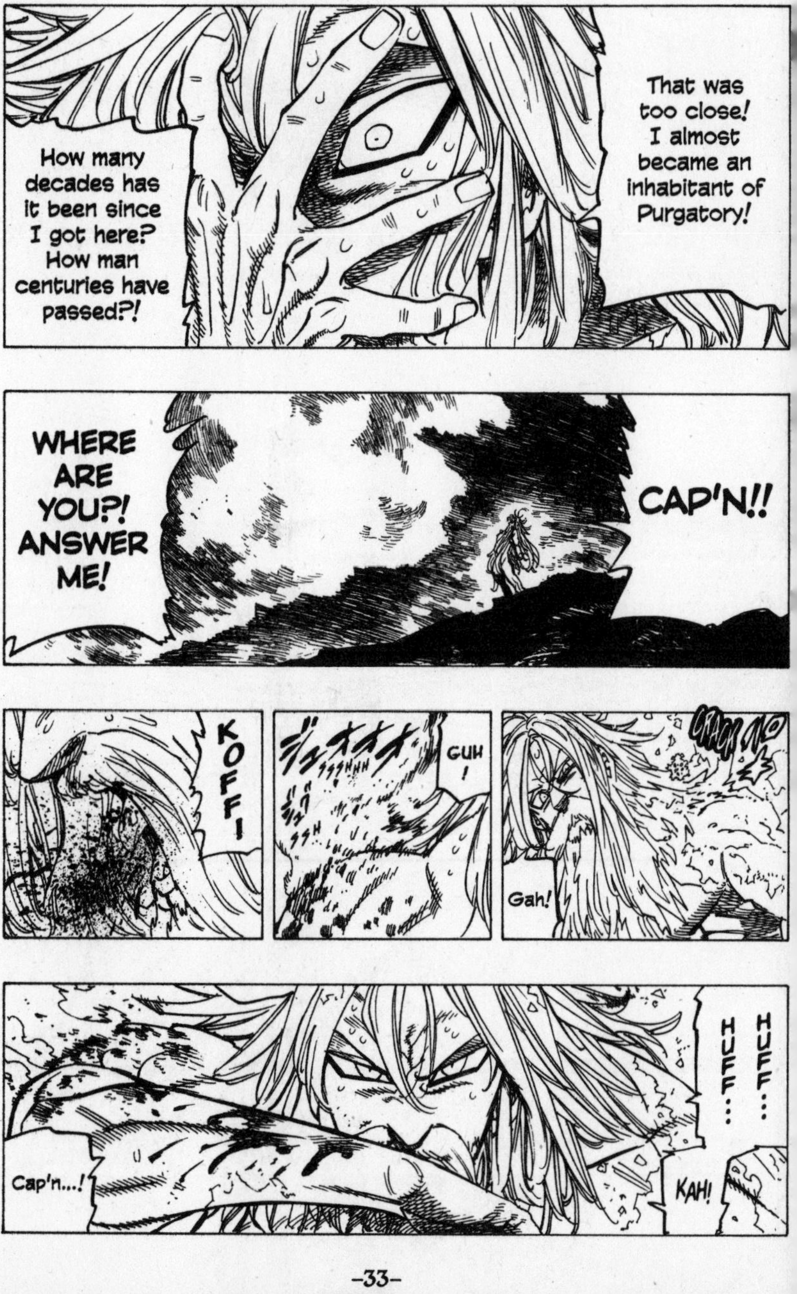
That was too close! I almost became an inhabitant of Purgatory!
How many decades has it been since I got here? How man centuries have passed?!
CAP'N!!
WHERE ARE YOU?! ANSWER ME!
Gah!
GUH!
KOFF!
HUFF... HUFF...
KAH!
Cap'n...!

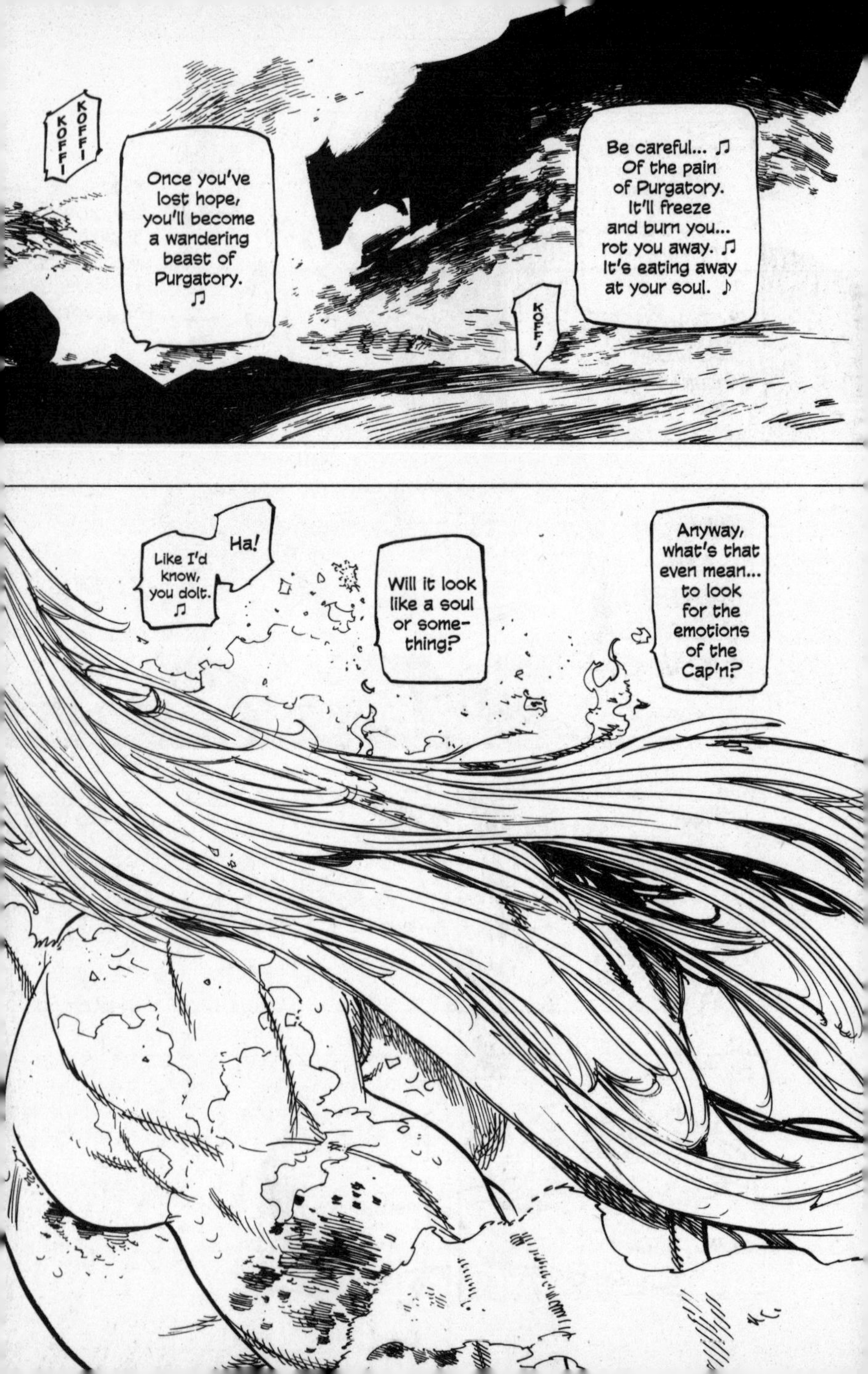
Be careful... ♫ Of the pain of Purgatory. It'll freeze and burn you... rot you away. ♫ It's eating away at your soul. ♪
KOFF!
Once you've lost hope, you'll become a wandering beast of Purgatory. ♫
KOFFI KOFFI
Anyway, what's that even mean... to look for the emotions of the Cap'n?
Will it look like a soul or some-thing?
Ha!
Like I'd know, you dolt. ♫

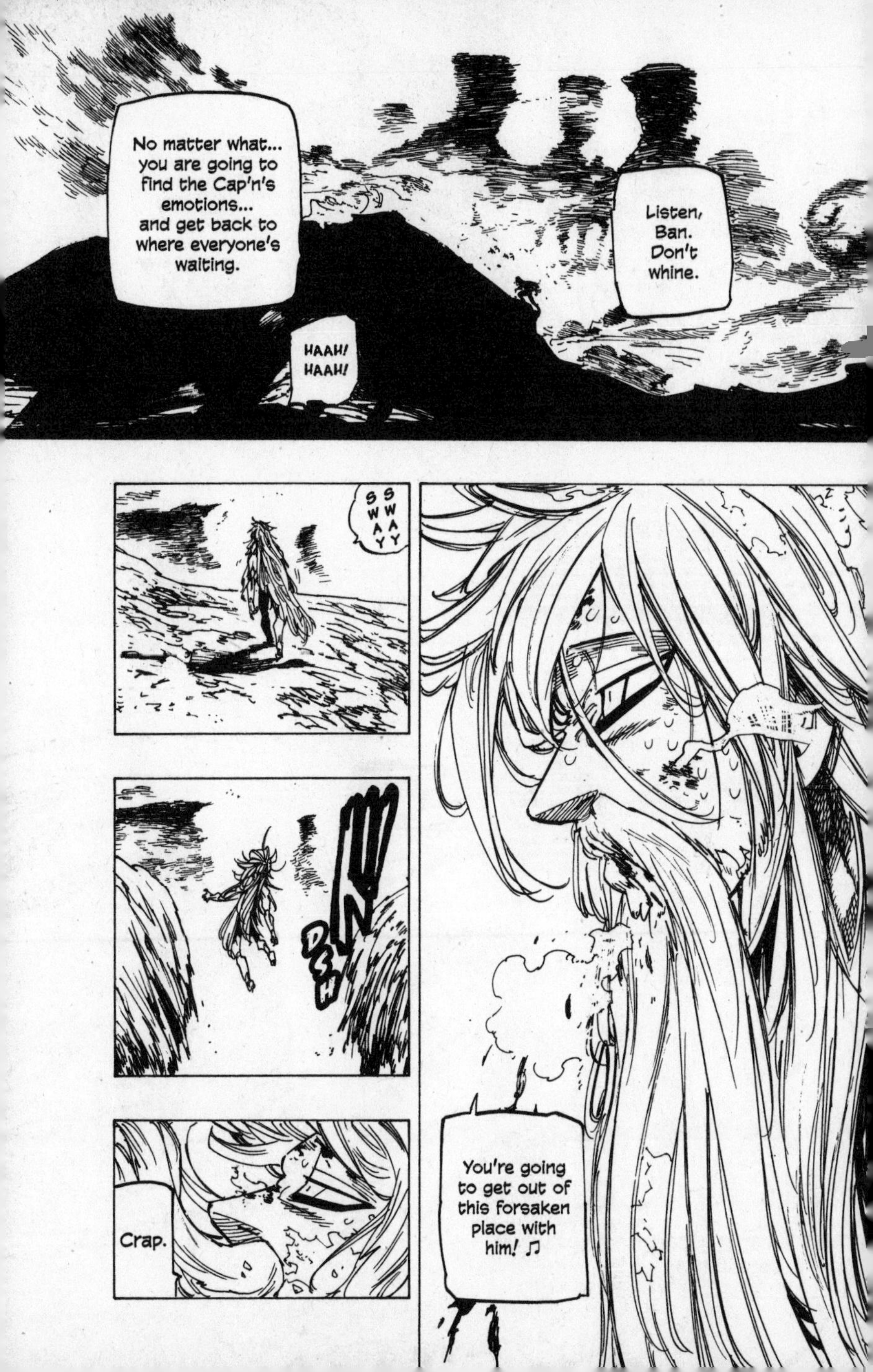
Listen, Ban. Don't whine.
No matter what... you are going to find the Cap'n's emotions... and get back to where everyone's waiting.
HAAH! HAAH!
You're going to get out of this forsaken place with him! ♫
SWAY SWAY
DASH
Crap.

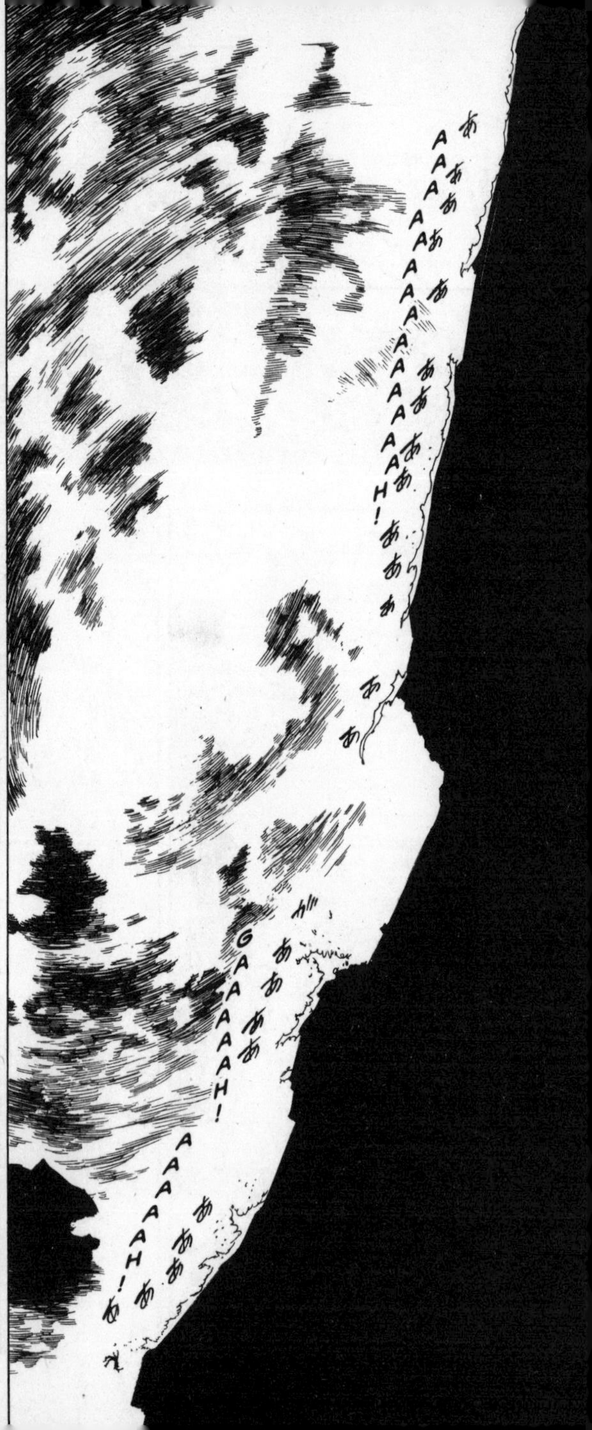
AAAAAAAAAAAAAAH!
ああああああああああああああ
GAAAAAAH!
ががあああ
AAAAAH!
あああああ

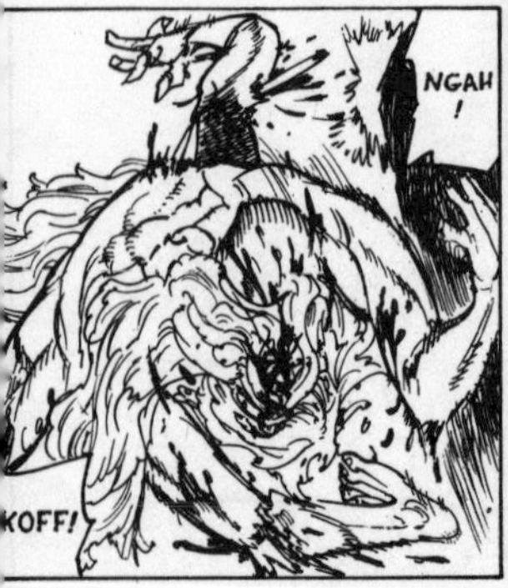
NGAH!
KOFF!

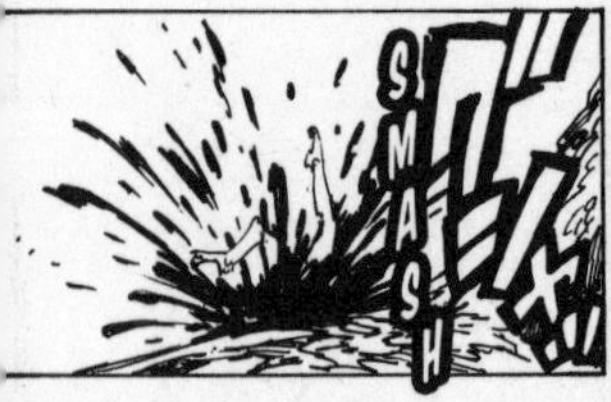
SMASH

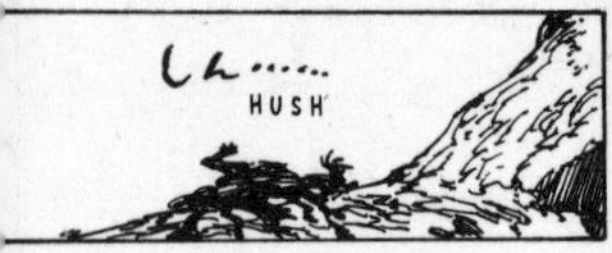
しん……
HUSH

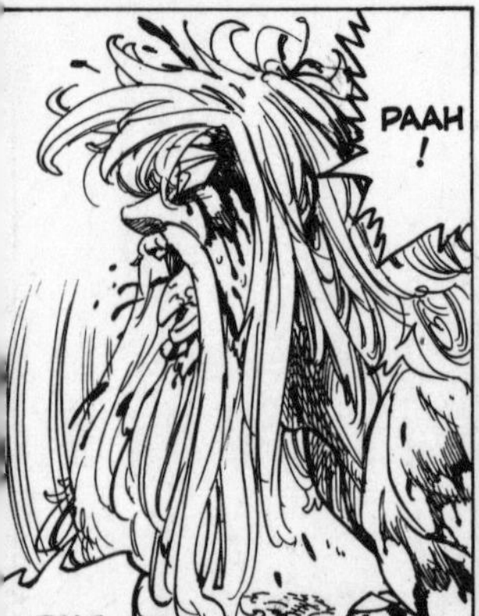
PAAH!
THAT HURT!!

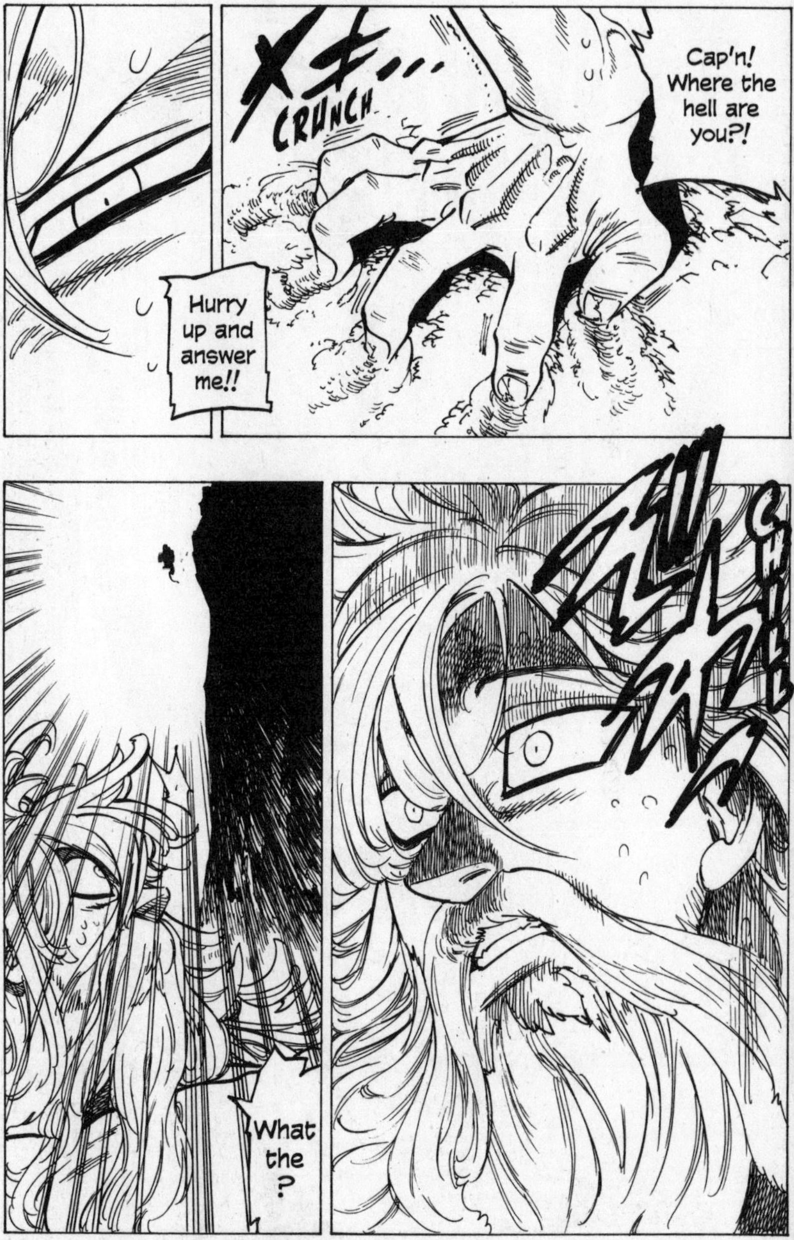
Cap'n! Where the hell are you?!
メキ…
CRUNCH
Hurry up and answer me!!
CHILL
What the ?

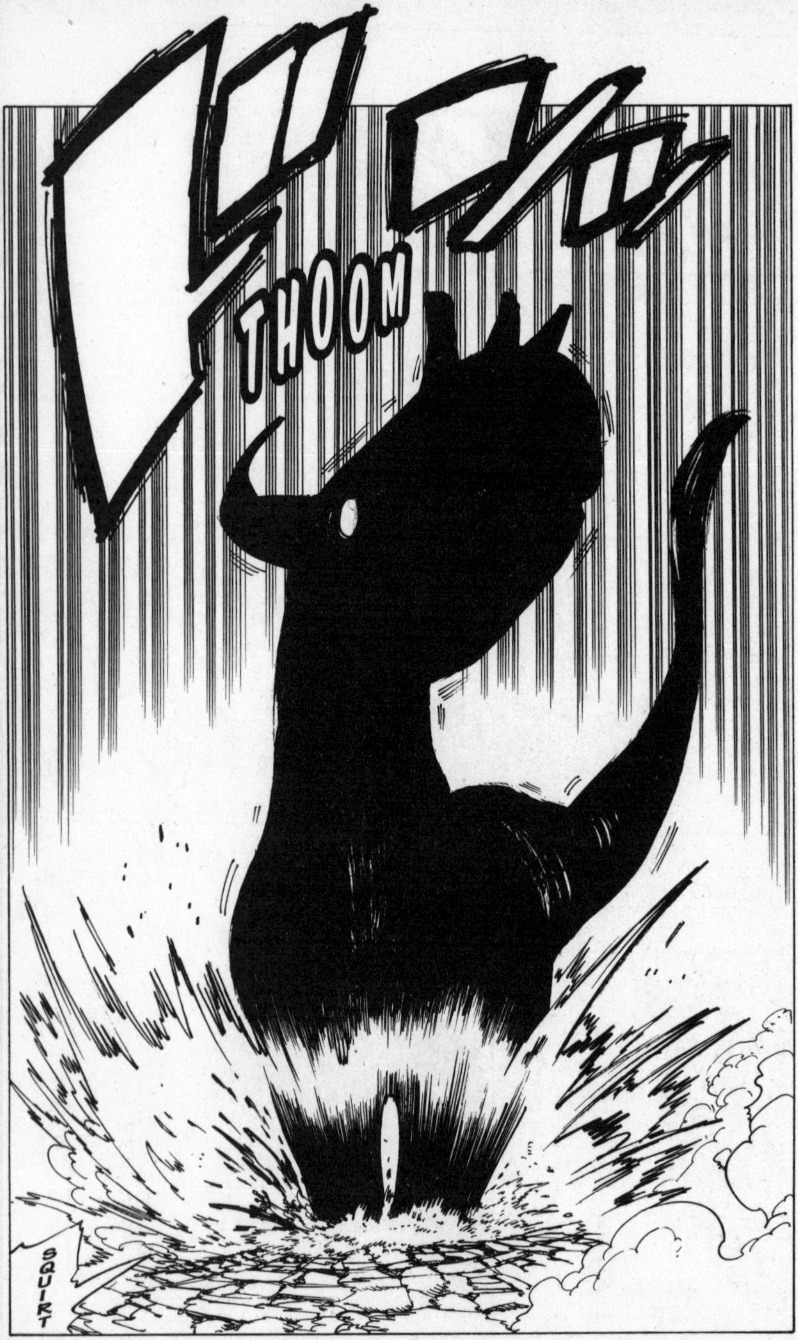
THOOM
SQUIRT

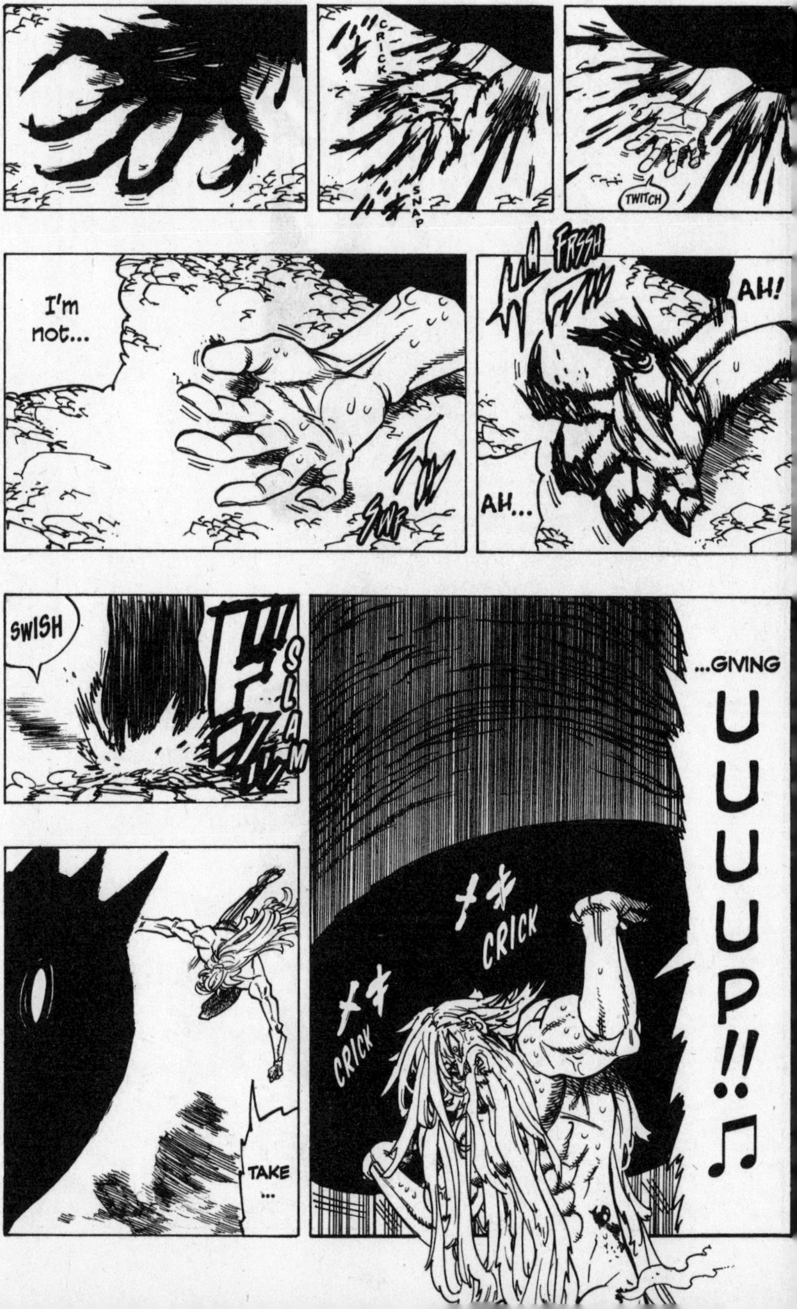
TWITCH
CRICK
SNAP
FRSSH
AH!
AH...
I'm not...
SWF
...GIVING
UUUUP!!♫
メキ
CRICK
メキ
CRICK
SWISH
SLAM
TAKE
...

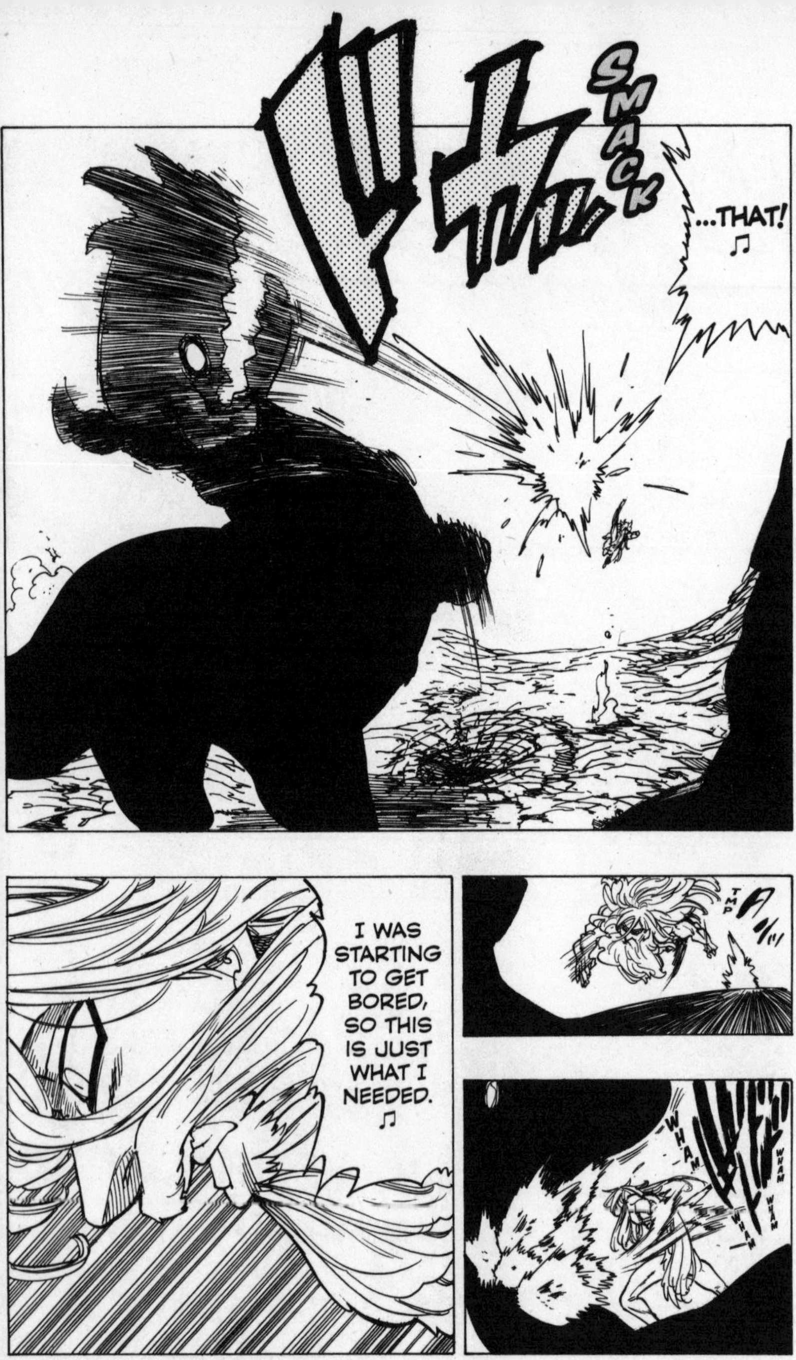
SMACK
...THAT! ♫
I WAS STARTING TO GET BORED, SO THIS IS JUST WHAT I NEEDED. ♫
TMP
WHAM
WHAM
WHAM
WHAM

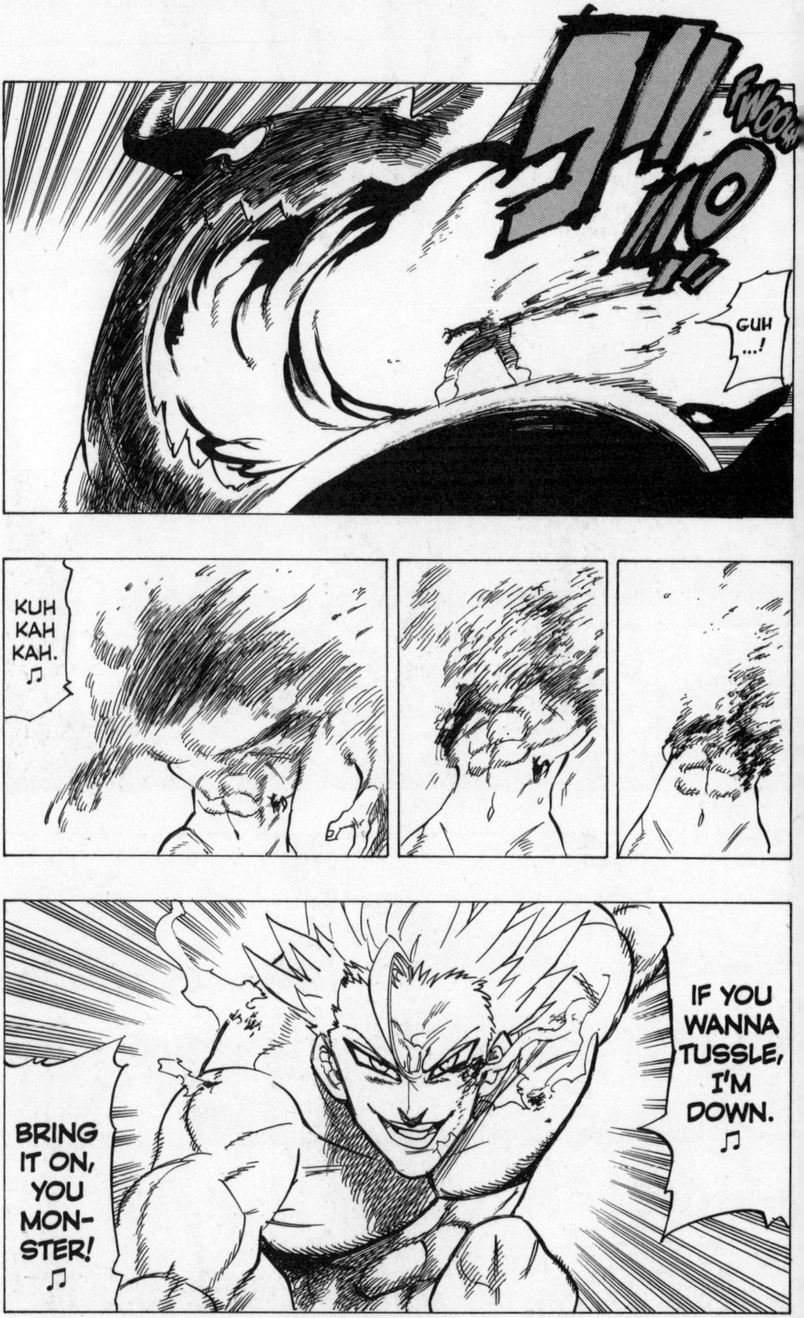
FWOOM
GUH ...!
KUH KAH KAH. ♫
IF YOU WANNA TUSSLE, I'M DOWN. ♫
BRING IT ON, YOU MON-STER! ♫

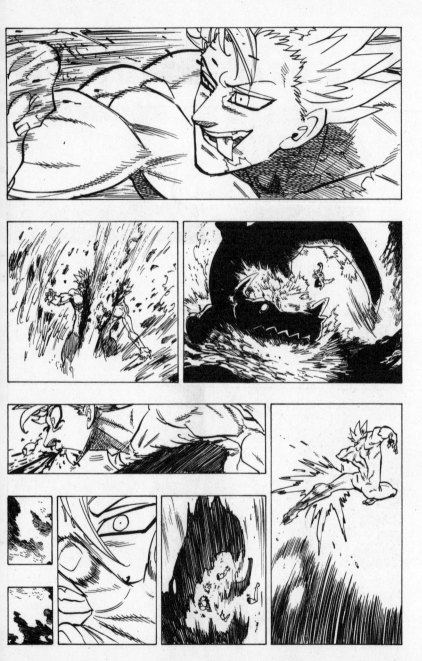

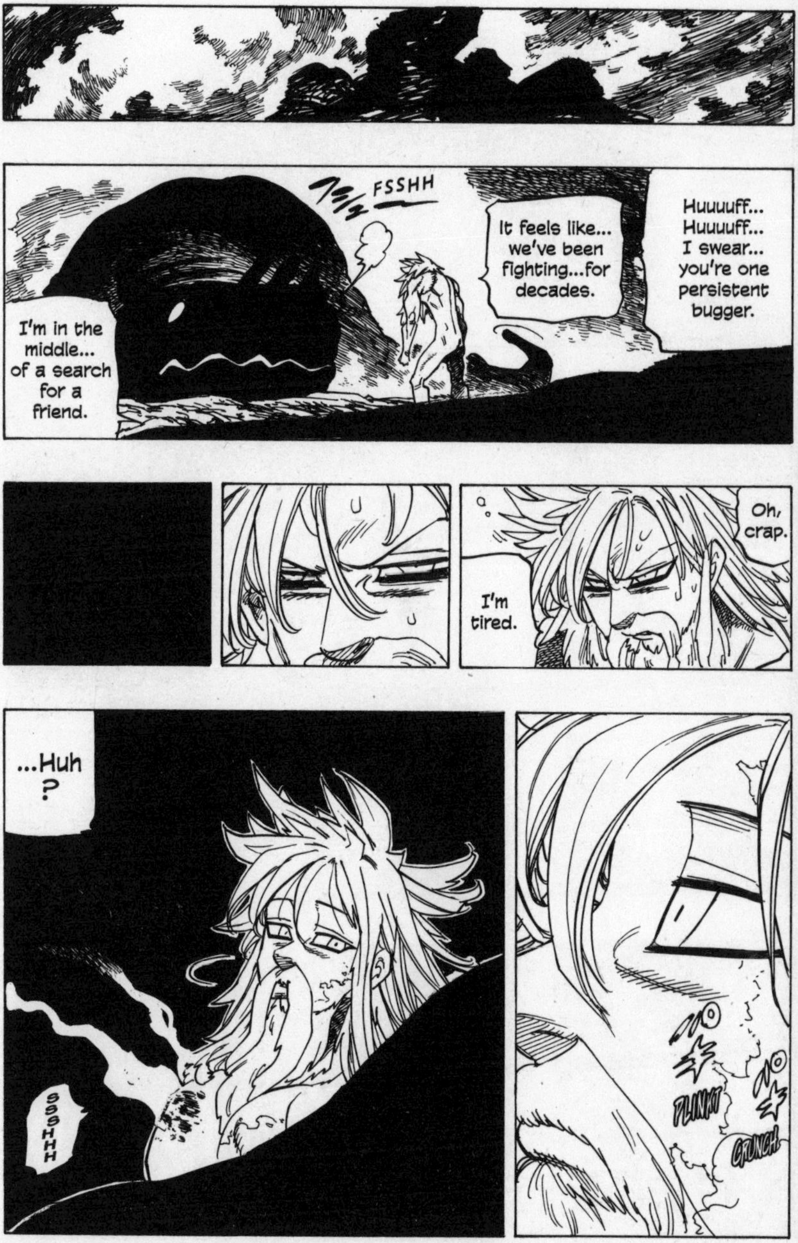
Huuuuff... Huuuuff... I swear... you're one persistent bugger.
FSSHH
It feels like... we've been fighting...for decades.
I'm in the middle... of a search for a friend.
Oh, crap.
I'm tired.
PLINK
CRUNCH
...Huh?
SSSHHH

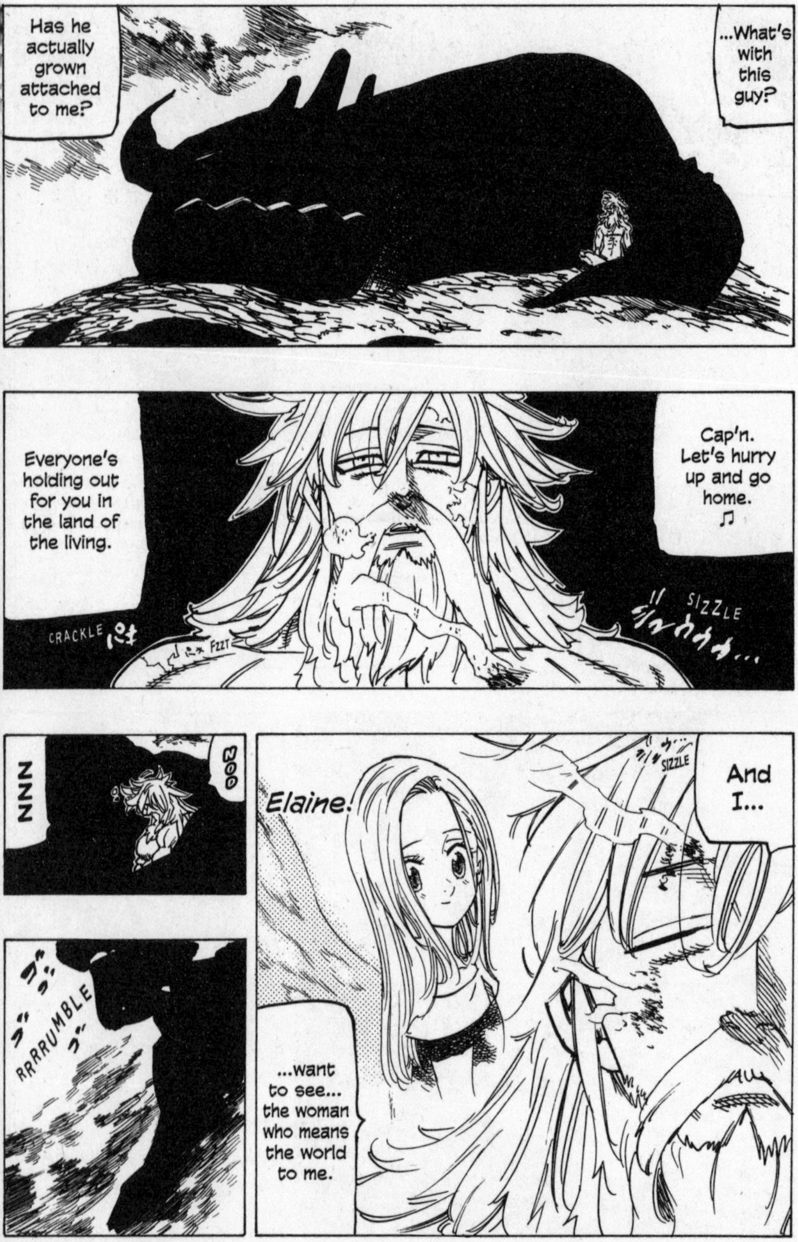

...What's with this guy?
Has he actually grown attached to me?
Cap'n. Let's hurry up and go home. ♫
Everyone's holding out for you in the land of the living.
SIZZLE
FZZT
CRACKLE
SIZZLE
And I...
Elaine!
...want to see... the woman who means the world to me.
NOD
NNN
RRRRUMBLE

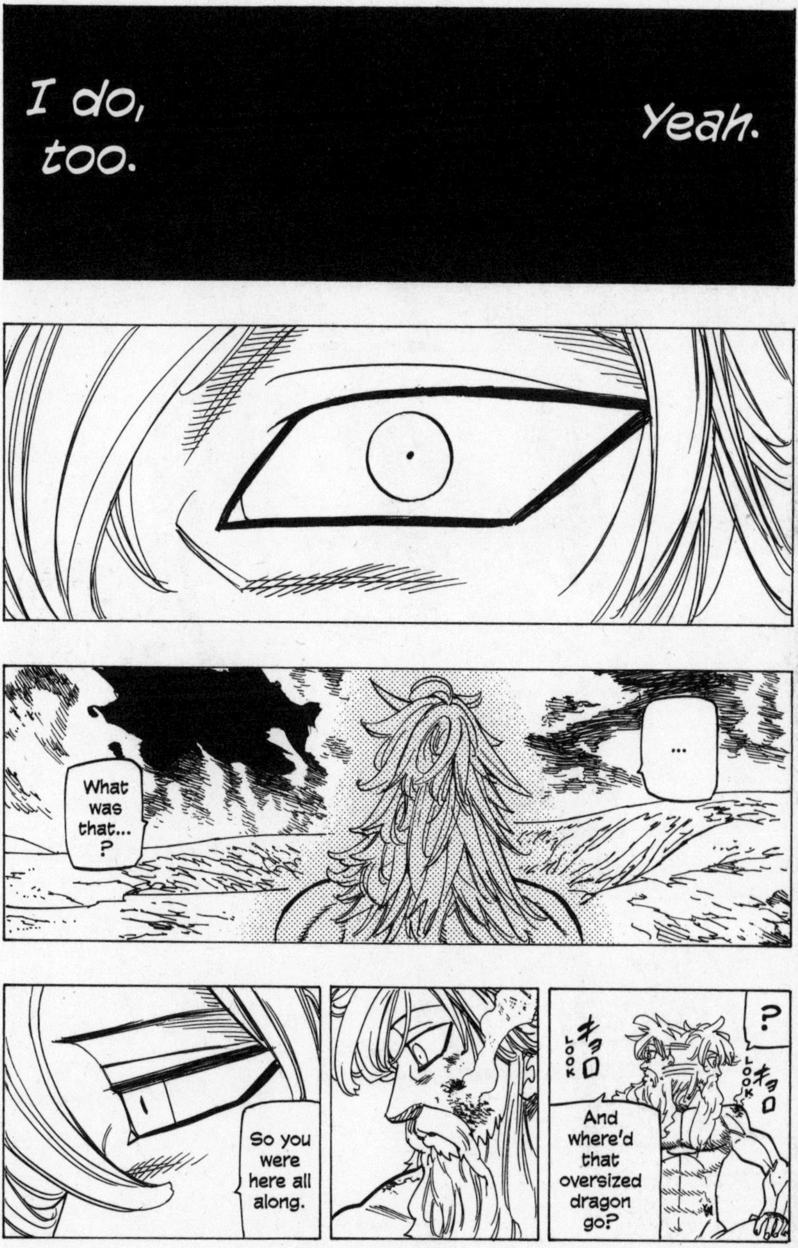
Yeah.
I do, too.
...
What was that...?
?
キョロ LOOK
キョロ LOOK
And where'd that oversized dragon go?
So you were here all along.

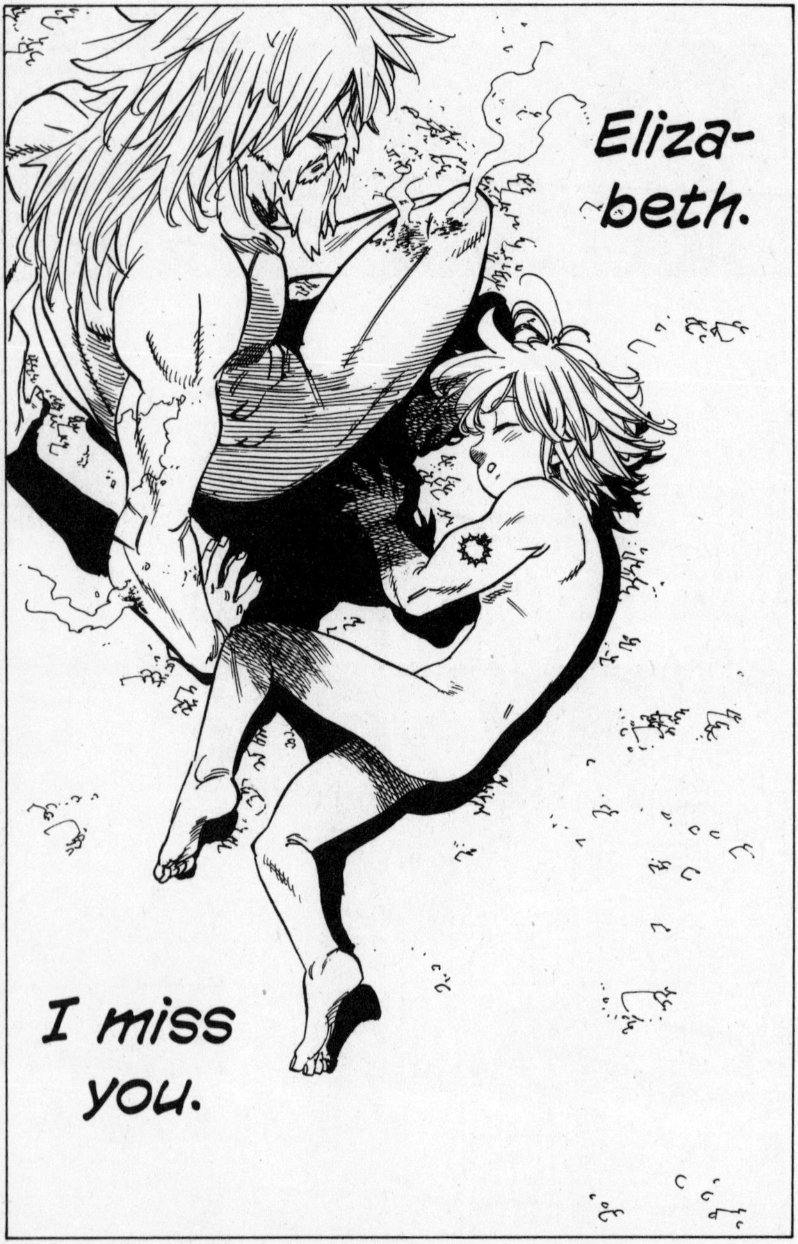
Eliza-
beth.
I miss
you.

Chapter 269 - Purgatory Life

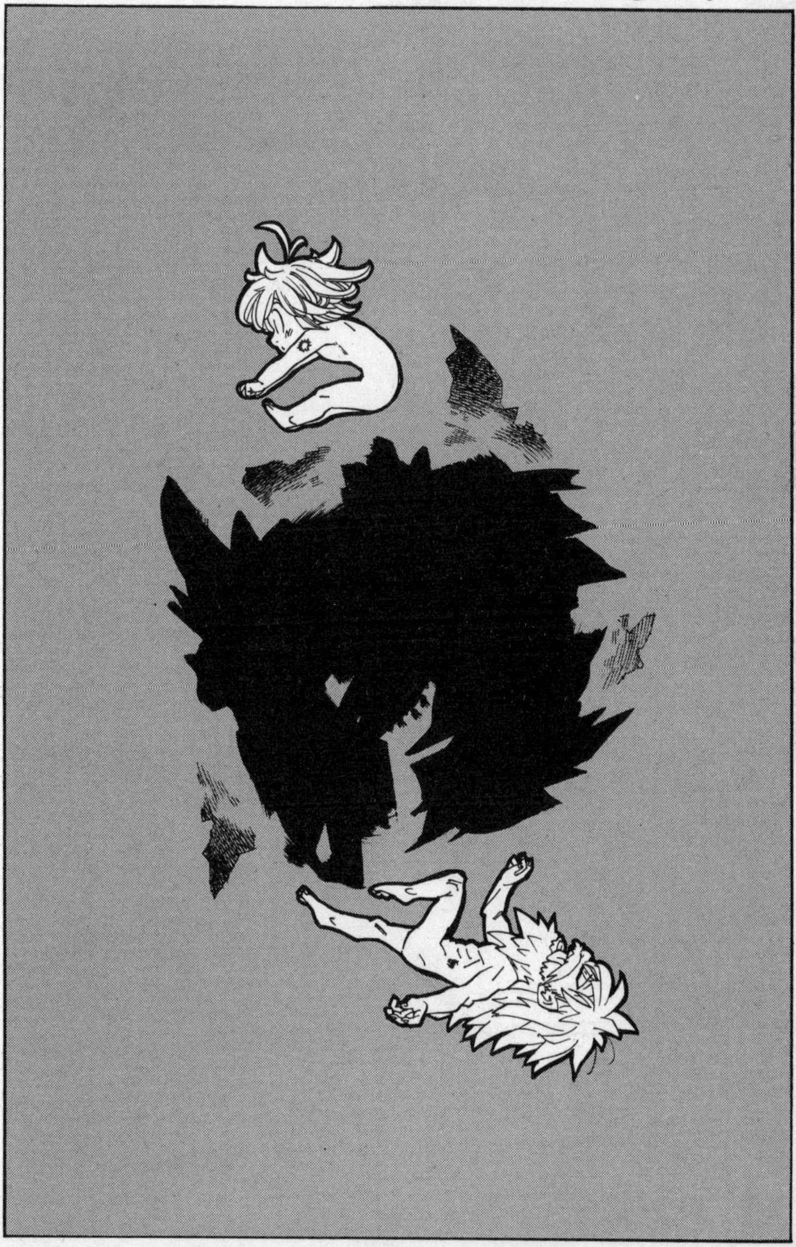

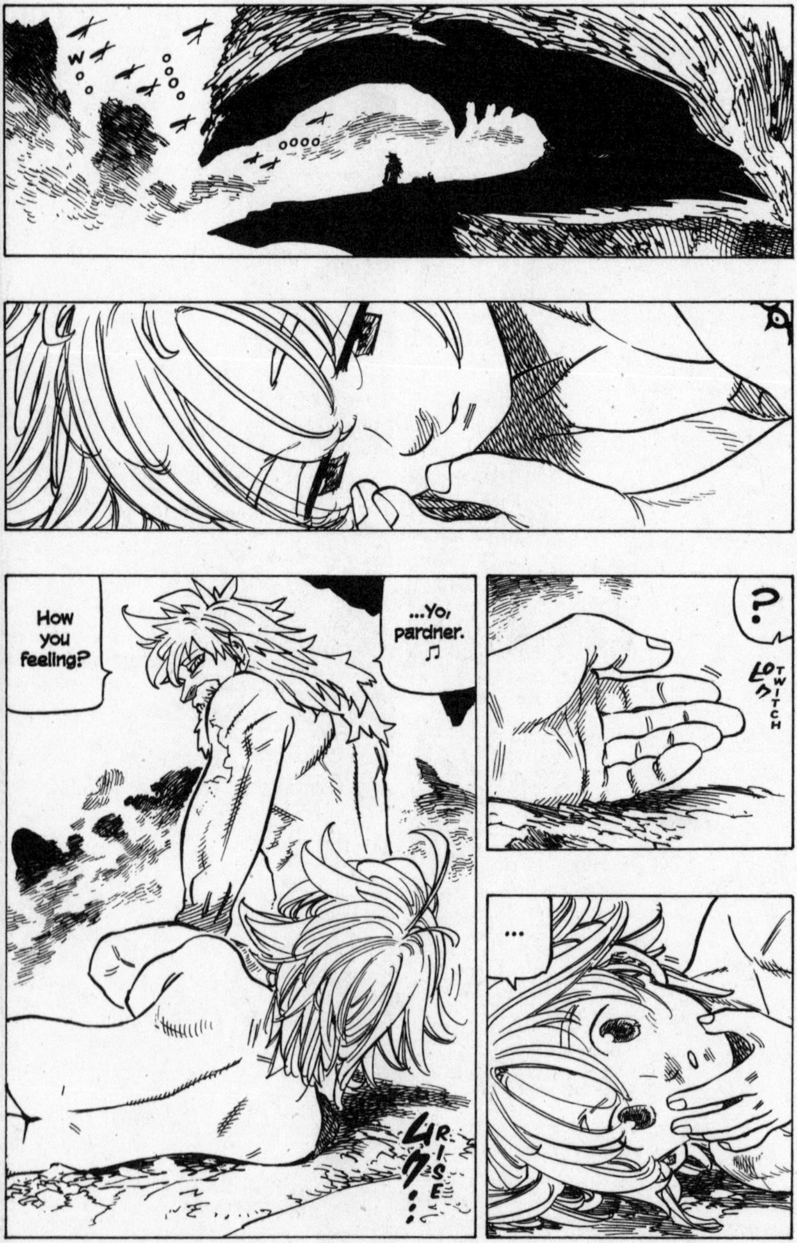
?
TWITCH
...
...Yo, pardner. ♫
How you feeling?
RISE

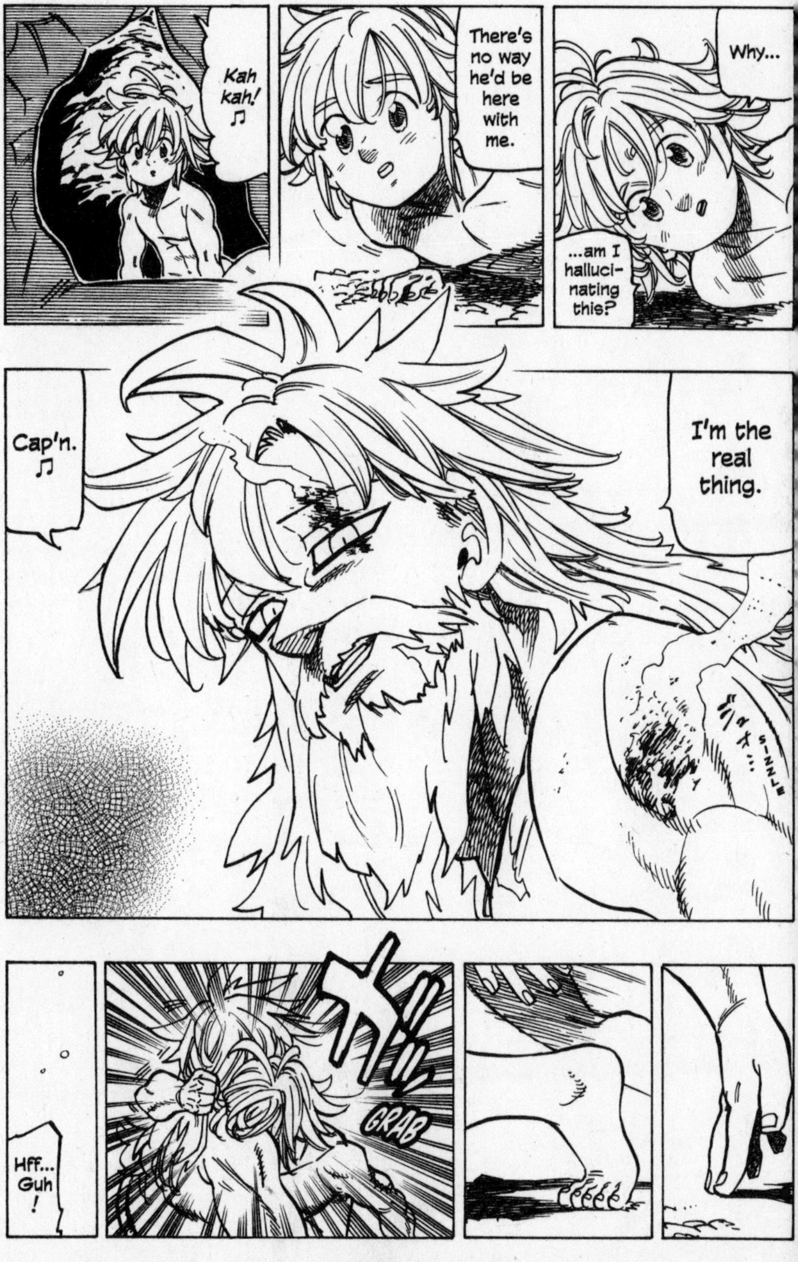
Why...
...am I hallucinating this?
There's no way he'd be here with me.
Kah kah! ♫
I'm the real thing.
SIZZLE
Cap'n. ♫
GRAB
Hff... Guh!

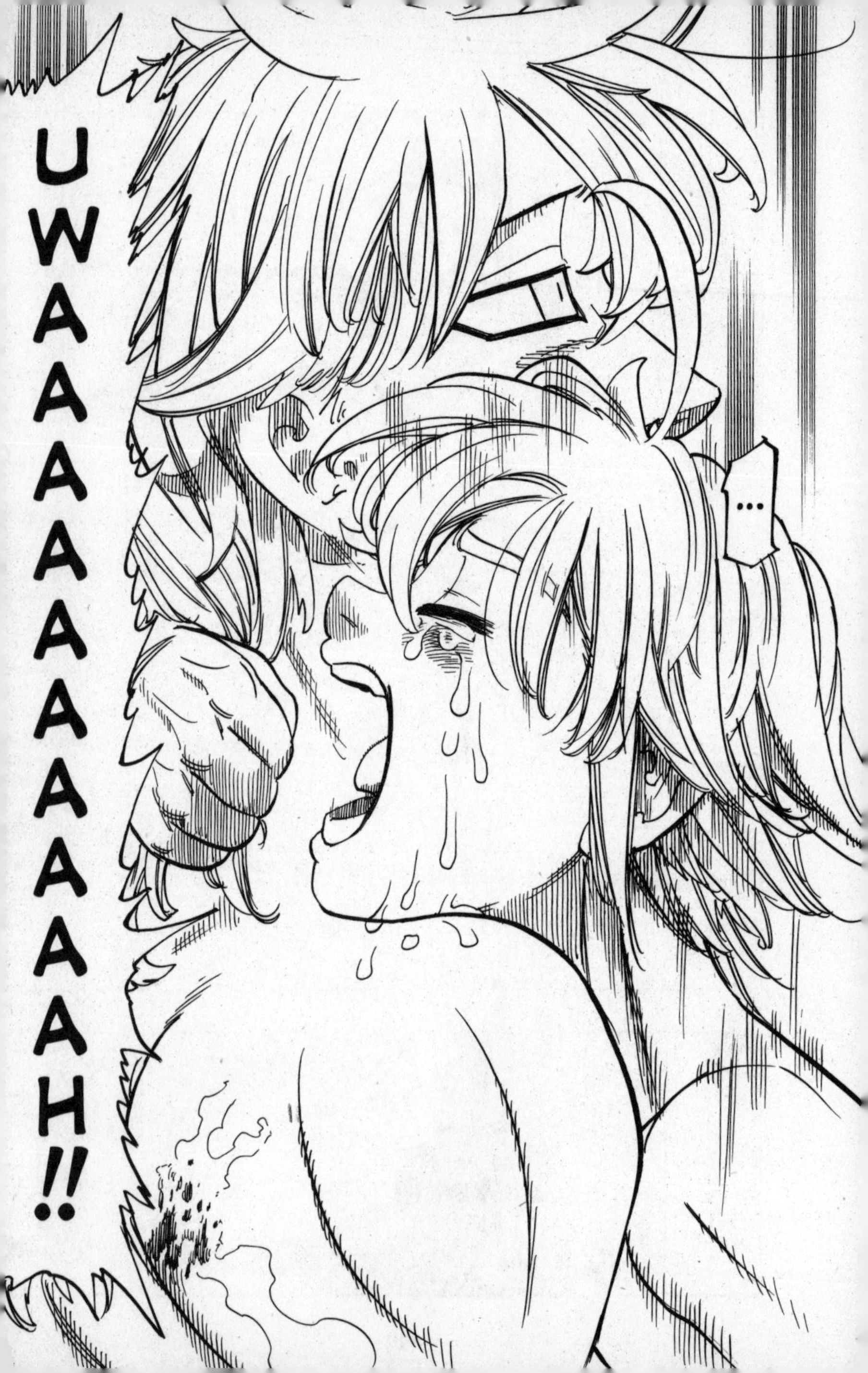
...
UWAAAAAAAAAH!!

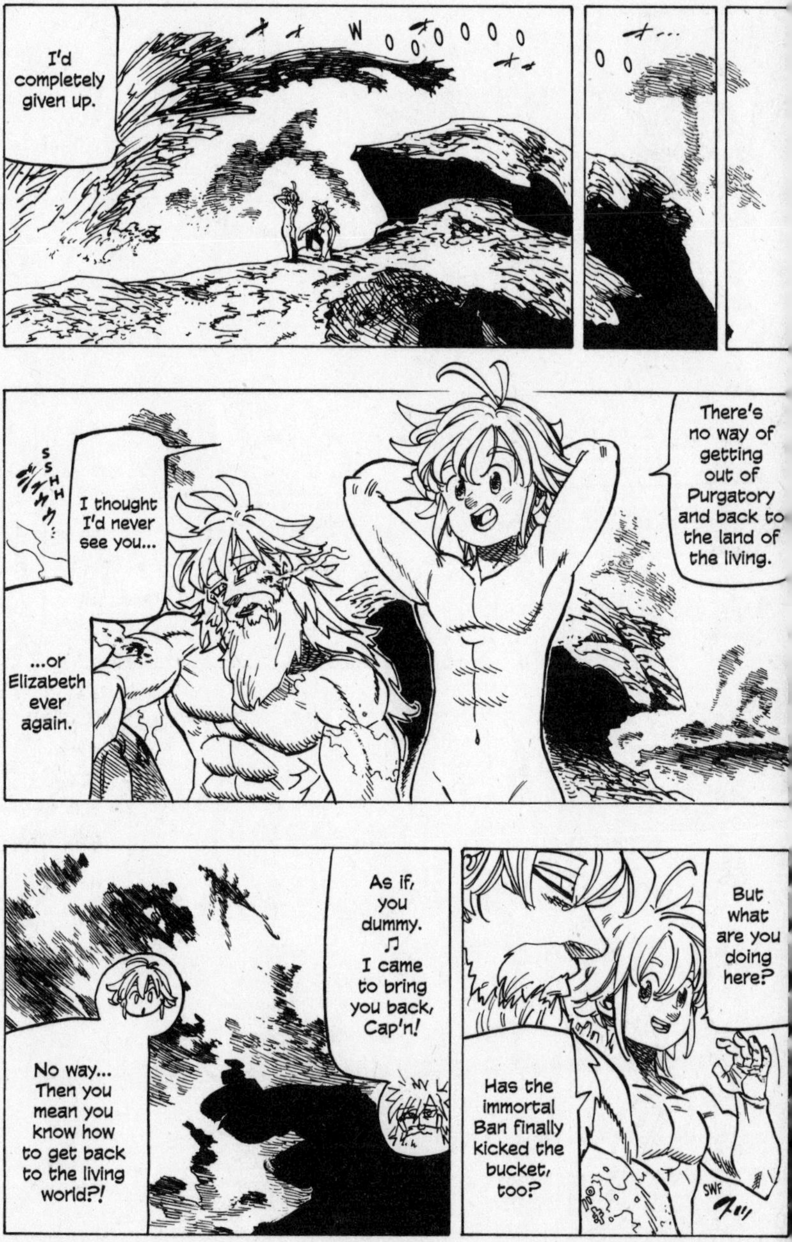

OO
WOOOOOO
I'd completely given up.
There's no way of getting out of Purgatory and back to the land of the living.
SSHH
I thought I'd never see you...
...or Elizabeth ever again.
But what are you doing here?
Has the immortal Ban finally kicked the bucket, too?
SWF
As if, you dummy. ♫ I came to bring you back, Cap'n!
No way... Then you mean you know how to get back to the living world?!

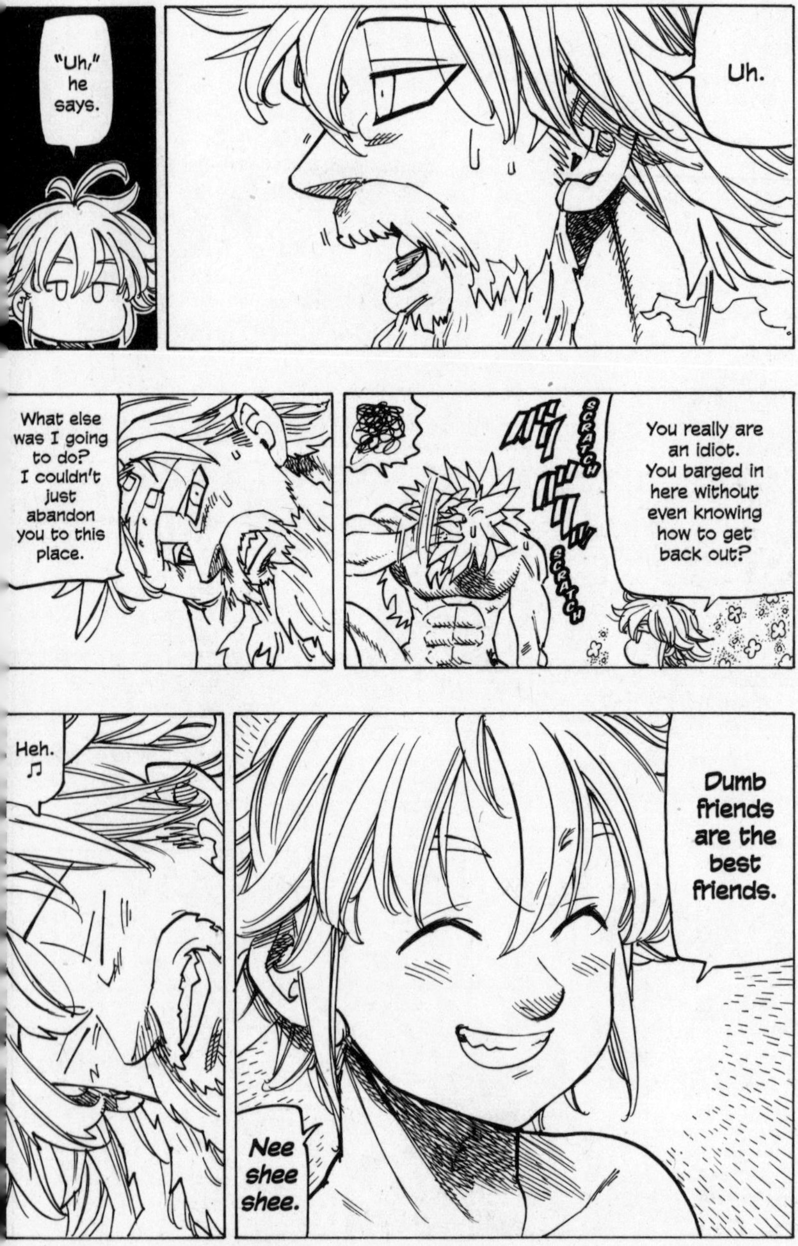
Uh.
"Uh," he says.
You really are an idiot. You barged in here without even knowing how to get back out?
SCRATCH
SCRATCH
What else was I going to do? I couldn't just abandon you to this place.
Dumb friends are the best friends.
Nee shee shee.
Heh. ♫

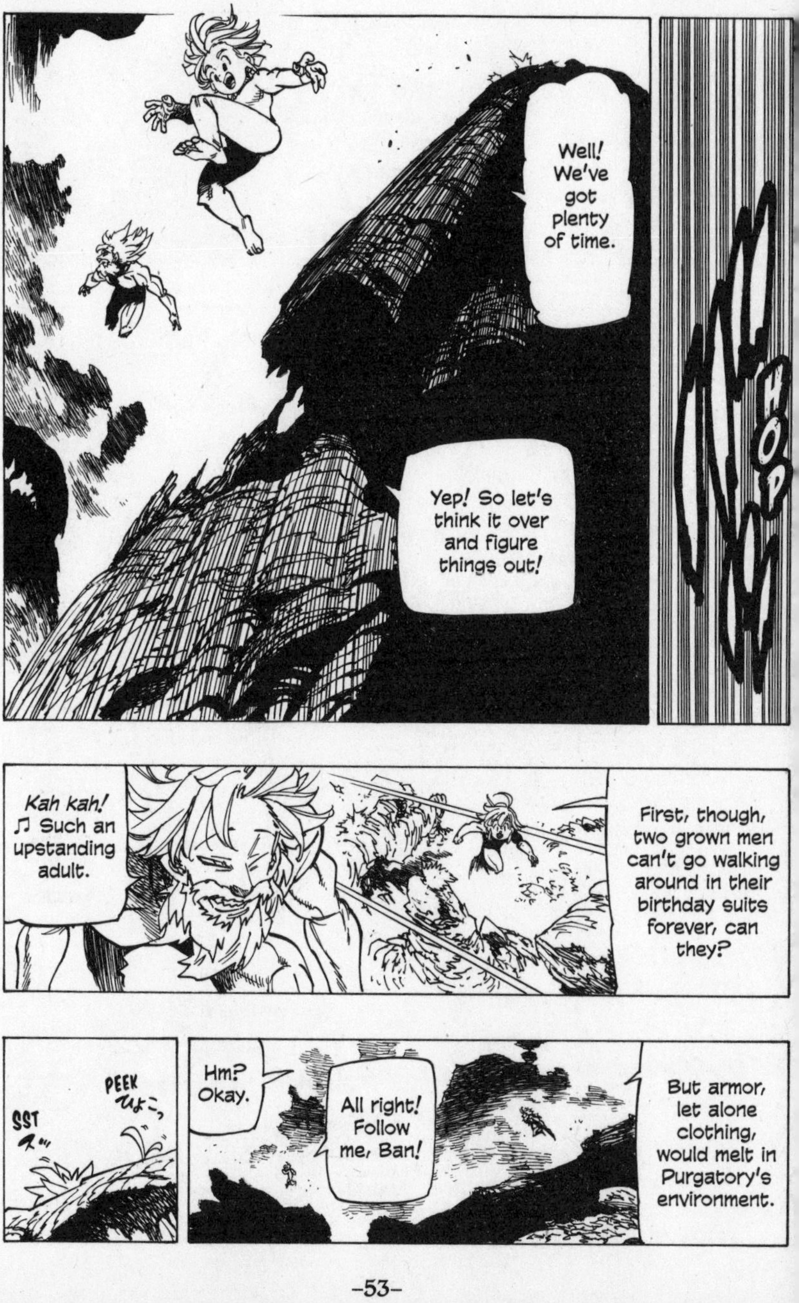
HOP
Well! We've got plenty of time.
Yep! So let's think it over and figure things out!
First, though, two grown men can't go walking around in their birthday suits forever, can they?
Kah kah! ♫ Such an upstanding adult.
But armor, let alone clothing, would melt in Purgatory's environment.
All right! Follow me, Ban!
Hm? Okay.
PEEK
SST

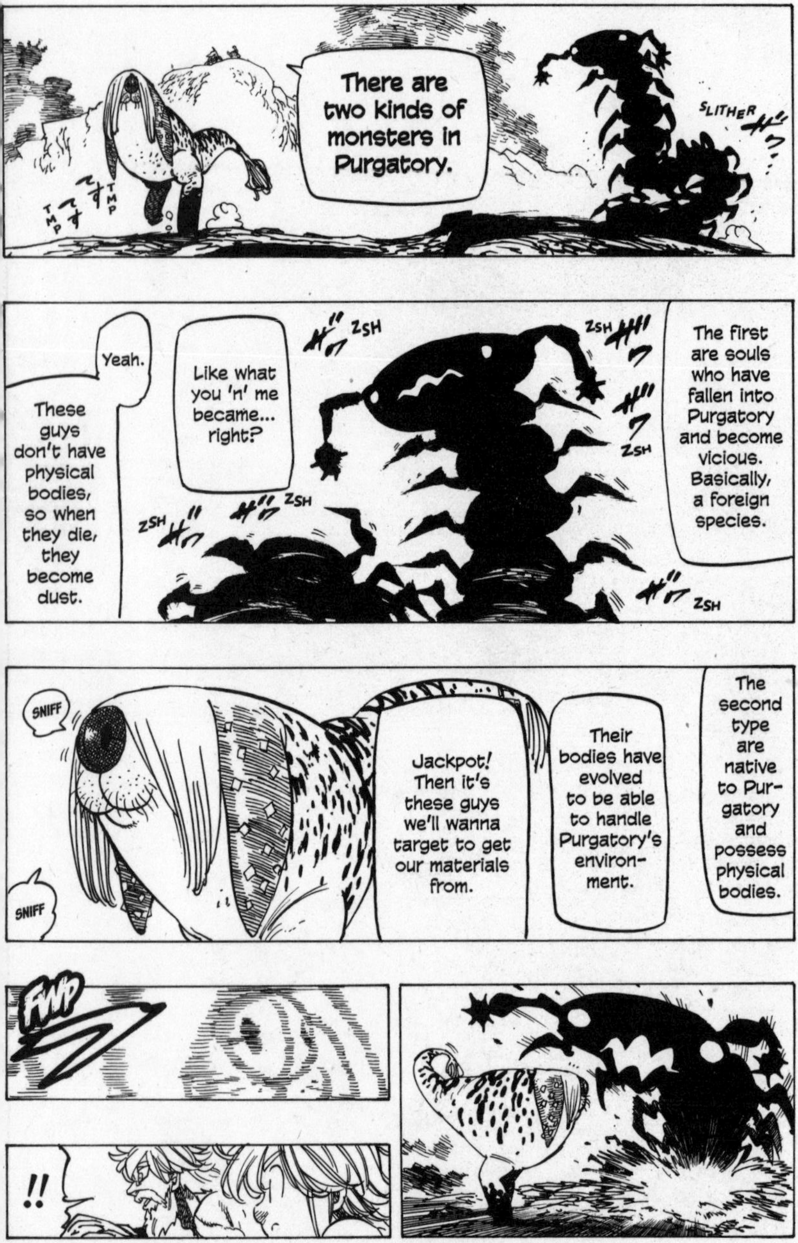
SLITHER
There are two kinds of monsters in Purgatory.
TMP TMP
The first are souls who have fallen into Purgatory and become vicious. Basically, a foreign species.
ZSH
ZSH
ZSH
ZSH
ZSH
ZSH
Like what you 'n' me became... right?
Yeah.
These guys don't have physical bodies, so when they die, they become dust.
The second type are native to Purgatory and possess physical bodies.
Their bodies have evolved to be able to handle Purgatory's environment.
Jackpot! Then it's these guys we'll wanna target to get our materials from.
SNIFF
SNIFF
FWP
!!

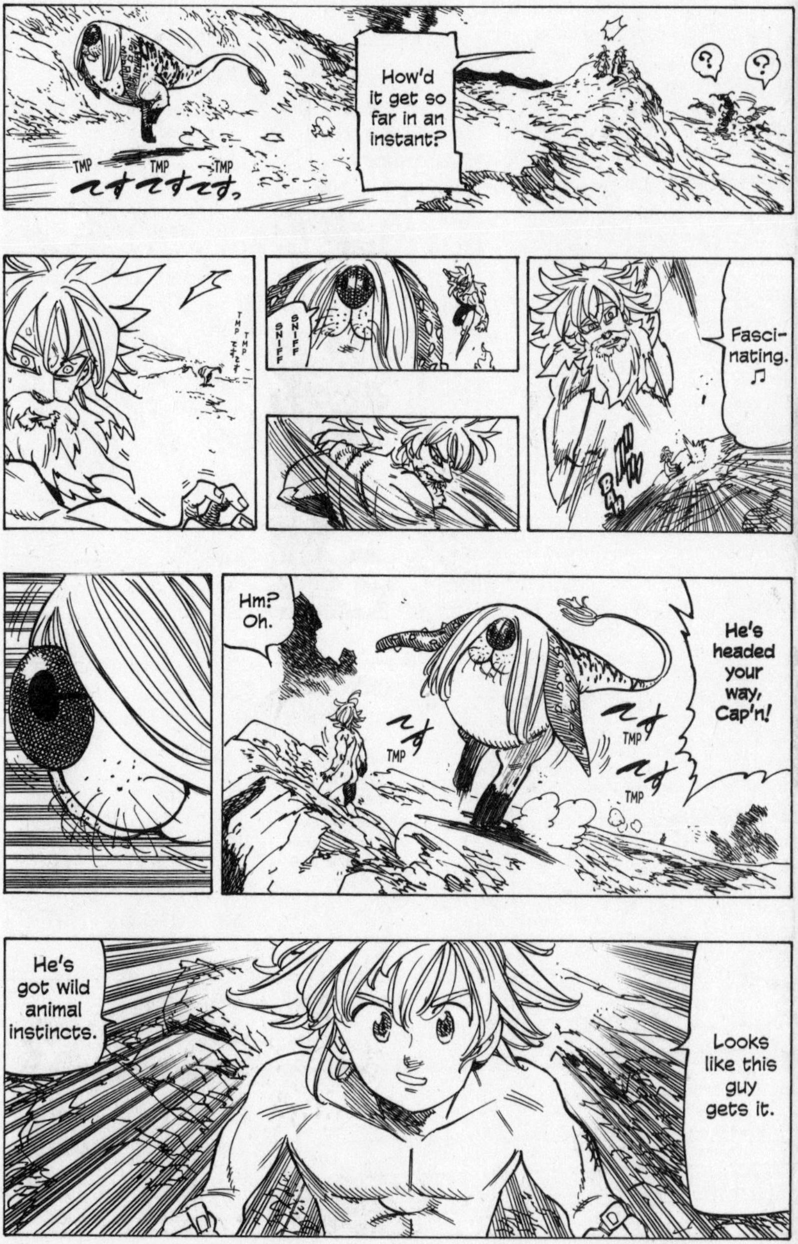

?
?
How'd it get so far in an instant?
TMP
TMP
TMP
Fasci-nating. ♫
SNIFF
SNIFF
TMP
TMP
He's headed your way, Cap'n!
Hm? Oh.
TMP
TMP
TMP
Looks like this guy gets it.
He's got wild animal instincts.

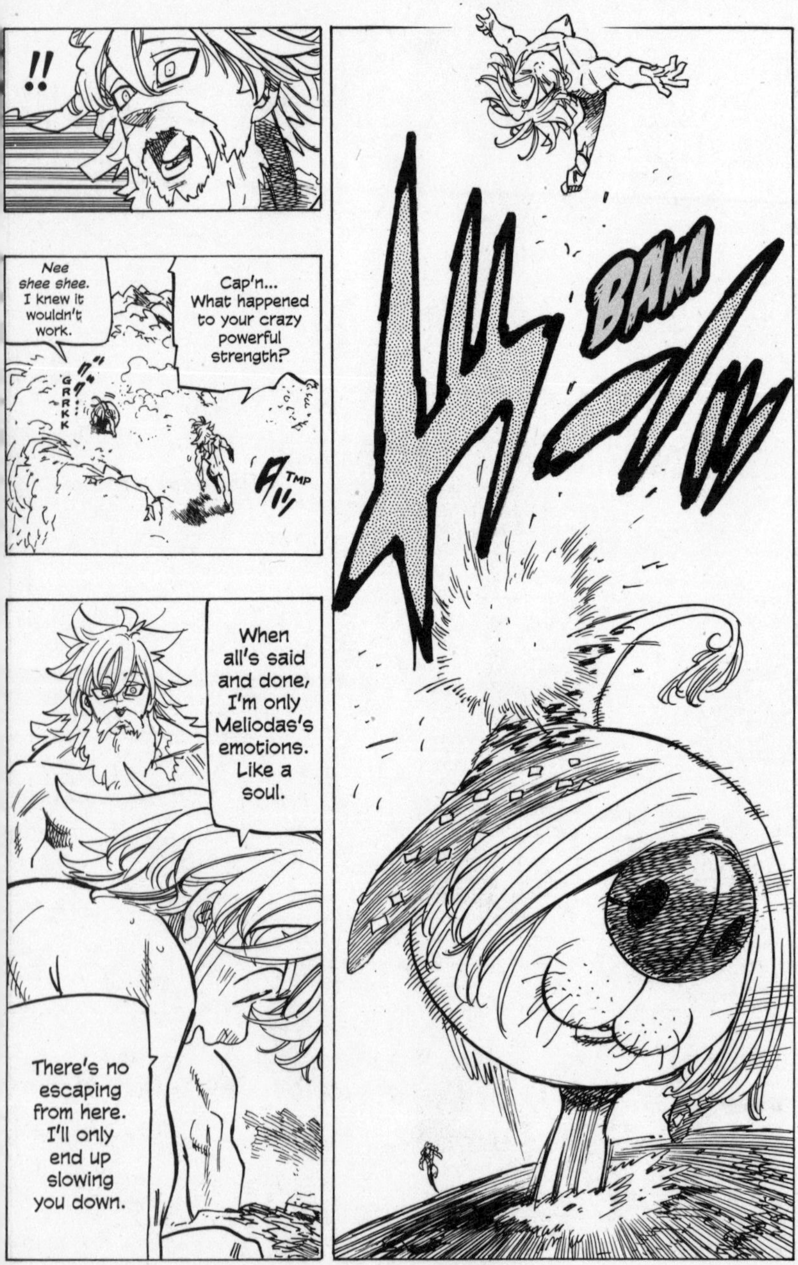
BAM
!!
Cap'n... What happened to your crazy powerful strength?
Nee shee shee. I knew it wouldn't work.
TMP
GRRKK
When all's said and done, I'm only Meliodas's emotions. Like a soul.
There's no escaping from here. I'll only end up slowing you down.

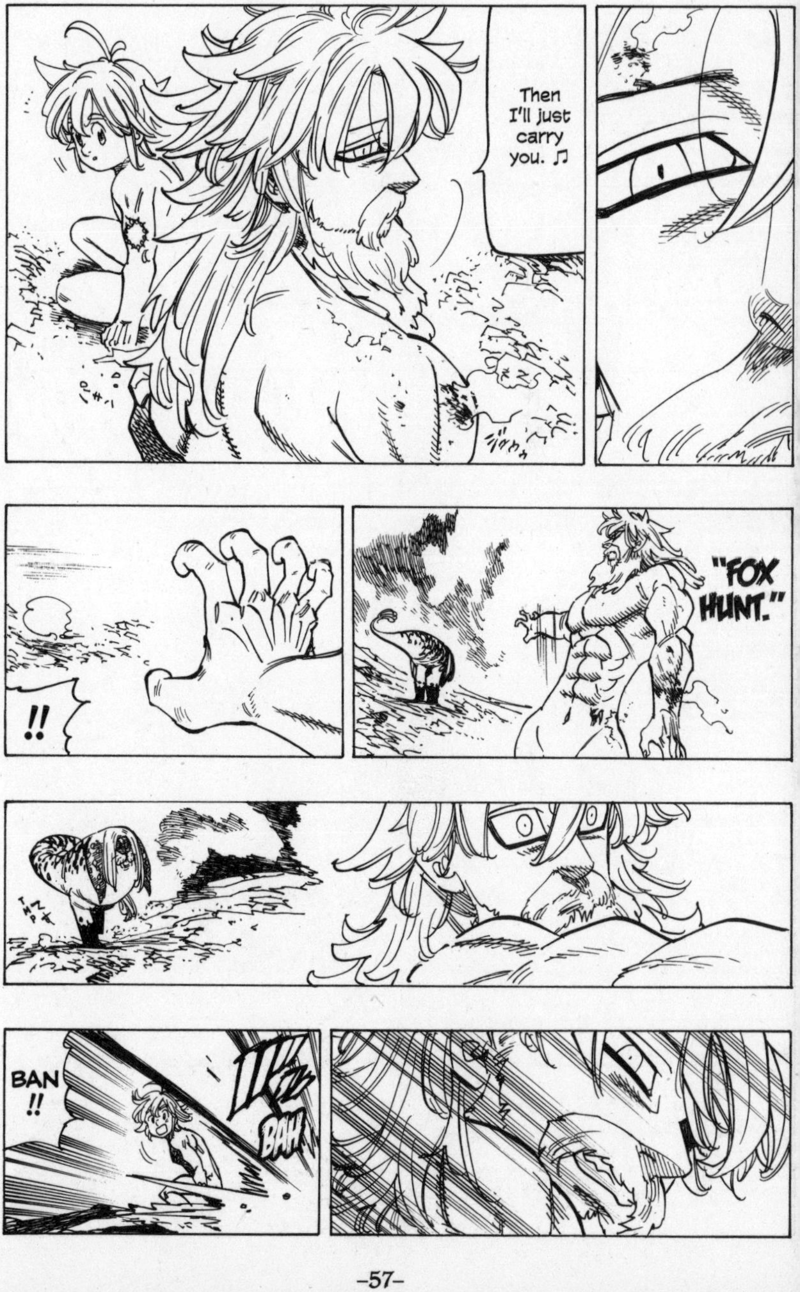
Then I'll just carry you. ♫
"FOX HUNT."
!!
BAH
BAN !!

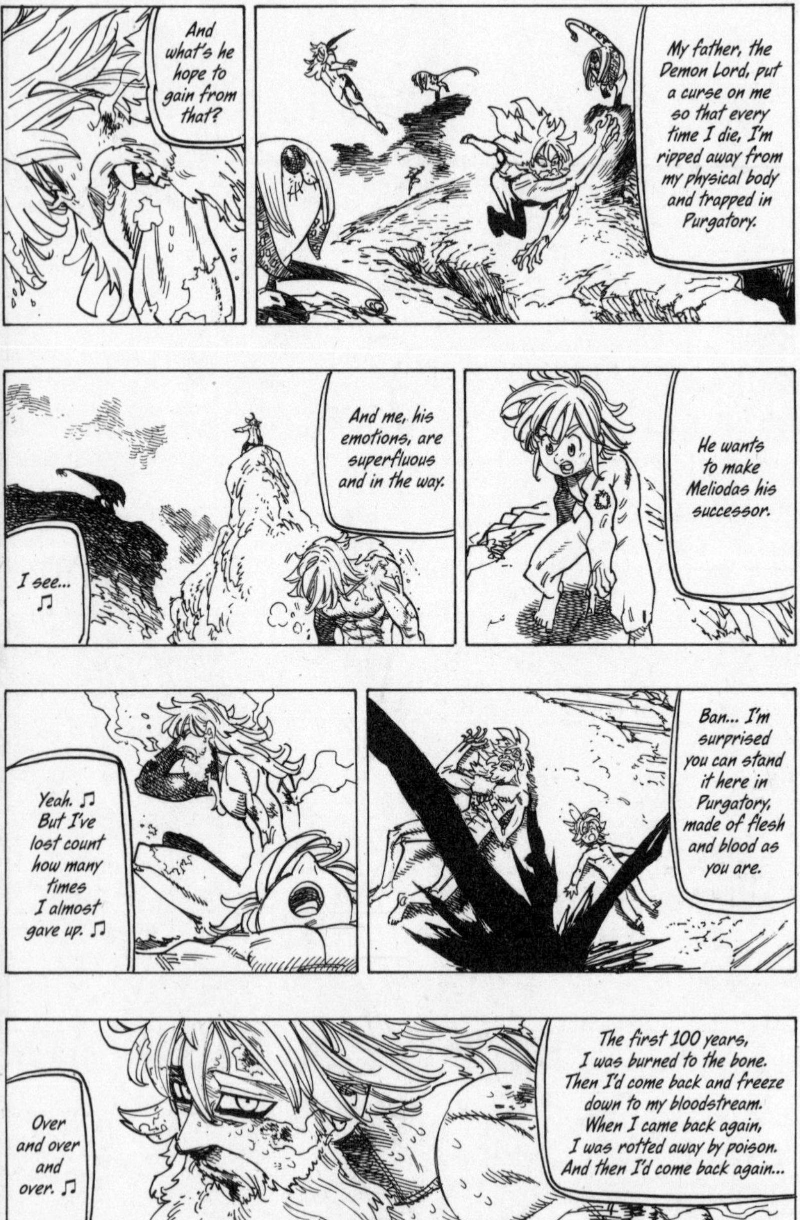
My father, the Demon Lord, put a curse on me so that every time I die, I'm ripped away from my physical body and trapped in Purgatory.
And what's he hope to gain from that?
He wants to make Meliodas his successor.
And me, his emotions, are superfluous and in the way.
I see... ♫
Ban... I'm surprised you can stand it here in Purgatory, made of flesh and blood as you are.
Yeah. ♫ But I've lost count how many times I almost gave up. ♫
The first 100 years, I was burned to the bone. Then I'd come back and freeze down to my bloodstream. When I came back again, I was rotted away by poison. And then I'd come back again...
Over and over and over. ♫

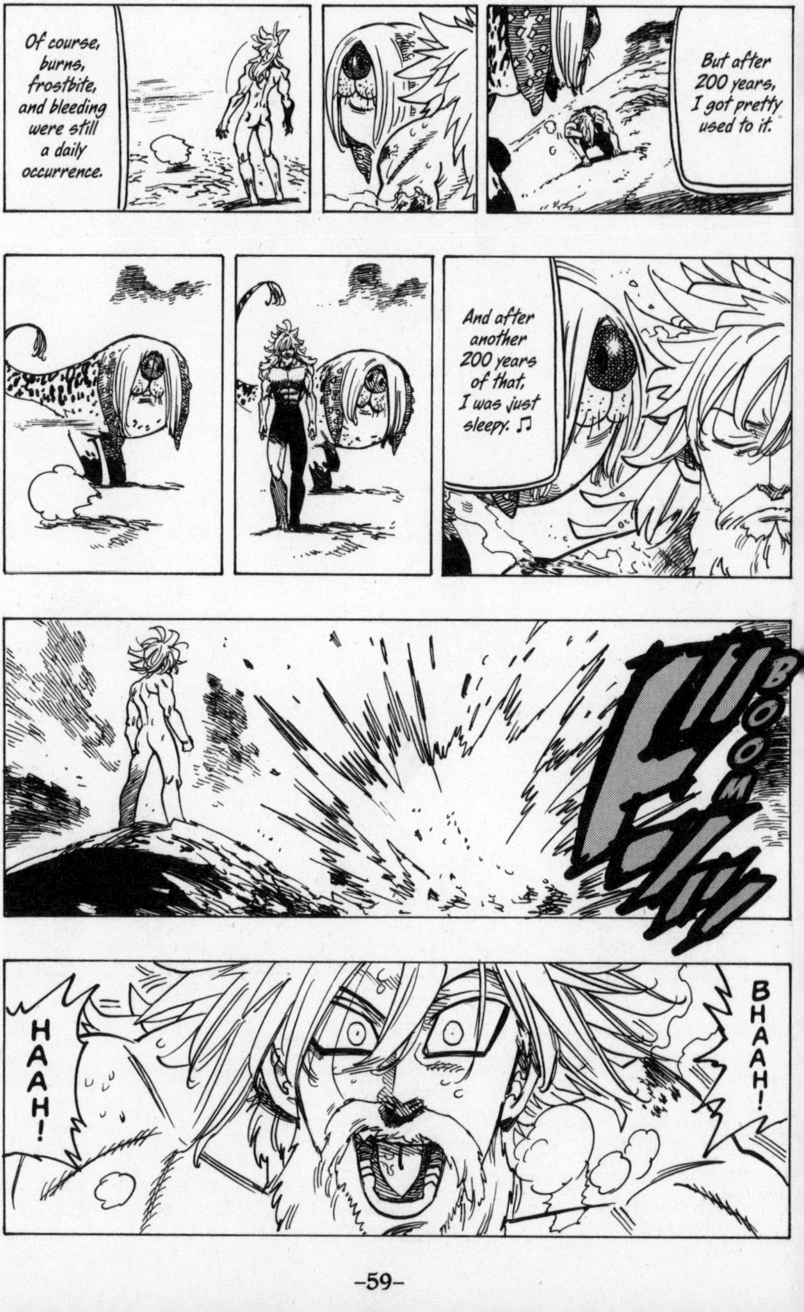

But after 200 years, I got pretty used to it.
Of course, burns, frostbite, and bleeding were still a daily occurrence.
And after another 200 years of that, I was just sleepy. ♫
BOOOM
BHAAH!
HAAH!

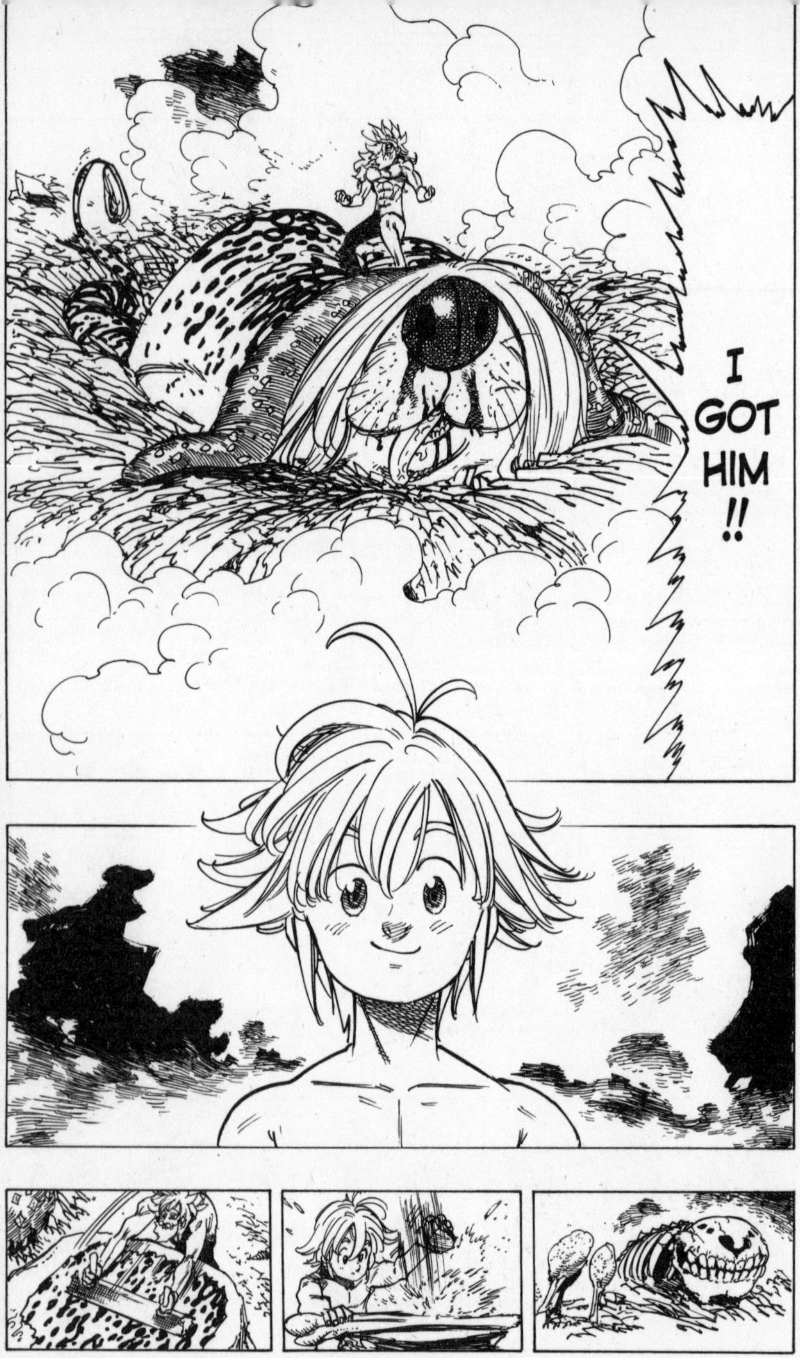
I GOT HIM !!

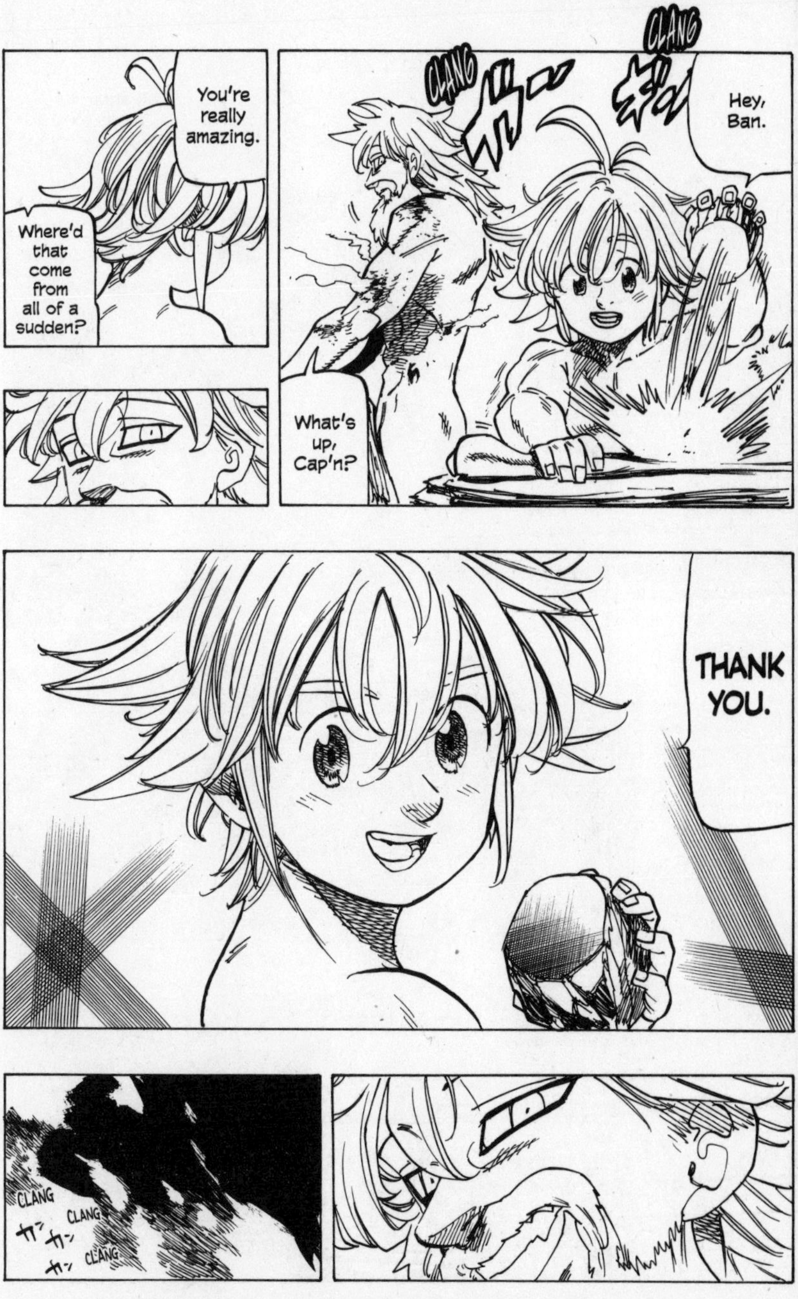

CLANG
Hey, Ban.
CLANG
What's up, Cap'n?
You're really amazing.
Where'd that come from all of a sudden?
THANK YOU.
CLANG
CLANG
CLANG

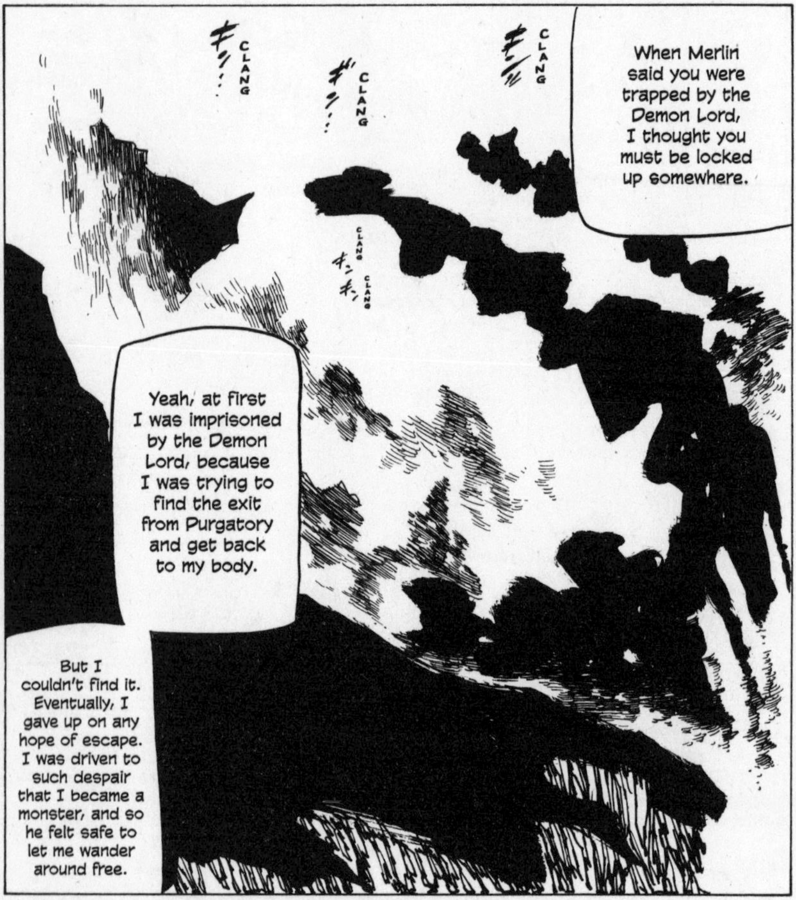
CLANG
CLANG
CLANG
When Merlin said you were trapped by the Demon Lord, I thought you must be locked up somewhere.
CLANG
CLANG
Yeah, at first I was imprisoned by the Demon Lord, because I was trying to find the exit from Purgatory and get back to my body.
But I couldn't find it. Eventually, I gave up on any hope of escape. I was driven to such despair that I became a monster, and so he felt safe to let me wander around free.

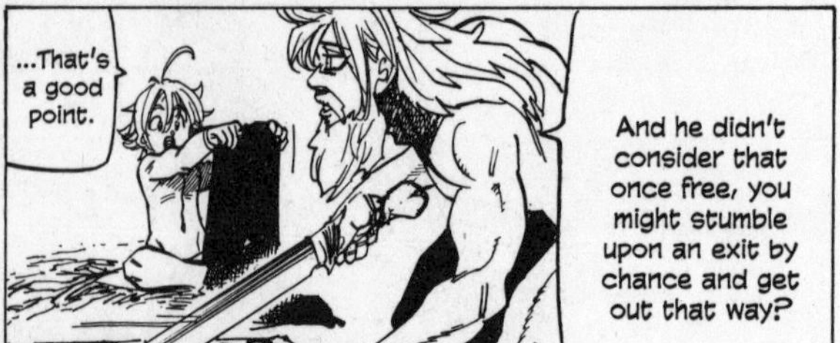
And he didn't consider that once free, you might stumble upon an exit by chance and get out that way?
...That's a good point.

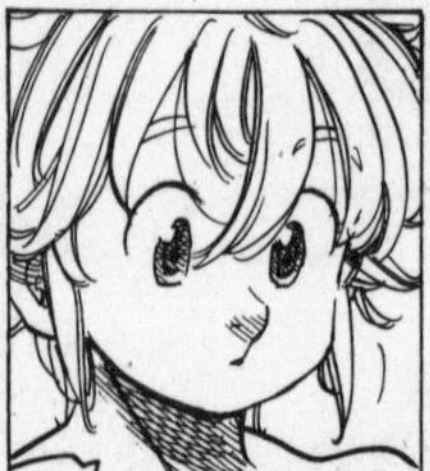
!!

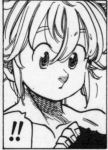

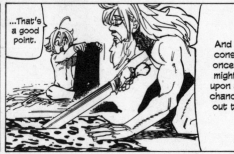

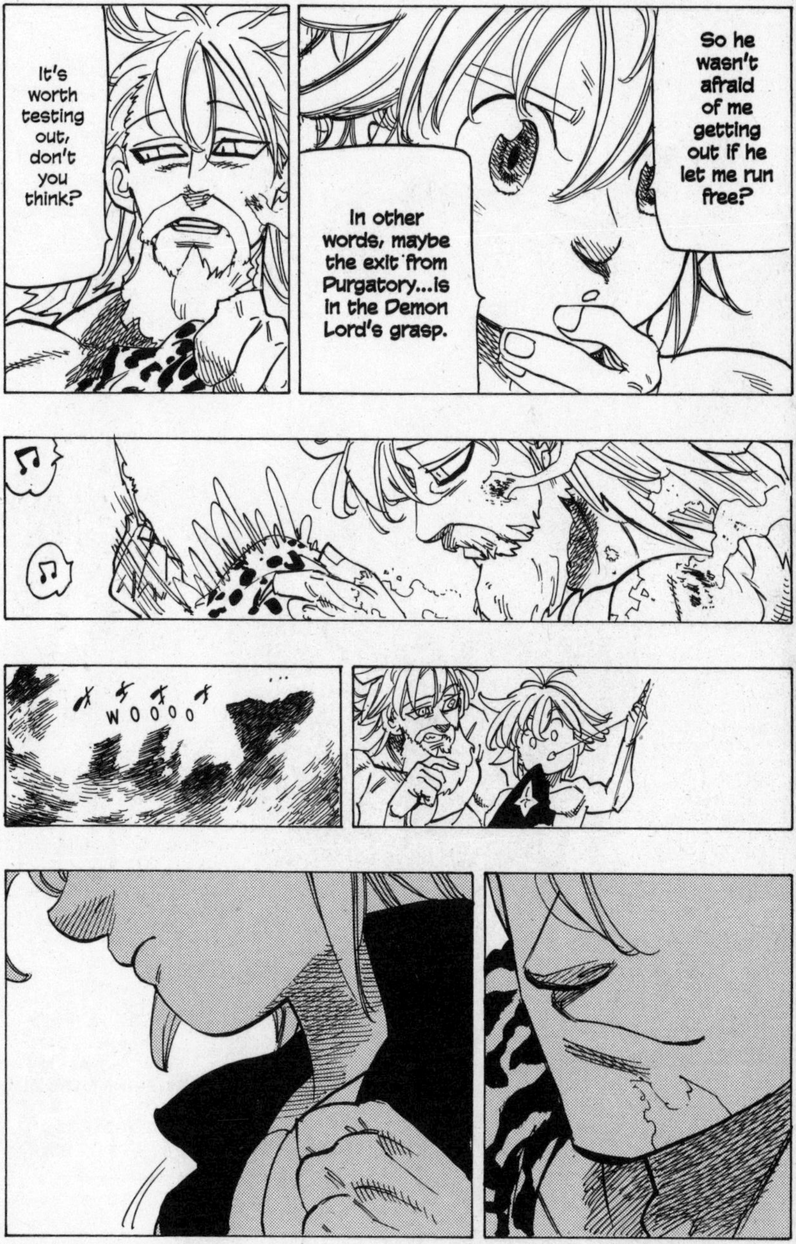
So he wasn't afraid of me getting out if he let me run free?
In other words, maybe the exit from Purgatory...is in the Demon Lord's grasp.
It's worth testing out, don't you think?
♪
♪
WOOOO
...

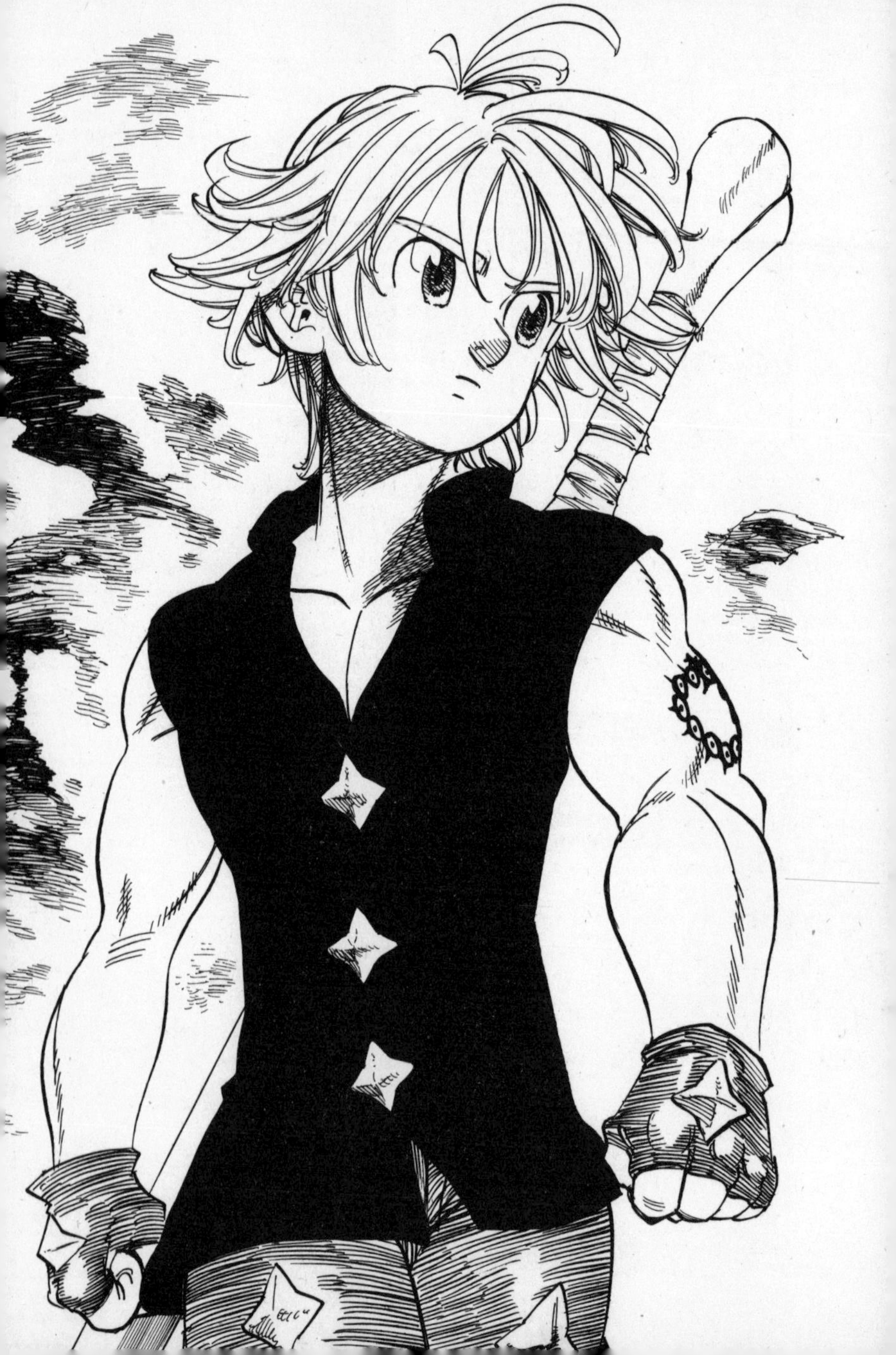

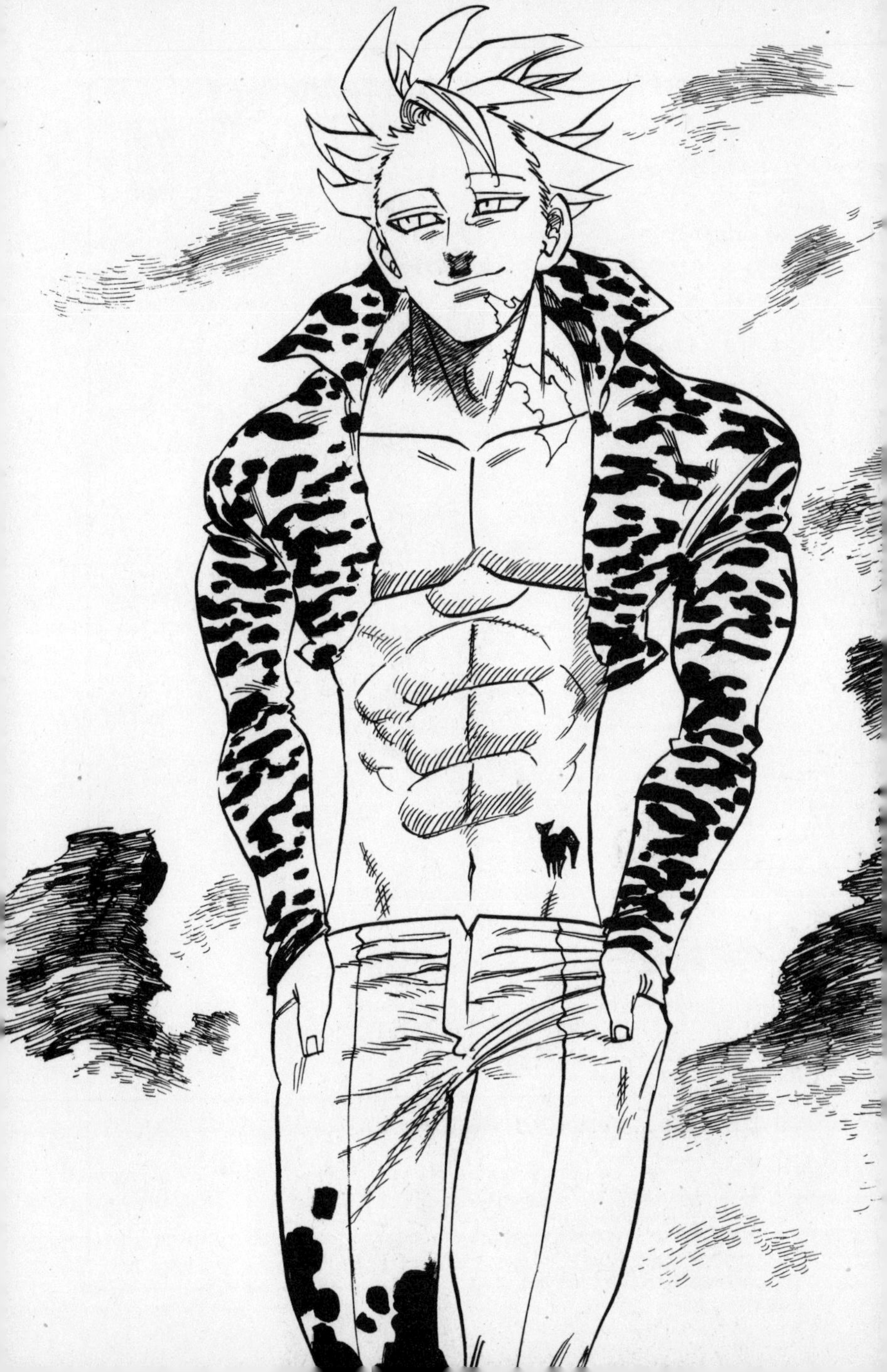

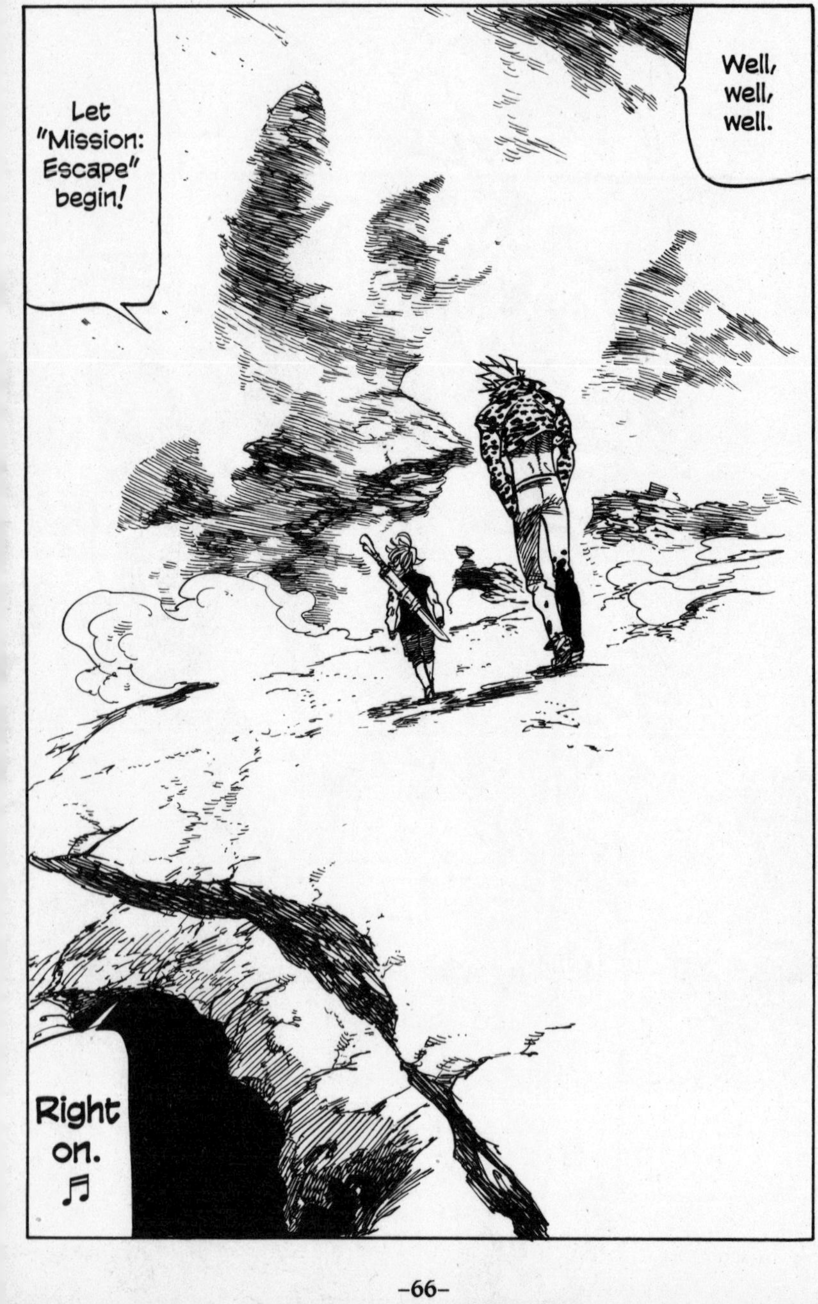
Well, well, well.
Let "Mission: Escape" begin!
Right on. ♬

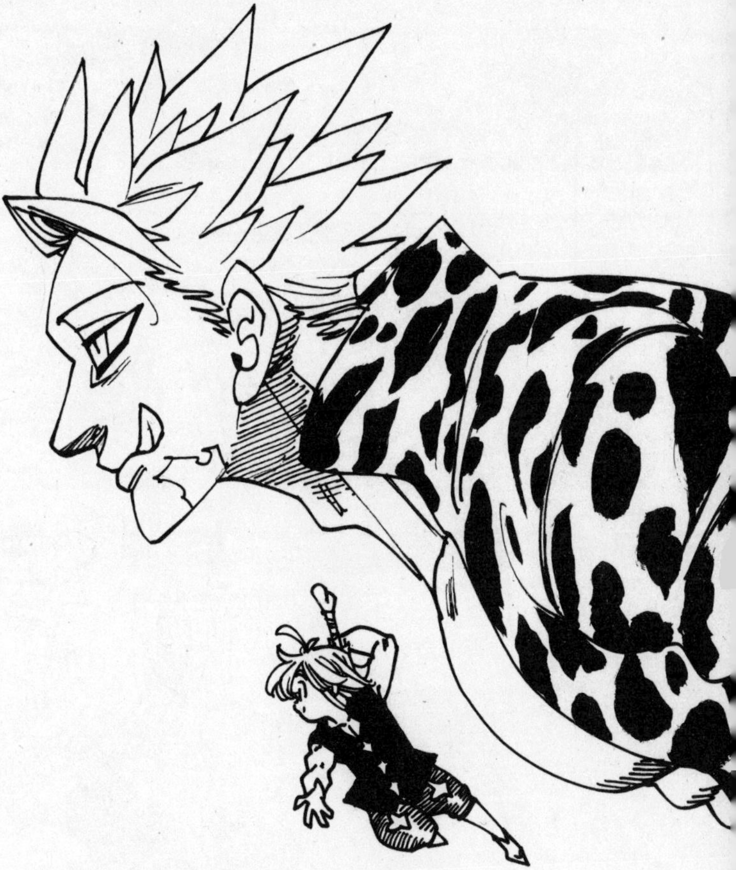

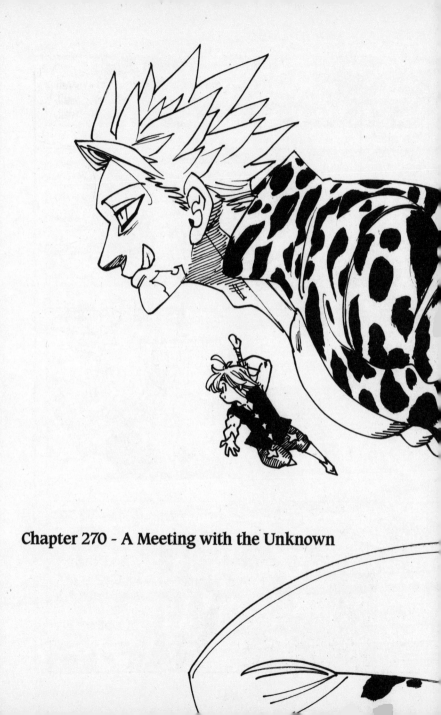

Chapter 270 - A Meeting with the Unknown

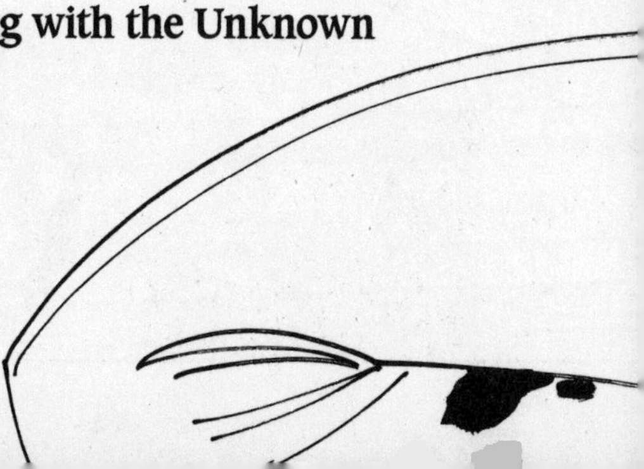

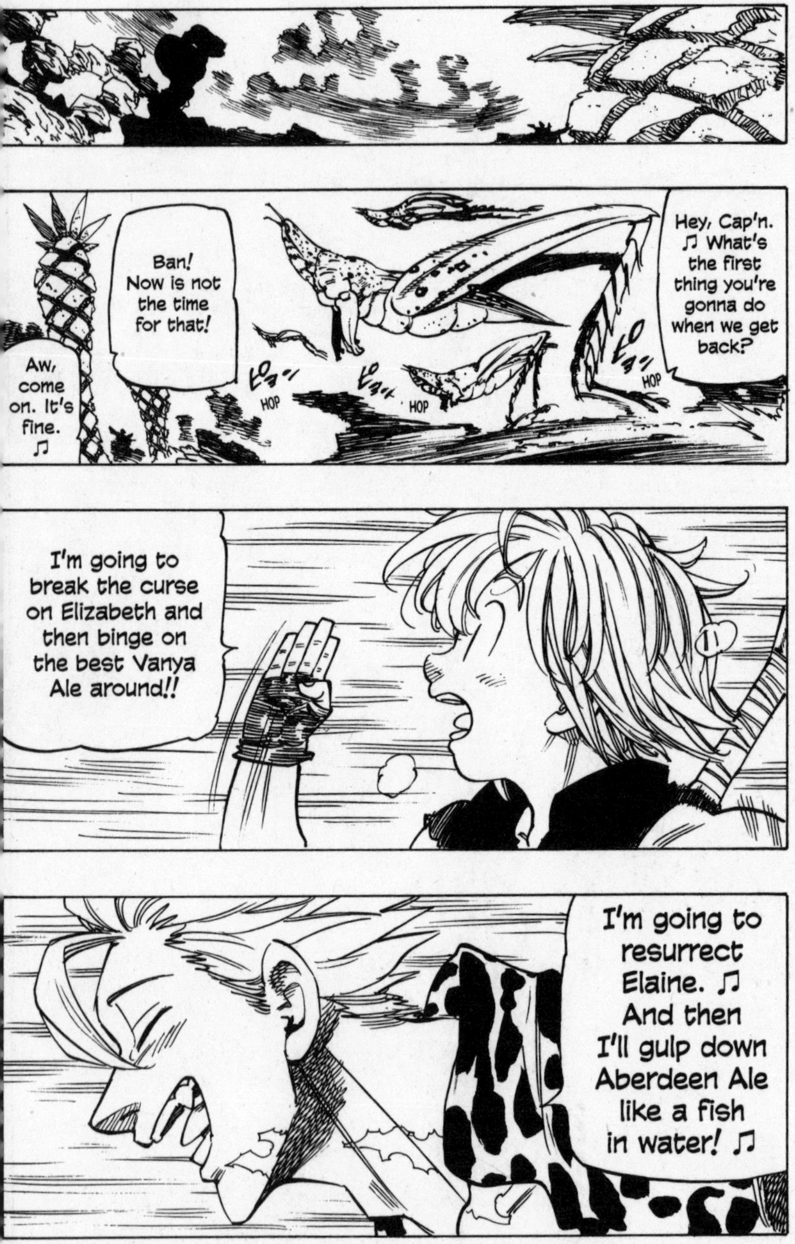
Hey, Cap'n. ♫ What's the first thing you're gonna do when we get back?
HOP
Ban! Now is not the time for that!
HOP
HOP
Aw, come on. It's fine. ♫
I'm going to break the curse on Elizabeth and then binge on the best Vanya Ale around!!
I'm going to resurrect Elaine. ♫ And then I'll gulp down Aberdeen Ale like a fish in water! ♫

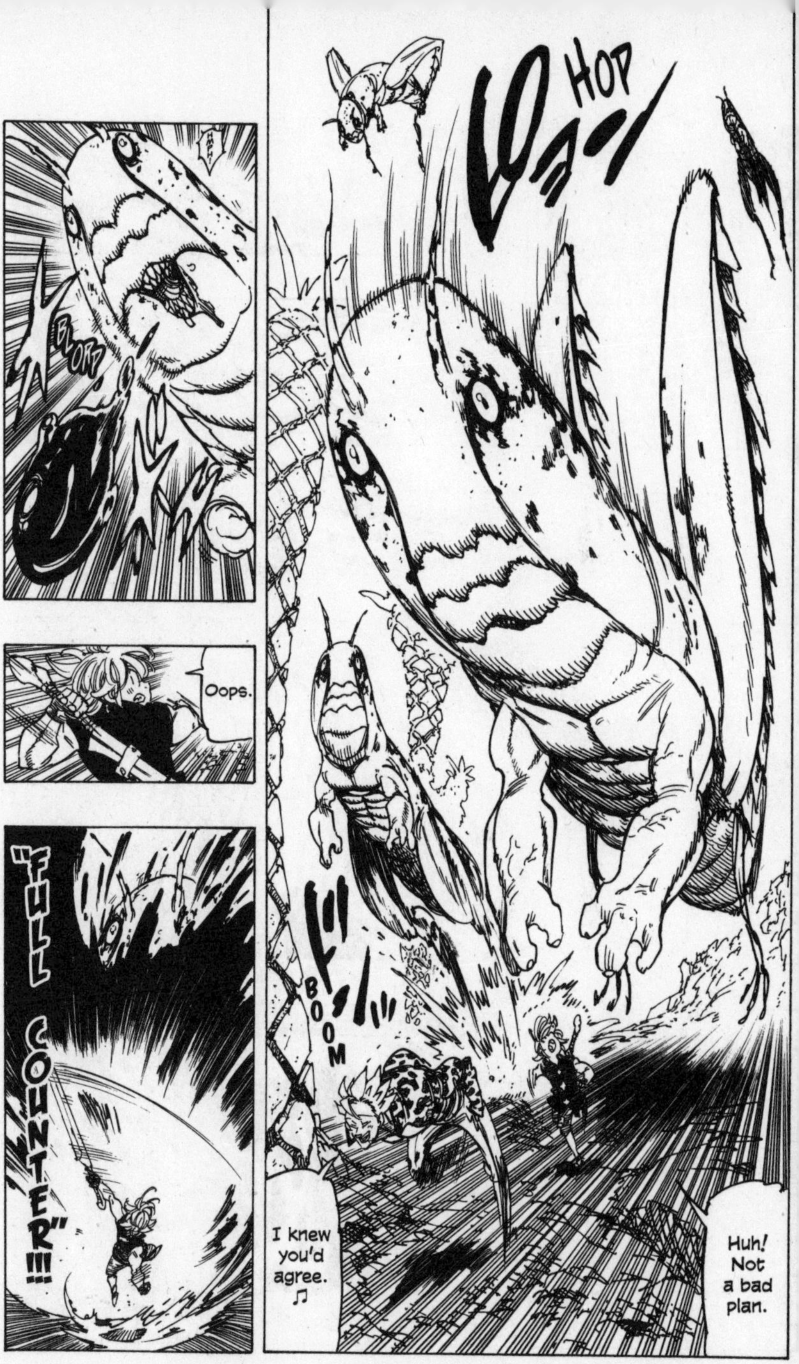
HOP
BOOM
Huh! Not a bad plan.
I knew you'd agree. ♫
HMPH!
BLORP
Oops.
"FULL COUNTER"!!!

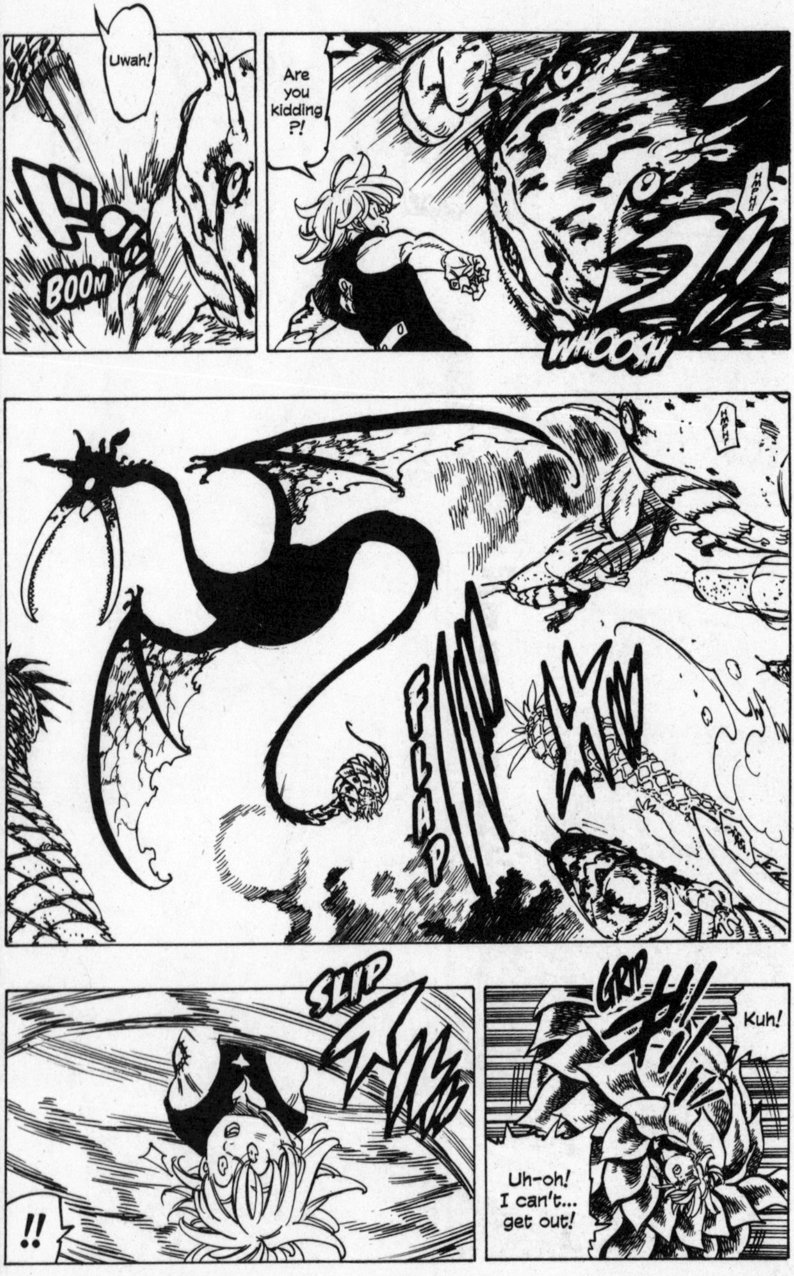
HMPH!!
Are you kidding?!
WHOOSH
Uwah!
BOOM
HMPH
FLAP
GRIP
Kuh!
Uh-oh! I can't... get out!
SLIP
!!

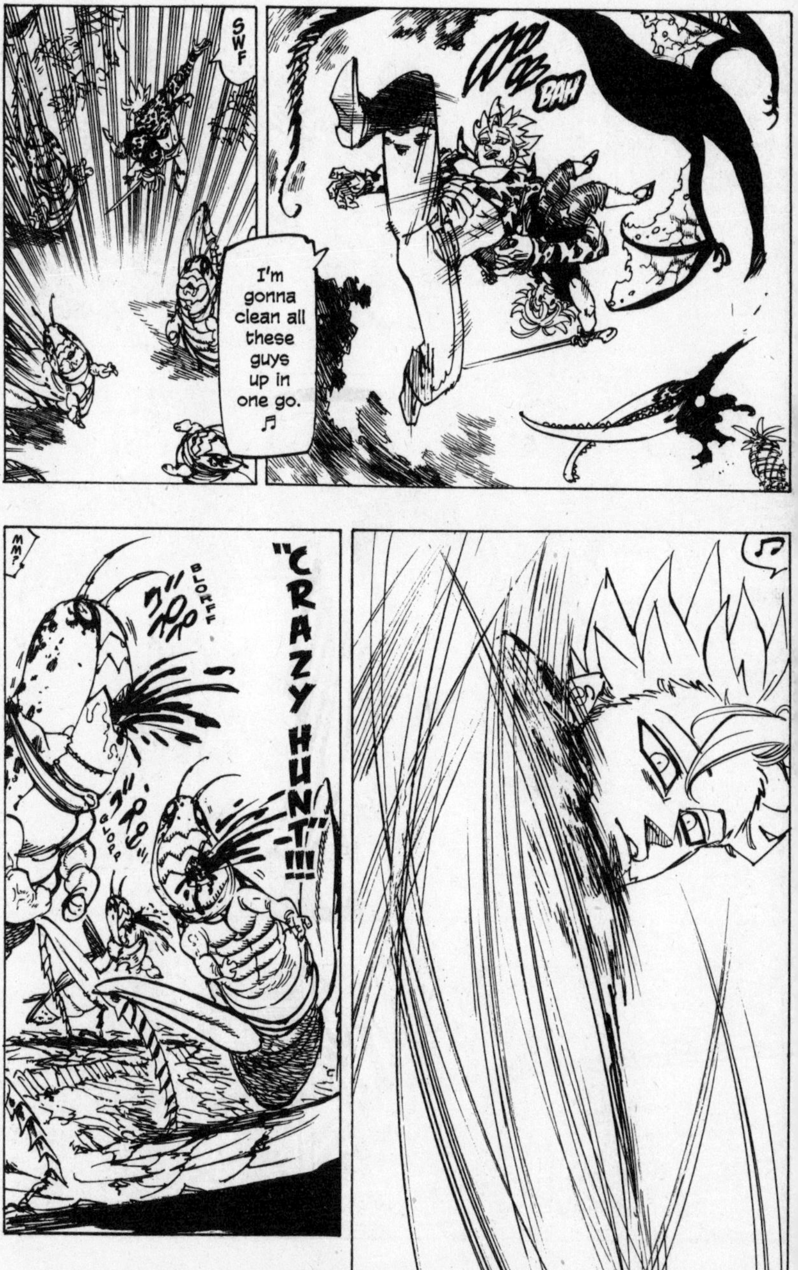
BAH
SWF
I'm gonna clean all these guys up in one go. ♫
♫
"CRAZY HUNT"!!!
BLORFF
MM?
GLOPP

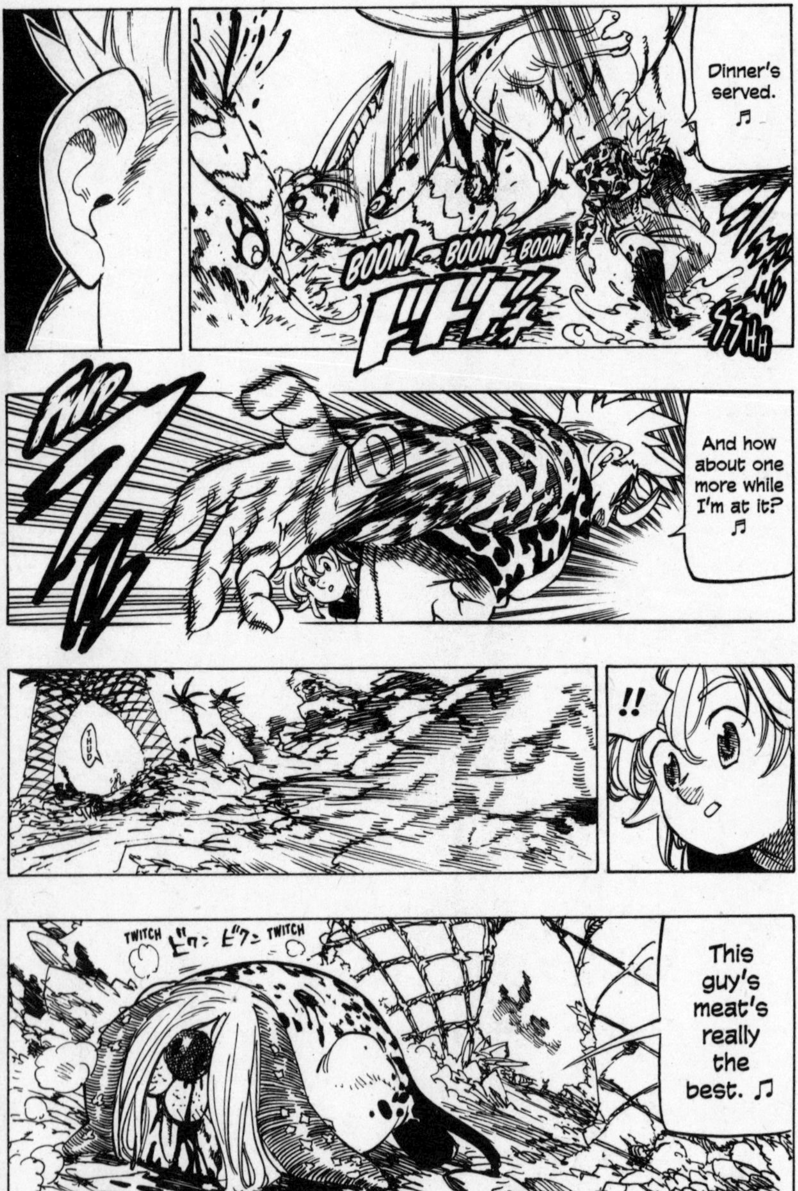
Dinner's served. ♫
BOOM BOOM BOOM
ドドドッ
SSHH
FWIP
And how about one more while I'm at it? ♫
!!
THUD
TWITCH ビクン ビクン TWITCH
This guy's meat's really the best. ♫

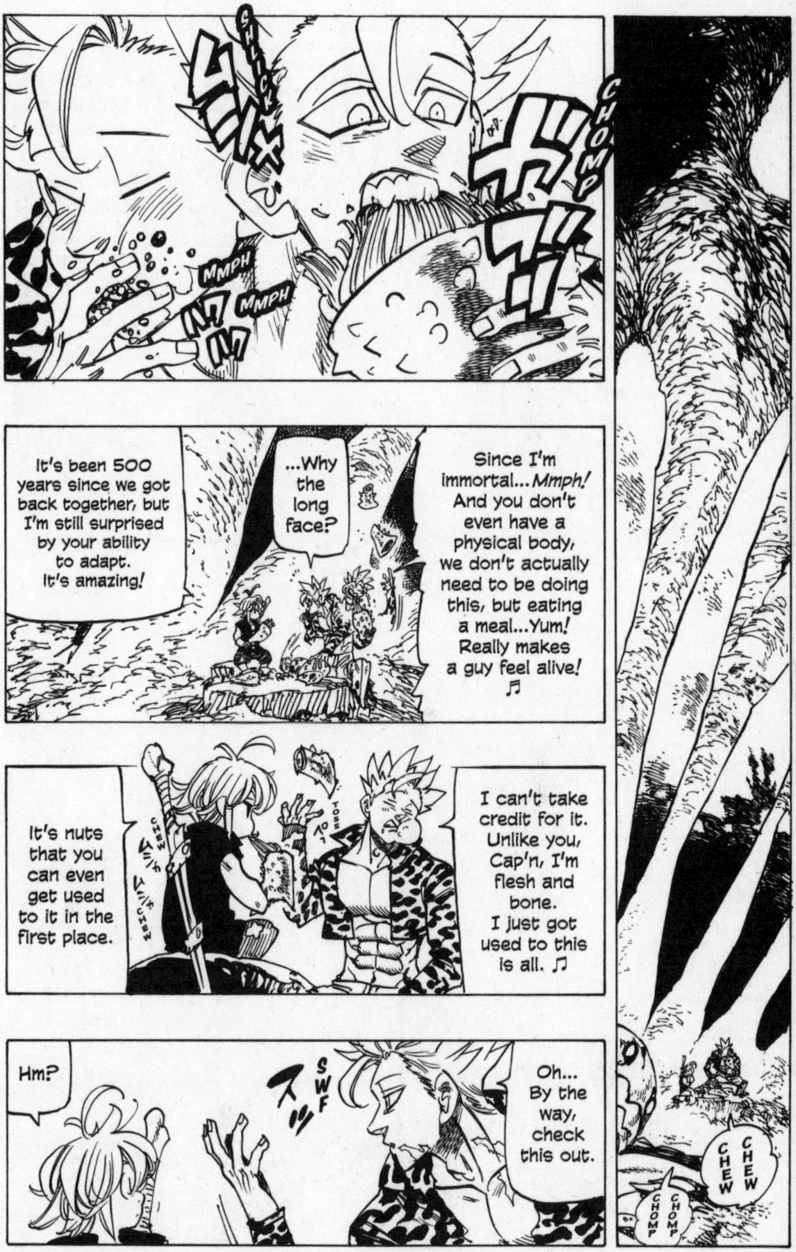
CHEW CHEW
CHOMP CHOMP
CHOMP
SHLICK
MMPH
MMPH
Since I'm immortal... *Mmph!* And you don't even have a physical body, we don't actually need to be doing this, but eating a meal... Yum! Really makes a guy feel alive! ♫
...Why the long face?
It's been 500 years since we got back together, but I'm still surprised by your ability to adapt. It's amazing!
I can't take credit for it. Unlike you, Cap'n, I'm flesh and bone. I just got used to this is all. ♫
TOSS
CHEW
CHEW
It's nuts that you can even get used to it in the first place.
Oh... By the way, check this out.
SWF
Hm?

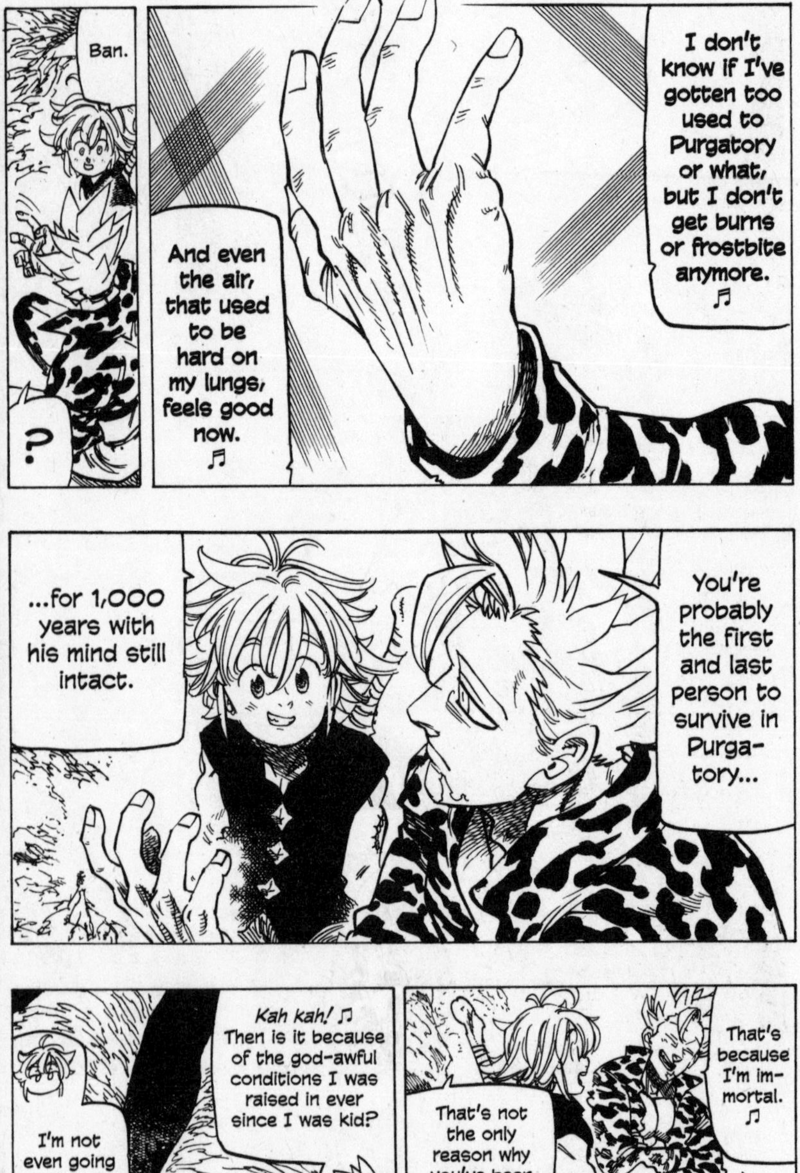
I don't know if I've gotten too used to Purgatory or what, but I don't get burns or frostbite anymore. ♬
And even the air, that used to be hard on my lungs, feels good now. ♬
Ban.
?
You're probably the first and last person to survive in Purga-tory...
...for 1,000 years with his mind still intact.
That's because I'm im-mortal. ♬
That's not the only reason why you've been able to stand it in here.
Kah kah! ♬ Then is it because of the god-awful conditions I was raised in ever since I was kid?
I'm not even going to touch that.

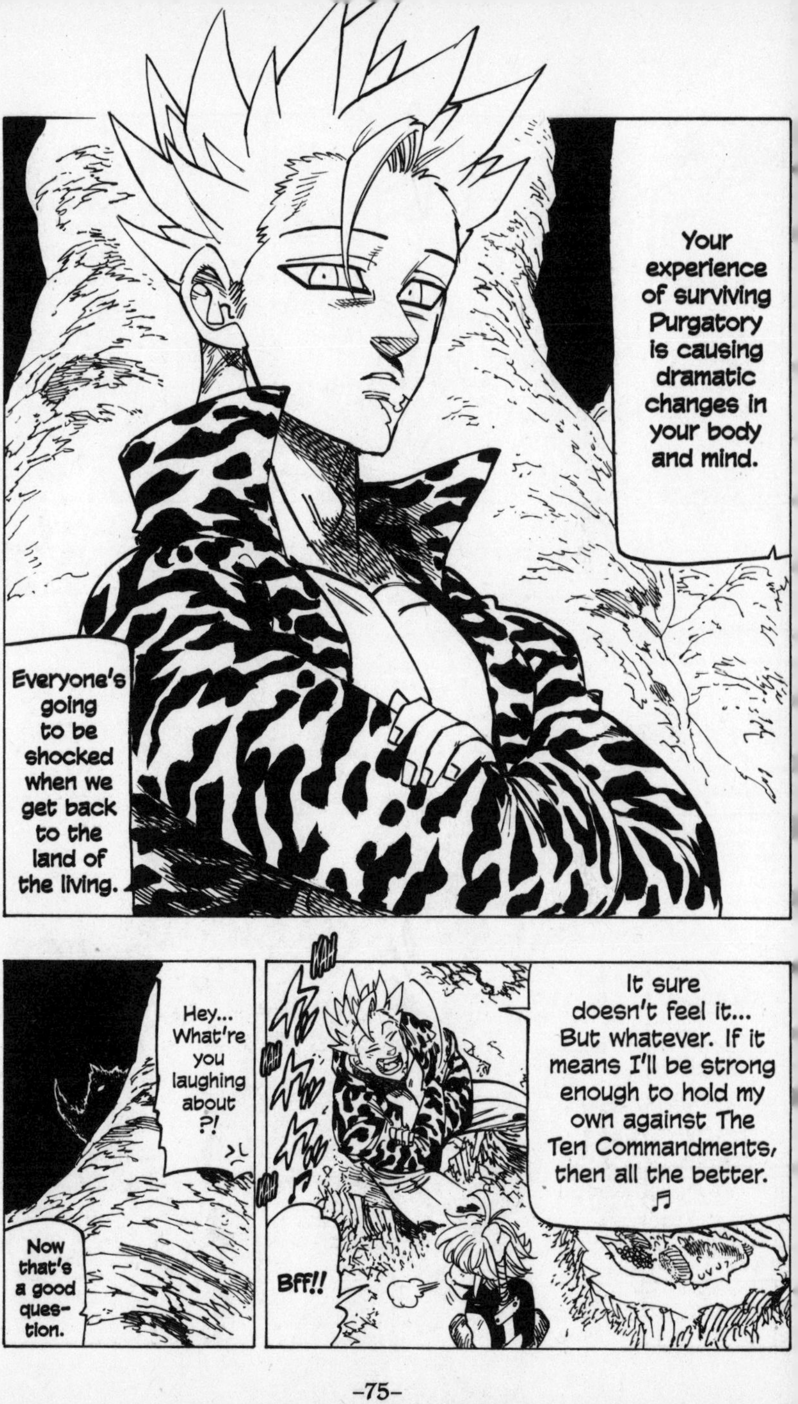
Your experience of surviving Purgatory is causing dramatic changes in your body and mind.
Everyone's going to be shocked when we get back to the land of the living.
It sure doesn't feel it... But whatever. If it means I'll be strong enough to hold my own against The Ten Commandments, then all the better. ♫
KAH
KAH
KAH
Bff!!
Hey... What're you laughing about ?!
Now that's a good ques-tion.

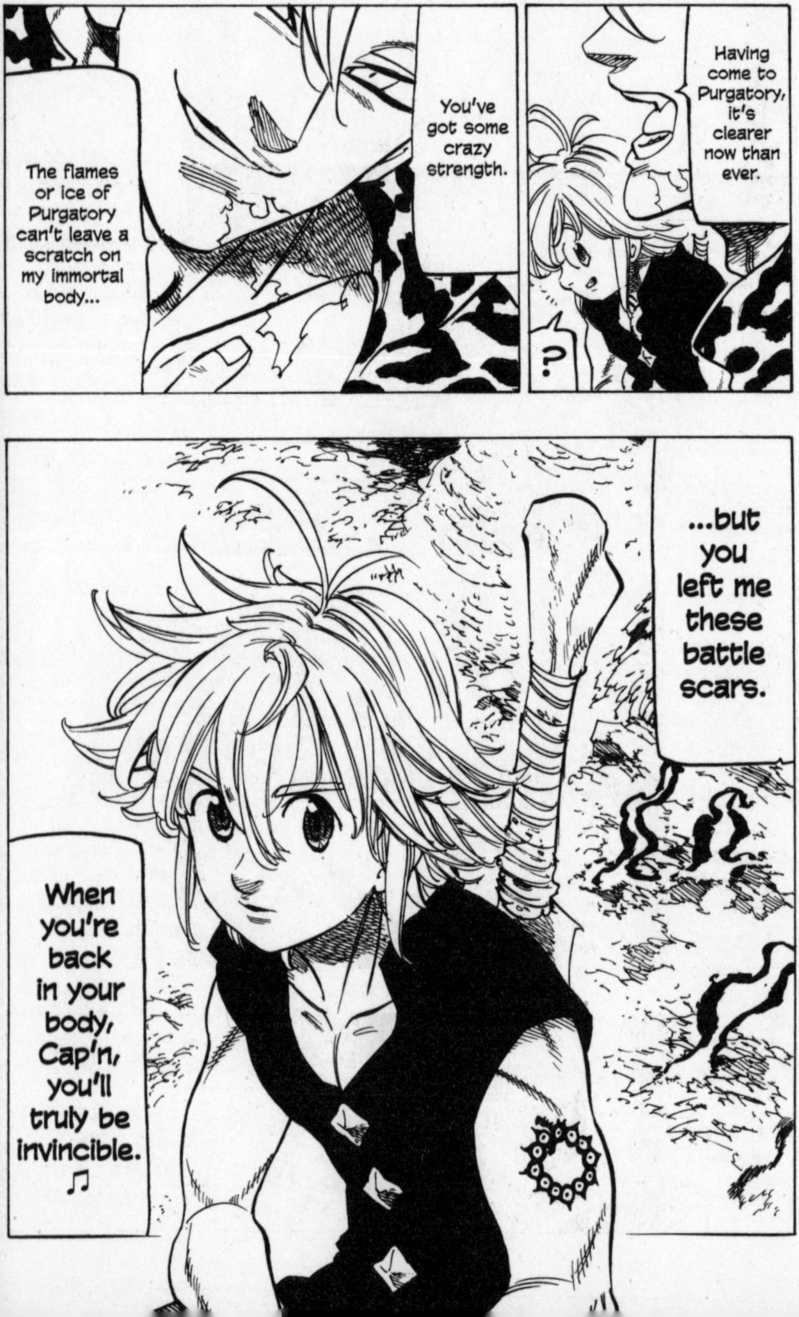
Having come to Purgatory, it's clearer now than ever.
?
You've got some crazy strength.
The flames or ice of Purgatory can't leave a scratch on my immortal body...
...but you left me these battle scars.
When you're back in your body, Cap'n, you'll truly be invincible. ♫

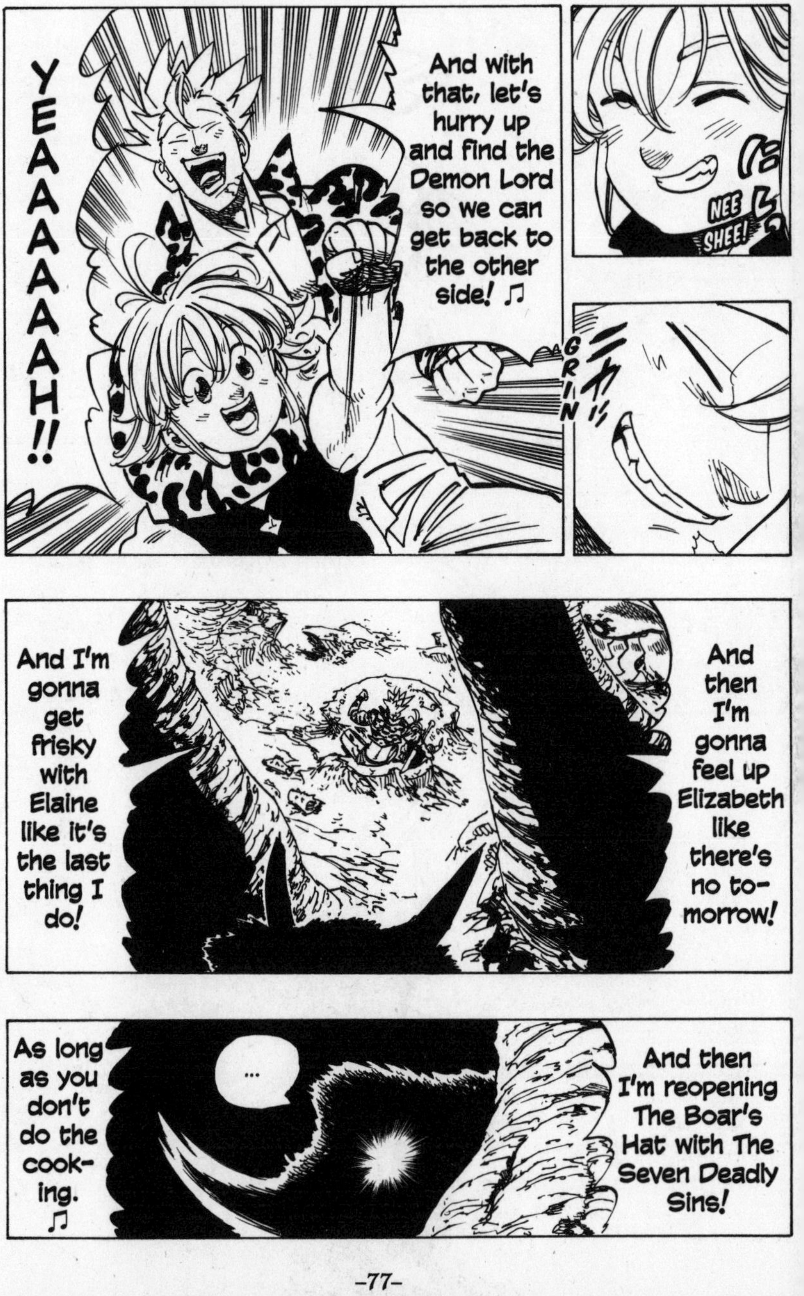
NEE SHEE!
GRIN
And with that, let's hurry up and find the Demon Lord so we can get back to the other side! ♫
YEAAAAAAAH!!
And then I'm gonna feel up Elizabeth like there's no to-morrow!
And I'm gonna get frisky with Elaine like it's the last thing I do!
And then I'm reopening The Boar's Hat with The Seven Deadly Sins!
...
As long as you don't do the cook-ing. ♫

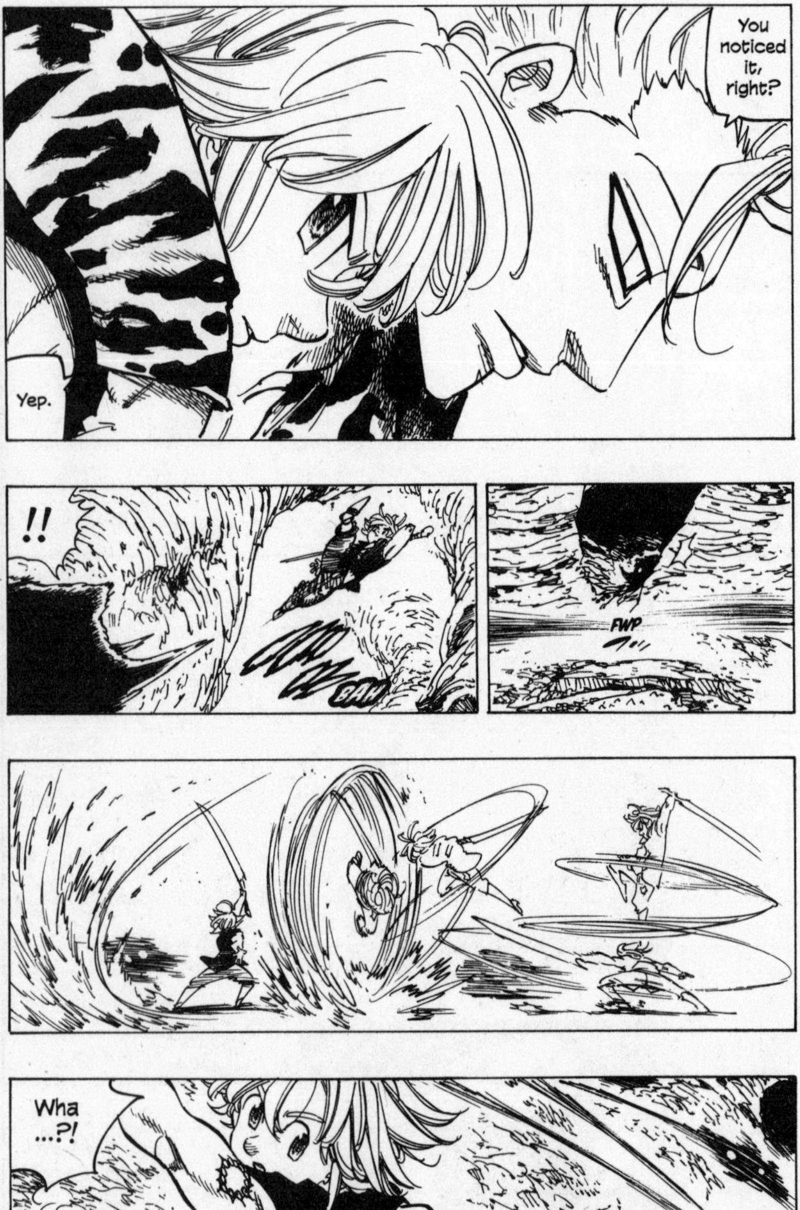
You noticed it, right?
Yep.
FWP
!!
BAH
Wha ...?!

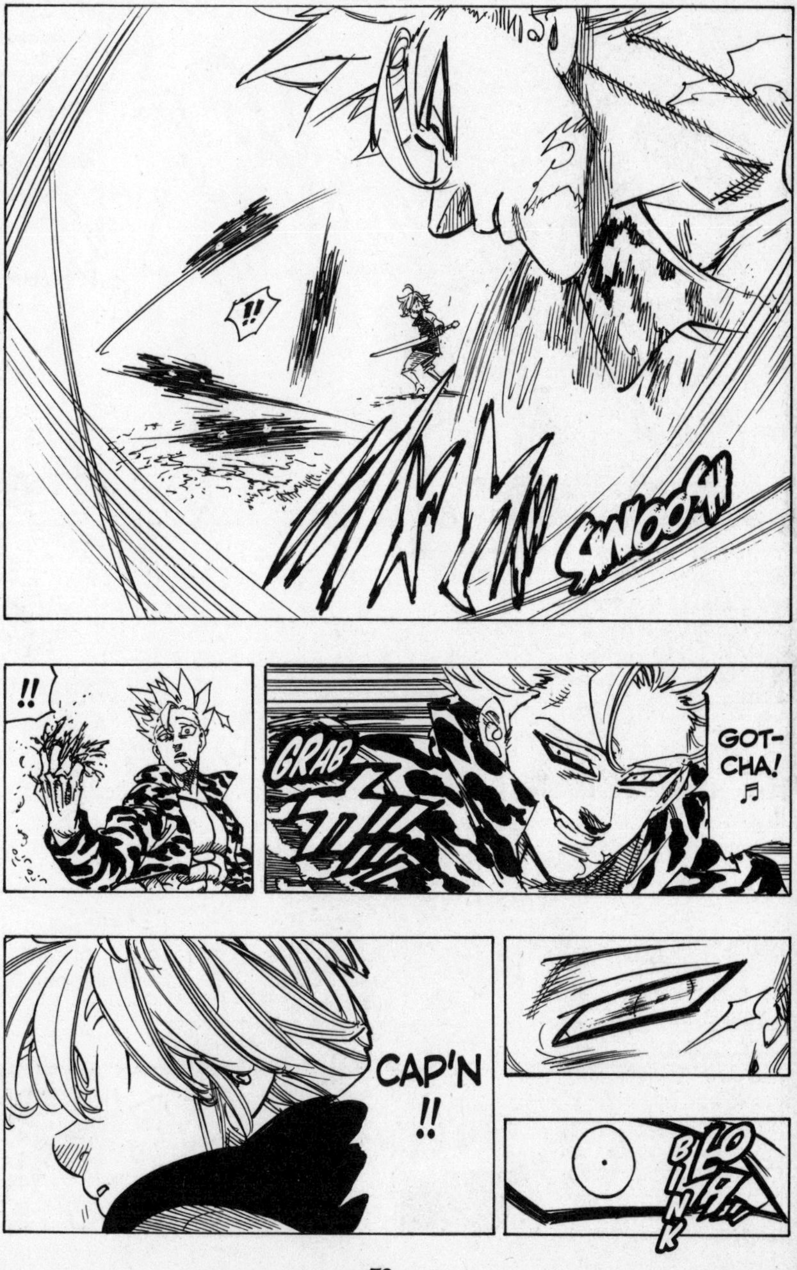
!!
SWOOSH
GOT-CHA! ♬
GRAB
!!
BLINK
CAP'N !!

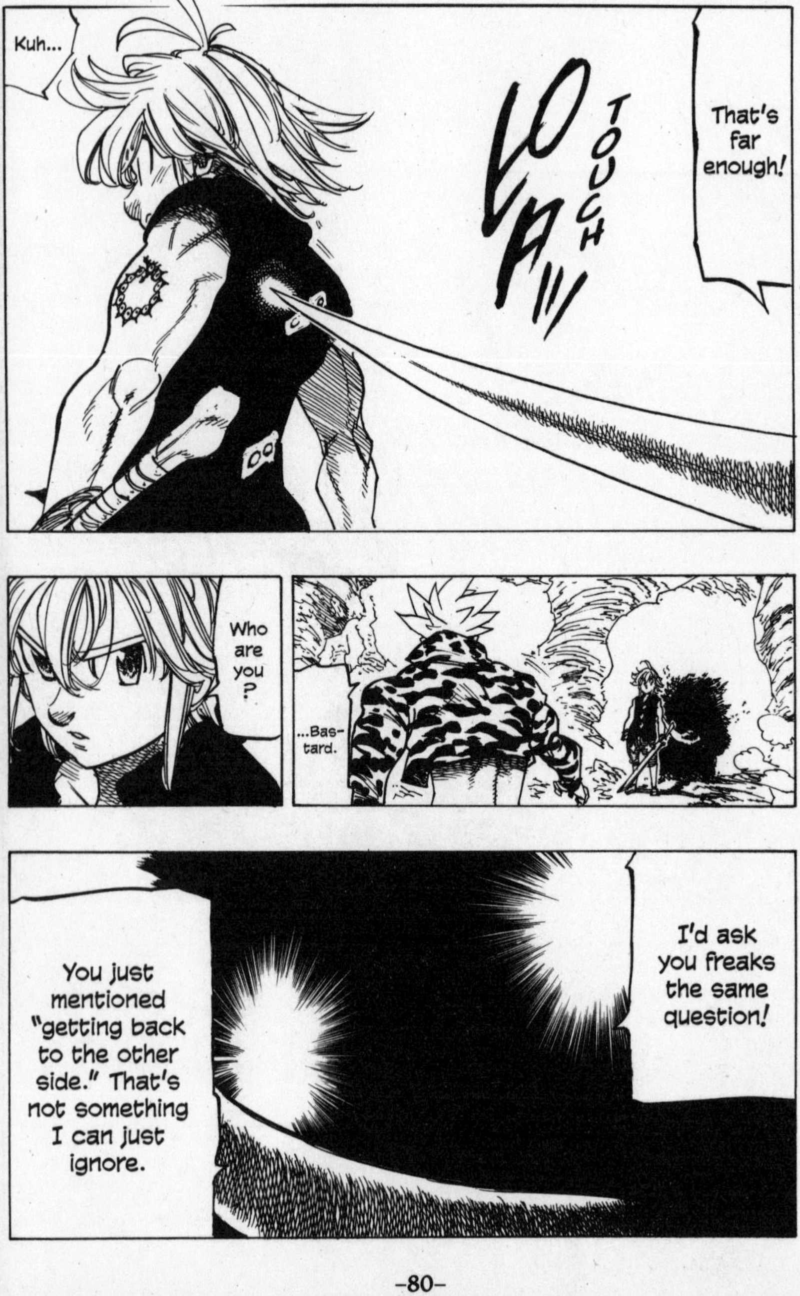

That's far enough!
TOUCH
Kuh...
...Bas-tard.
Who are you?
I'd ask you freaks the same question!
You just mentioned "getting back to the other side." That's not something I can just ignore.

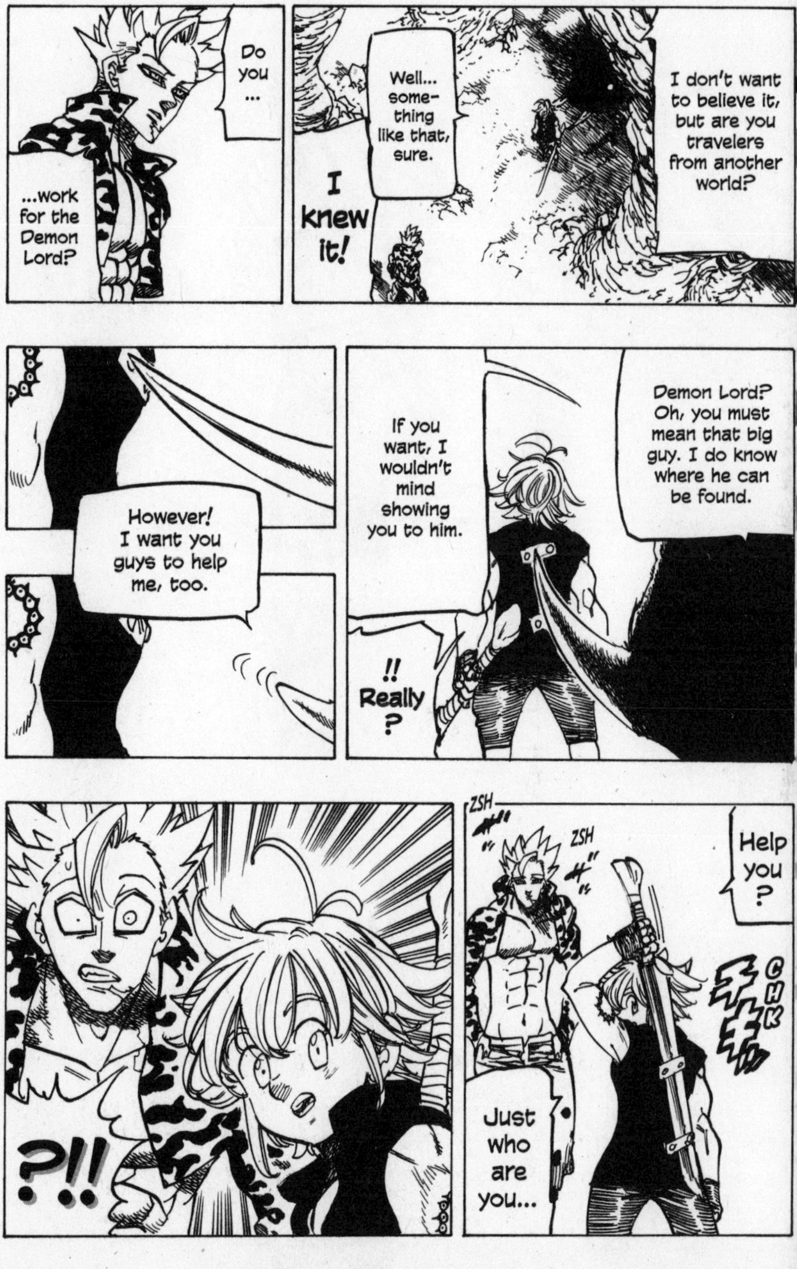
I don't want to believe it, but are you travelers from another world?
Well... something like that, sure.
I knew it!
Do you ...
...work for the Demon Lord?
Demon Lord? Oh, you must mean that big guy. I do know where he can be found.
If you want, I wouldn't mind showing you to him.
!! Really ?
However! I want you guys to help me, too.
Help you ?
ZSH
ZSH
CHK
Just who are you...
?!!

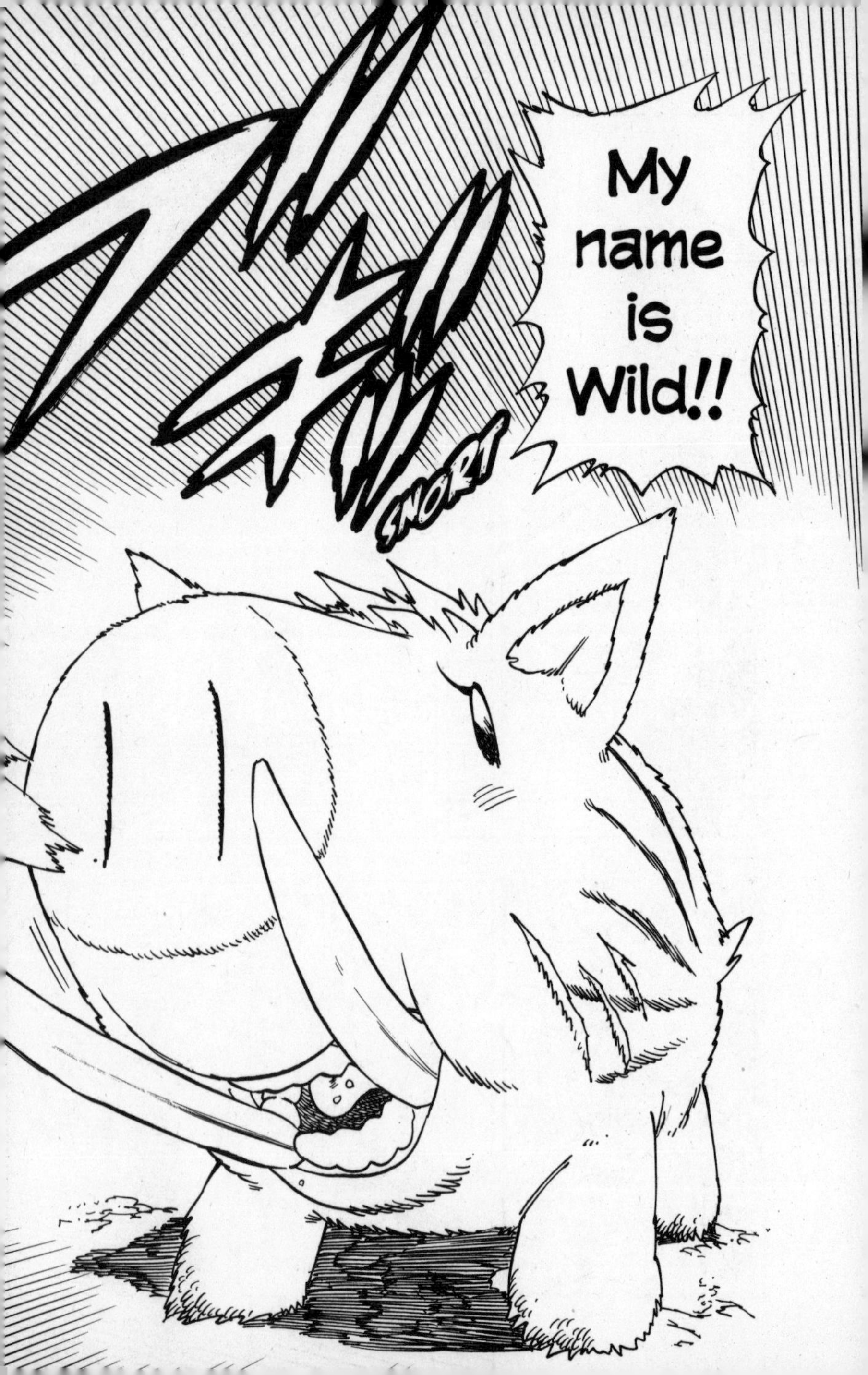
My name is Wild!!
SNORT

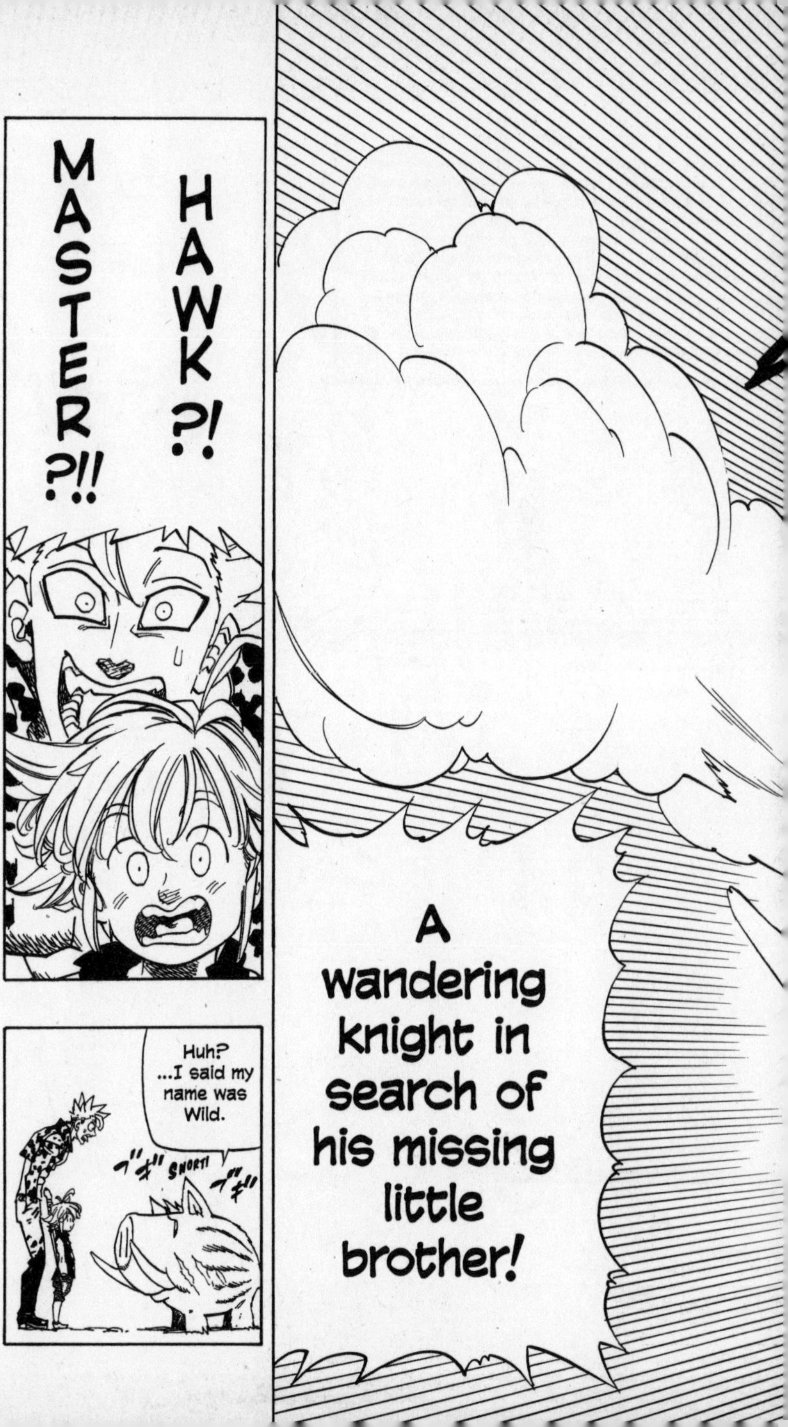
A wandering knight in search of his missing little brother!
HAWK?!
MASTER?!!
Huh? ...I said my name was Wild.
SNORT!

Second only to "The Ten Commandments" in terms of sheer power, The "Six Knights of Black" are a legion of Demons who were too cocky and therefore were forsaken by the Demon Lord. The designs for "Derocchio," "Dahaka," and "Atra" didn't change that much compared to the final versions. The backstory for "Pump" is that he's a nephew of Galland's so after thinking up a version where he looks like Galland except without horns and then a polar opposite version where he's super short, we decided on something completely different from either of those. "Gara" was at first designed to be the opposite but equal counterpart to King's fatty version.

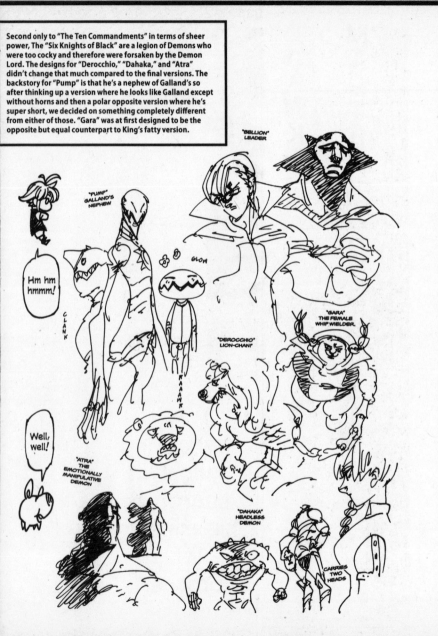

"BELLION" LEADER

"PUMP" GALLAND'S NEPHEW

GLOW

Hm hm hmmm!

CLANK

RAAAAAK

"GARA" THE FEMALE WHIP WIELDER.

"DEROCCHIO" LION-CHAN!

Well, well!

"ATRA" THE EMOTIONALLY MANIPULATIVE DEMON

"DAHAKA" HEADLESS DEMON

CARRIES TWO HEADS

Chapter 271 - A Single-Minded Love

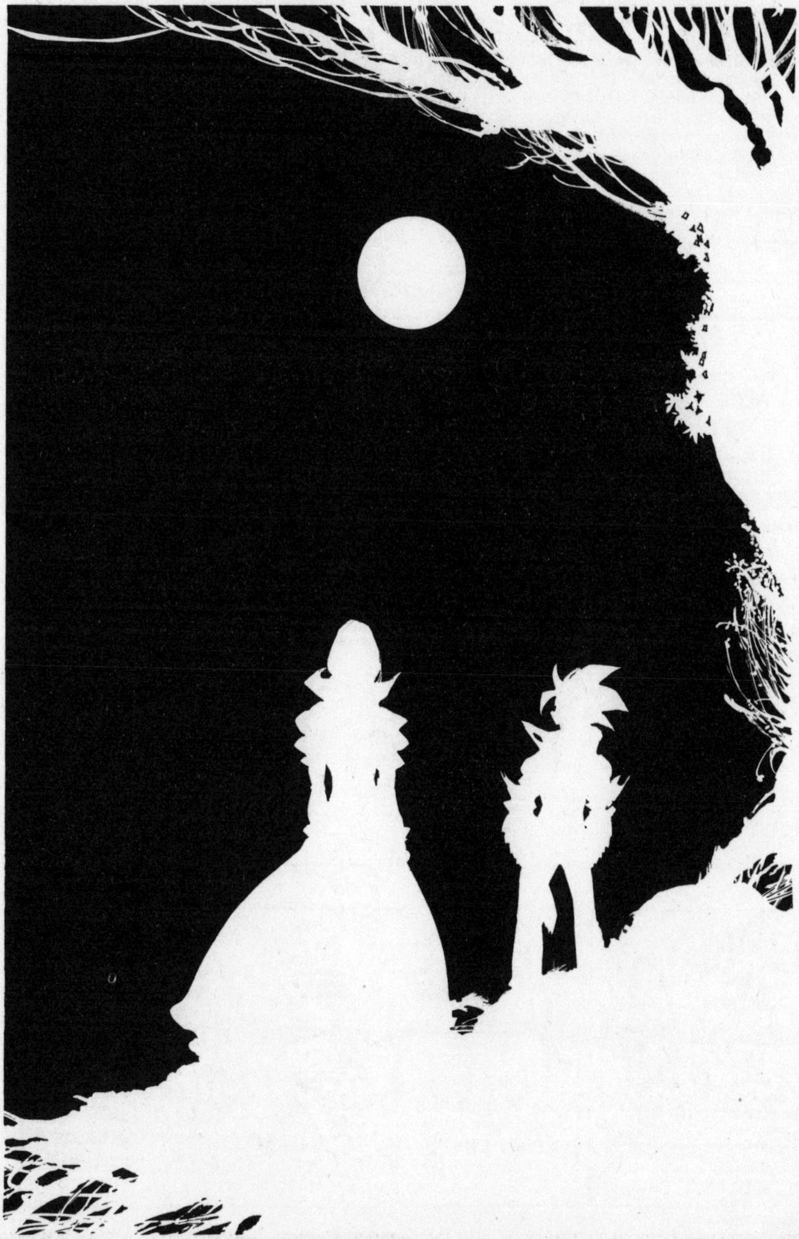

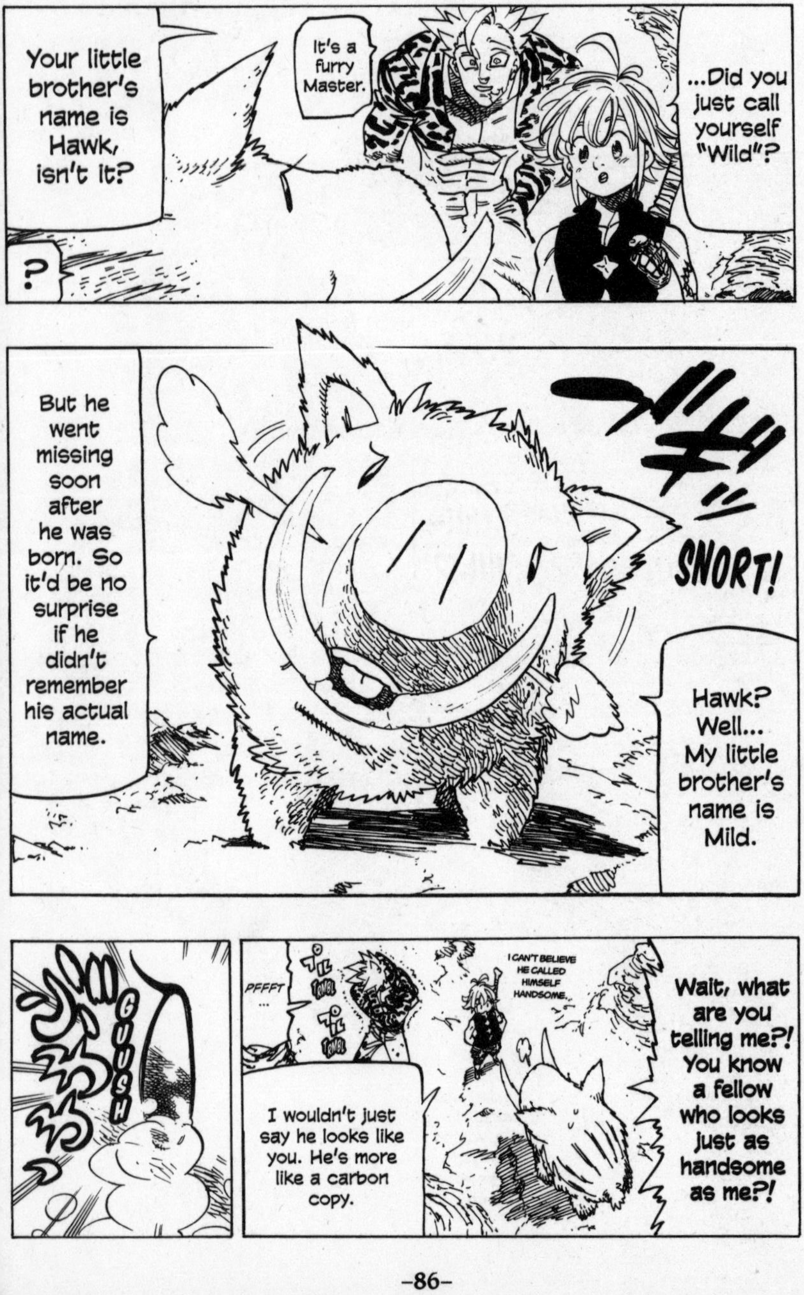
...Did you just call yourself "Wild"?
It's a furry Master.
Your little brother's name is Hawk, isn't it?
?
SNORT!
Hawk? Well... My little brother's name is Mild.
But he went missing soon after he was born. So it'd be no surprise if he didn't remember his actual name.
Wait, what are you telling me?! You know a fellow who looks just as handsome as me?!
I CAN'T BELIEVE HE CALLED HIMSELF HANDSOME...
TRMBL
TRMBL
PFFFT ...
I wouldn't just say he looks like you. He's more like a carbon copy.
GUUSH

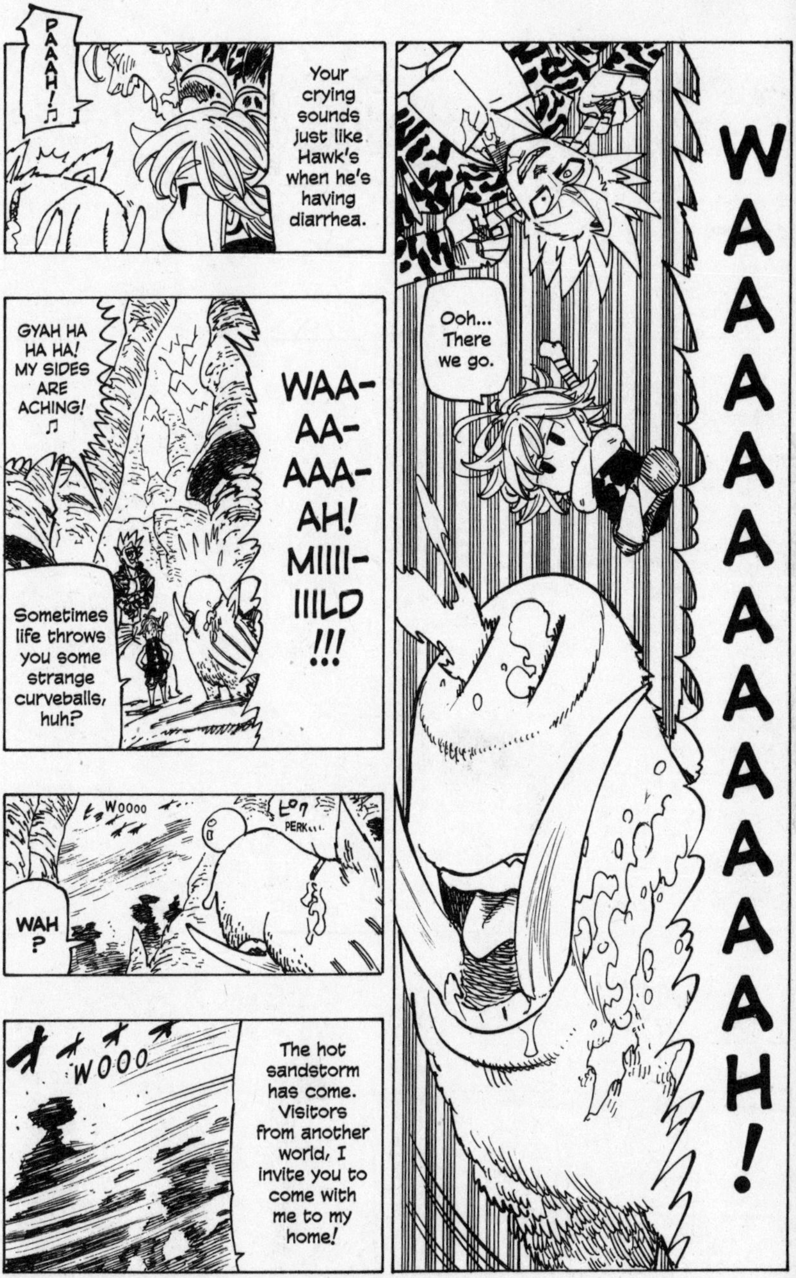

WAAAAAAAAAH!
Ooh... There we go.
Your crying sounds just like Hawk's when he's having diarrhea.
PAAAH!♫
WAA-AA-AAA-AH! MIIIII-IIILD!!!
GYAH HA HA HA! MY SIDES ARE ACHING! ♫
Sometimes life throws you some strange curveballs, huh?
PERK
WOOOO
WAH?
The hot sandstorm has come. Visitors from another world, I invite you to come with me to my home!
WOOO

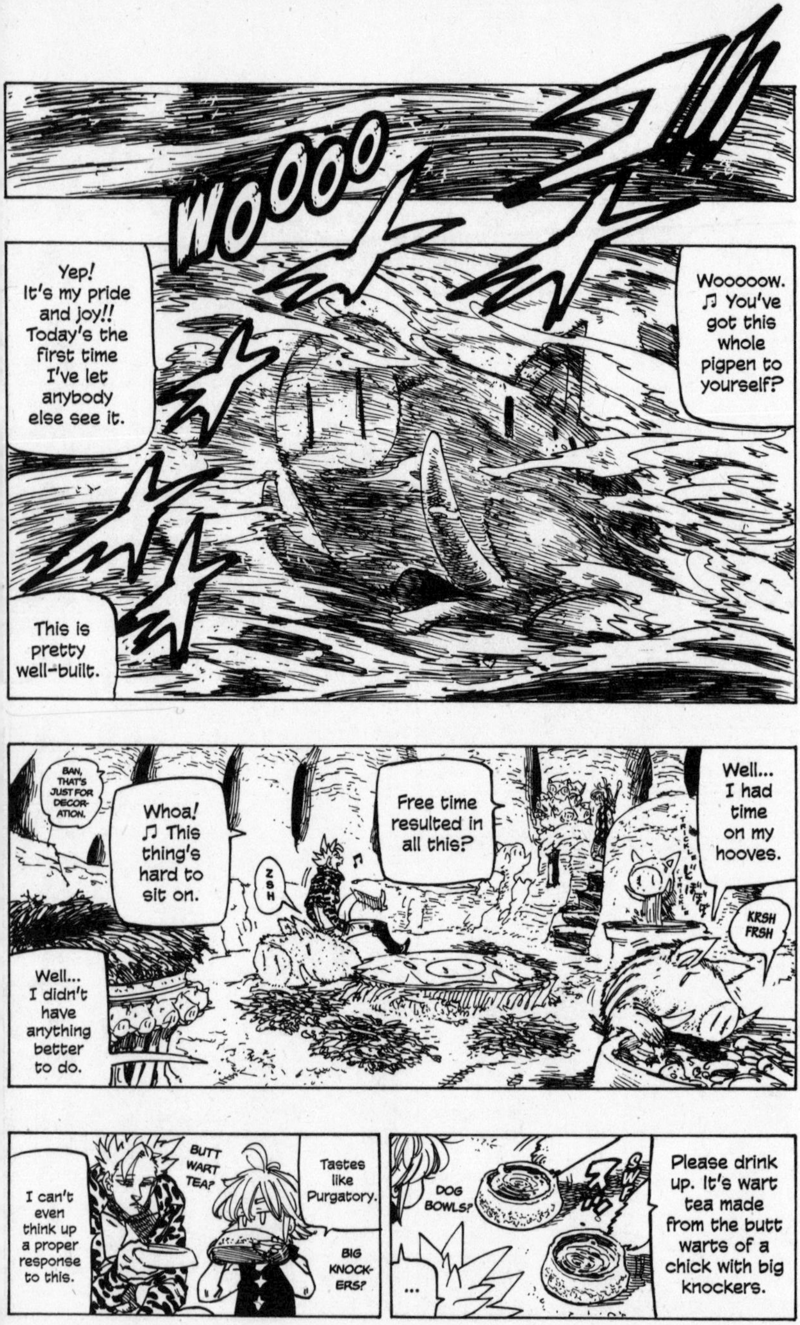

WOOOO
Wooooow. ♫ You've got this whole pigpen to yourself?
Yep! It's my pride and joy!! Today's the first time I've let anybody else see it.
This is pretty well-built.
Well... I had time on my hooves.
TRICKLE TRICKLE
KRSH FRSH
Free time resulted in all this?
Whoa! ♫ This thing's hard to sit on.
ZSH
BAN, THAT'S JUST FOR DECORATION.
Well... I didn't have anything better to do.
Please drink up. It's wart tea made from the butt warts of a chick with big knockers.
DOG BOWLS?
...
Tastes like Purgatory.
BUTT WART TEA?
BIG KNOCKERS?
I can't even think up a proper response to this.

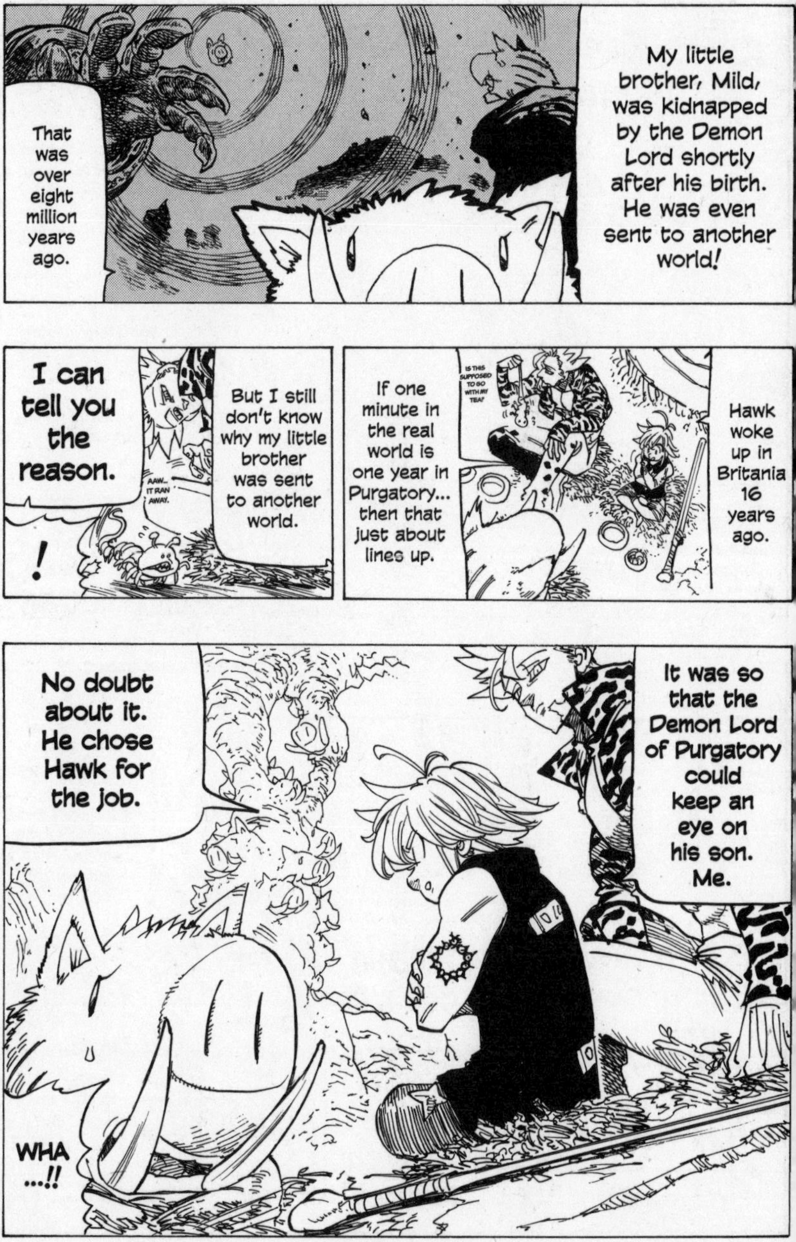
My little brother, Mild, was kidnapped by the Demon Lord shortly after his birth. He was even sent to another world!
That was over eight million years ago.
Hawk woke up in Britania 16 years ago.
IS THIS SUPPOSED TO GO WITH MY TEA?!
If one minute in the real world is one year in Purgatory... then that just about lines up.
But I still don't know why my little brother was sent to another world.
AAW... IT RAN AWAY.
I can tell you the reason.
!
It was so that the Demon Lord of Purgatory could keep an eye on his son. Me.
No doubt about it. He chose Hawk for the job.
WHA ...!!

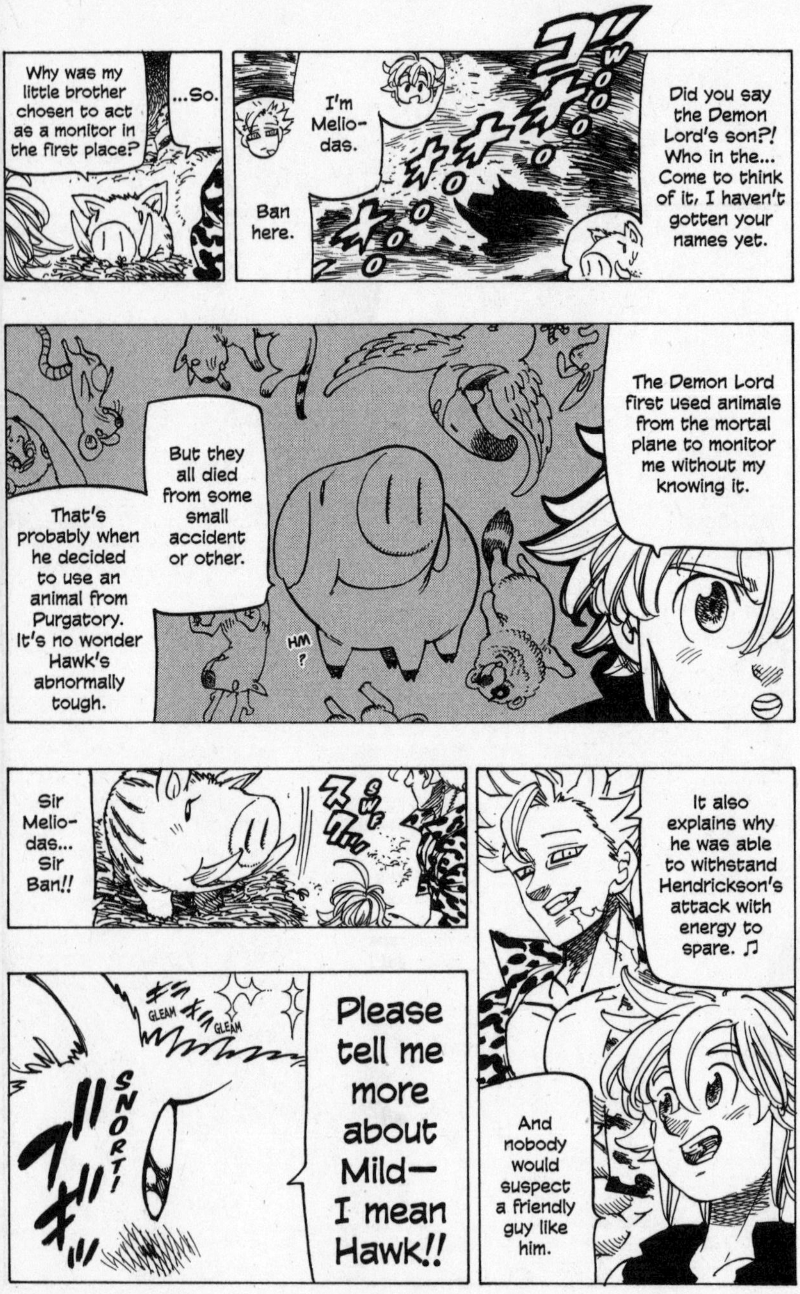

Did you say the Demon Lord's son?! Who in the... Come to think of it, I haven't gotten your names yet.
WOOOOOOO
I'm Melio-das.
Ban here.
...So.
Why was my little brother chosen to act as a monitor in the first place?
The Demon Lord first used animals from the mortal plane to monitor me without my knowing it.
But they all died from some small accident or other.
That's probably when he decided to use an animal from Purgatory. It's no wonder Hawk's abnormally tough.
HM ?
It also explains why he was able to withstand Hendrickson's attack with energy to spare. ♫
And nobody would suspect a friendly guy like him.
SWF
Sir Melio-das... Sir Ban!!
Please tell me more about Mild— I mean Hawk!!
GLEAM
GLEAM
SNORT!

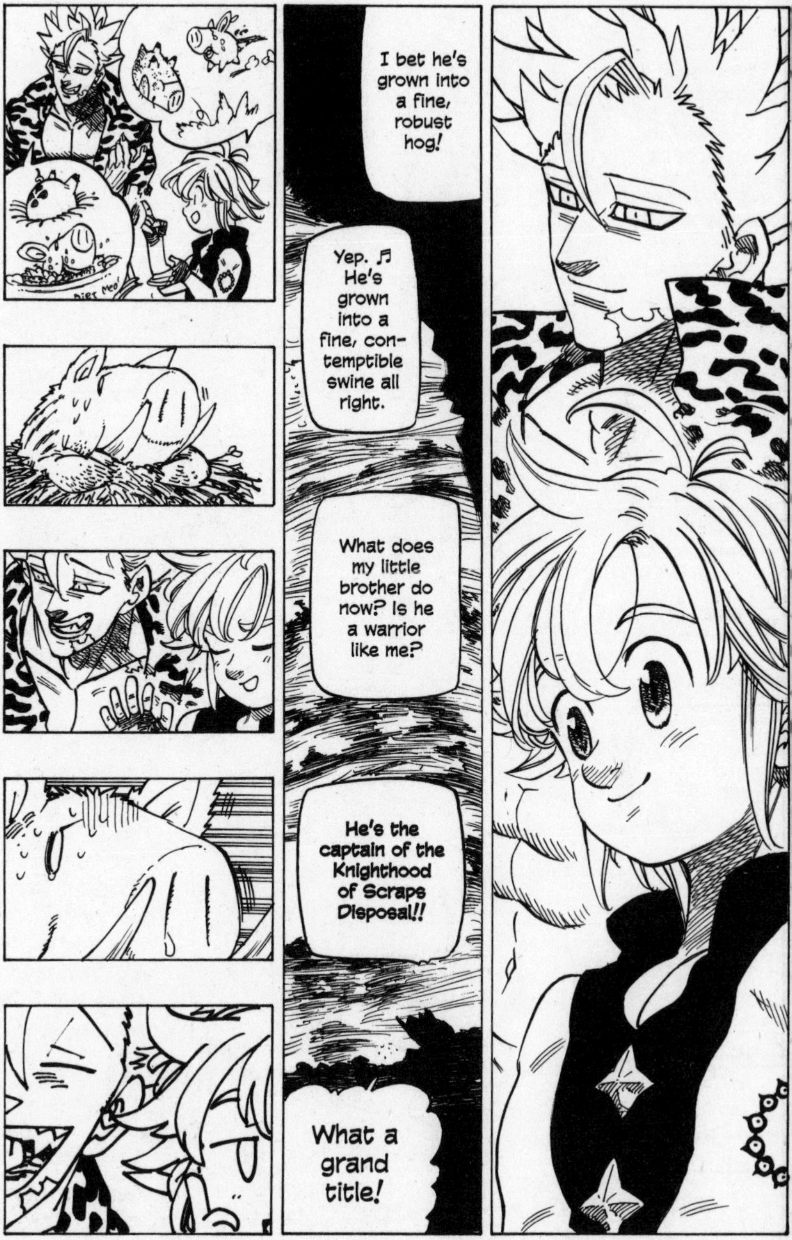
I bet he's grown into a fine, robust hog!
Yep. ♬ He's grown into a fine, contemptible swine all right.
What does my little brother do now? Is he a warrior like me?
He's the captain of the Knighthood of Scraps Disposal!!
What a grand title!

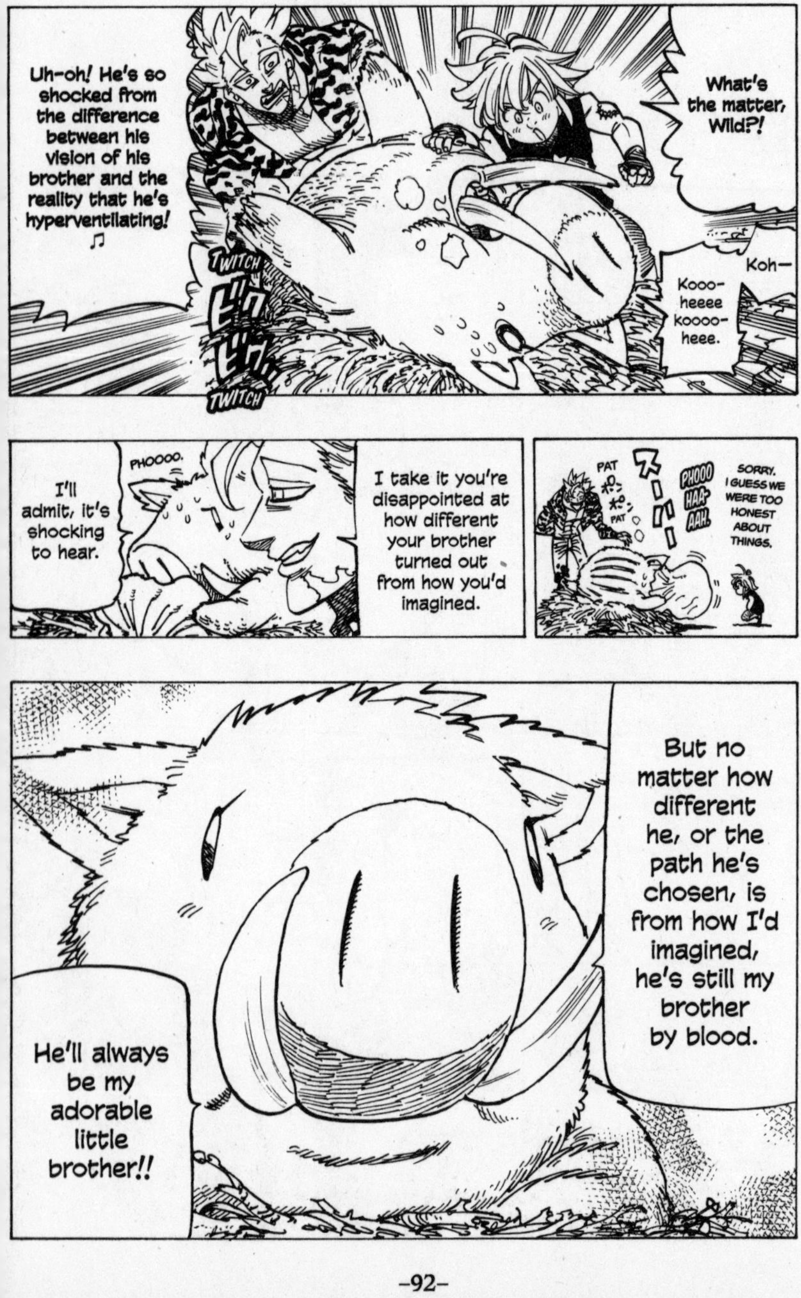

What's the matter, Wild?!
Koh—
Kooo-heeee kooooheee.
Uh-oh! He's so shocked from the difference between his vision of his brother and the reality that he's hyperventilating! ♫
TWITCH
TWITCH
SORRY. I GUESS WE WERE TOO HONEST ABOUT THINGS.
PHOOO HAA AAH.
PAT
PAT
I take it you're disappointed at how different your brother turned out from how you'd imagined.
PHOOOO.
I'll admit, it's shocking to hear.
But no matter how different he, or the path he's chosen, is from how I'd imagined, he's still my brother by blood.
He'll always be my adorable little brother!!

...That's right.

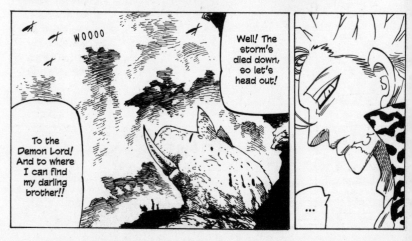

WOOOO

Well! The storm's died down, so let's head out!

To the Demon Lord! And to where I can find my darling brother!!

...

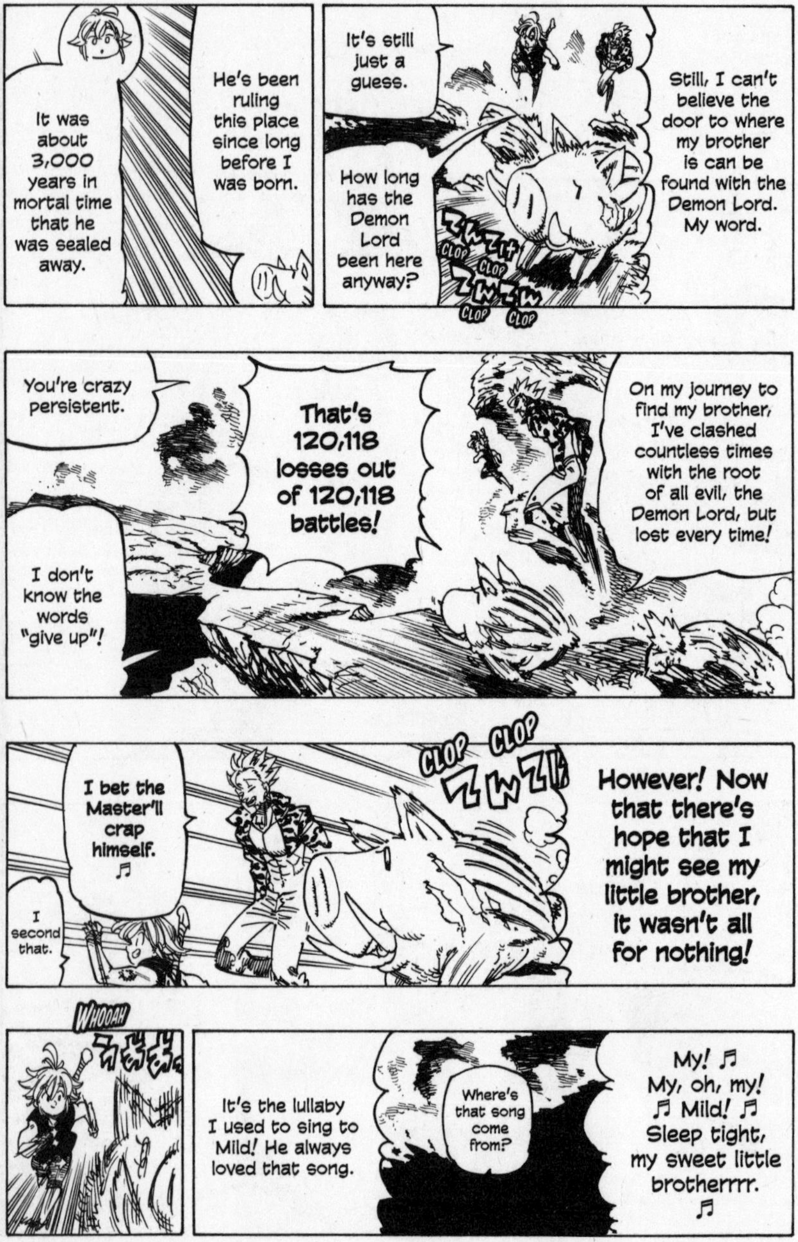
Still, I can't believe the door to where my brother is can be found with the Demon Lord. My word.
It's still just a guess.
How long has the Demon Lord been here anyway?
CLOP CLOP CLOP CLOP
He's been ruling this place since long before I was born.
It was about 3,000 years in mortal time that he was sealed away.
On my journey to find my brother, I've clashed countless times with the root of all evil, the Demon Lord, but lost every time!
That's 120,118 losses out of 120,118 battles!
You're crazy persistent.
I don't know the words "give up"!
CLOP CLOP
However! Now that there's hope that I might see my little brother, it wasn't all for nothing!
I bet the Master'll crap himself. ♫
I second that.
My! ♫ My, oh, my! ♫ Mild! ♫ Sleep tight, my sweet little brotherrrr. ♫
Where's that song come from?
It's the lullaby I used to sing to Mild! He always loved that song.
WHOOAH

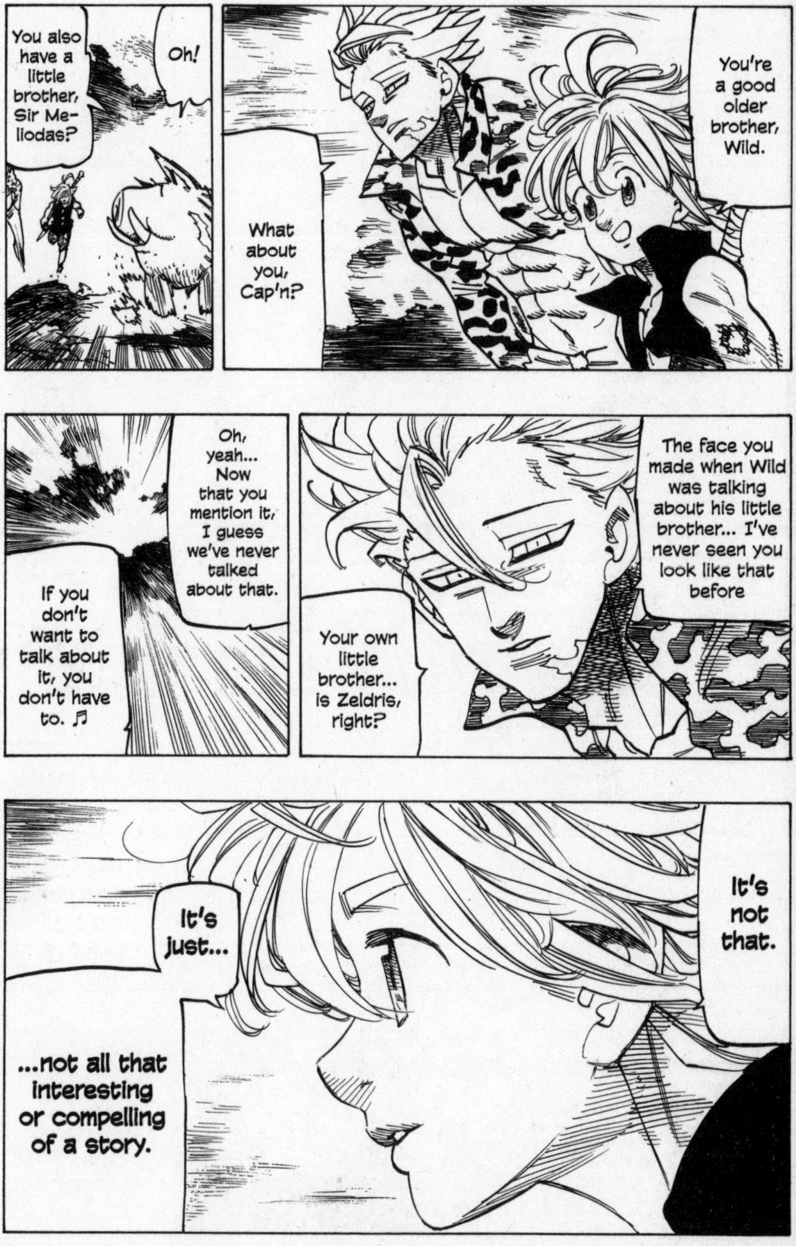
You're a good older brother, Wild.
What about you, Cap'n?
Oh!
You also have a little brother, Sir Meliodas?
The face you made when Wild was talking about his little brother... I've never seen you look like that before
Your own little brother... is Zeldris, right?
Oh, yeah... Now that you mention it, I guess we've never talked about that.
If you don't want to talk about it, you don't have to. ♫
It's not that.
It's just...
...not all that interesting or compelling of a story.

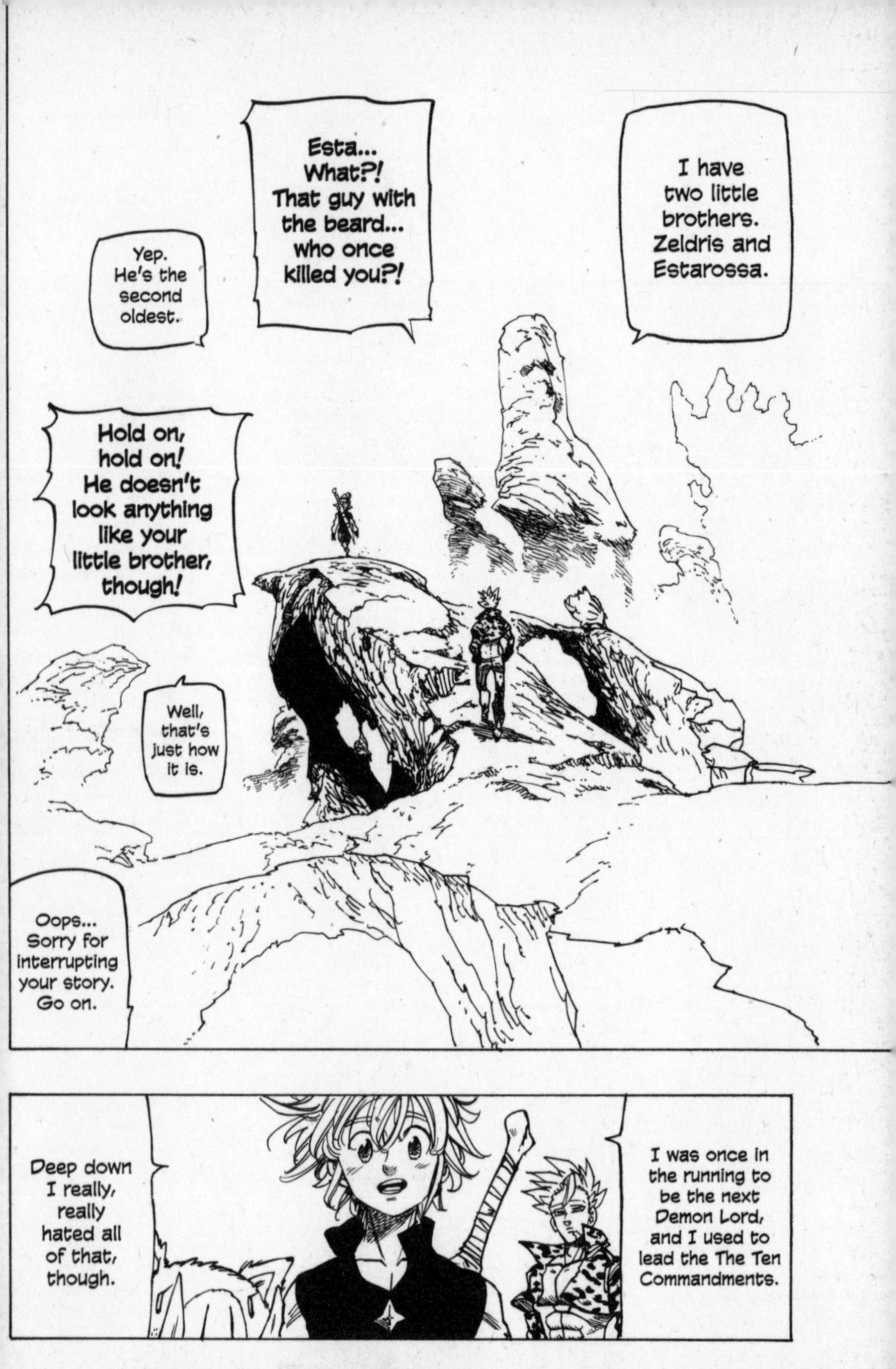
I have two little brothers. Zeldris and Estarossa.
Esta... What?! That guy with the beard... who once killed you?!
Yep. He's the second oldest.
Hold on, hold on! He doesn't look anything like your little brother, though!
Well, that's just how it is.
Oops... Sorry for interrupting your story. Go on.
I was once in the running to be the next Demon Lord, and I used to lead the The Ten Commandments.
Deep down I really, really hated all of that, though.

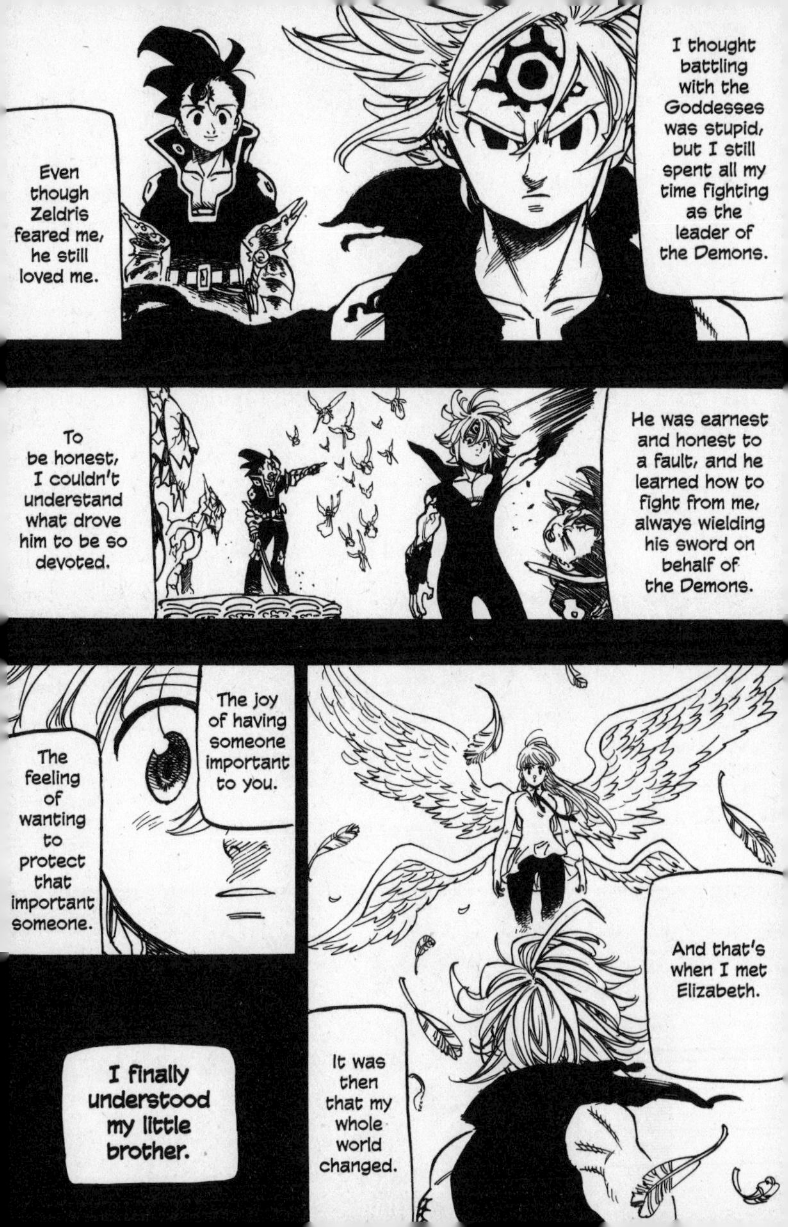
I thought battling with the Goddesses was stupid, but I still spent all my time fighting as the leader of the Demons.
Even though Zeldris feared me, he still loved me.
He was earnest and honest to a fault, and he learned how to fight from me, always wielding his sword on behalf of the Demons.
To be honest, I couldn't understand what drove him to be so devoted.
And that's when I met Elizabeth.
It was then that my whole world changed.
The joy of having someone important to you.
The feeling of wanting to protect that important someone.
I finally understood my little brother.

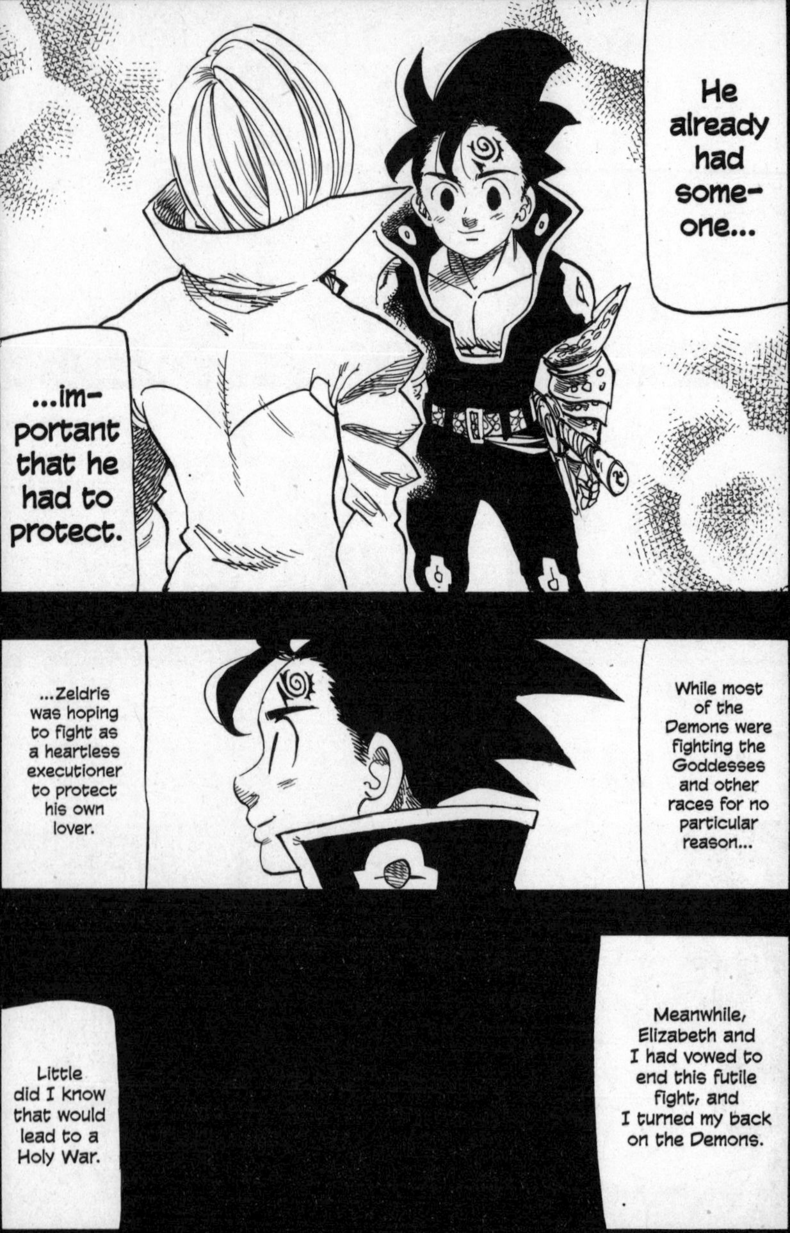
He already had some-one...
...im-portant that he had to protect.
While most of the Demons were fighting the Goddesses and other races for no particular reason...
...Zeldris was hoping to fight as a heartless executioner to protect his own lover.
Meanwhile, Elizabeth and I had vowed to end this futile fight, and I turned my back on the Demons.
Little did I know that would lead to a Holy War.

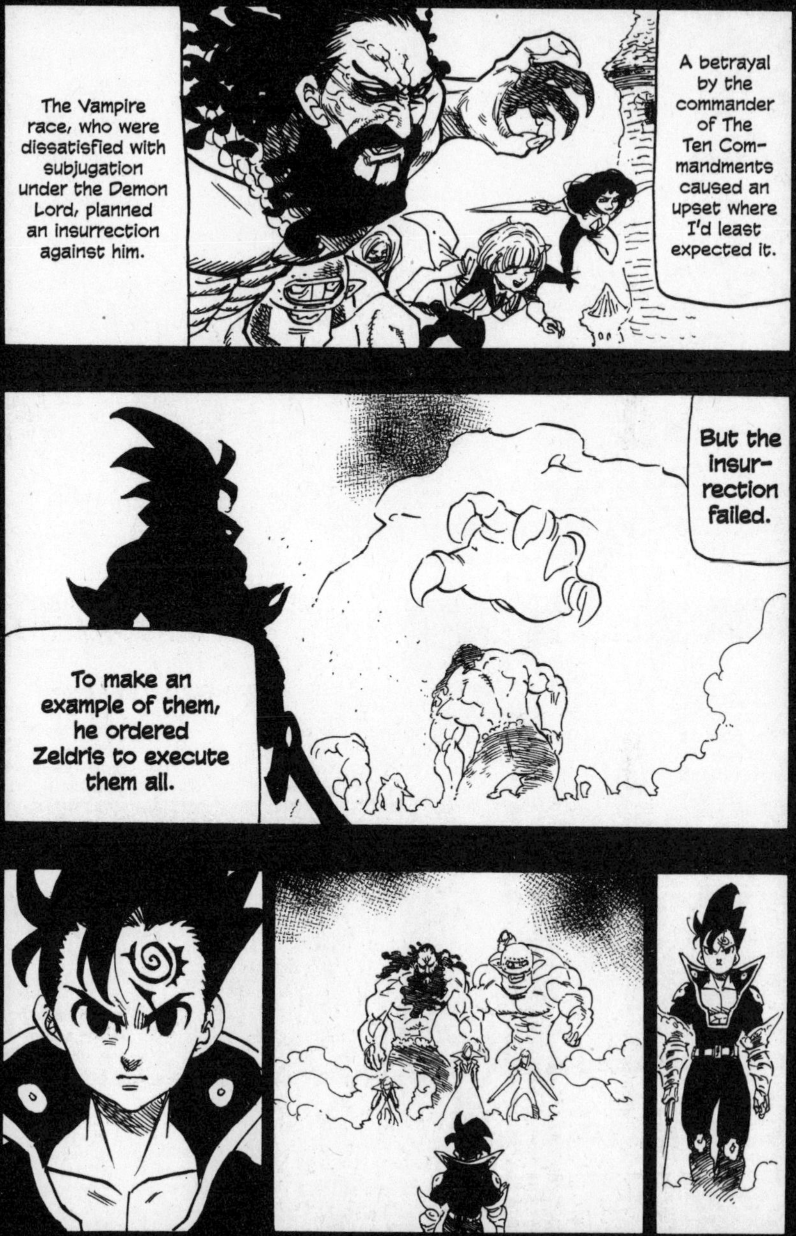
A betrayal by the commander of The Ten Commandments caused an upset where I'd least expected it.
The Vampire race, who were dissatisfied with subjugation under the Demon Lord, planned an insurrection against him.
But the insurrection failed.
To make an example of them, he ordered Zeldris to execute them all.

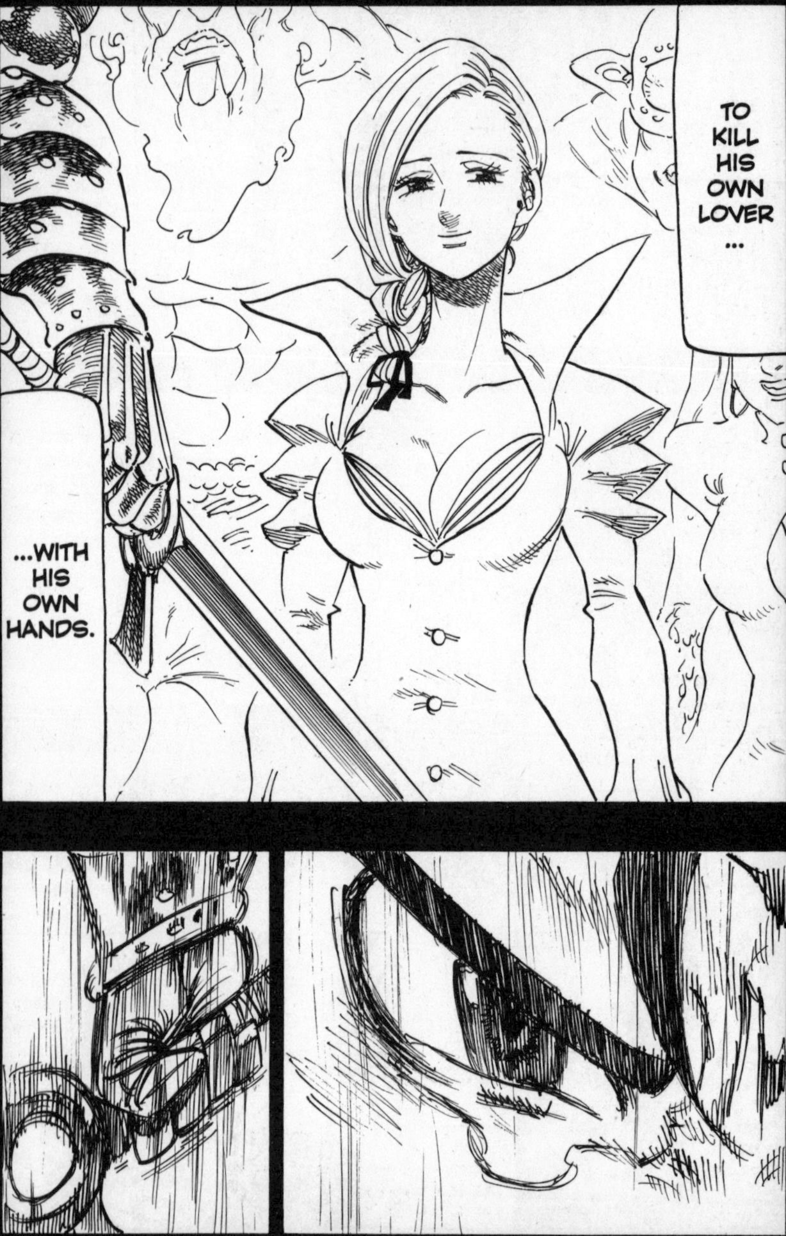
TO KILL HIS OWN LOVER ...
...WITH HIS OWN HANDS.

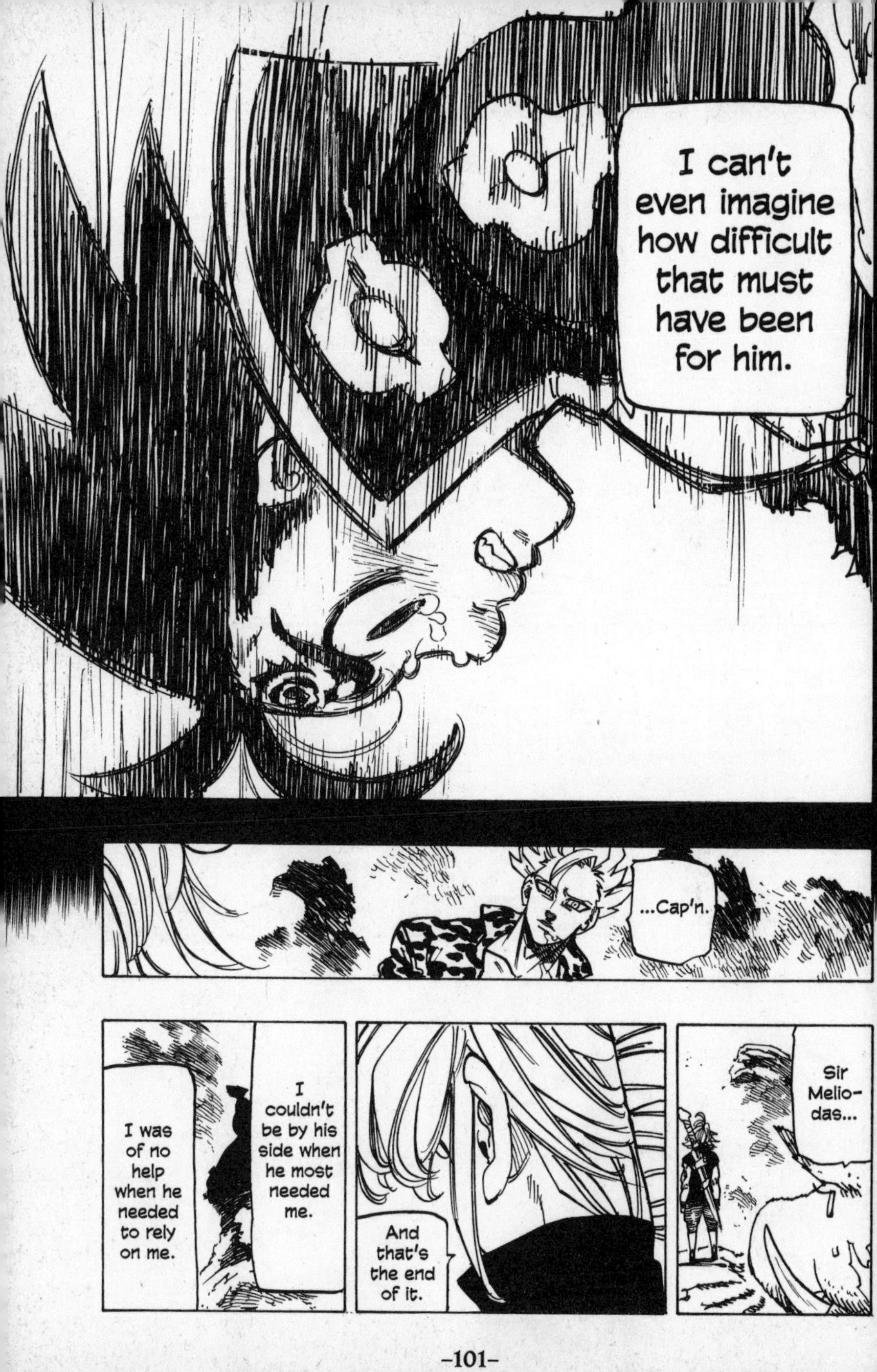
I can't even imagine how difficult that must have been for him.
...Cap'n.
Sir Melio-das...
And that's the end of it.
I couldn't be by his side when he most needed me.
I was of no help when he needed to rely on me.

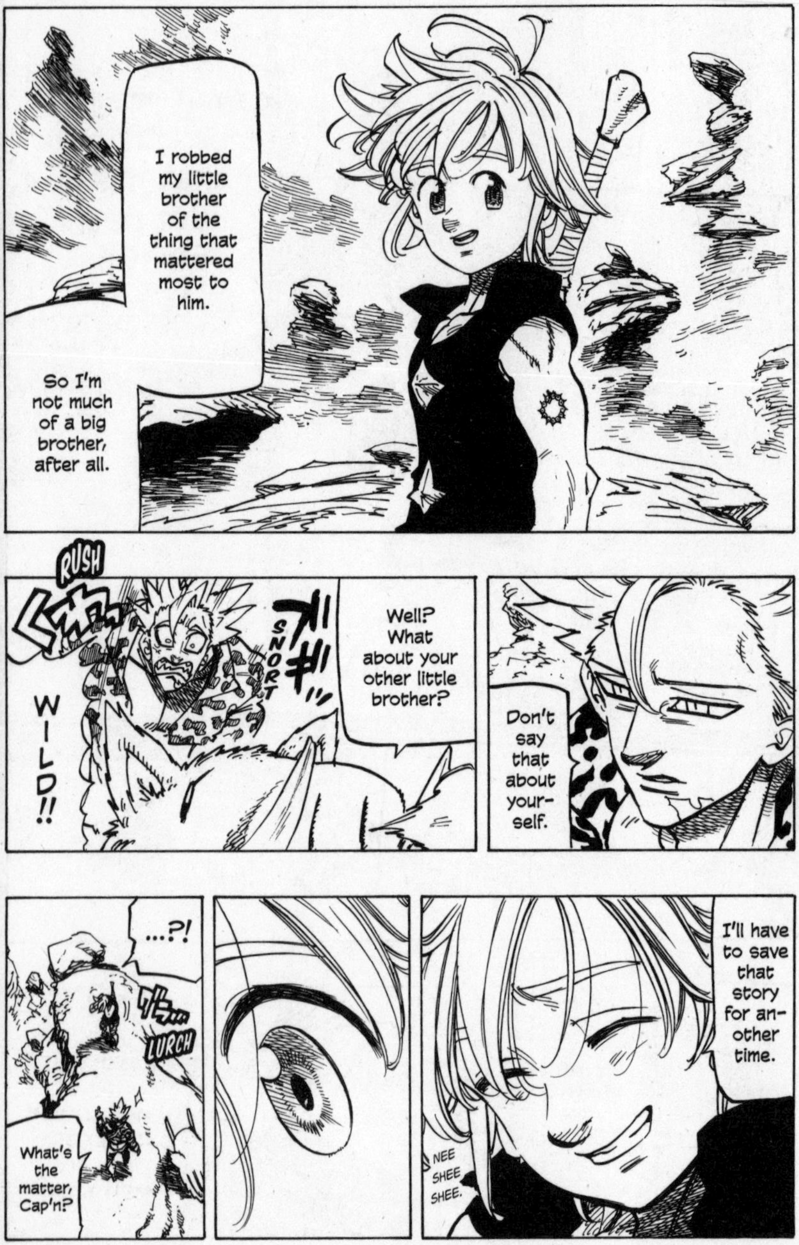
I robbed my little brother of the thing that mattered most to him.
So I'm not much of a big brother, after all.
Don't say that about your-self.
Well? What about your other little brother?
SNORT
RUSH
WILD!!
I'll have to save that story for an-other time.
NEE SHEE SHEE.
...?!
LURCH
What's the matter, Cap'n?

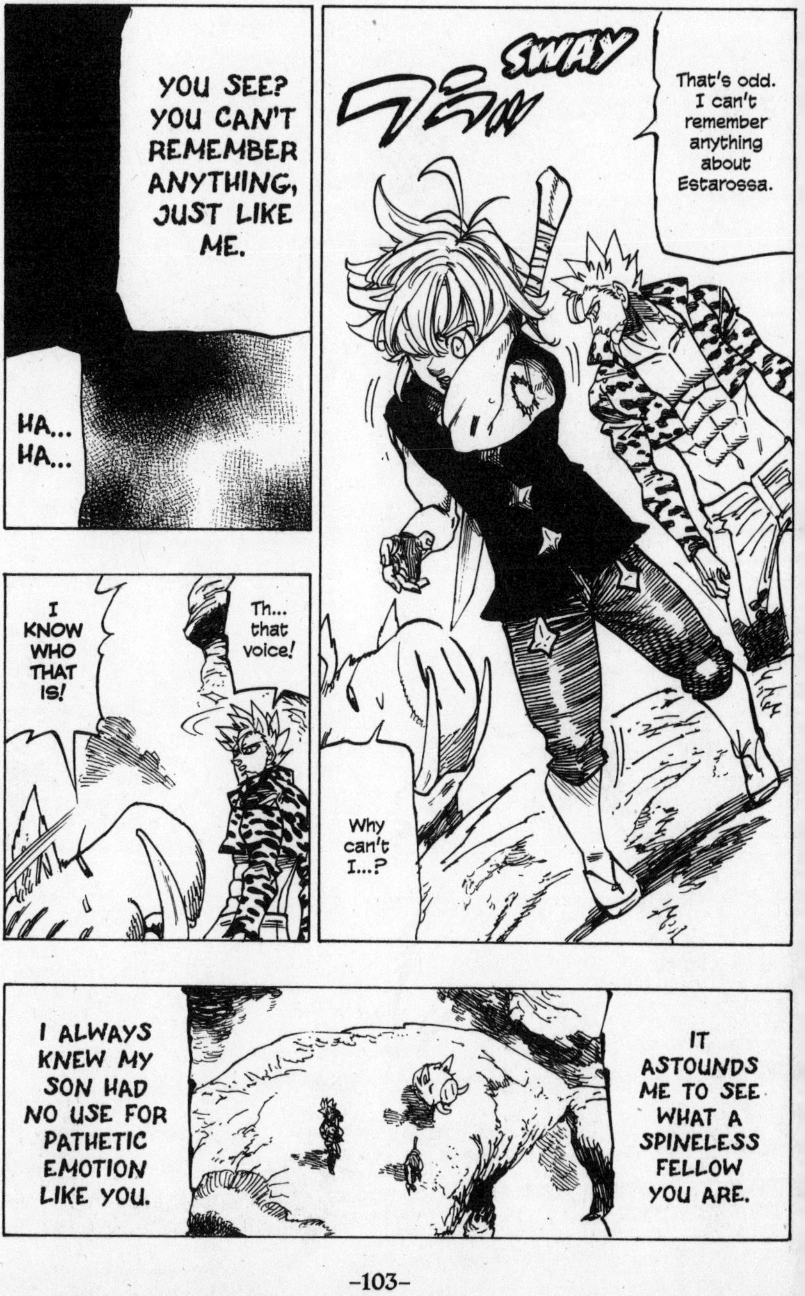
That's odd. I can't remember anything about Estarossa.
SWAY
Why can't I...?
YOU SEE? YOU CAN'T REMEMBER ANYTHING, JUST LIKE ME.
HA... HA...
Th... that voice!
I KNOW WHO THAT IS!
IT ASTOUNDS ME TO SEE WHAT A SPINELESS FELLOW YOU ARE.
I ALWAYS KNEW MY SON HAD NO USE FOR PATHETIC EMOTION LIKE YOU.

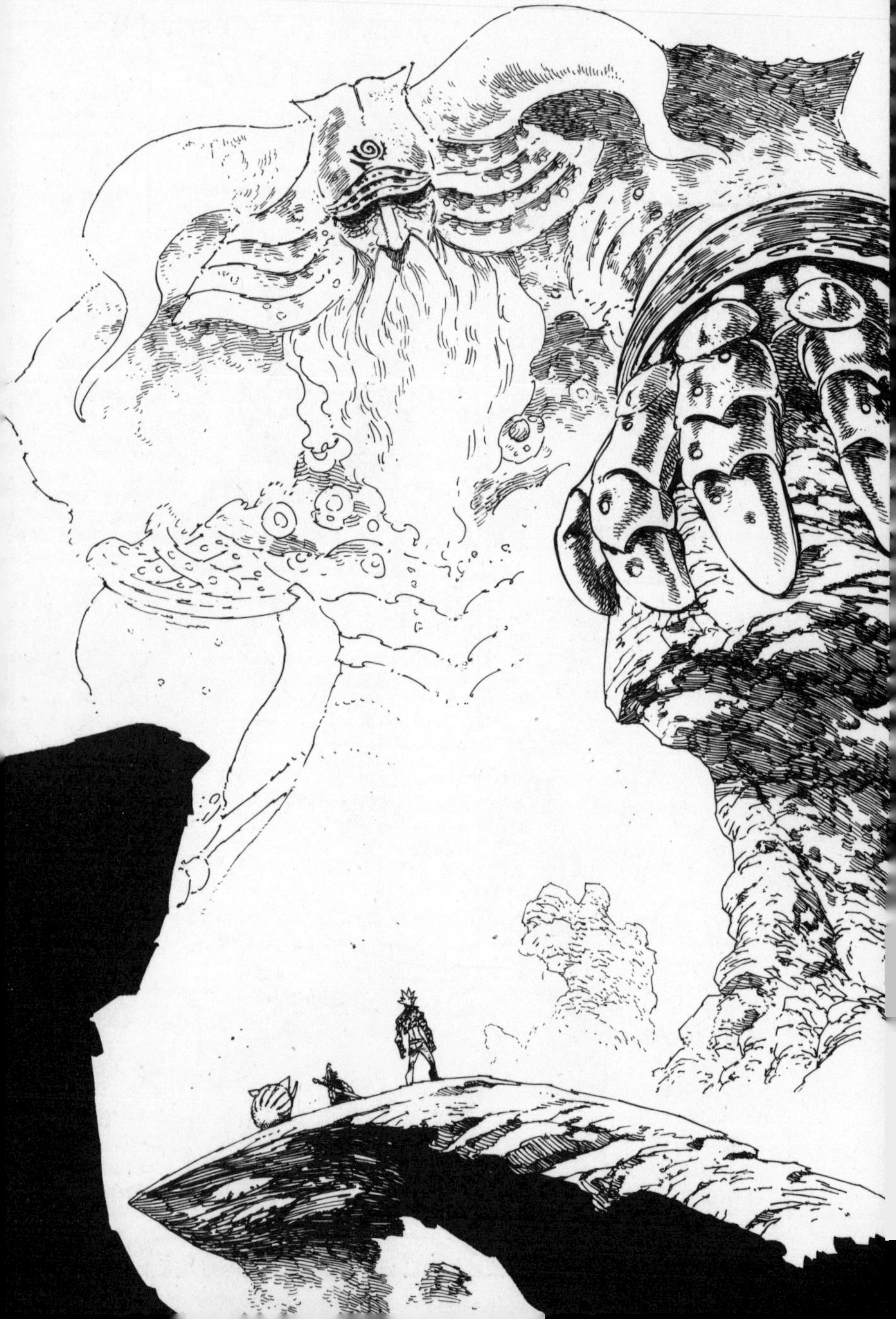

Chapter 272 - Eternal Battle

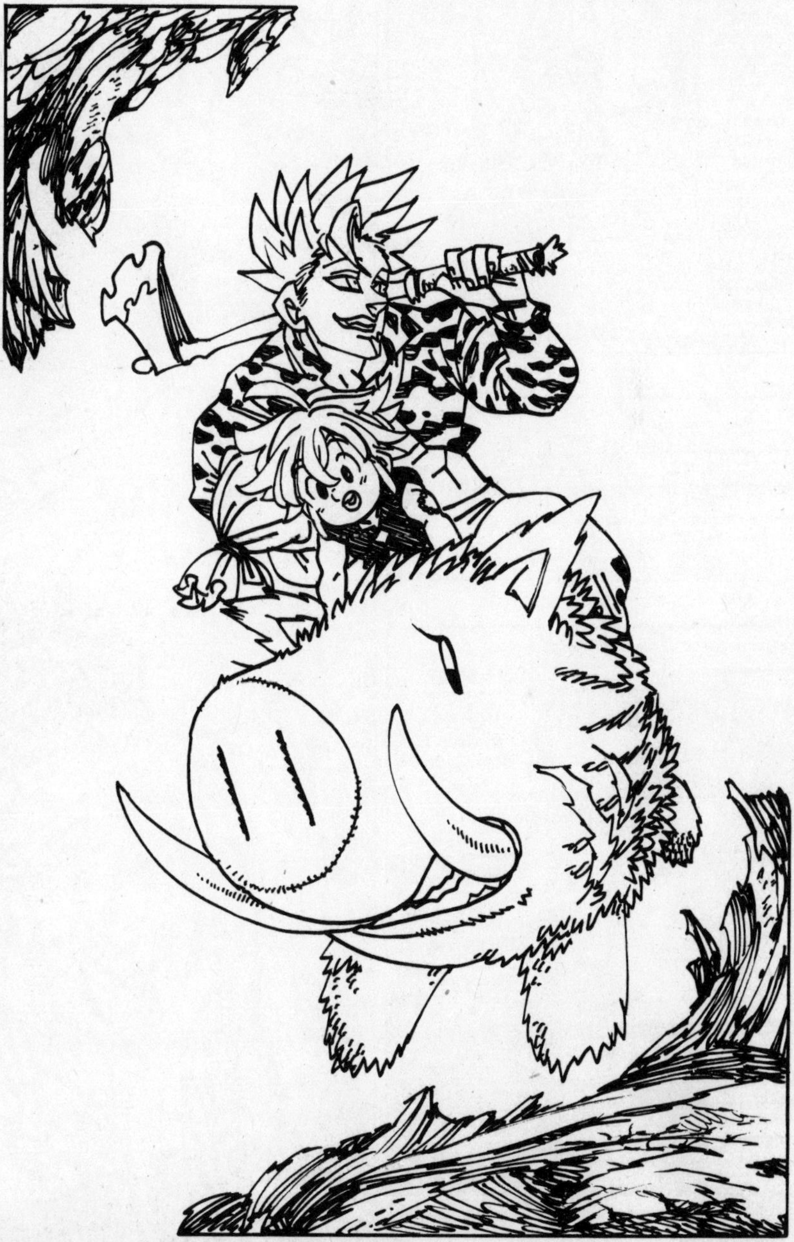

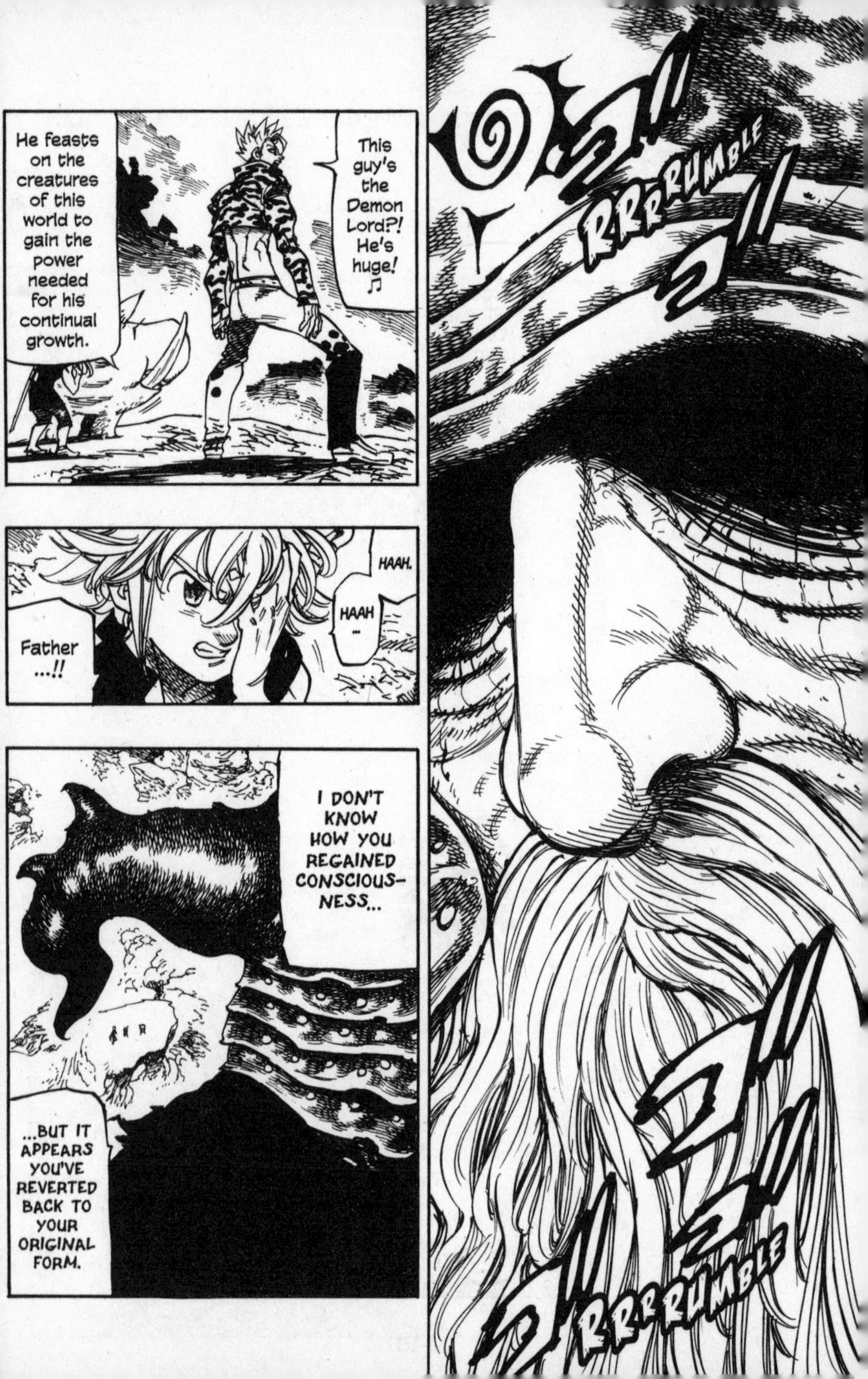
RRRRUMBLE
RRRRUMBLE
This guy's the Demon Lord?! He's huge! ♫
He feasts on the creatures of this world to gain the power needed for his continual growth.
HAAH.
HAAH ...
Father ...!!
I DON'T KNOW HOW YOU REGAINED CONSCIOUS-NESS...
...BUT IT APPEARS YOU'VE REVERTED BACK TO YOUR ORIGINAL FORM.

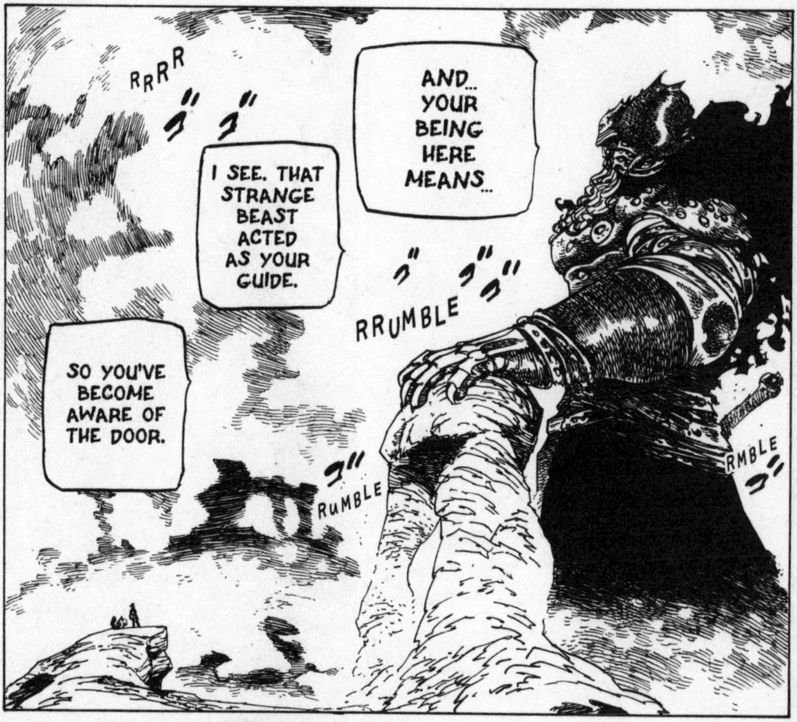
AND... YOUR BEING HERE MEANS...
RRRR
I SEE. THAT STRANGE BEAST ACTED AS YOUR GUIDE.
RRUMBLE
RMBLE
SO YOU'VE BECOME AWARE OF THE DOOR.
RUMBLE

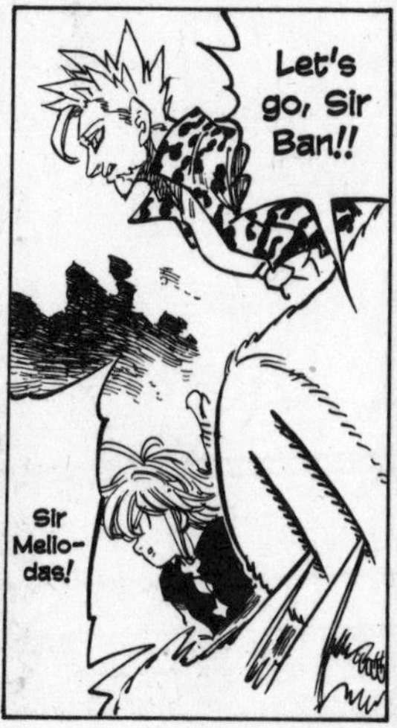
Let's go, Sir Ban!!
Sir Melio-das!

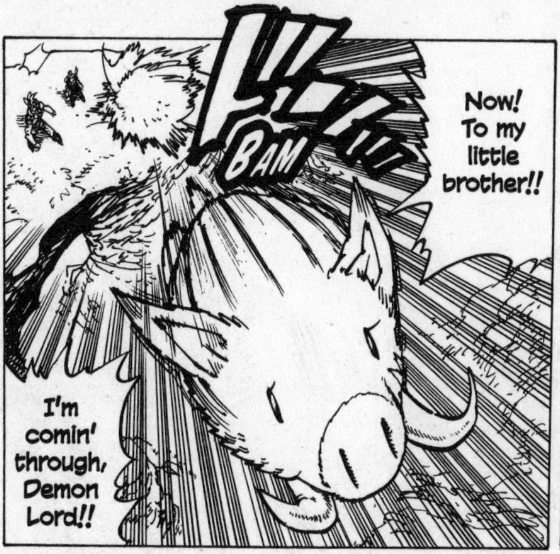
Now! To my little brother!!
BAM
I'm comin' through, Demon Lord!!

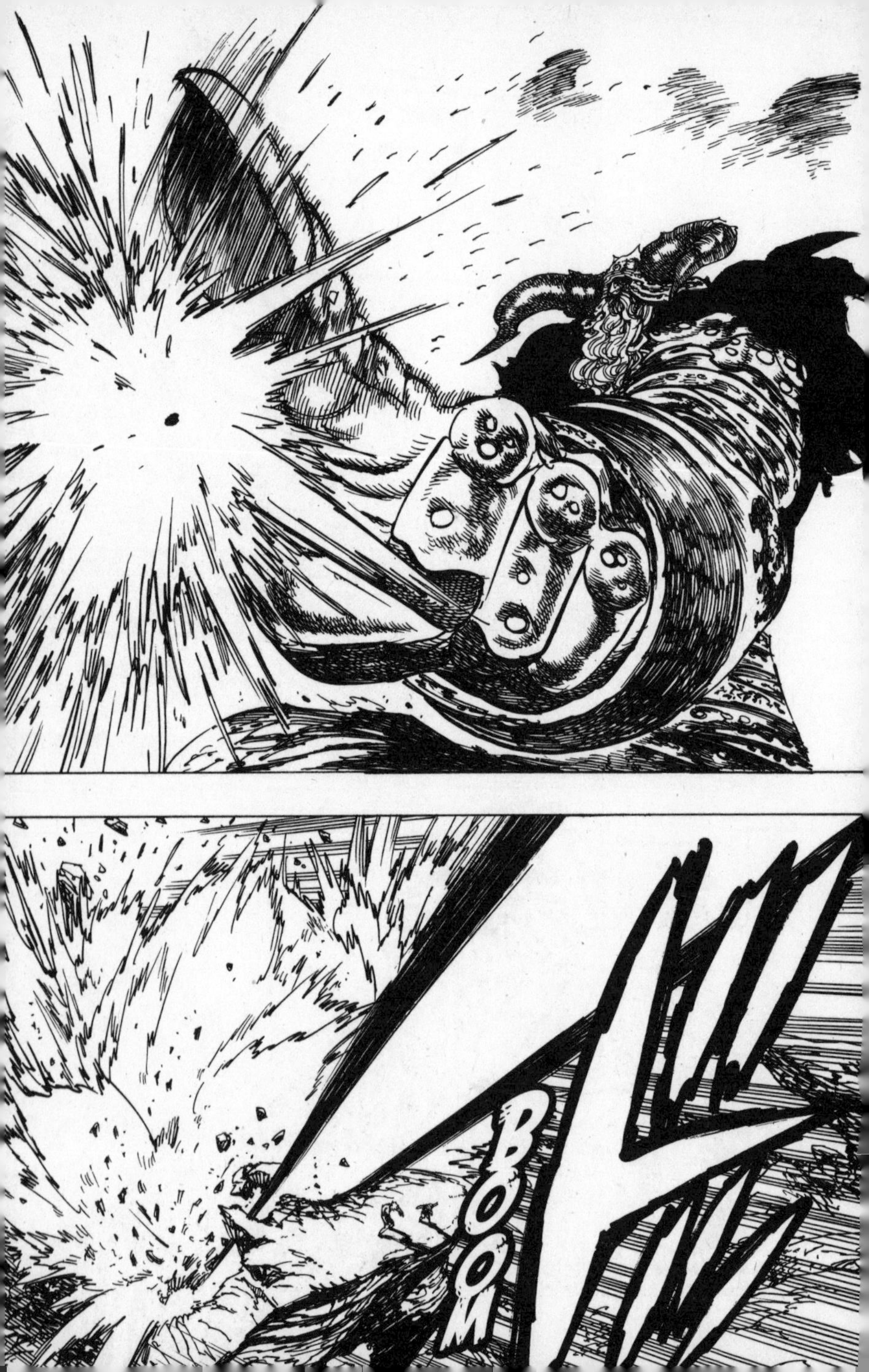
BOOM

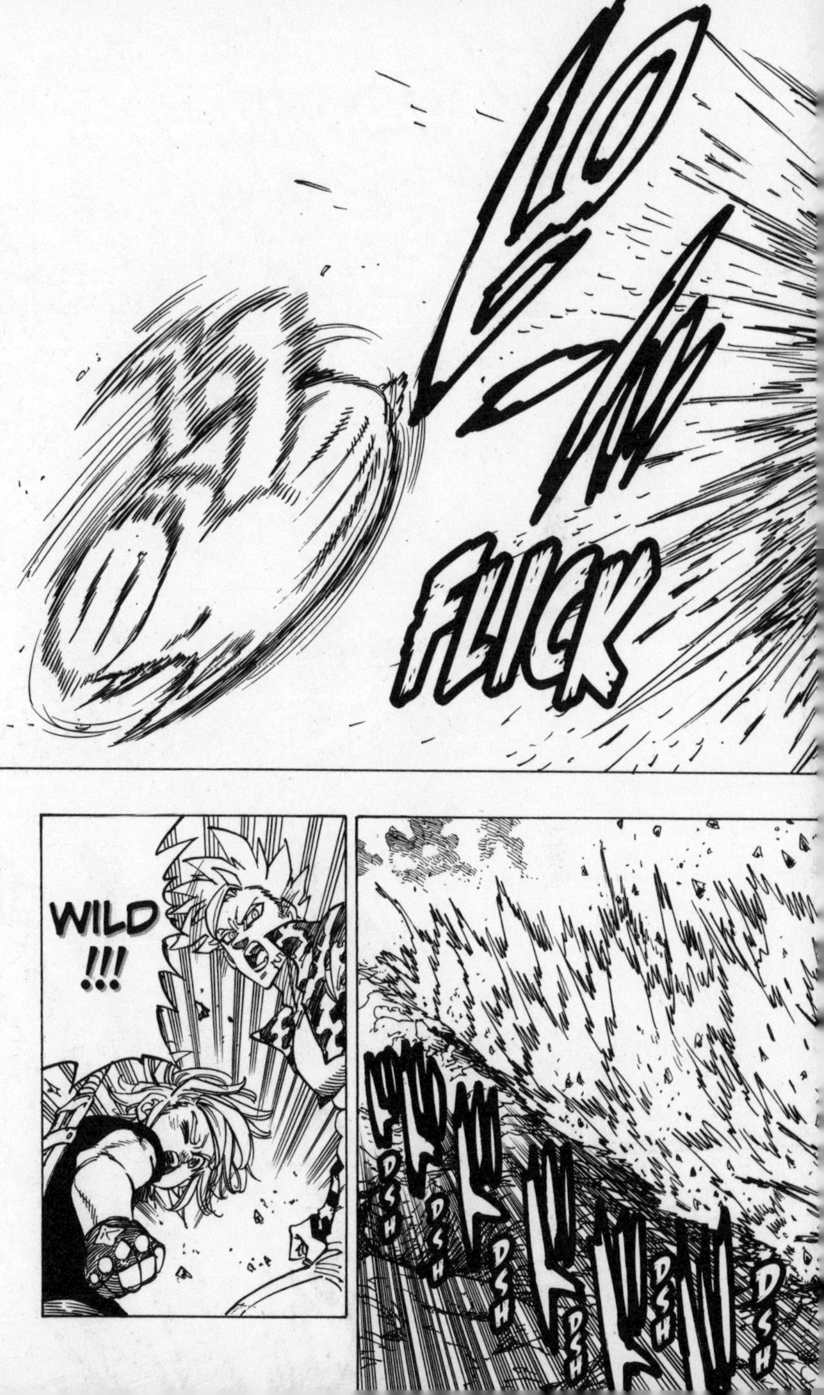
FLICK
DSH
DSH
DSH
DSH
DSH
DSH
DSH
WILD !!!

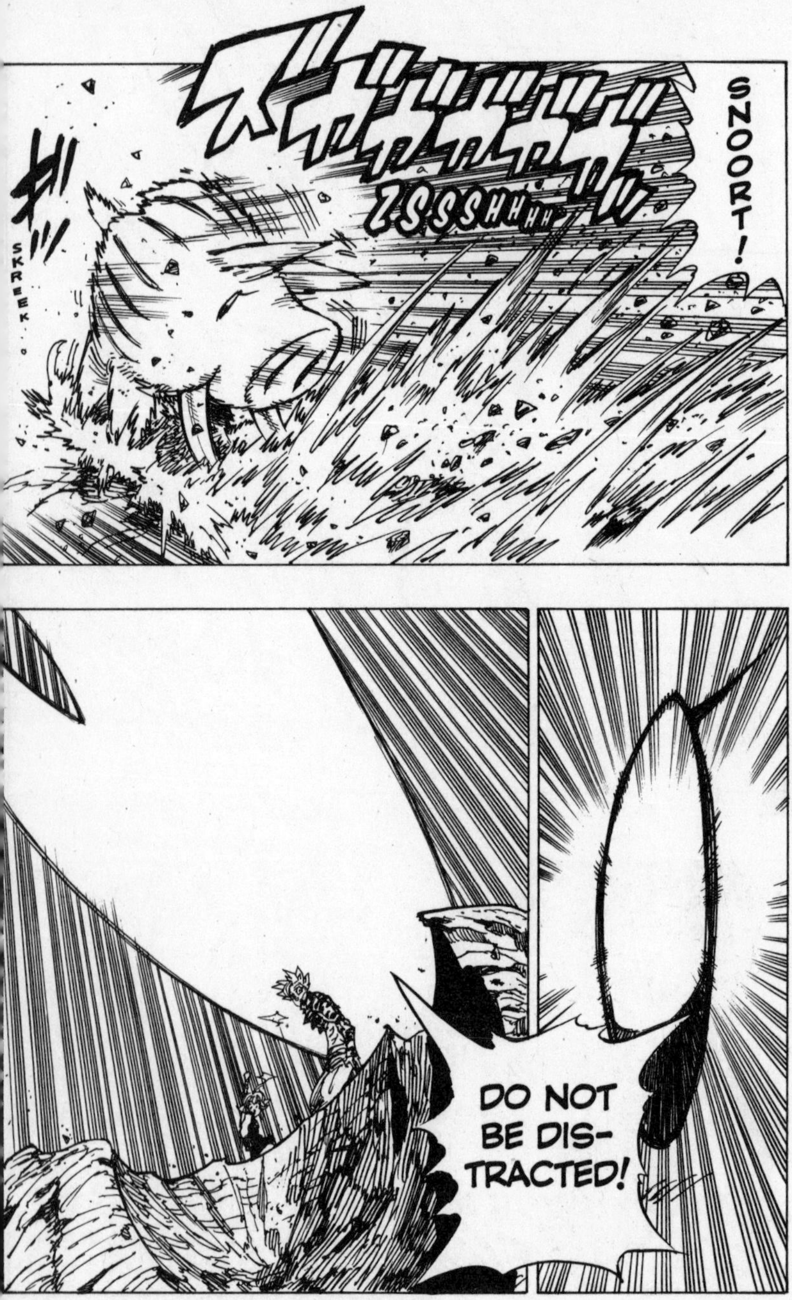
SNOORT!
ZSSSHHHHH
SKREEK...
DO NOT BE DIS-TRACTED!

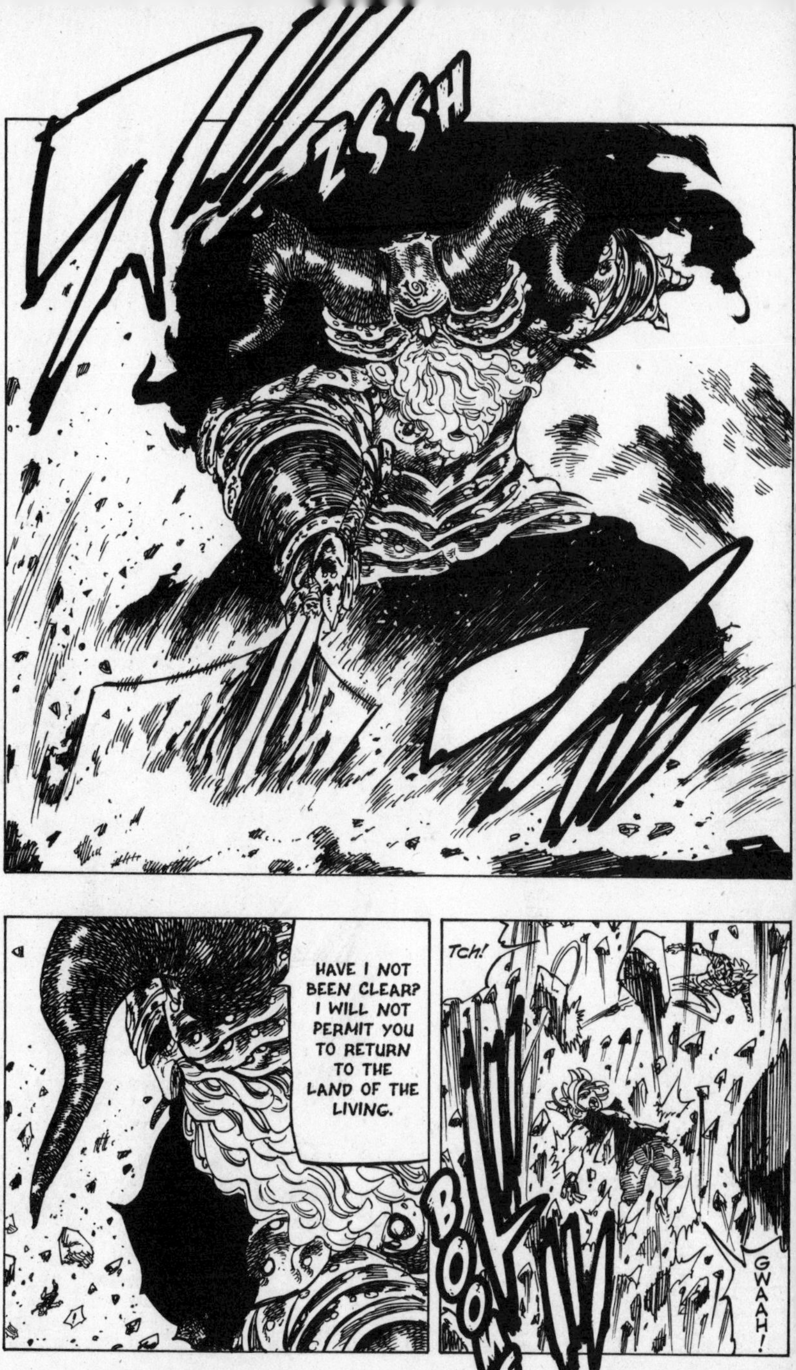
ZSSH
Tch!
BOOMF
GWAAH!
HAVE I NOT BEEN CLEAR? I WILL NOT PERMIT YOU TO RETURN TO THE LAND OF THE LIVING.

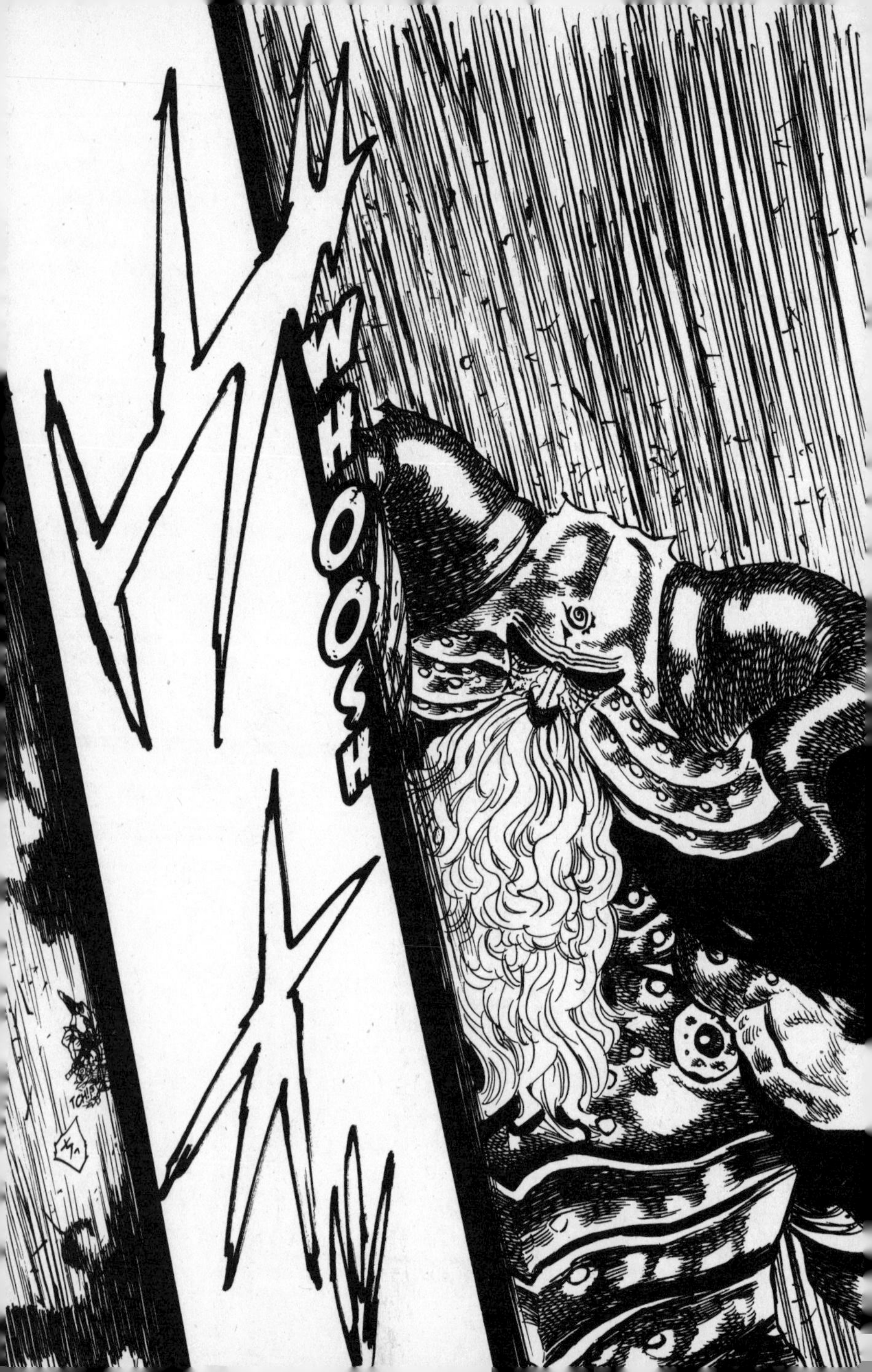
WHOOSH
TCH!?

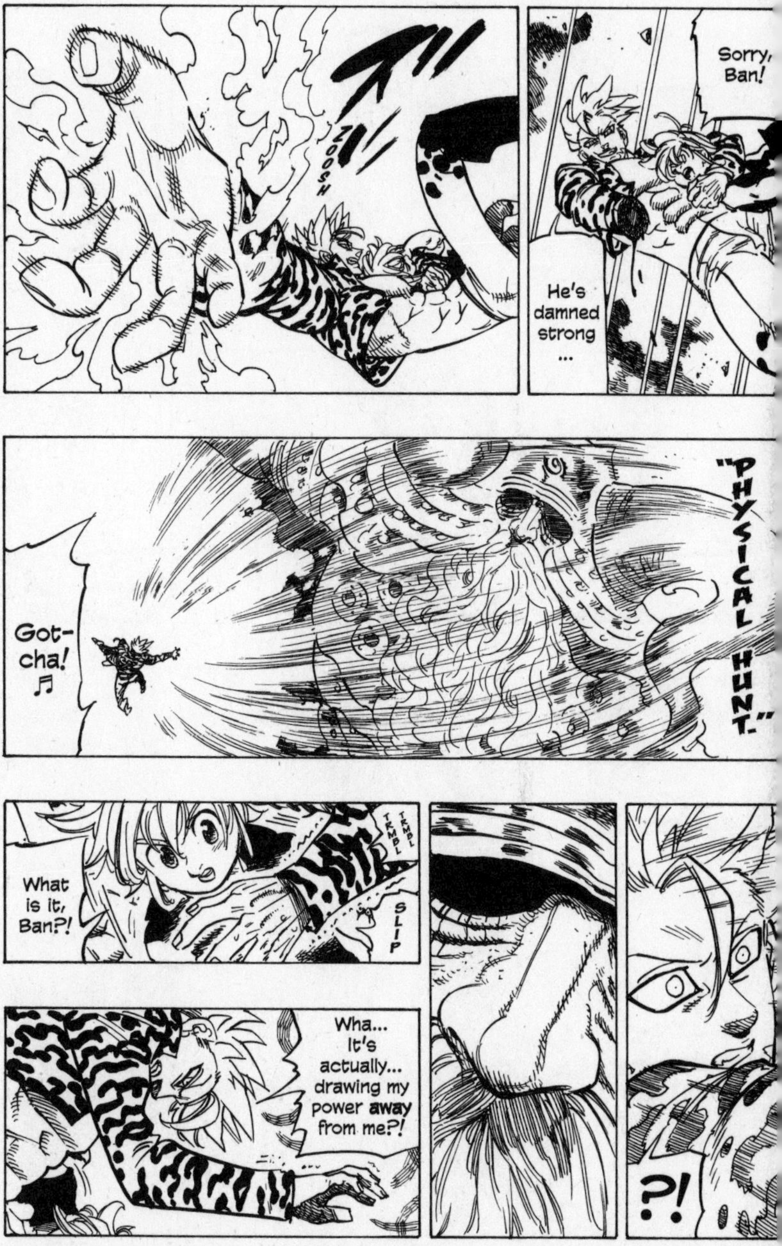
Sorry, Ban!
He's damned strong ...
ZOOSH
"PHYSICAL HUNT."
Got-cha! ♫
?!
TRMBL TRMBL
What is it, Ban?!
SLIP
Wha... It's actually... drawing my power away from me?!

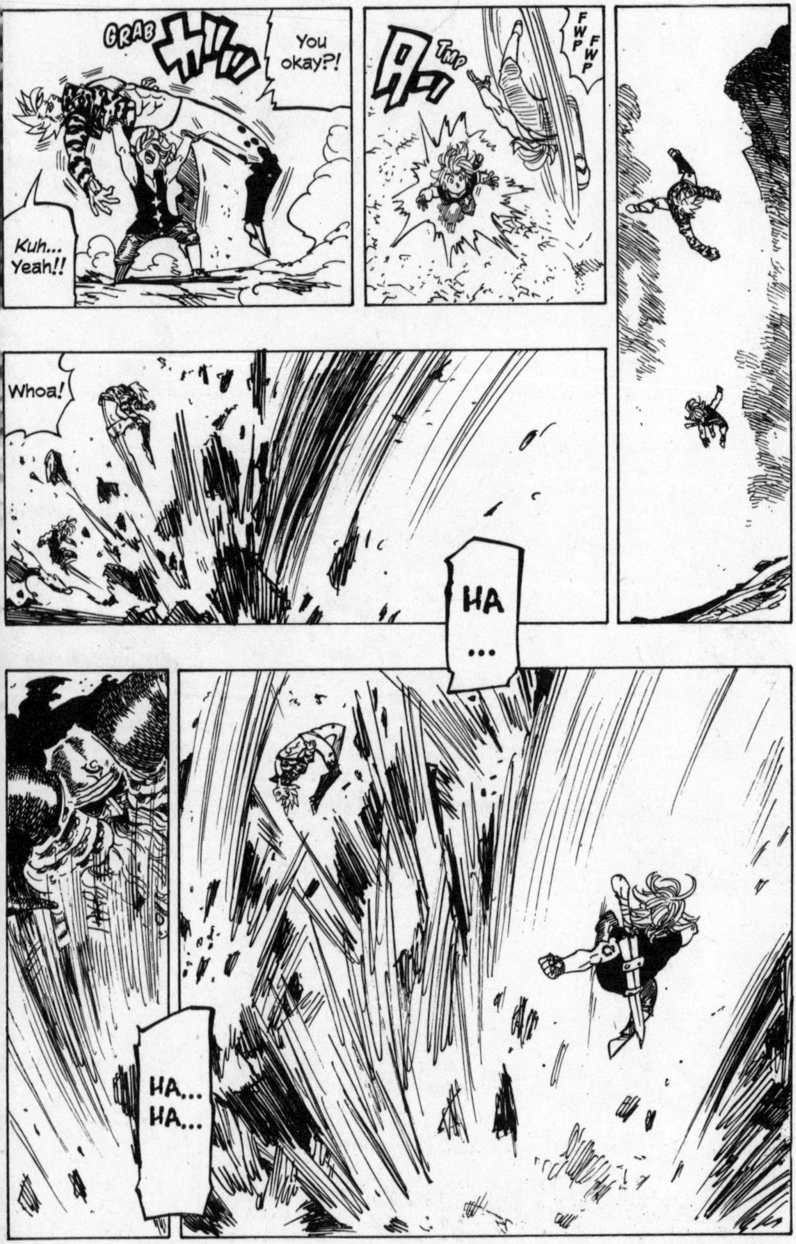
FWP FWP
TMP
You okay?!
GRAB
Kuh... Yeah!!
Whoa!
HA...
HA... HA...

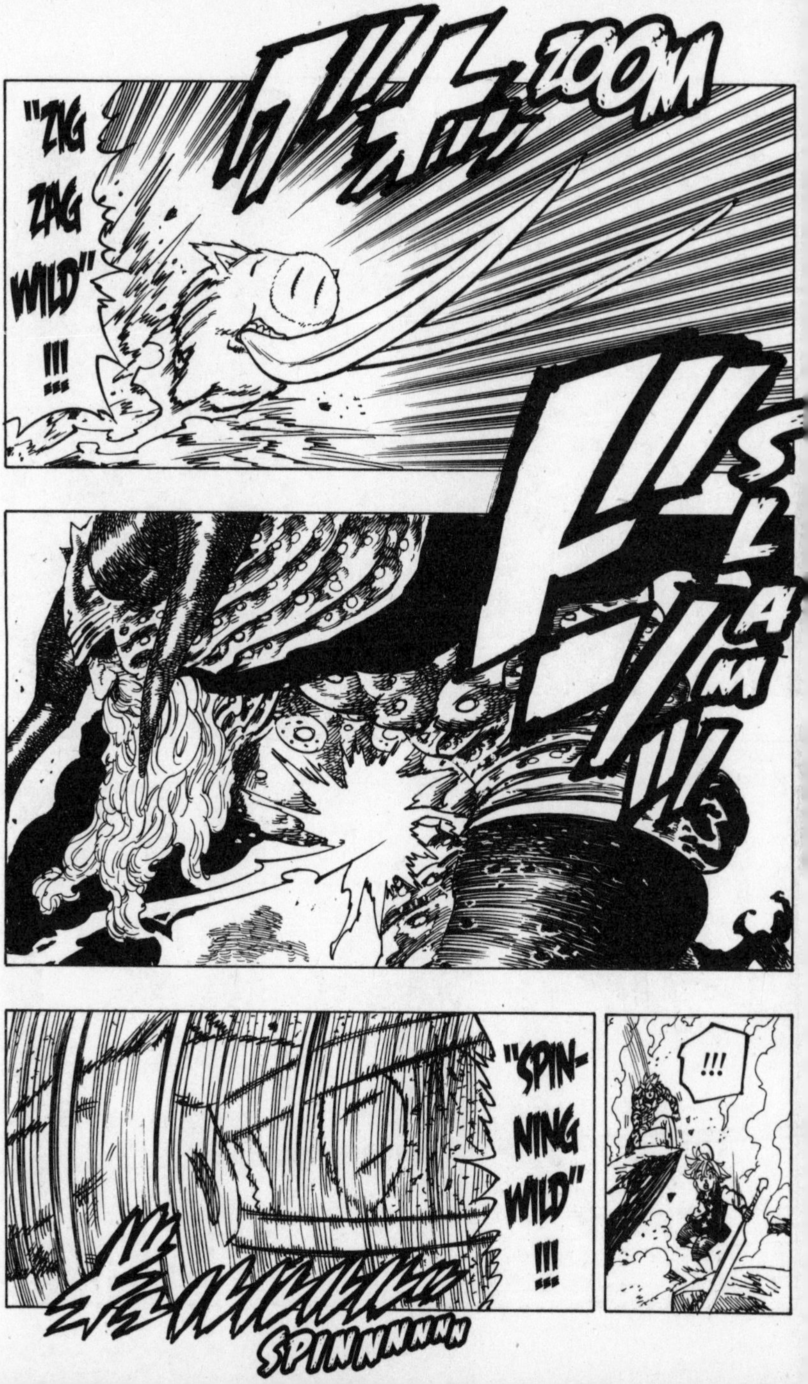
ZOOM
"ZIG ZAG WILD"!!!
SLAM
!!!
"SPIN-NING WILD"!!!
SPINNNNNNN

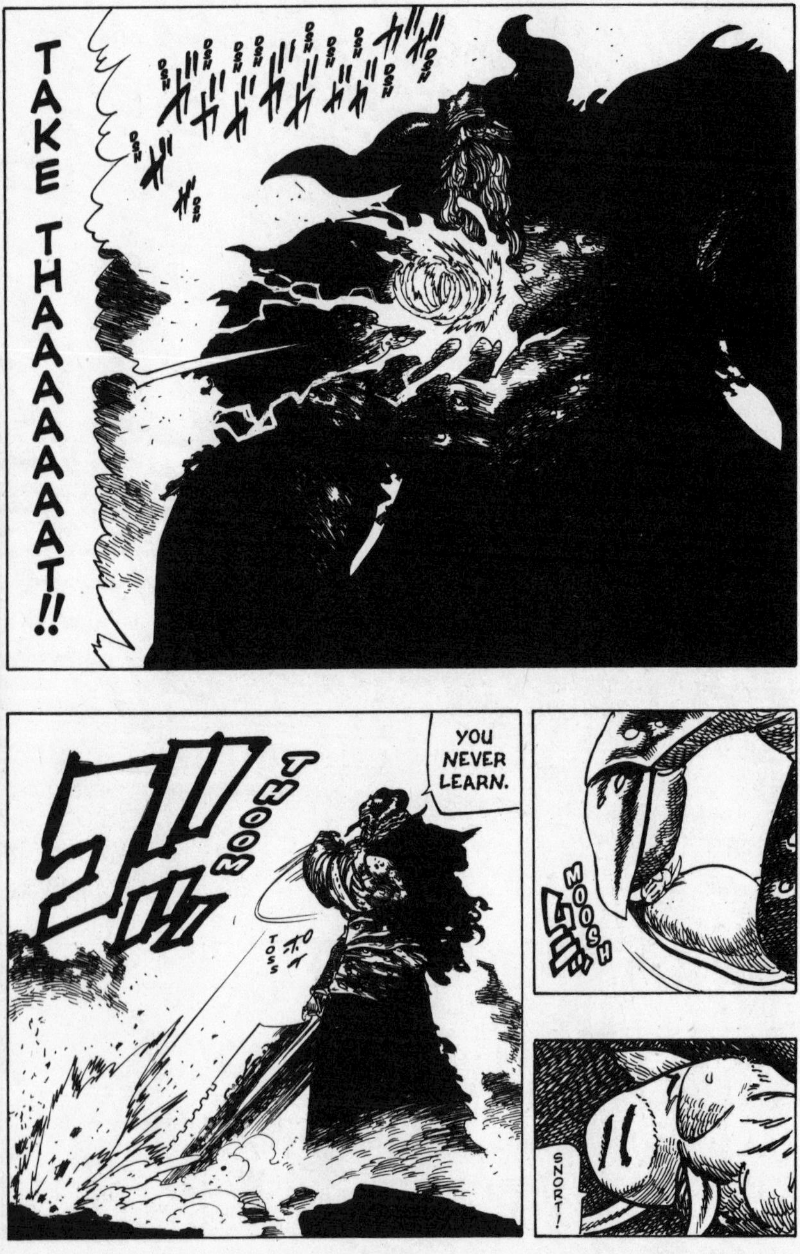
DSH
TAKE THAAAAAAAAT!!
MOOSH
SNORT!
YOU NEVER LEARN.
THOOOM
TOSS

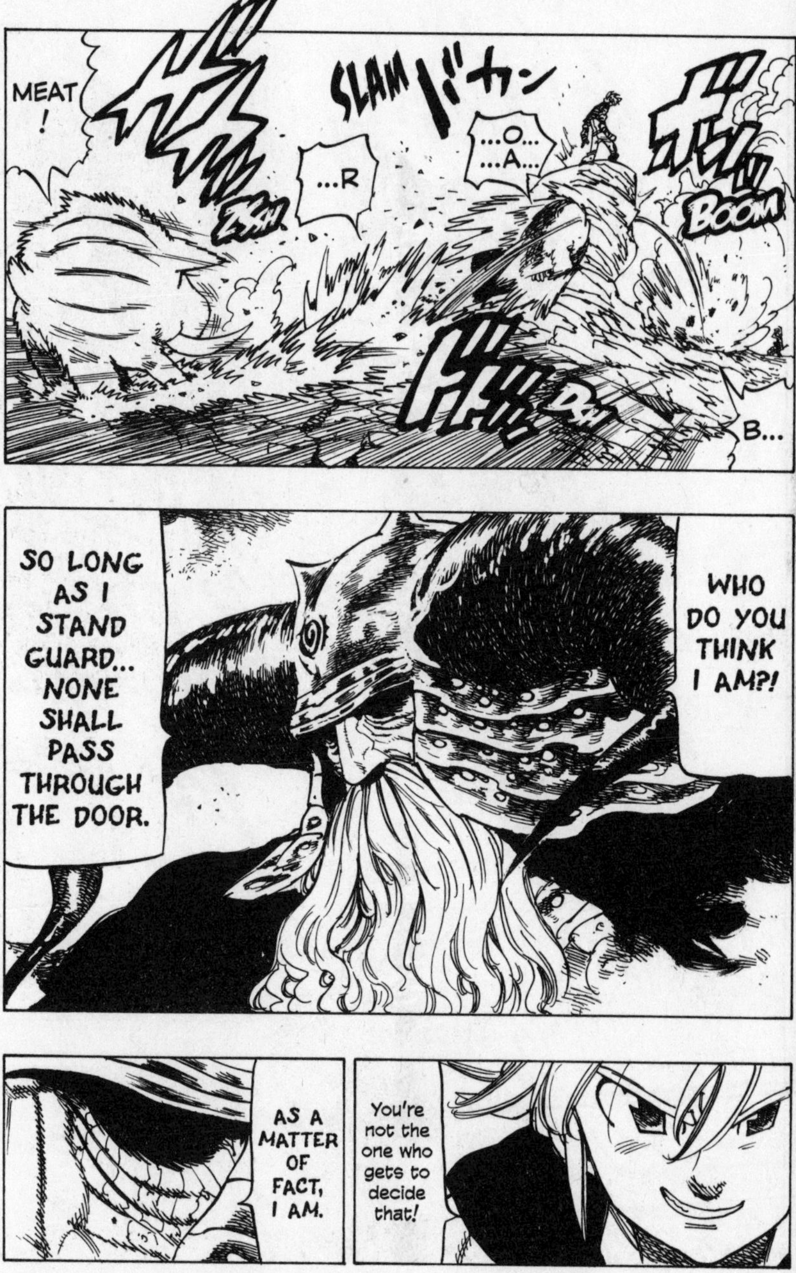
BOOM
...O...
...A...
SLAM
バカン
...R
MEAT!
DSH
B...
WHO DO YOU THINK I AM?!
SO LONG AS I STAND GUARD... NONE SHALL PASS THROUGH THE DOOR.
You're not the one who gets to decide that!
AS A MATTER OF FACT, I AM.

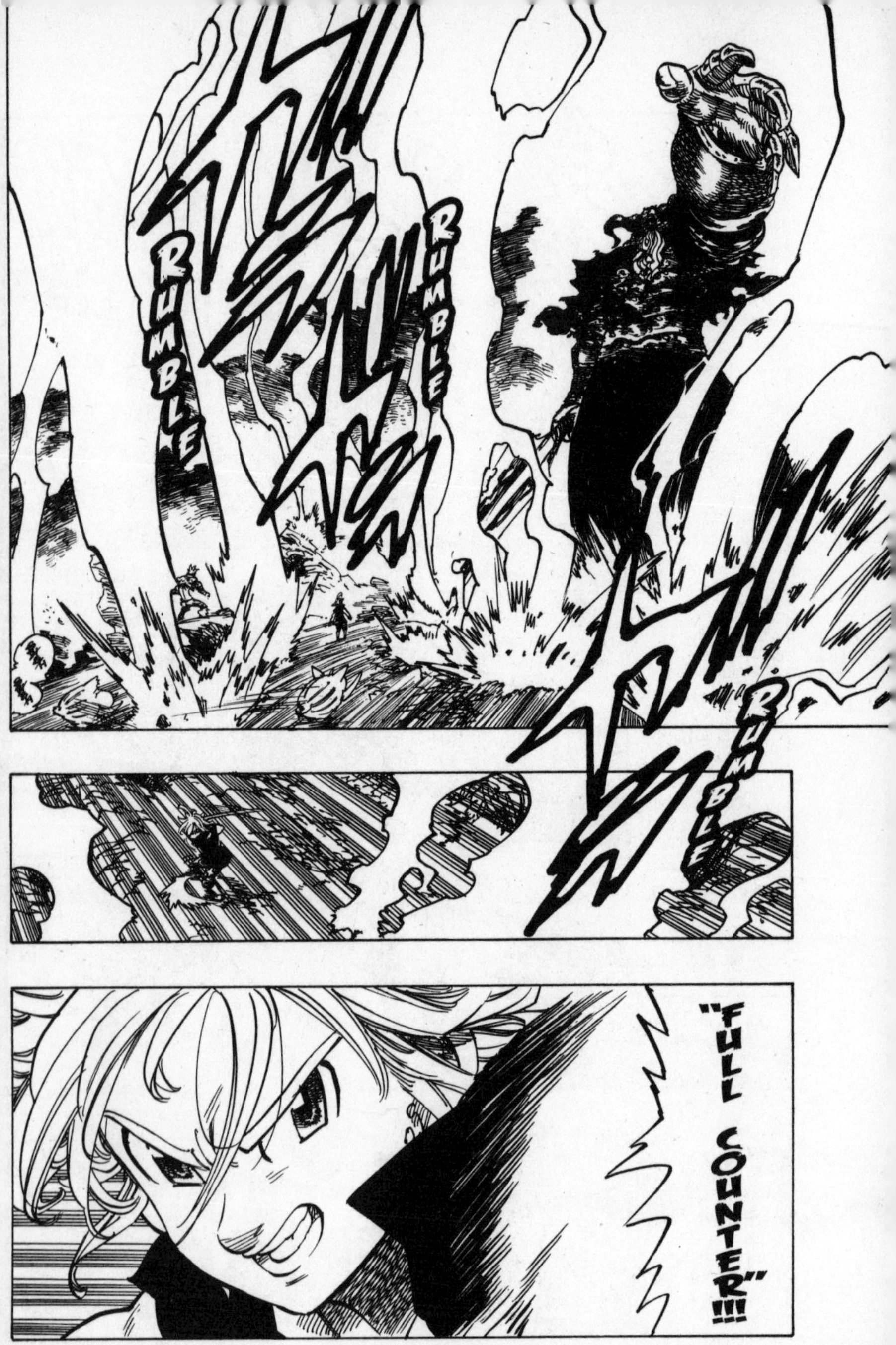
RUMBLE
RUMBLE
RUMBLE
"FULL COUNTER"!!!

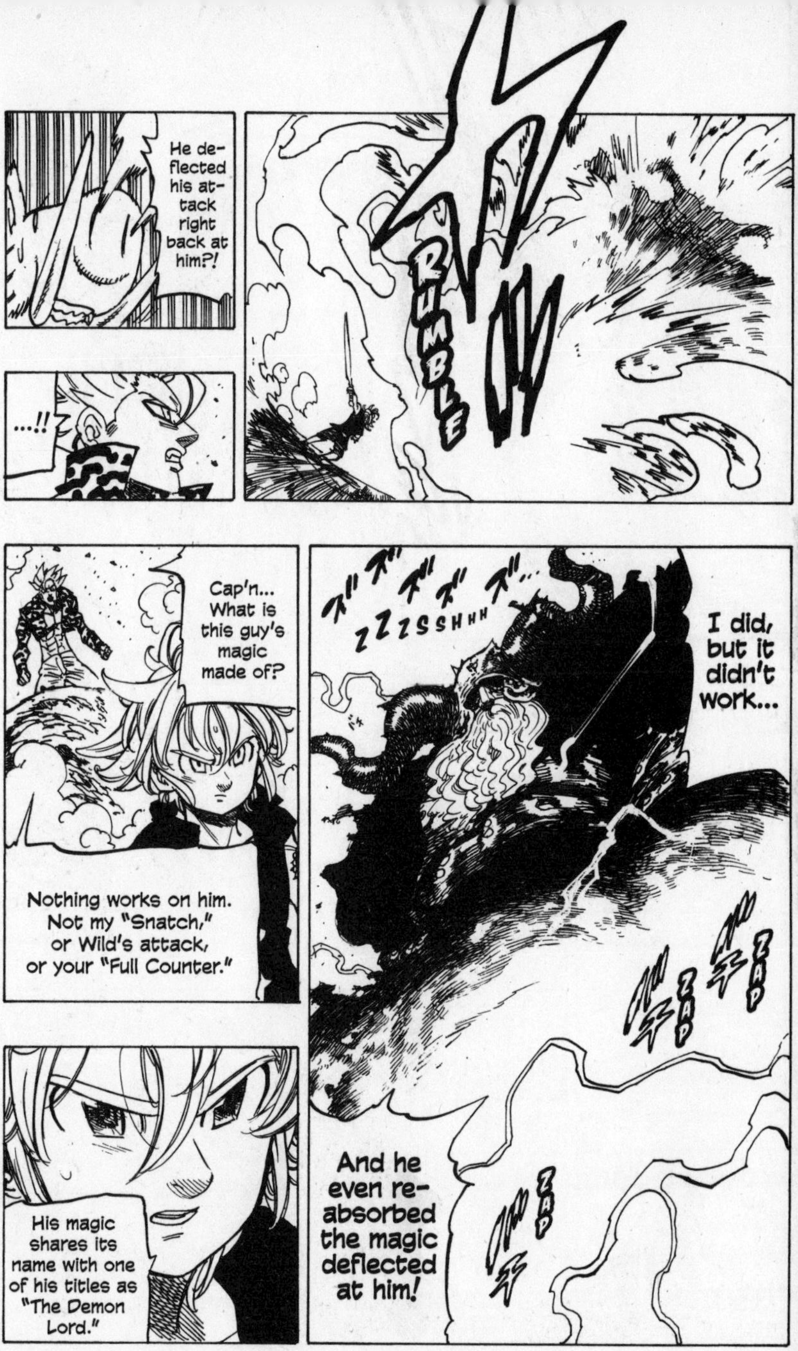
RUMBLE
He deflected his attack right back at him?!
...!!
ZZZSSHHH
I did, but it didn't work...
ZAP
ZAP
And he even reabsorbed the magic deflected at him!
ZAP
Cap'n... What is this guy's magic made of?
Nothing works on him. Not my "Snatch," or Wild's attack, or your "Full Counter."
His magic shares its name with one of his titles as "The Demon Lord."

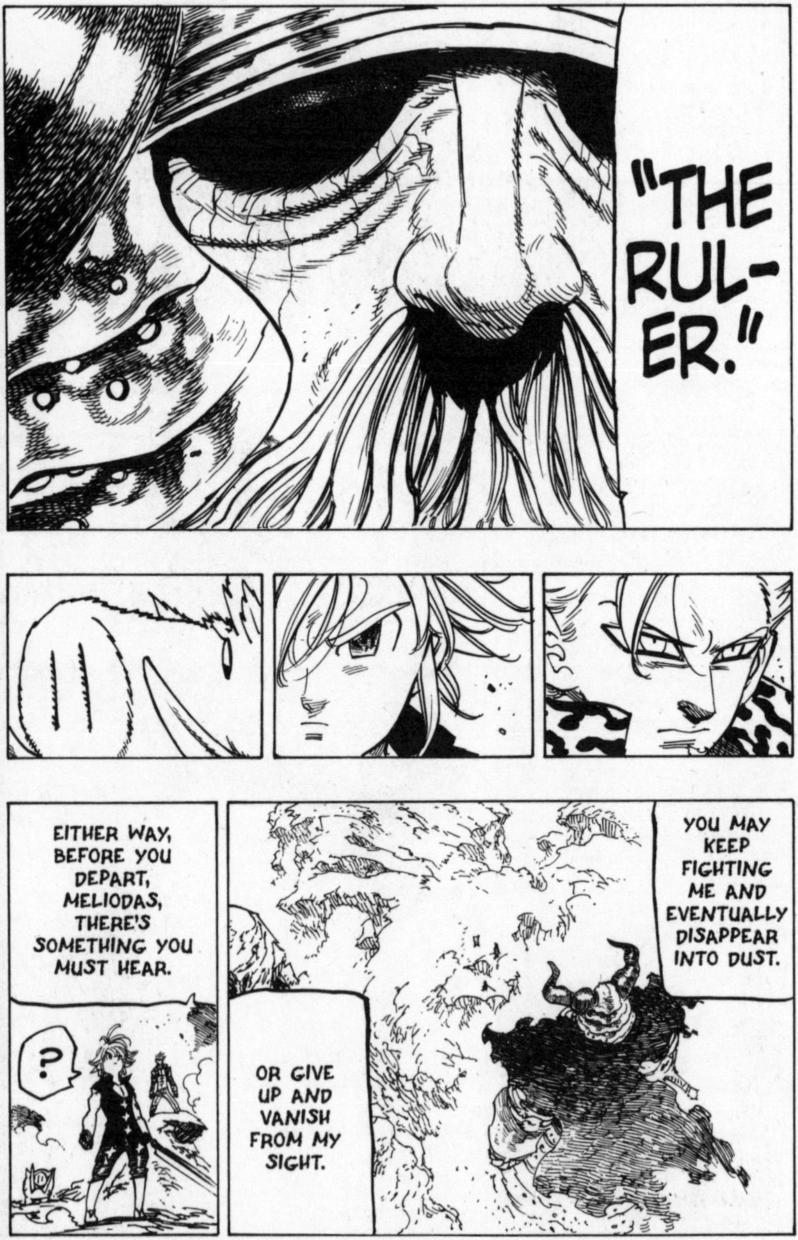
"THE RULER."
YOU MAY KEEP FIGHTING ME AND EVENTUALLY DISAPPEAR INTO DUST.
OR GIVE UP AND VANISH FROM MY SIGHT.
EITHER WAY, BEFORE YOU DEPART, MELIODAS, THERE'S SOMETHING YOU MUST HEAR.
?

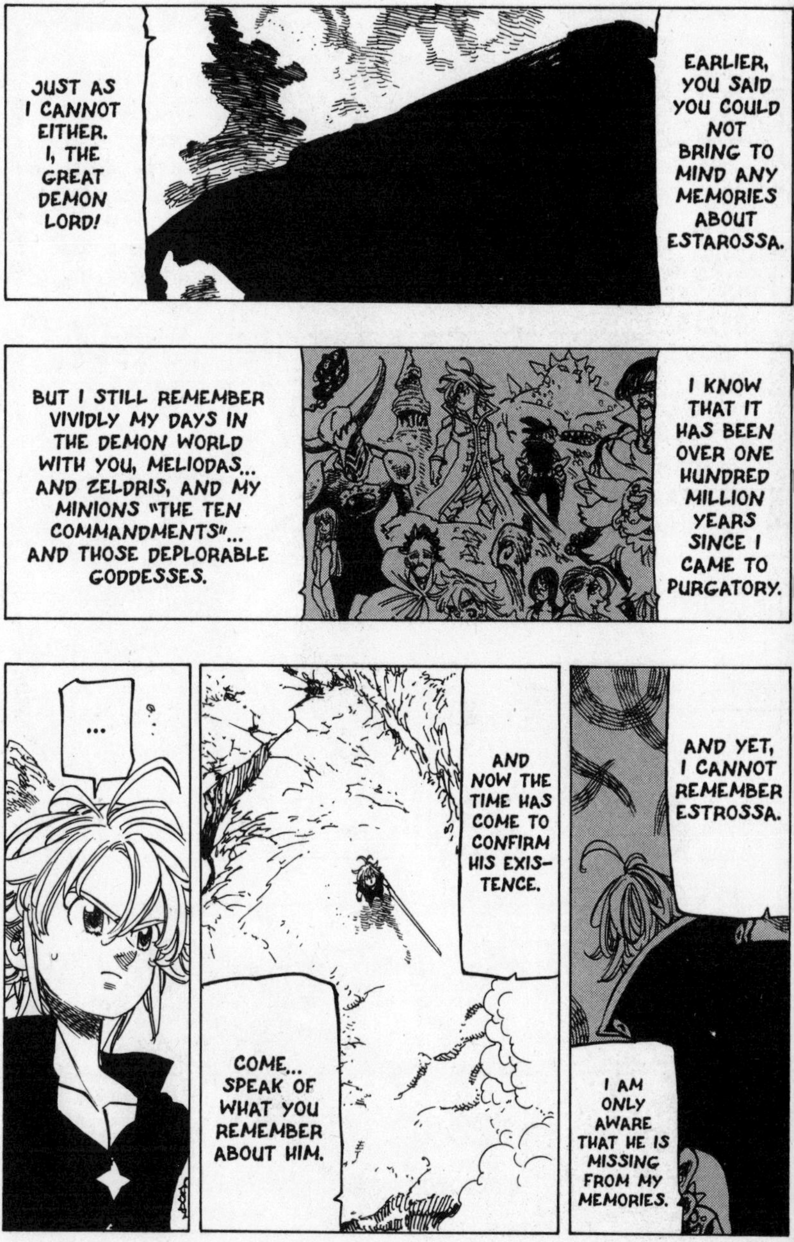
EARLIER, YOU SAID YOU COULD NOT BRING TO MIND ANY MEMORIES ABOUT ESTAROSSA.
JUST AS I CANNOT EITHER. I, THE GREAT DEMON LORD!
I KNOW THAT IT HAS BEEN OVER ONE HUNDRED MILLION YEARS SINCE I CAME TO PURGATORY.
BUT I STILL REMEMBER VIVIDLY MY DAYS IN THE DEMON WORLD WITH YOU, MELIODAS... AND ZELDRIS, AND MY MINIONS "THE TEN COMMANDMENTS"... AND THOSE DEPLORABLE GODDESSES.
AND YET, I CANNOT REMEMBER ESTROSSA.
I AM ONLY AWARE THAT HE IS MISSING FROM MY MEMORIES.
AND NOW THE TIME HAS COME TO CONFIRM HIS EXISTENCE.
COME... SPEAK OF WHAT YOU REMEMBER ABOUT HIM.
...

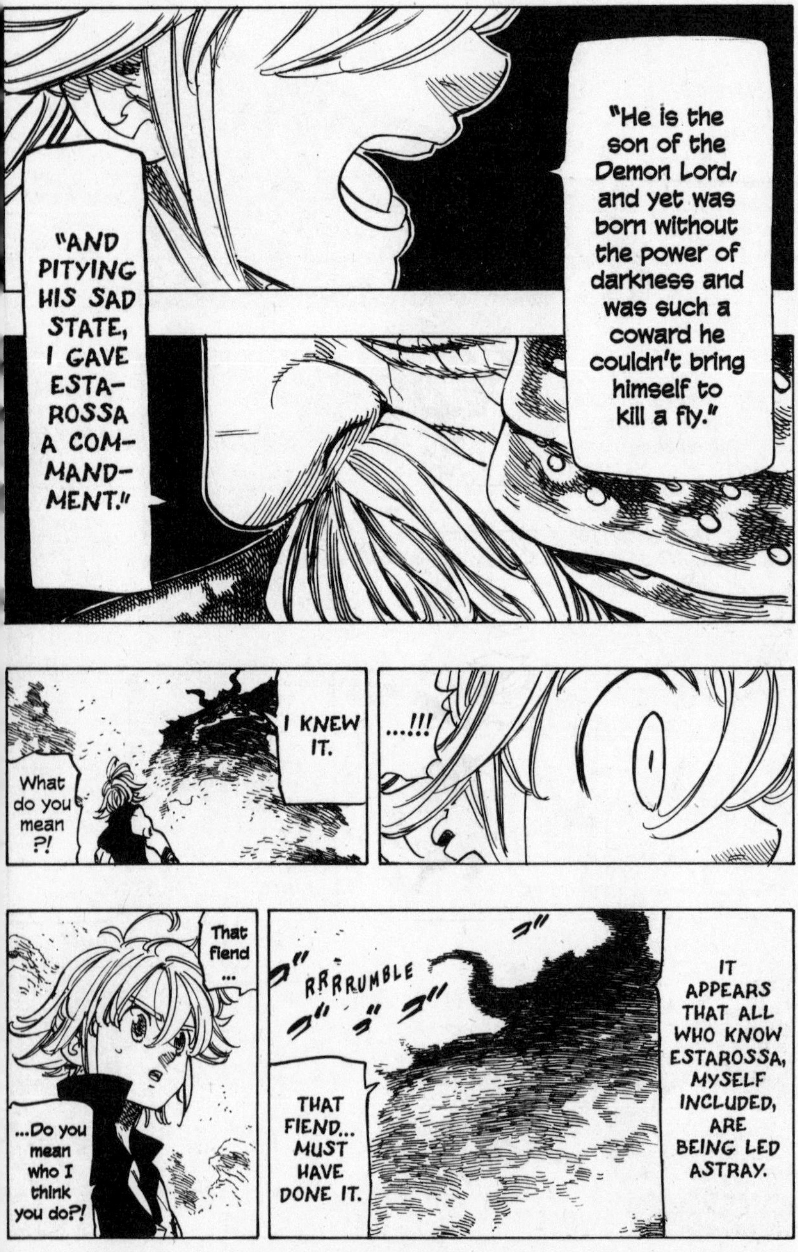
"He is the son of the Demon Lord, and yet was born without the power of darkness and was such a coward he couldn't bring himself to kill a fly."
"AND PITYING HIS SAD STATE, I GAVE ESTAROSSA A COMMANDMENT."
...!!!
I KNEW IT.
What do you mean?!
IT APPEARS THAT ALL WHO KNOW ESTAROSSA, MYSELF INCLUDED, ARE BEING LED ASTRAY.
RRRRUMBLE
THAT FIEND... MUST HAVE DONE IT.
That fiend ...
...Do you mean who I think you do?!

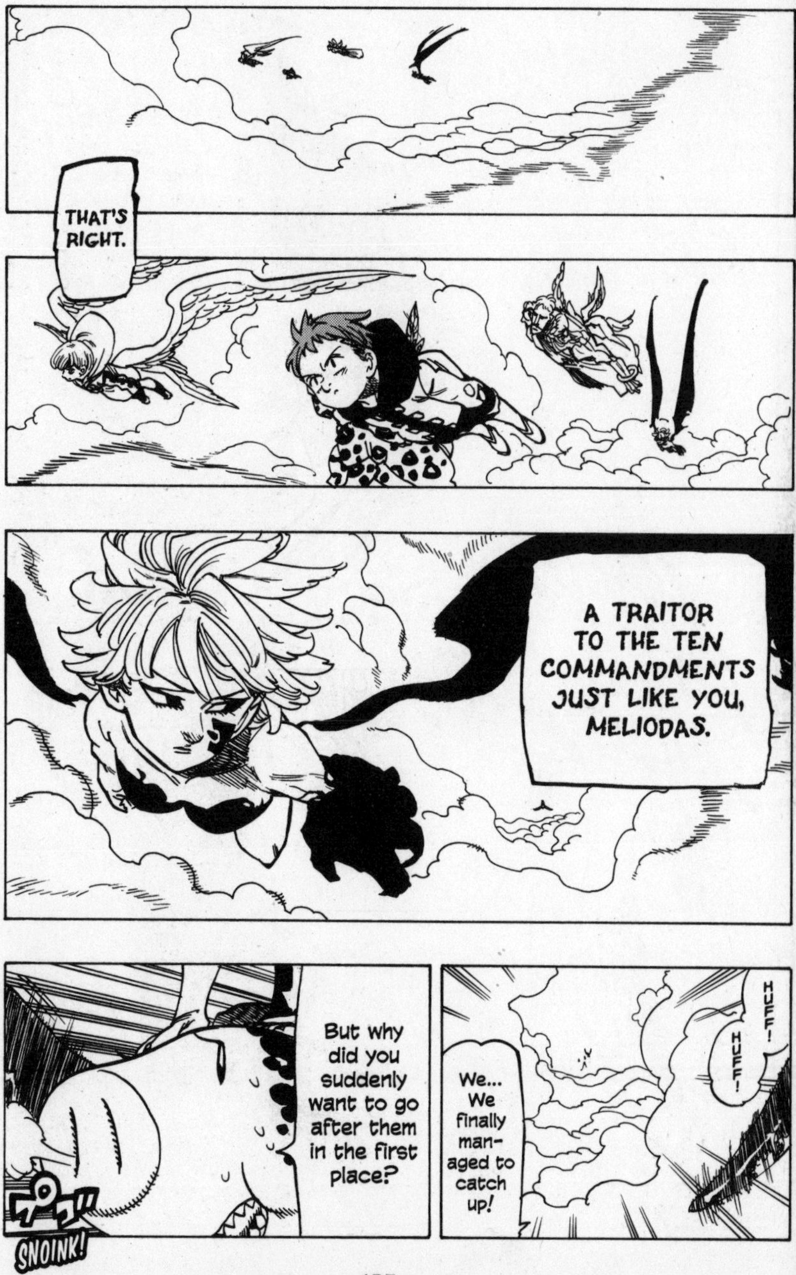
THAT'S RIGHT.
A TRAITOR TO THE TEN COMMANDMENTS JUST LIKE YOU, MELIODAS.
HUFF! HUFF!
We... We finally managed to catch up!
But why did you suddenly want to go after them in the first place?
SNOINK!

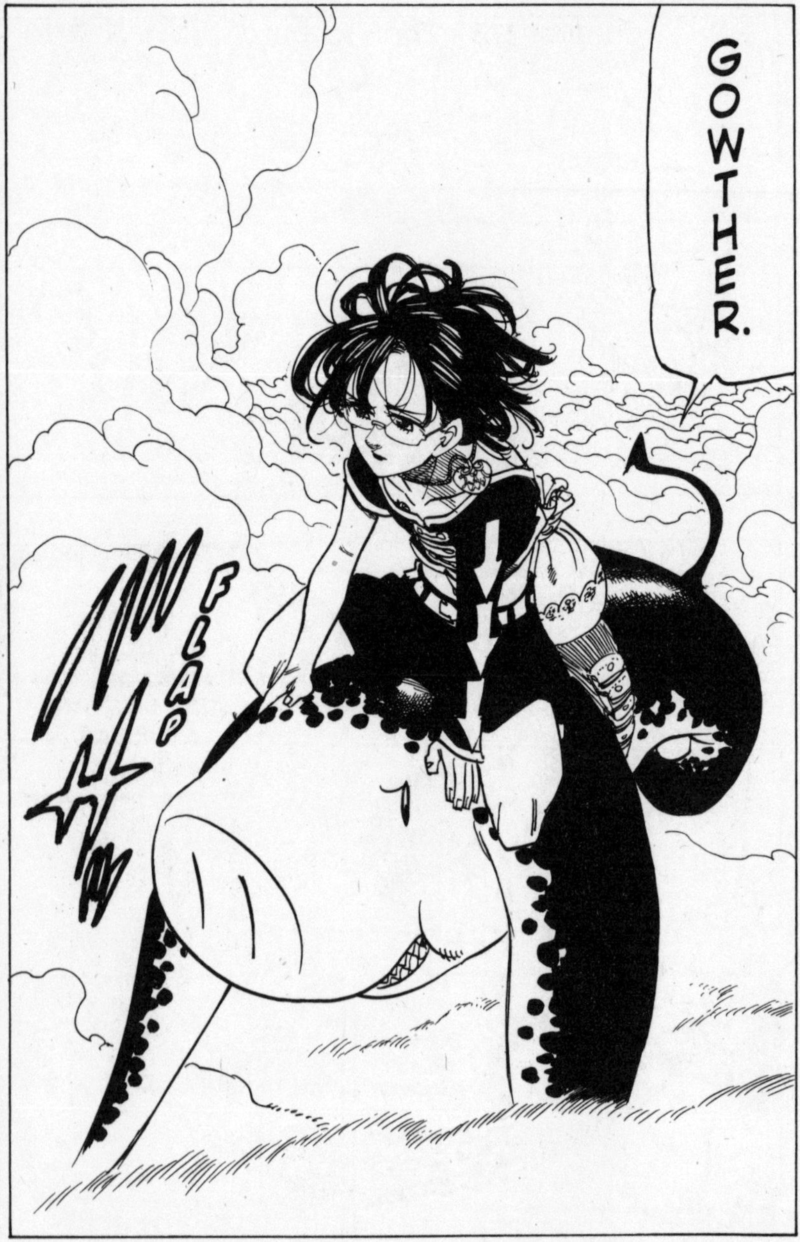
GOWTHER.
FLAP

Chapter 273 - The Victims of the Holy War

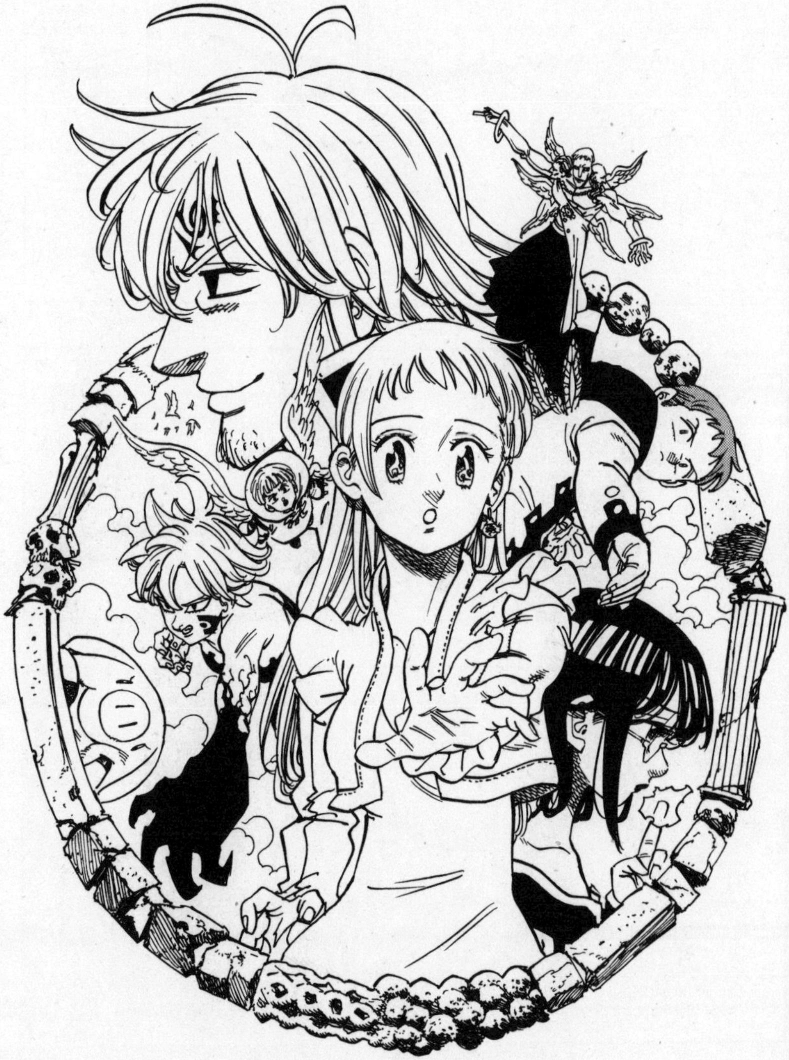

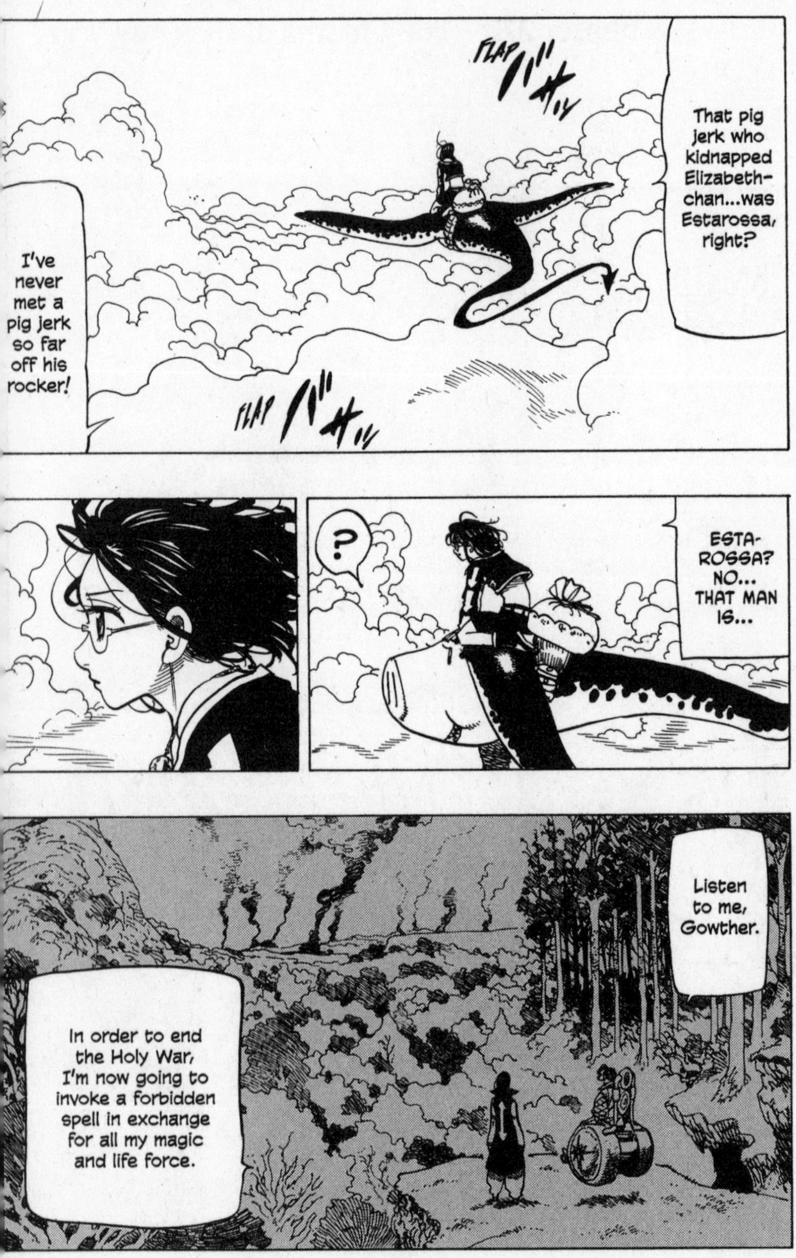
FLAP
That pig jerk who kidnapped Elizabeth-chan...was Estarossa, right?
I've never met a pig jerk so far off his rocker!
FLAP
ESTA-ROSSA? NO... THAT MAN IS...
?
Listen to me, Gowther.
In order to end the Holy War, I'm now going to invoke a forbidden spell in exchange for all my magic and life force.

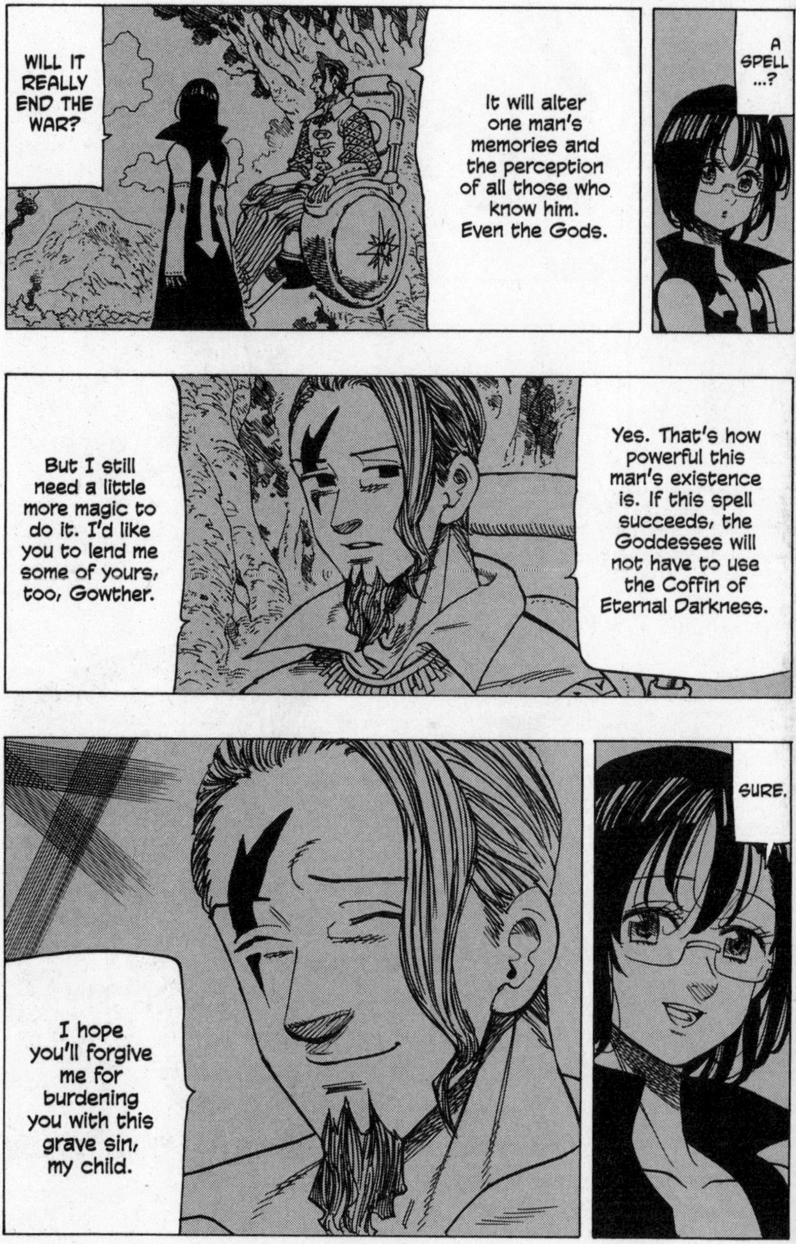
A SPELL ...?
It will alter one man's memories and the perception of all those who know him. Even the Gods.
WILL IT REALLY END THE WAR?
Yes. That's how powerful this man's existence is. If this spell succeeds, the Goddesses will not have to use the Coffin of Eternal Darkness.
But I still need a little more magic to do it. I'd like you to lend me some of yours, too, Gowther.
SURE.
I hope you'll forgive me for burdening you with this grave sin, my child.

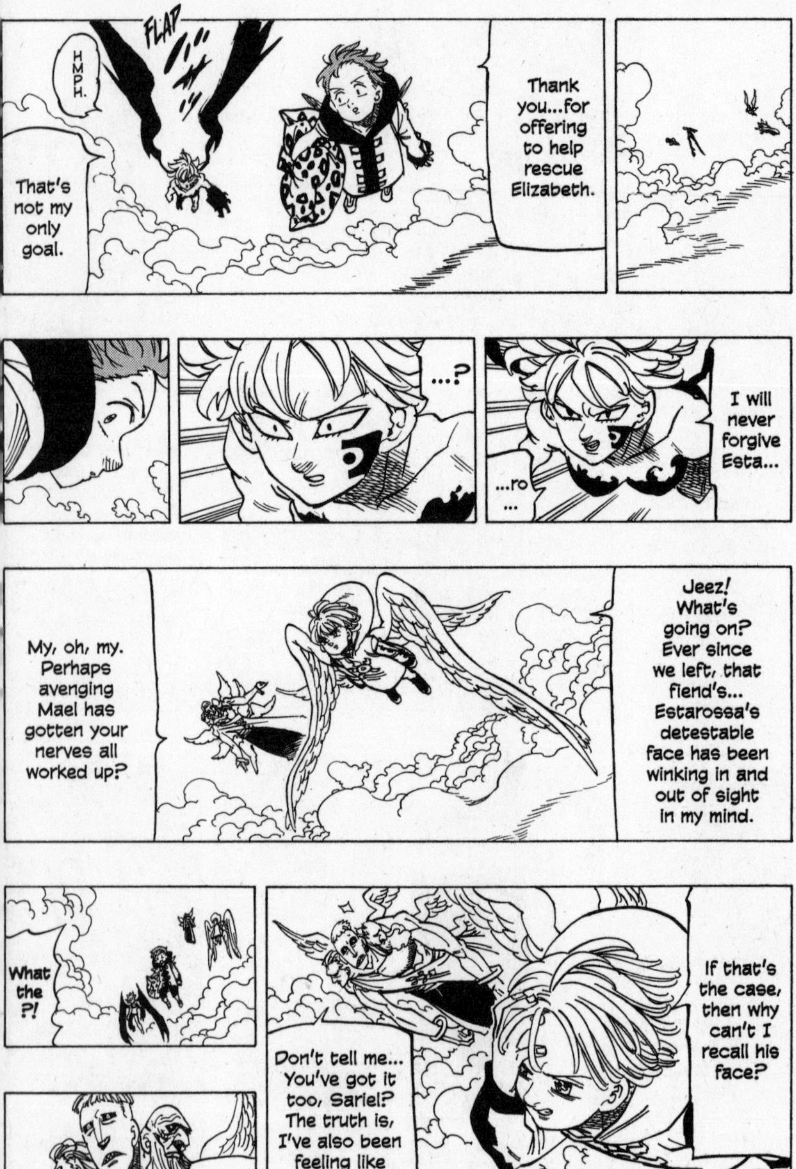
Thank you...for offering to help rescue Elizabeth.
FLAP
HMPH.
That's not my only goal.
I will never forgive Esta...
...ro ...
...?
Jeez! What's going on? Ever since we left, that fiend's... Estarossa's detestable face has been winking in and out of sight in my mind.
My, oh, my. Perhaps avenging Mael has gotten your nerves all worked up?
If that's the case, then why can't I recall his face?
Don't tell me... You've got it too, Sariel? The truth is, I've also been feeling like something's off for a while now.
What the ?!
This is...

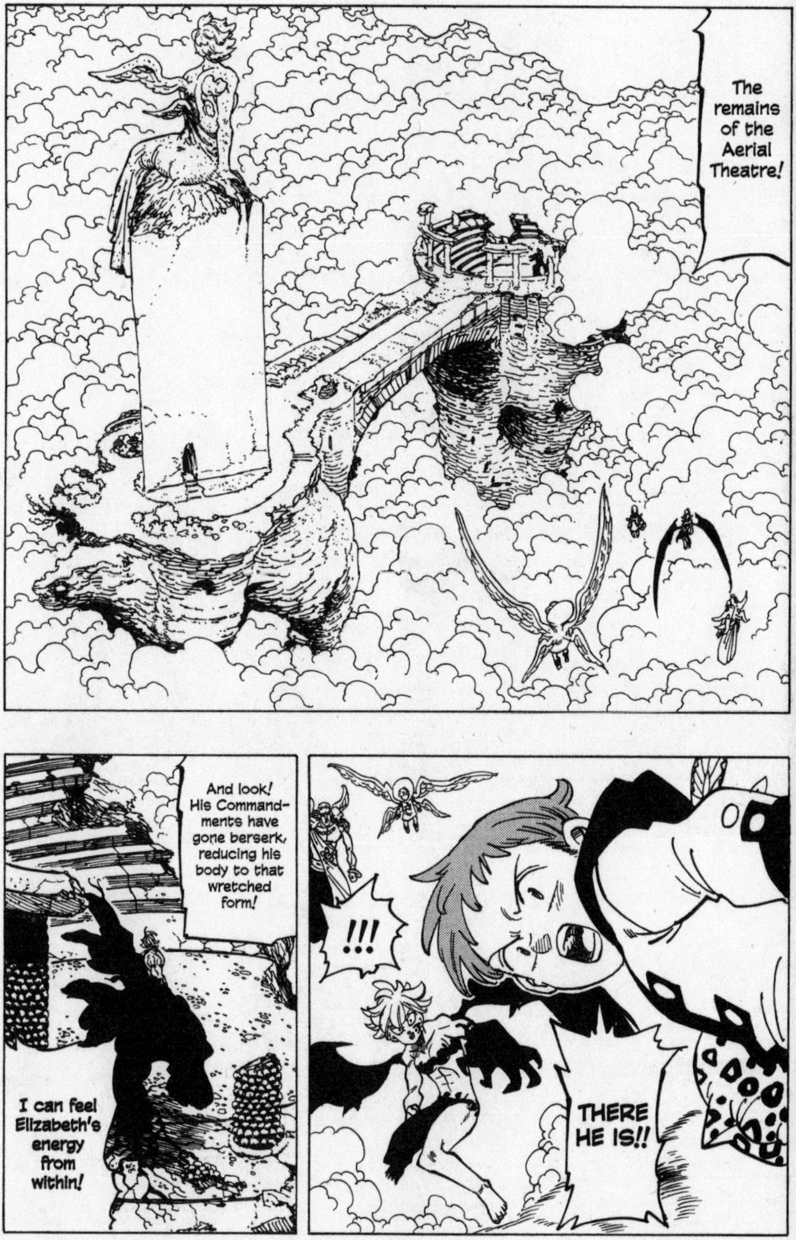
The remains of the Aerial Theatre!
!!!
THERE HE IS!!
And look! His Commandments have gone berserk, reducing his body to that wretched form!
I can feel Elizabeth's energy from within!

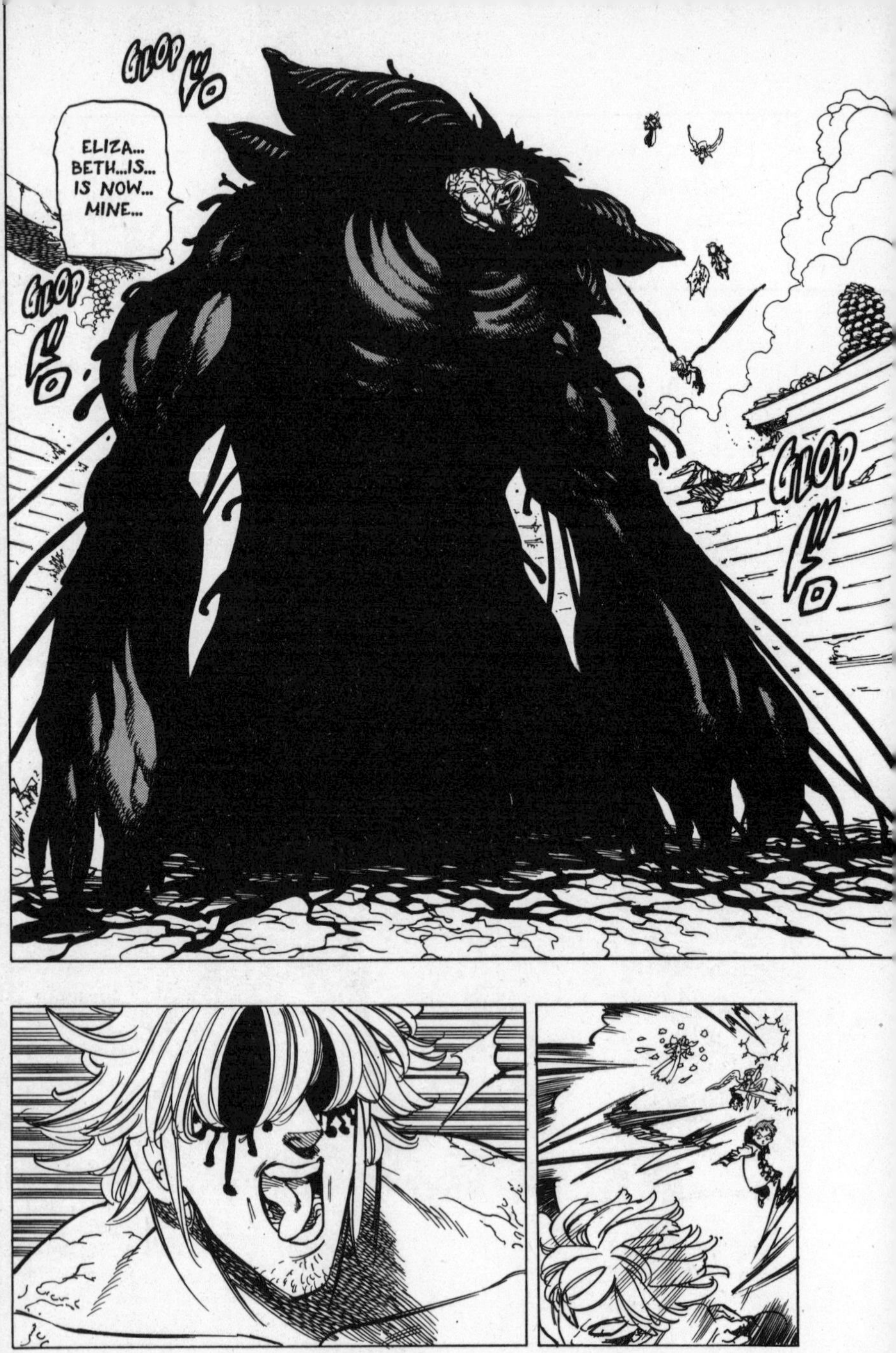
GLOP!!
ELIZA... BETH...IS... IS NOW... MINE...
GLOP!!
GLOP!!

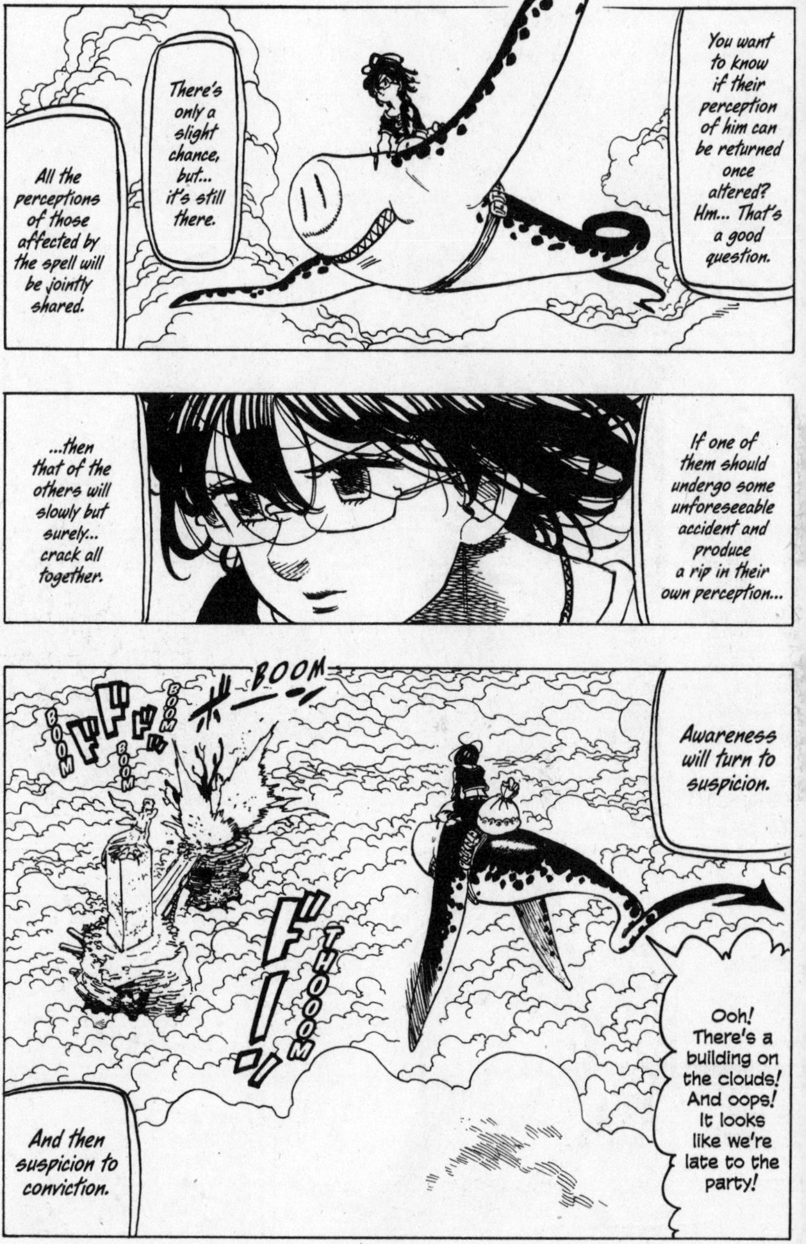
You want to know if their perception of him can be returned once altered? Hm... That's a good question.
There's only a slight chance, but... it's still there.
All the perceptions of those affected by the spell will be jointly shared.
If one of them should undergo some unforeseeable accident and produce a rip in their own perception...
...then that of the others will slowly but surely... crack all together.
Awareness will turn to suspicion.
BOOM
BOOM
BOOM
BOOM
THOOOOM
Ooh! There's a building on the clouds! And oops! It looks like we're late to the party!
And then suspicion to conviction.

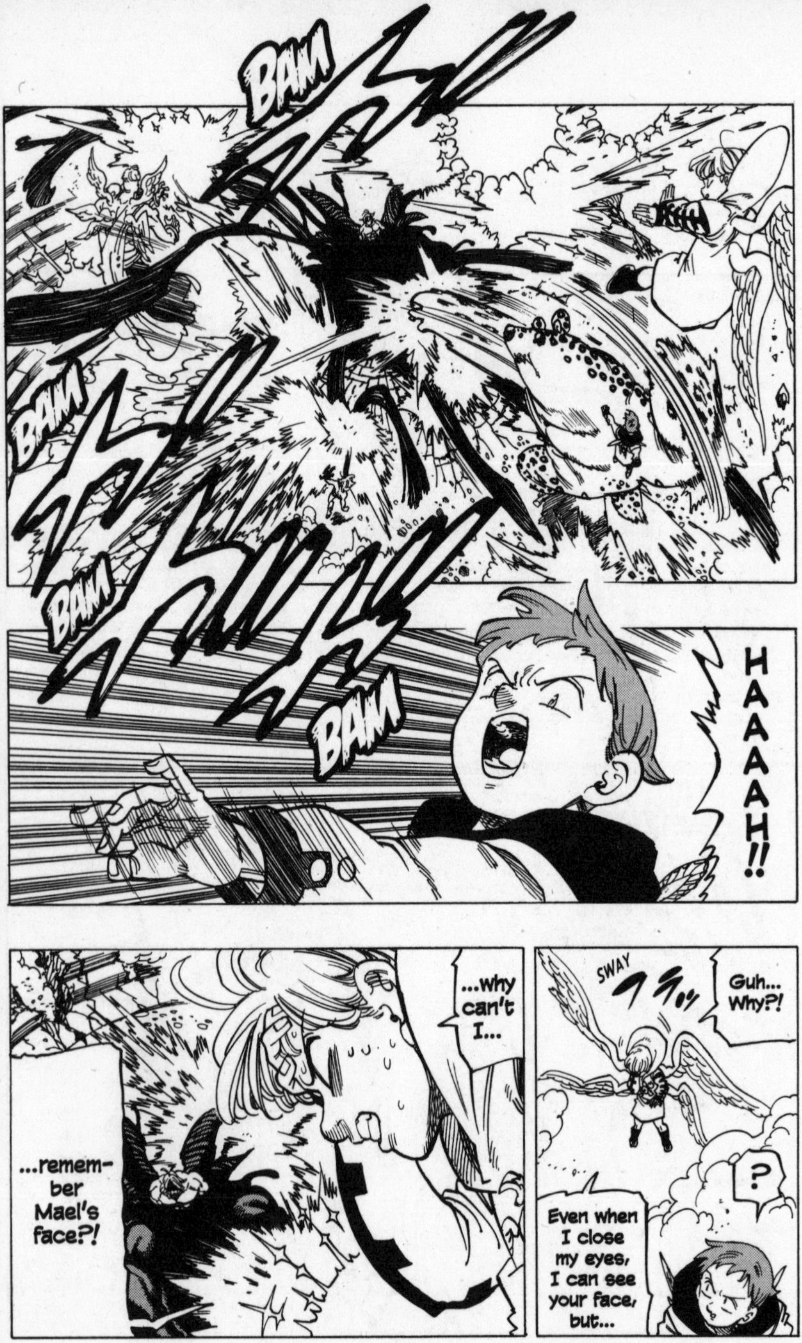
BAM
BAM
BAM
BAM
HAAAAAH!!
SWAY
Guh... Why?!
?
Even when I close my eyes, I can see your face, but...
...why can't I...
...remem-ber Mael's face?!

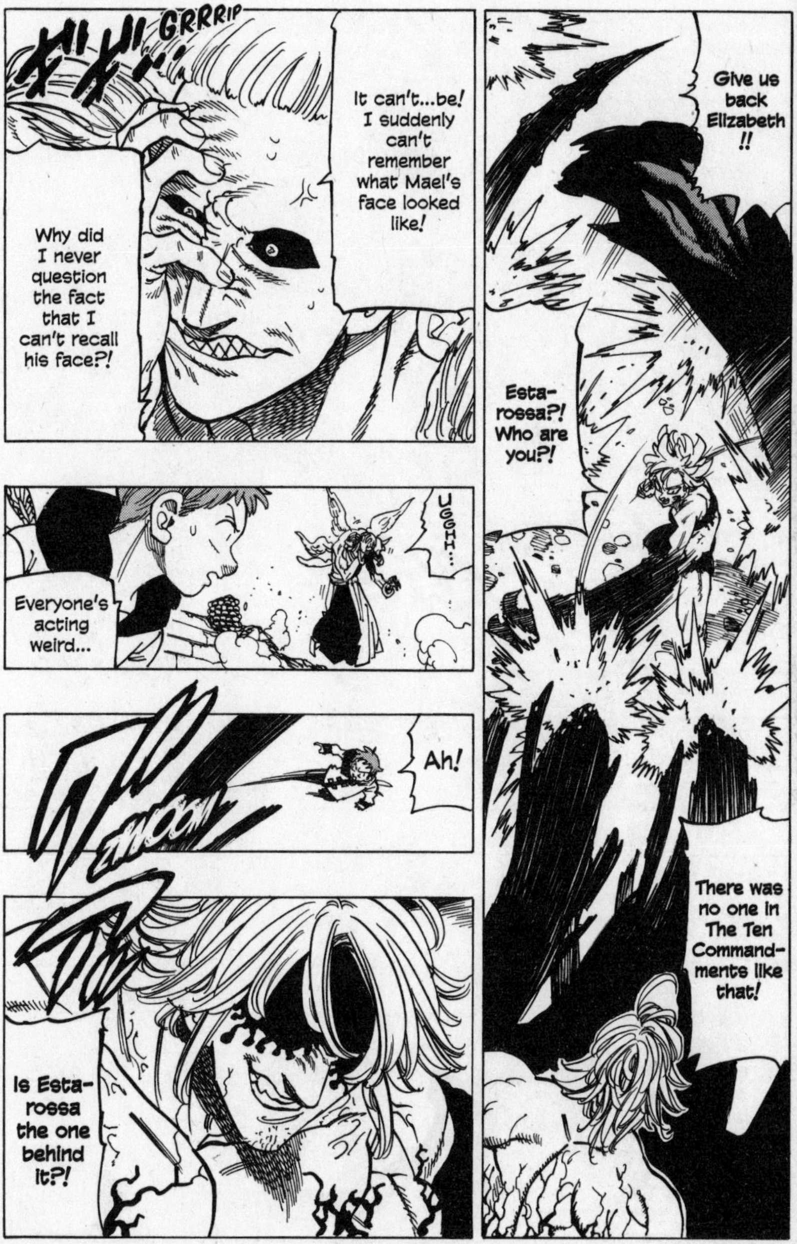
Give us back Elizabeth!!
Esta-rossa?! Who are you?!
There was no one in The Ten Command-ments like that!
GRRRIP
It can't...be! I suddenly can't remember what Mael's face looked like!
Why did I never question the fact that I can't recall his face?!
UGGHH...
Everyone's acting weird...
Ah!
WHOOM
Is Esta-rossa the one behind it?!

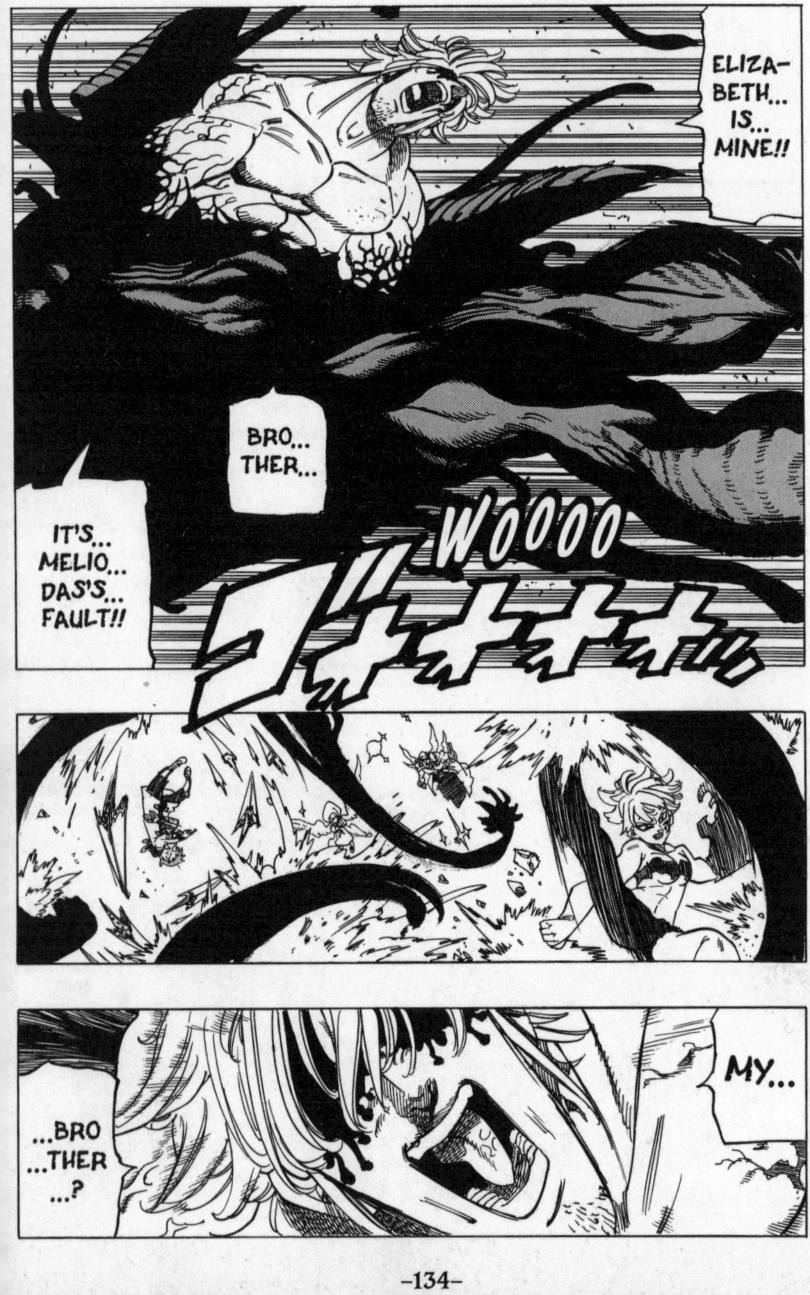
ELIZA-BETH... IS... MINE!!
BRO... THER...
IT'S... MELIO... DAS'S... FAULT!!
WOOOO
MY...
...BRO ...THER ...?

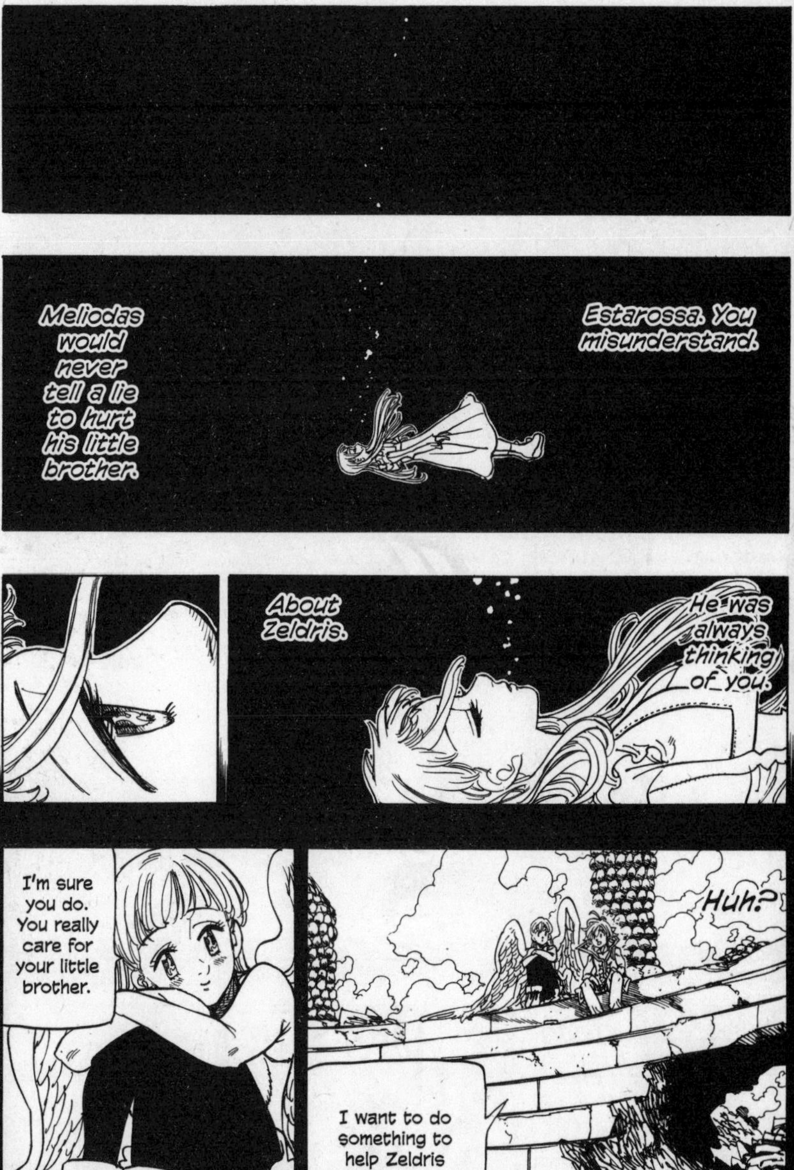
Estarossa. You misunderstand.
Meliodas would never tell a lie to hurt his little brother.
He was always thinking of you.
About Zeldris.
Huh?
I want to do something to help Zeldris and his girl.
I'm sure you do. You really care for your little brother.

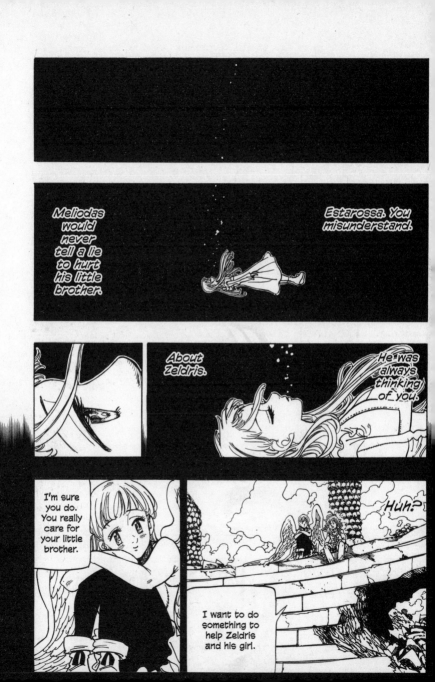

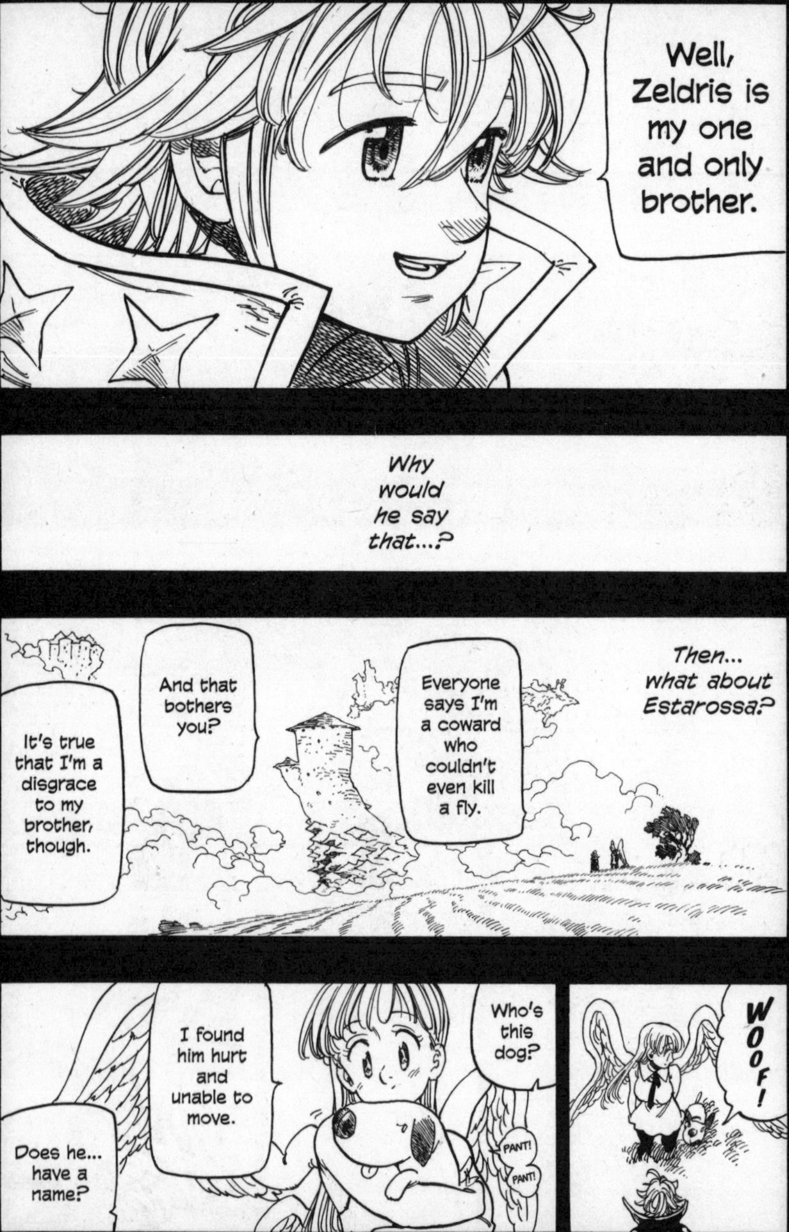
Well, Zeldris is my one and only brother.
Why would he say that...?
Then... what about Estarossa?
Everyone says I'm a coward who couldn't even kill a fly.
And that bothers you?
It's true that I'm a disgrace to my brother, though.
WOOF!
Who's this dog?
I found him hurt and unable to move.
PANT!
PANT!
Does he... have a name?

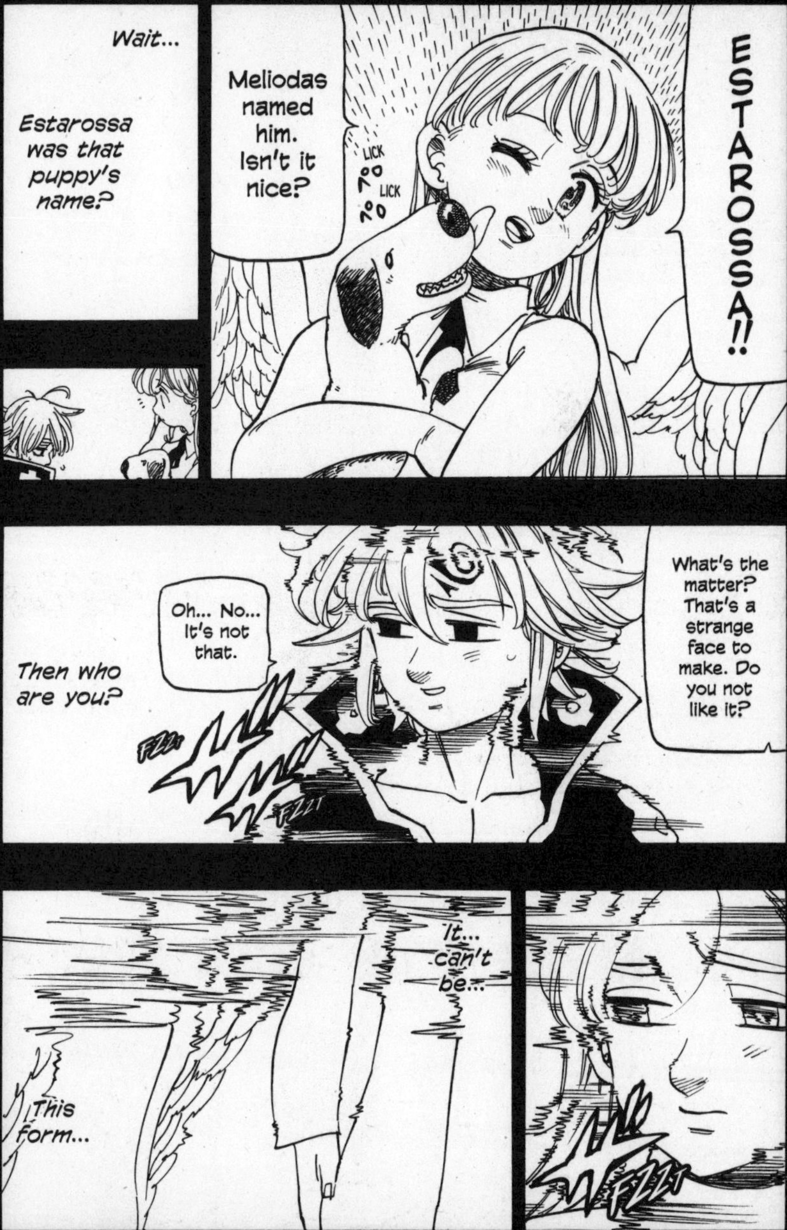
ESTAROSSA!!
Meliodas named him. Isn't it nice?
LICK LICK
Wait...
Estarossa was that puppy's name?
What's the matter? That's a strange face to make. Do you not like it?
Oh... No... It's not that.
Then who are you?
FZZT FZZT
FZZT
It... can't be...
This form...

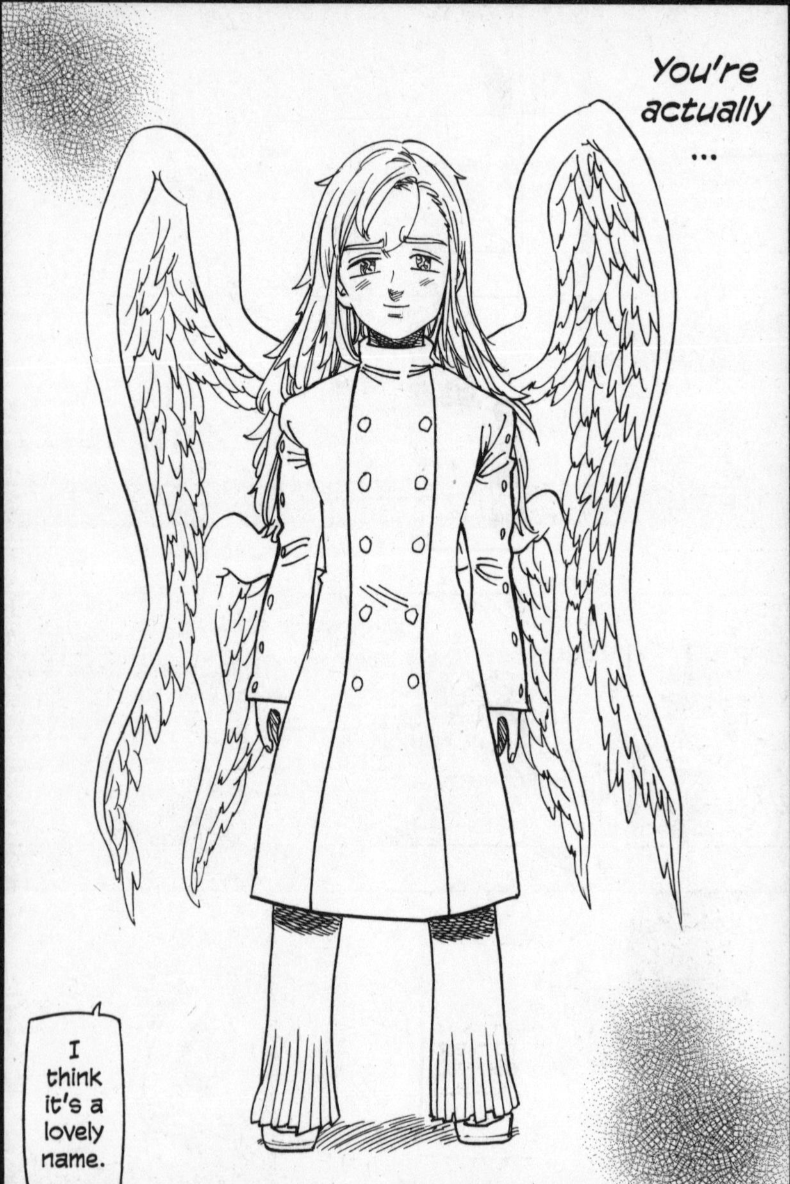
You're actually ...
I think it's a lovely name.

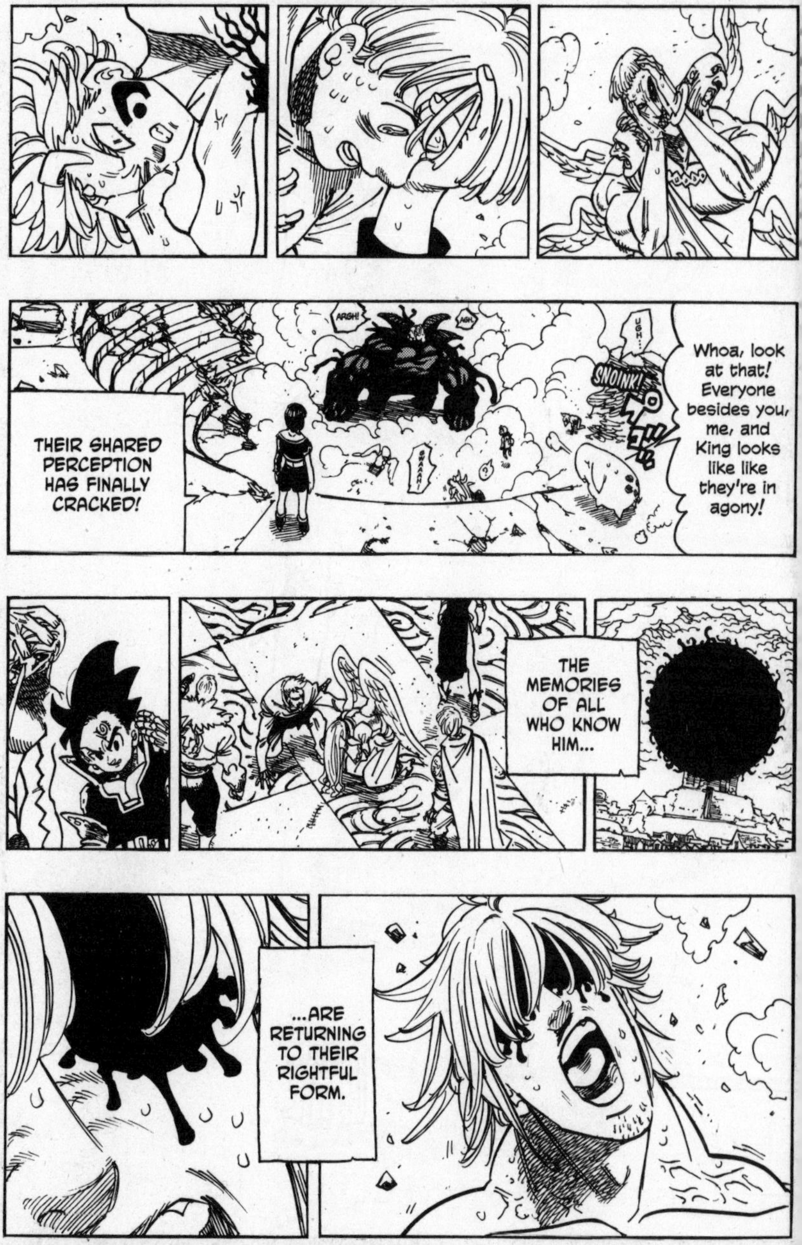
Whoa, look at that! Everyone besides you, me, and King looks like like they're in agony!
SNOINK!
UGH...
AGH
ARGH!
THEIR SHARED PERCEPTION HAS FINALLY CRACKED!
THE MEMORIES OF ALL WHO KNOW HIM...
...ARE RETURNING TO THEIR RIGHTFUL FORM.

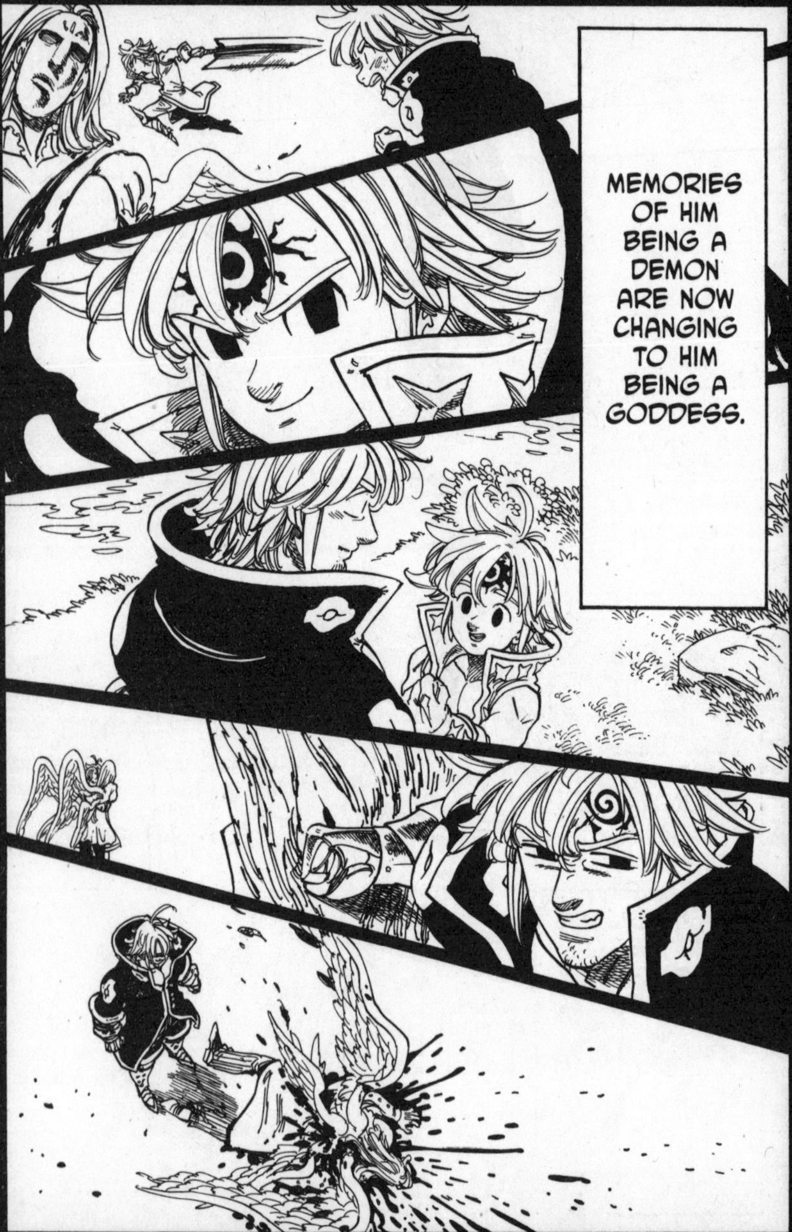
MEMORIES OF HIM BEING A DEMON ARE NOW CHANGING TO HIM BEING A GODDESS.

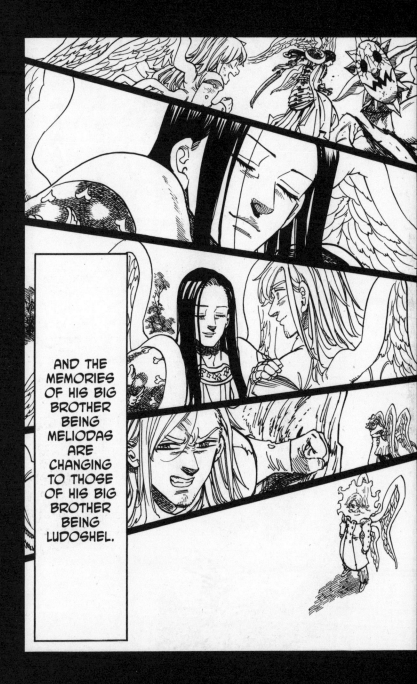

AND THE MEMORIES OF HIS BIG BROTHER BEING MELIODAS ARE CHANGING TO THOSE OF HIS BIG BROTHER BEING LUDOSHEL.

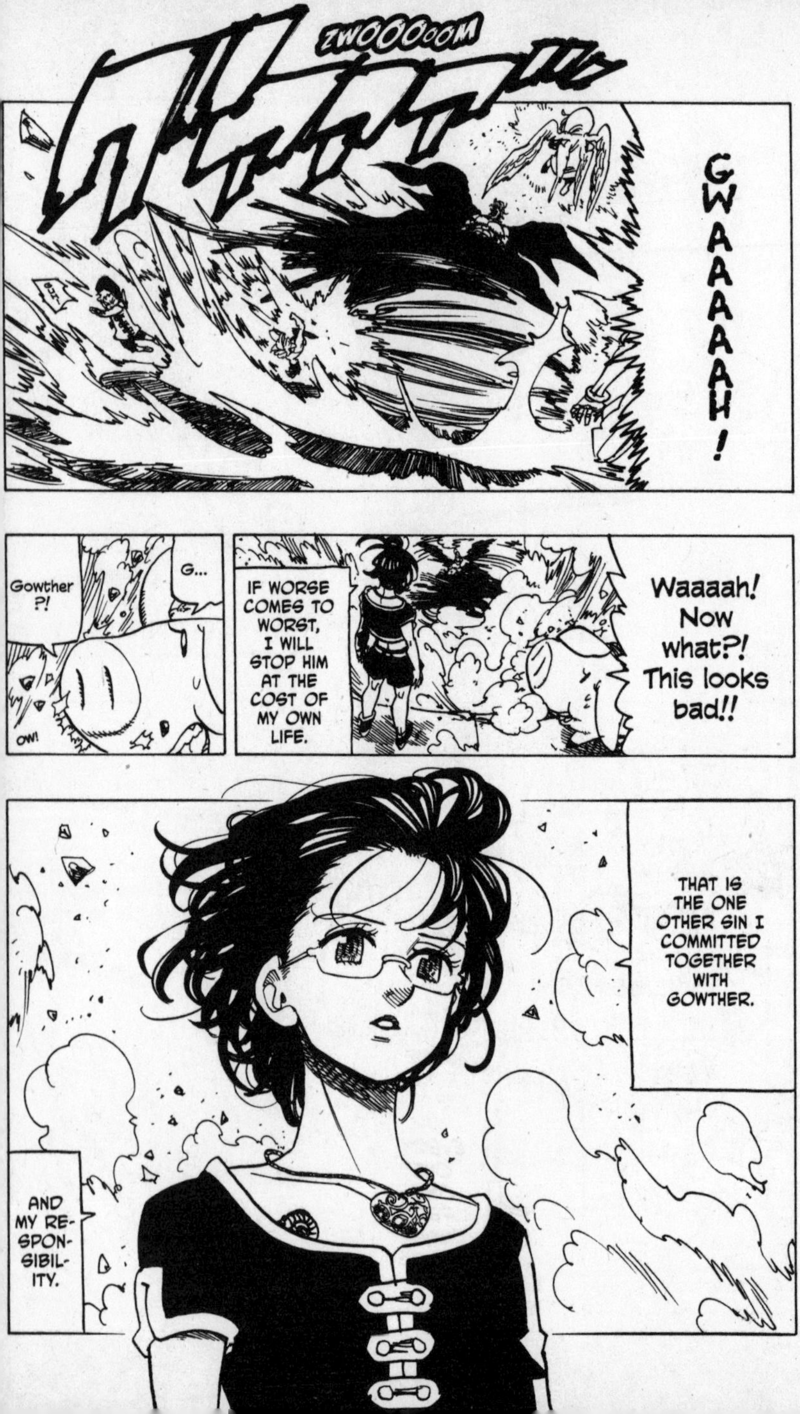
ZWOOOooM
GWAAAAAH!
Waaaah! Now what?! This looks bad!!
IF WORSE COMES TO WORST, I WILL STOP HIM AT THE COST OF MY OWN LIFE.
G...
Gowther ?!
OW!
THAT IS THE ONE OTHER SIN I COMMITTED TOGETHER WITH GOWTHER.
AND MY RE-SPON-SIBIL-ITY.

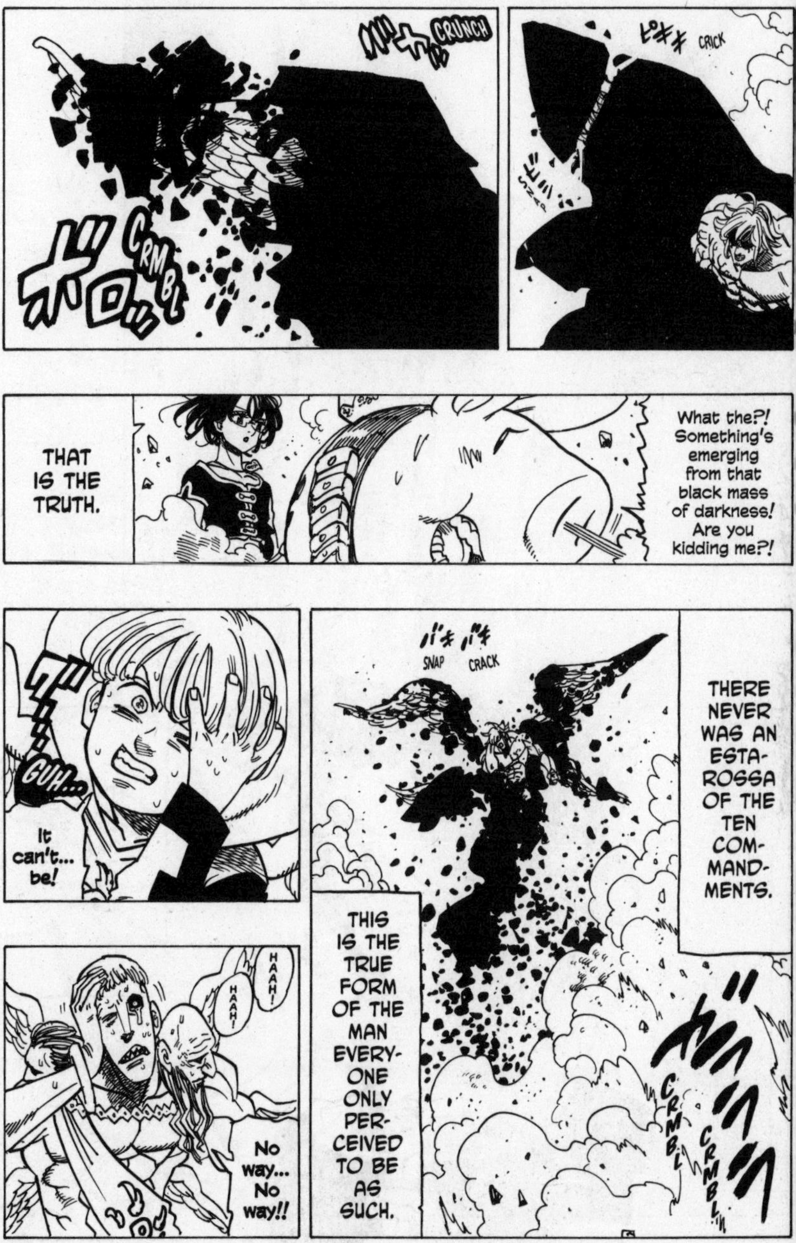
CRICK
CRUNCH
CRMBL
What the?! Something's emerging from that black mass of darkness! Are you kidding me?!
THAT IS THE TRUTH.
SNAP
CRACK
THERE NEVER WAS AN ESTA-ROSSA OF THE TEN COM-MAND-MENTS.
THIS IS THE TRUE FORM OF THE MAN EVERY-ONE ONLY PER-CEIVED TO BE AS SUCH.
CRMBL
CRMBL
GUH...
It can't... be!
HAAH!
HAAH!
No way... No way!!

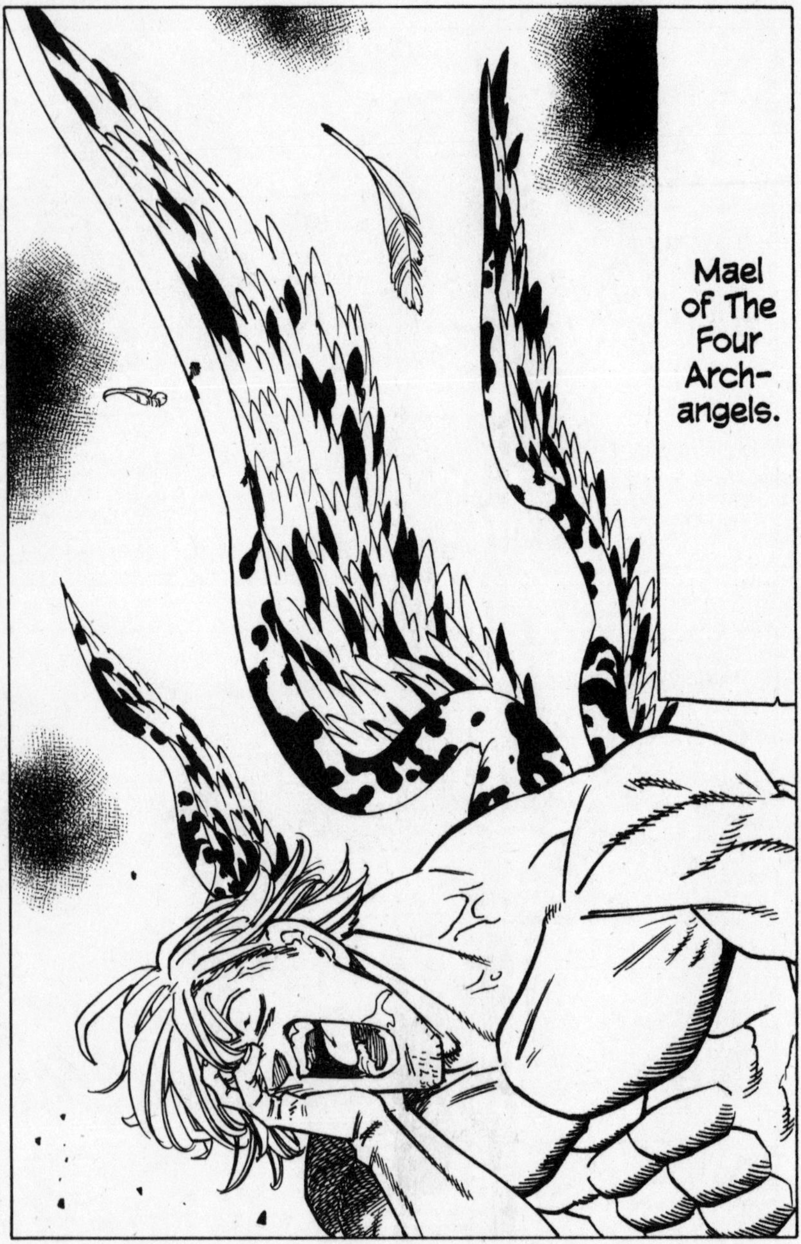
Mael of The Four Arch-angels.

Chapter 274 - The Despairing Fallen Angel Mael

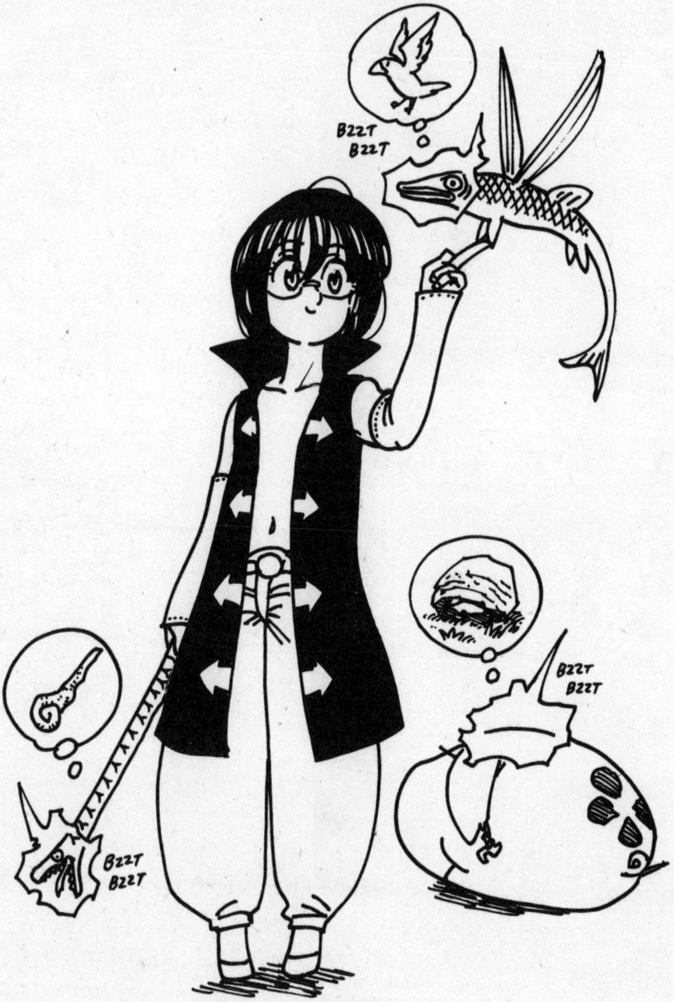
BZZT
BZZT
BZZT
BZZT
BZZT
BZZT

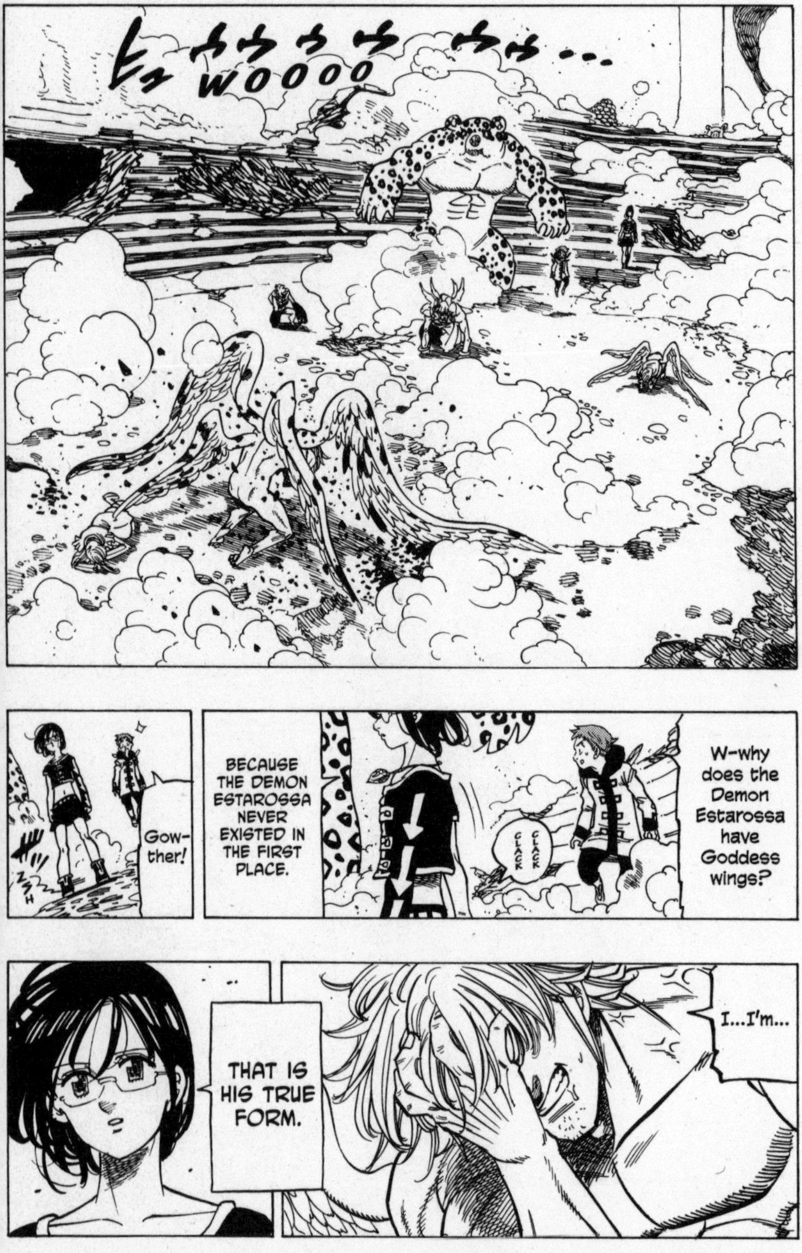
WOOOO
W-why does the Demon Estarossa have Goddess wings?
CLACK CLACK
BECAUSE THE DEMON ESTAROSSA NEVER EXISTED IN THE FIRST PLACE.
Gow-ther!
I...I'm...
THAT IS HIS TRUE FORM.

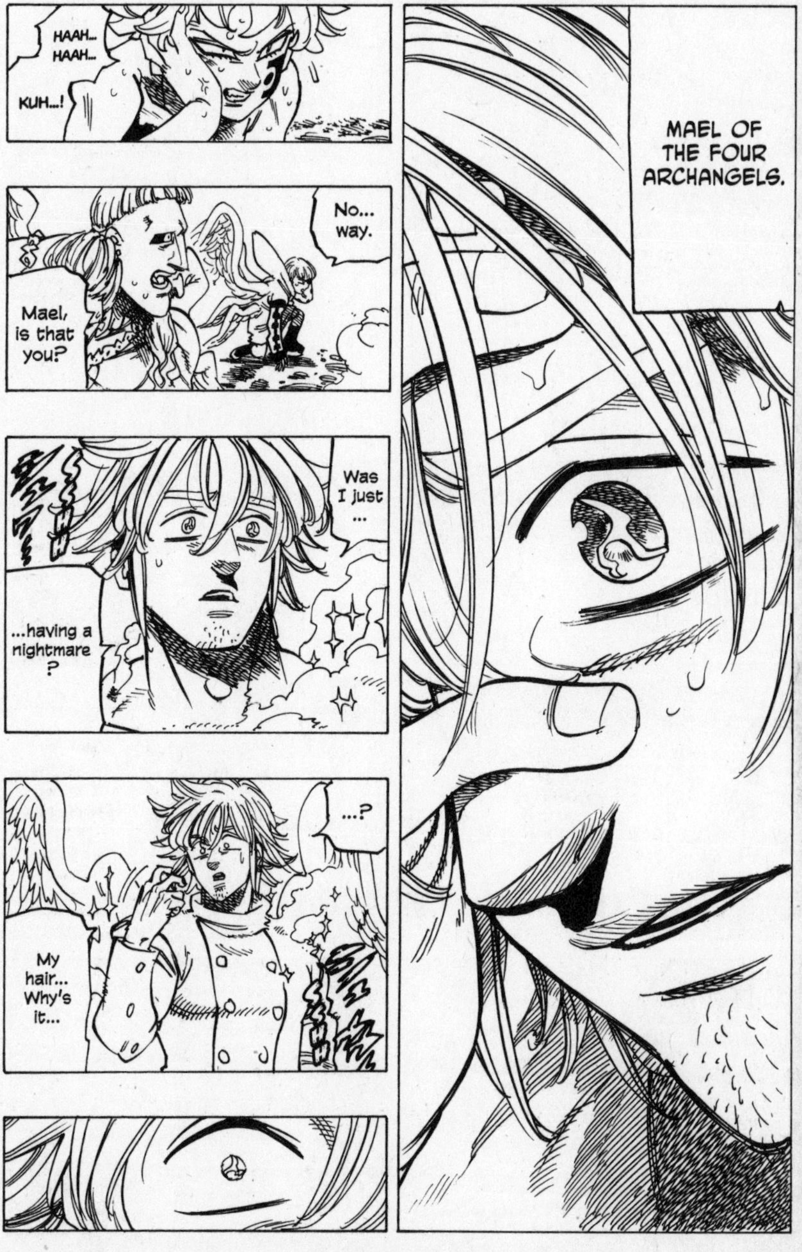
MAEL OF THE FOUR ARCHANGELS.
HAAH... HAAH...
KUH...!
No... way.
Mael, is that you?
Was I just ...
...having a nightmare ?
...?
My hair... Why's it...

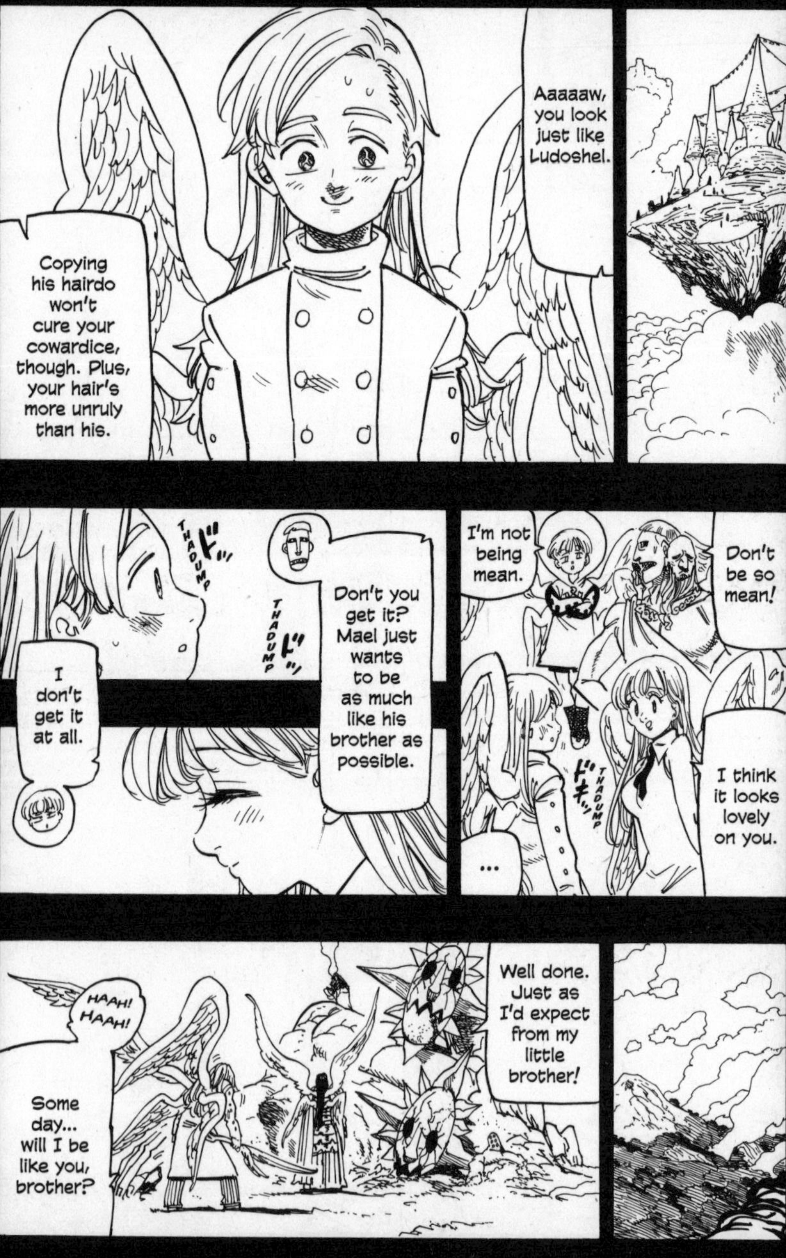
Aaaaaw, you look just like Ludoshel.
Copying his hairdo won't cure your cowardice, though. Plus, your hair's more unruly than his.
Don't be so mean!
I'm not being mean.
I think it looks lovely on you.
THADUMP
...
THADUMP
THADUMP
Don't you get it? Mael just wants to be as much like his brother as possible.
I don't get it at all.
Well done. Just as I'd expect from my little brother!
HAAH! HAAH!
Some day... will I be like you, brother?

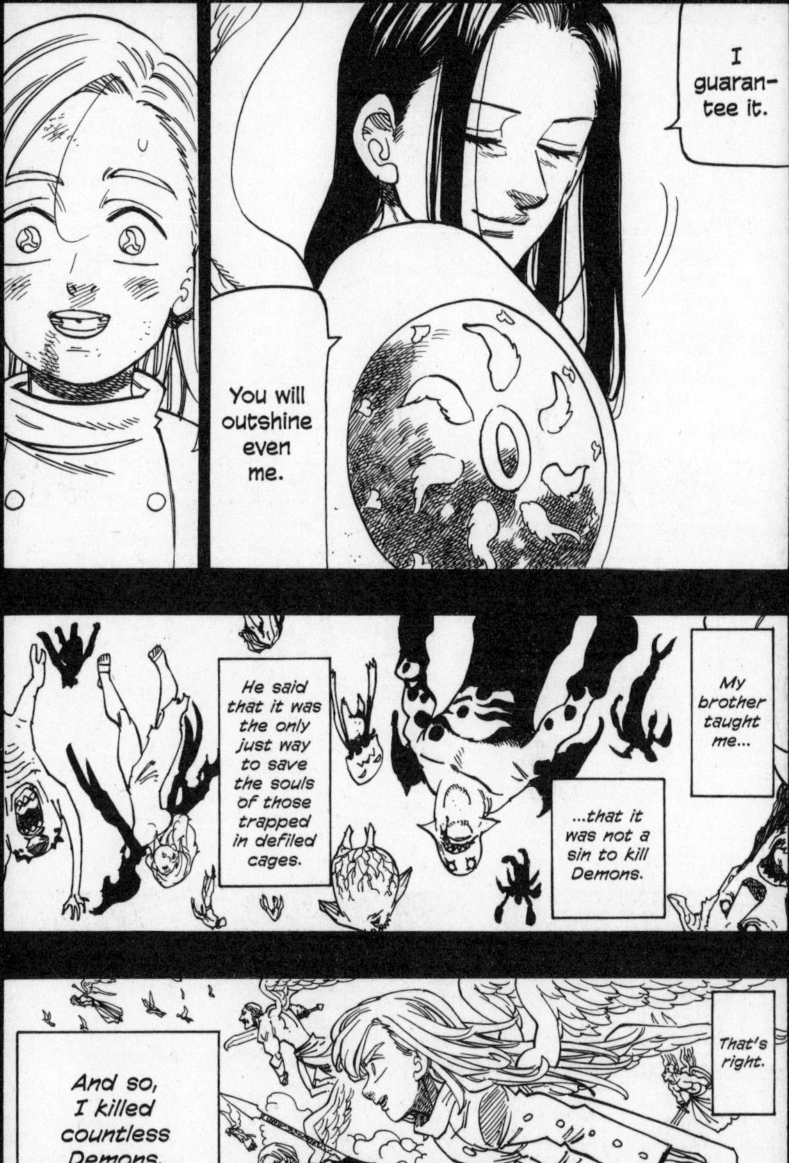
I guaran-tee it.
You will outshine even me.
My brother taught me...
...that it was not a sin to kill Demons.
He said that it was the only just way to save the souls of those trapped in defiled cages.
That's right.
And so, I killed countless Demons.

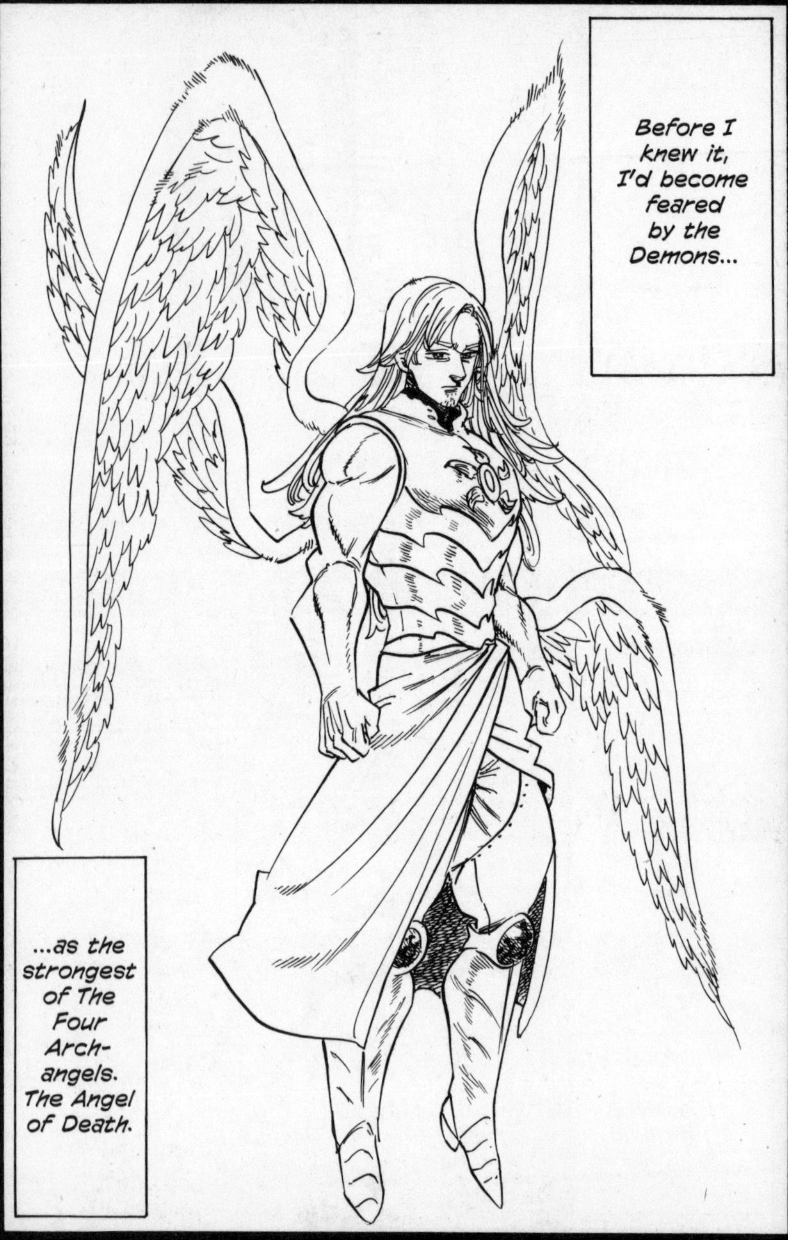
Before I knew it, I'd become feared by the Demons...
...as the strongest of The Four Arch-angels. The Angel of Death.

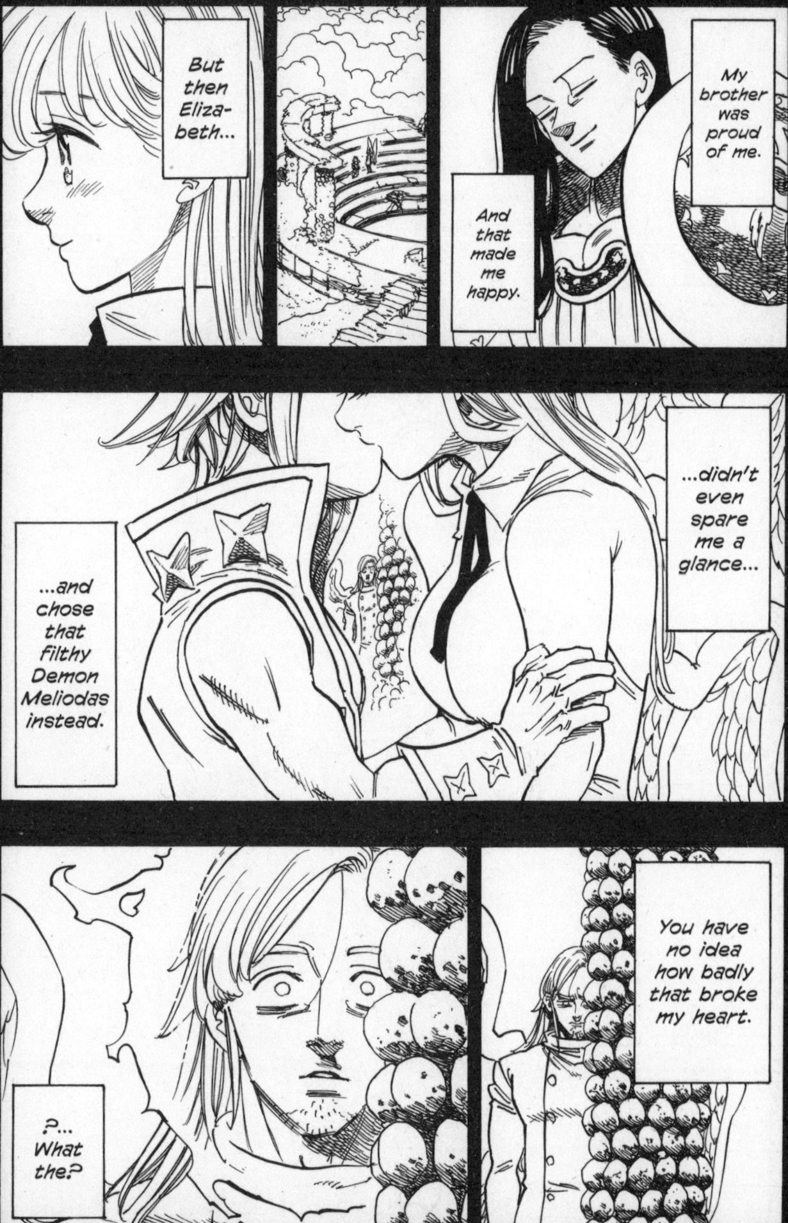
My brother was proud of me.
And that made me happy.
But then Eliza-beth...
...didn't even spare me a glance...
...and chose that filthy Demon Meliodas instead.
You have no idea how badly that broke my heart.
?... What the?

I am... Esta... rossa.
What am I saying?
My name is Mael!!
I've finally beaten the strongest of the Four Archangels Mael!
I killed myself? It can't be!!
Heh heh heh... Such a lowly form!
I'm not acting like myself. What am I seeing?!
I will offer this victory... to my great father, the Demon Lord.
I'm...I'm calling the Demon Lord... my father?! This is blasphemy! Aah! O Lord, forgive me!!

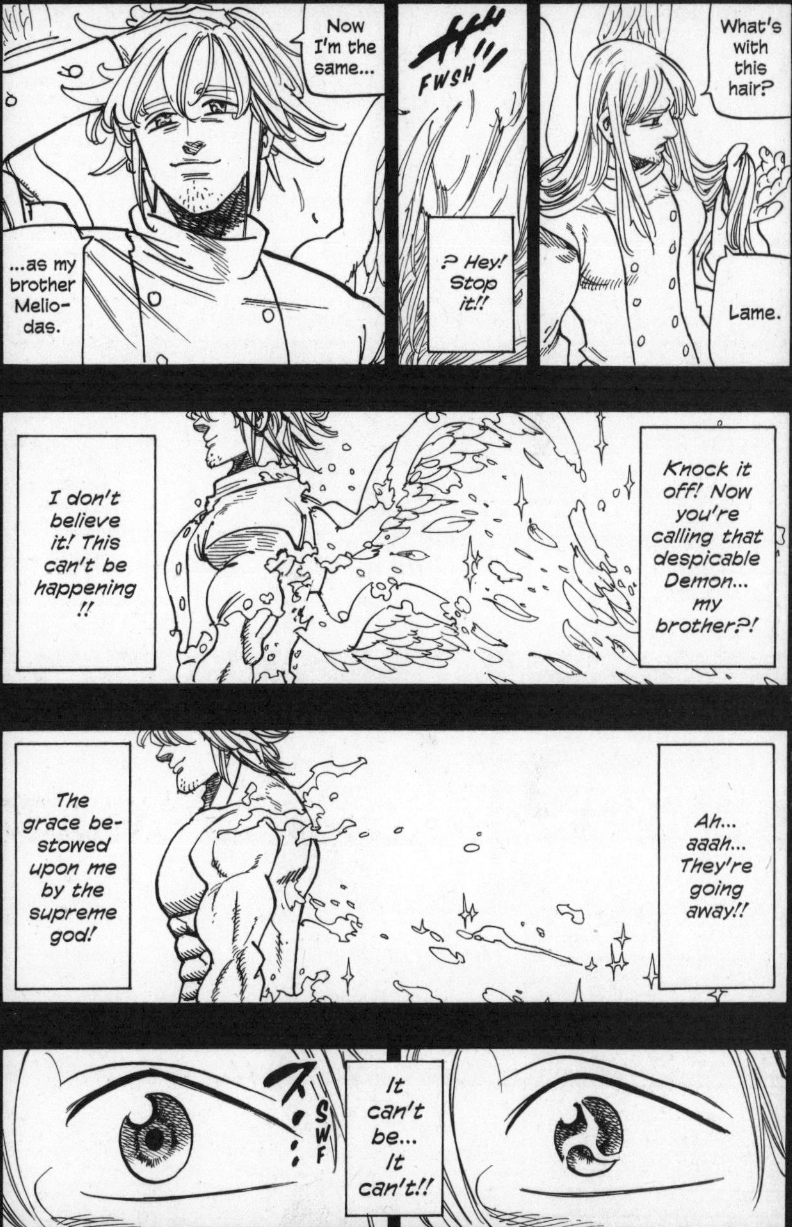
What's with this hair?
Lame.
FWSH
? Hey! Stop it!!
Now I'm the same...
...as my brother Melio-das.
Knock it off! Now you're calling that despicable Demon... my brother?!
I don't believe it! This can't be happening!!
Ah... aaah... They're going away!!
The grace be-stowed upon me by the supreme god!
It can't be... It can't!!
SWF

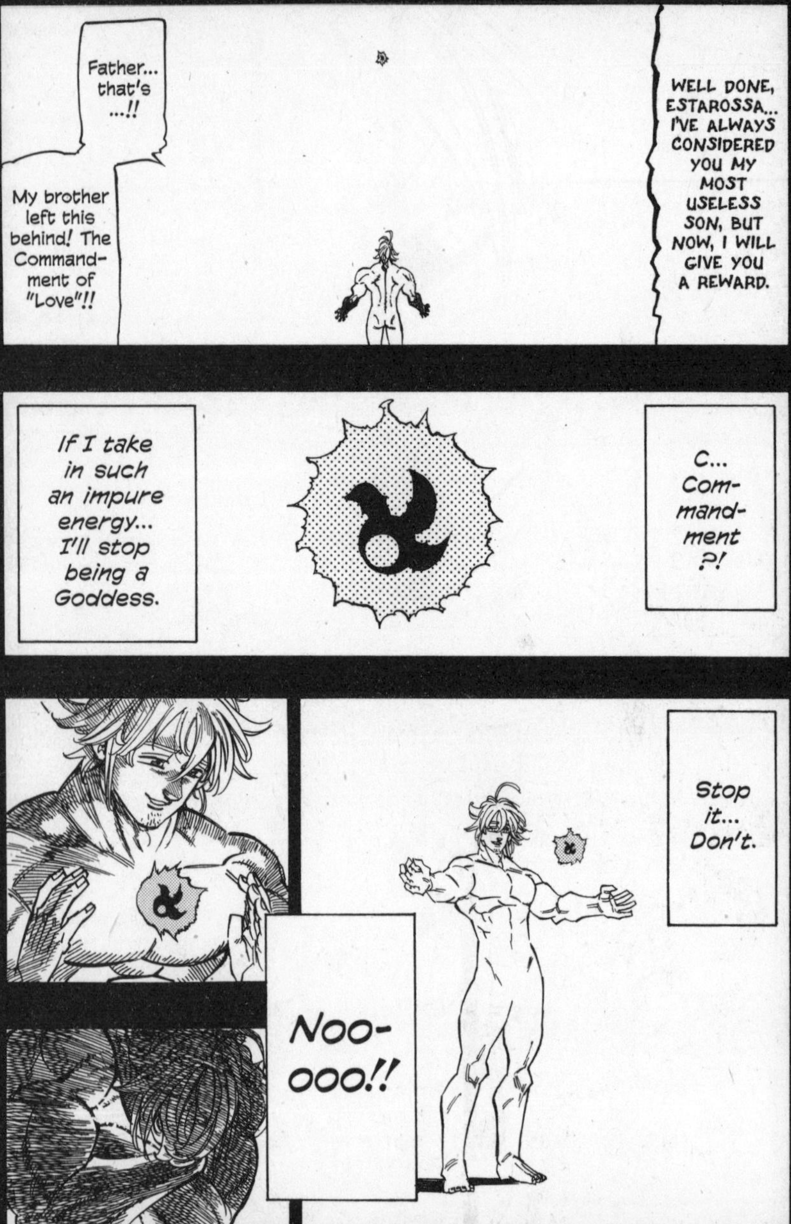
WELL DONE, ESTAROSSA... I'VE ALWAYS CONSIDERED YOU MY MOST USELESS SON, BUT NOW, I WILL GIVE YOU A REWARD.
Father... that's ...!!
My brother left this behind! The Command-ment of "Love"!!
C... Com-mand-ment ?!
If I take in such an impure energy... I'll stop being a Goddess.
Stop it... Don't.
Noo-ooo!!

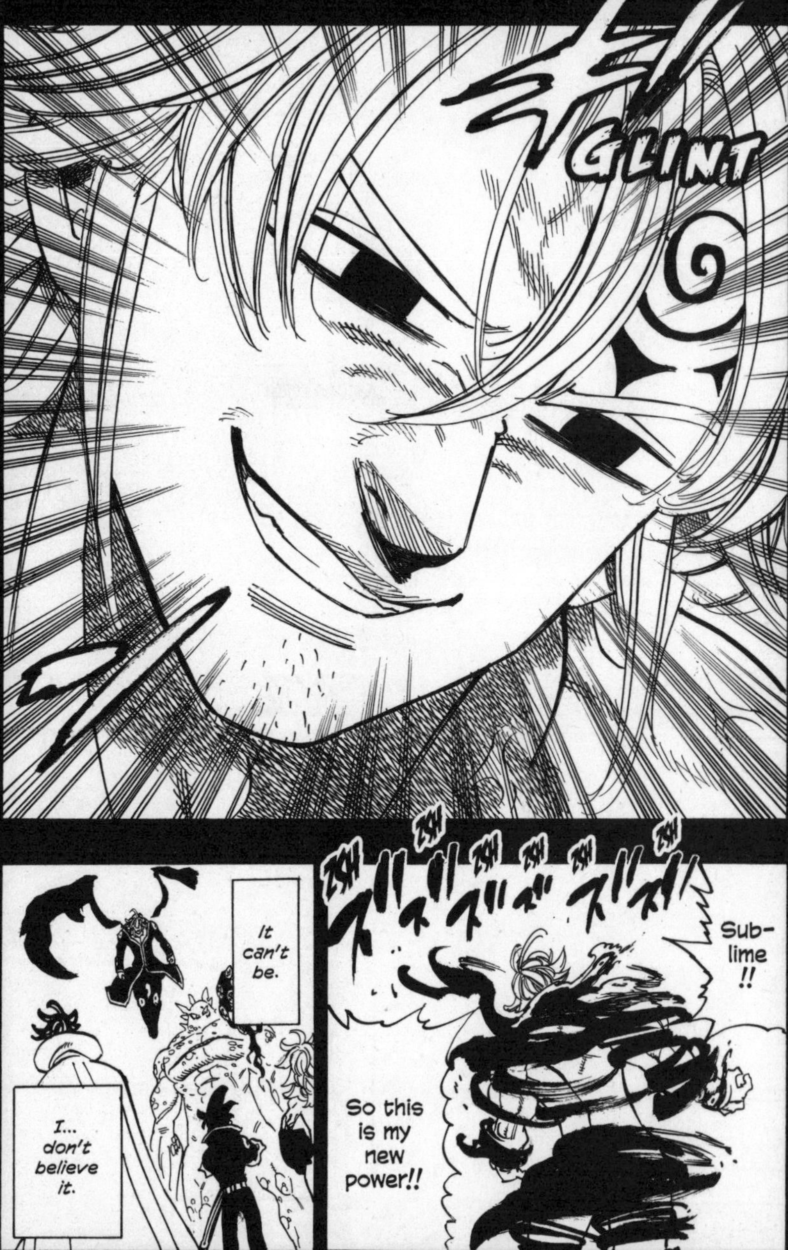
GLINT
ZSH ZSH ZSH ZSH ZSH ZSH
Sub-lime!!
So this is my new power!!
It can't be.
I... don't believe it.

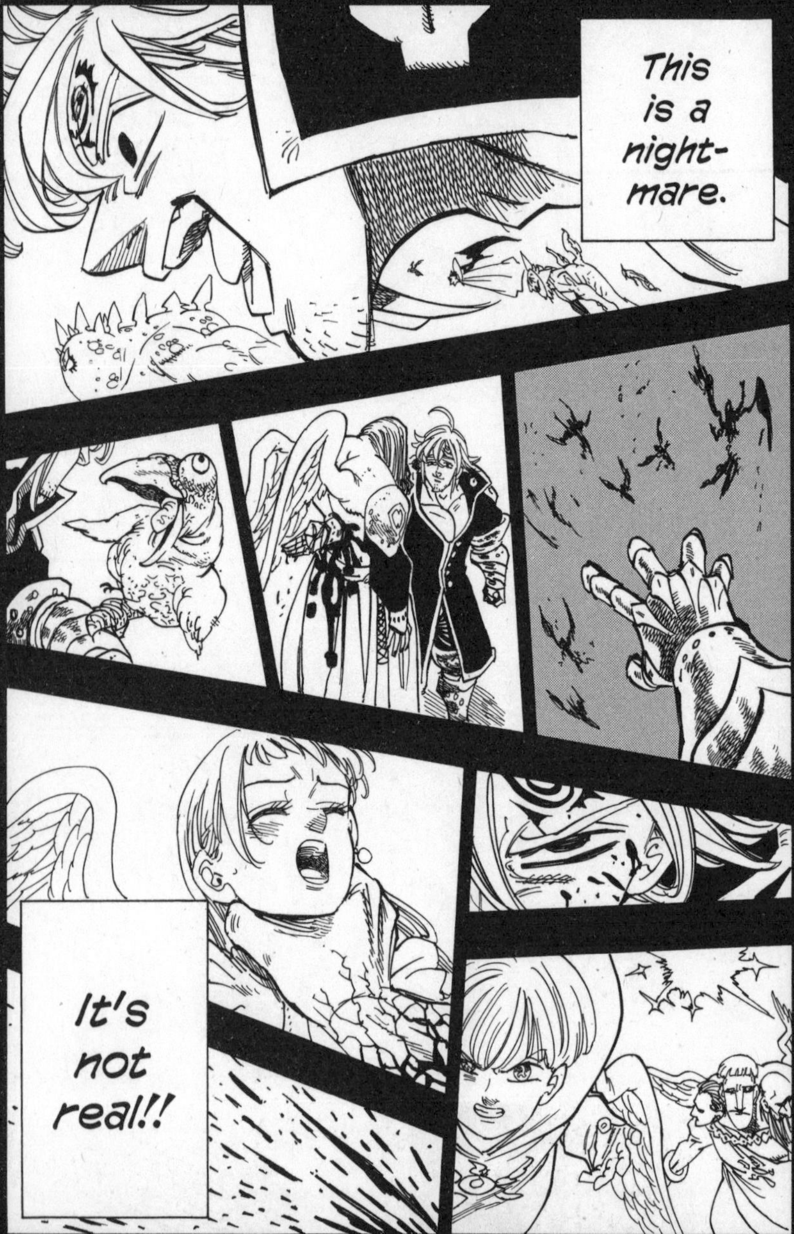
This is a night-mare.
It's not real!!

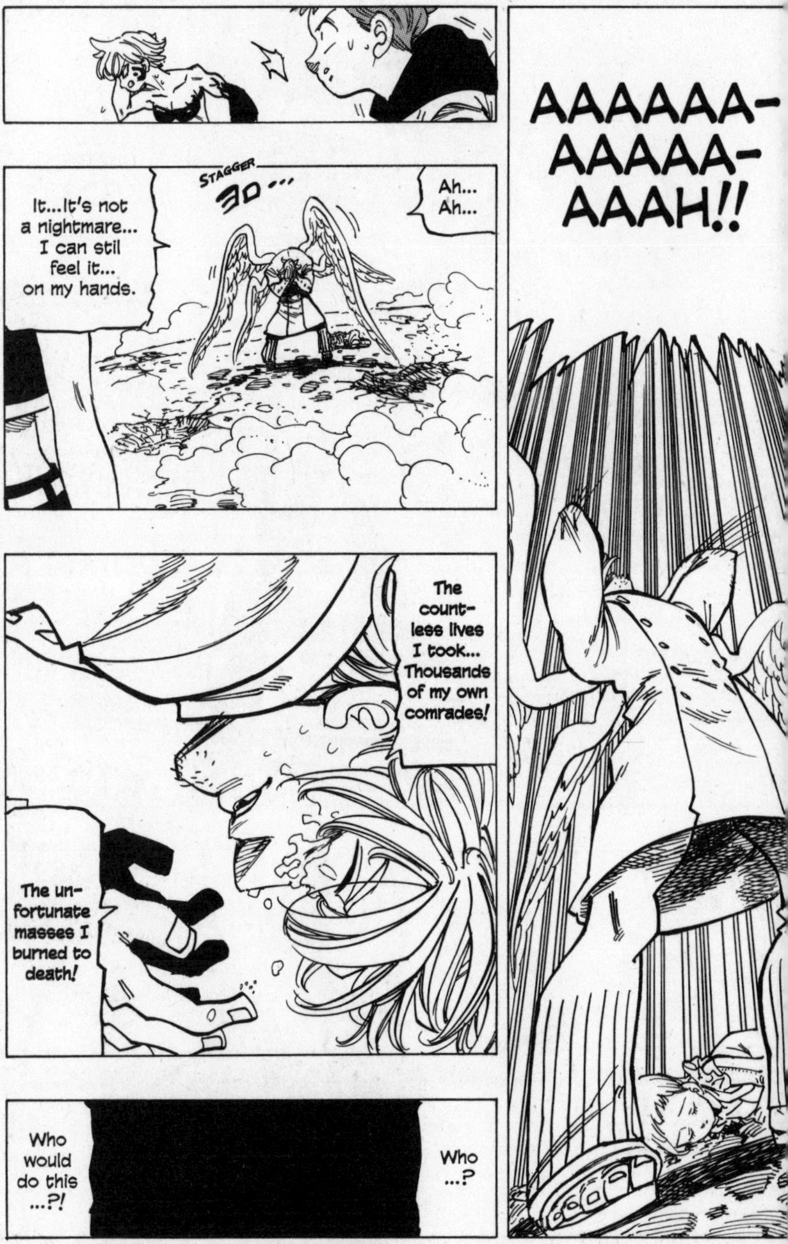

AAAAAA-AAAAA-AAAH!!
Ah... Ah...
STAGGER
It...It's not a nightmare... I can stil feel it... on my hands.
The count-less lives I took... Thousands of my own comrades!
The un-fortunate masses I burned to death!
Who ...?
Who would do this ...?!

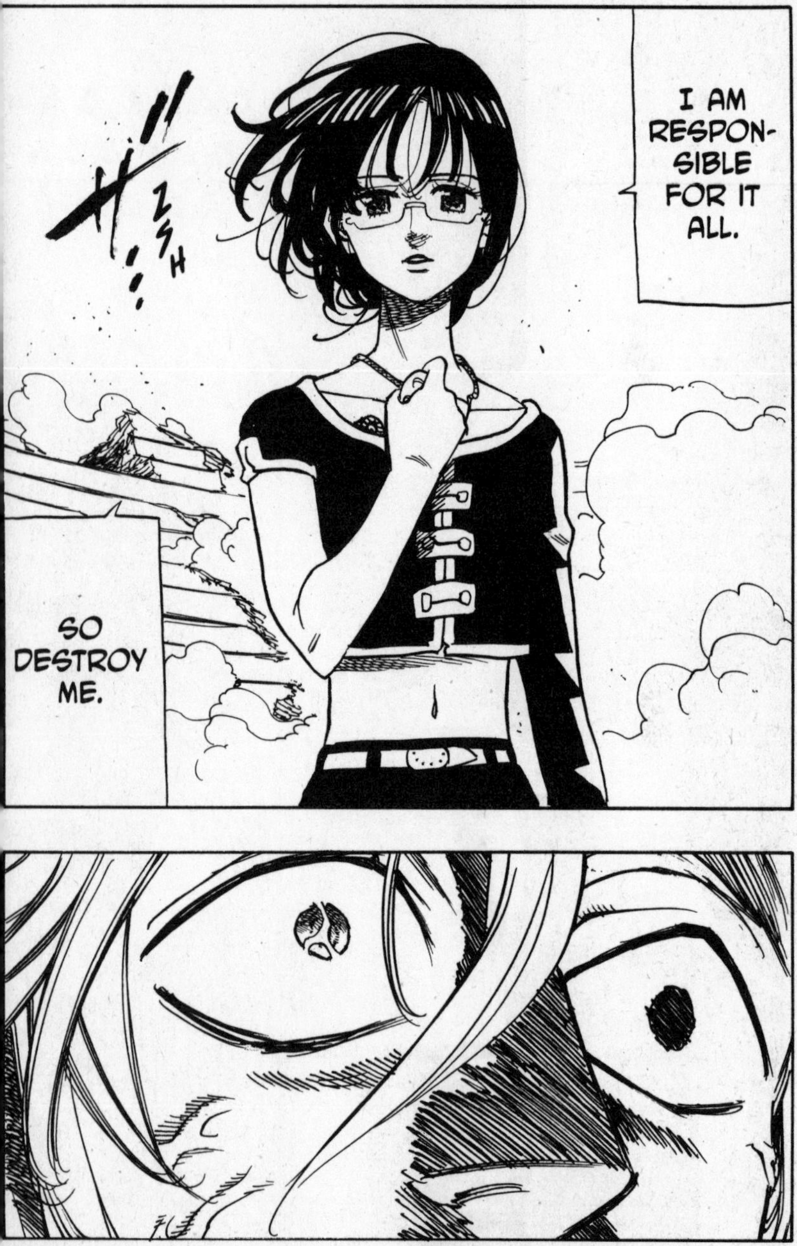
I AM RESPONSIBLE FOR IT ALL.
ZSH
SO DESTROY ME.

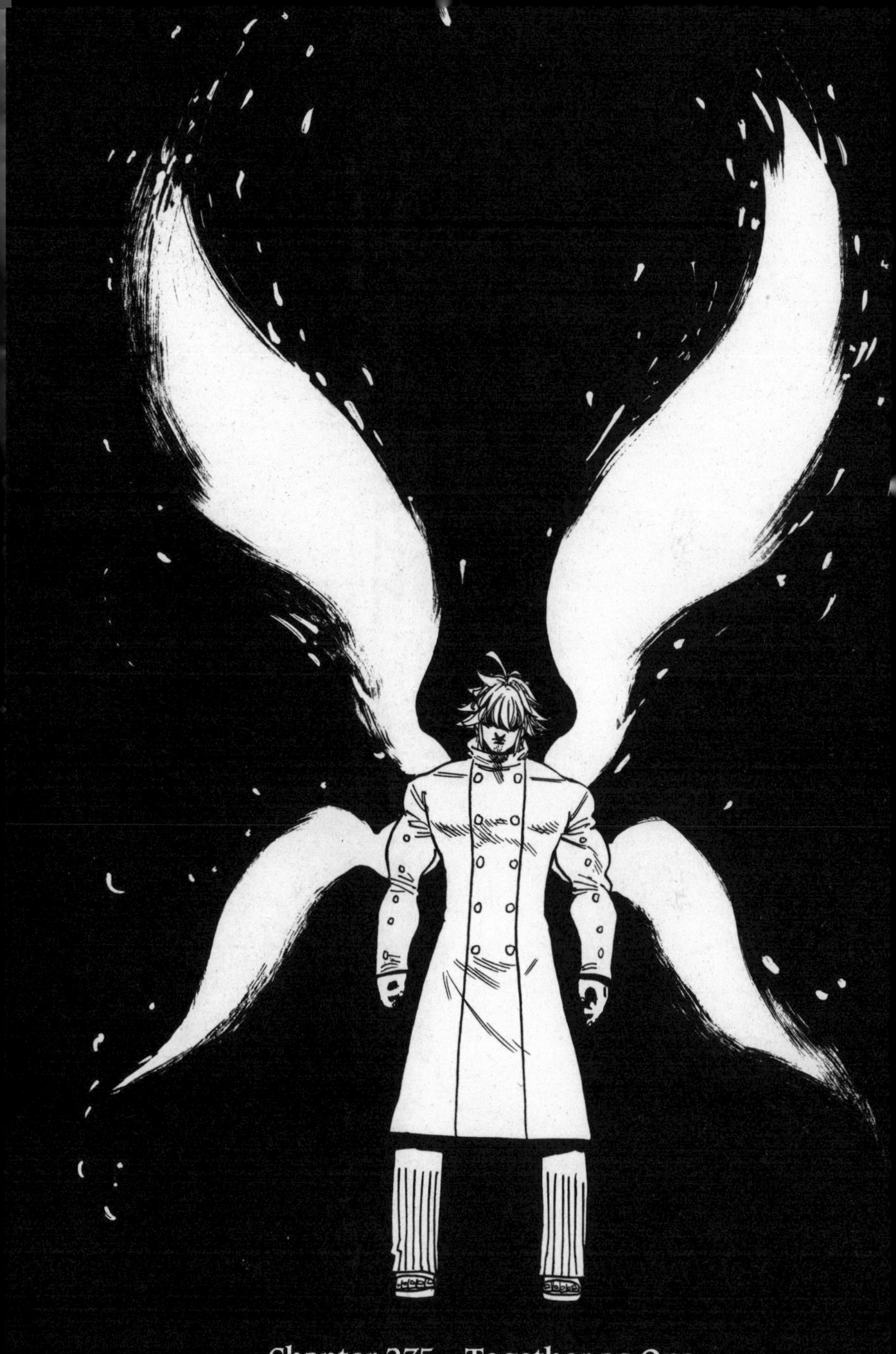

Chapter 275 - Together as One

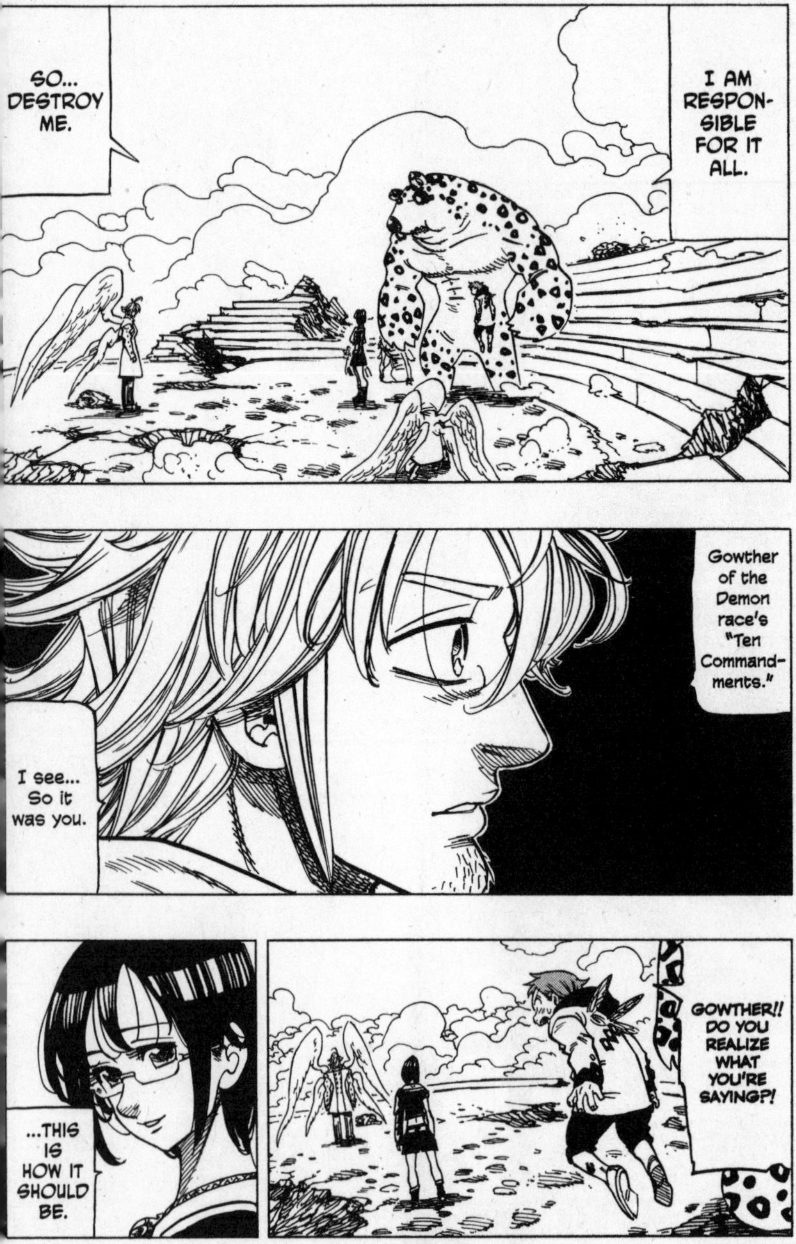
I AM RESPON-SIBLE FOR IT ALL.
SO... DESTROY ME.
Gowther of the Demon race's "Ten Command-ments."
I see... So it was you.
GOWTHER!! DO YOU REALIZE WHAT YOU'RE SAYING?!
...THIS IS HOW IT SHOULD BE.

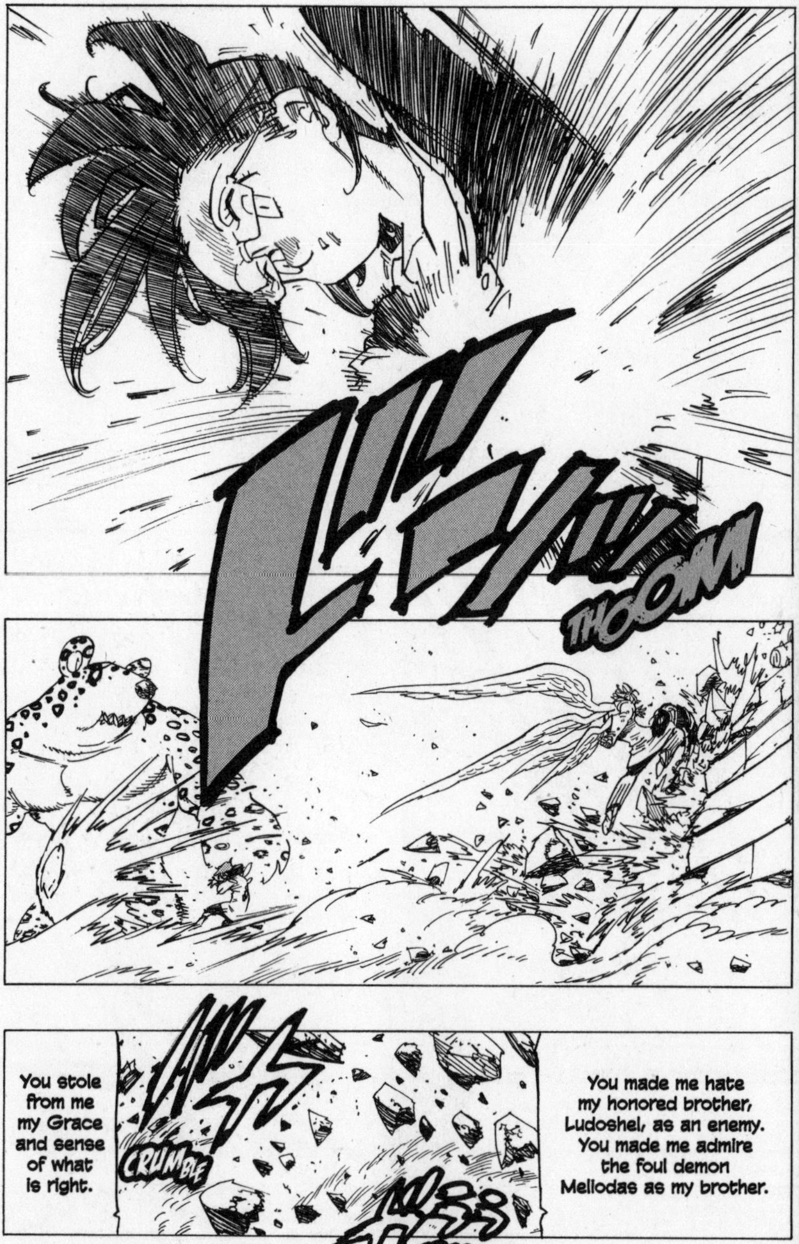
THOOM
You made me hate my honored brother, Ludoshel, as an enemy. You made me admire the foul demon Meliodas as my brother.
CRUMBLE
CRUNCH
You stole from me my Grace and sense of what is right.

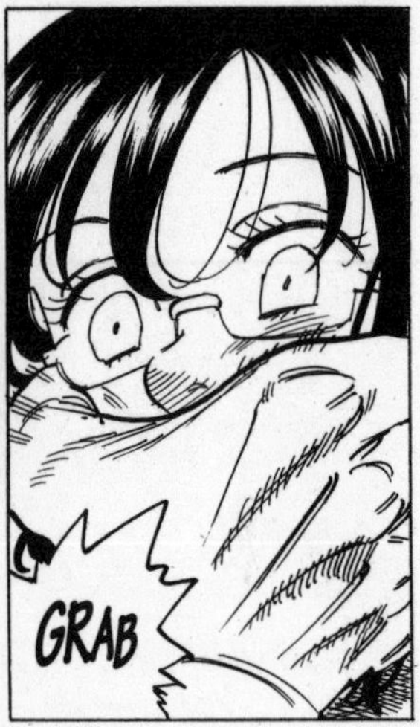
GRAB

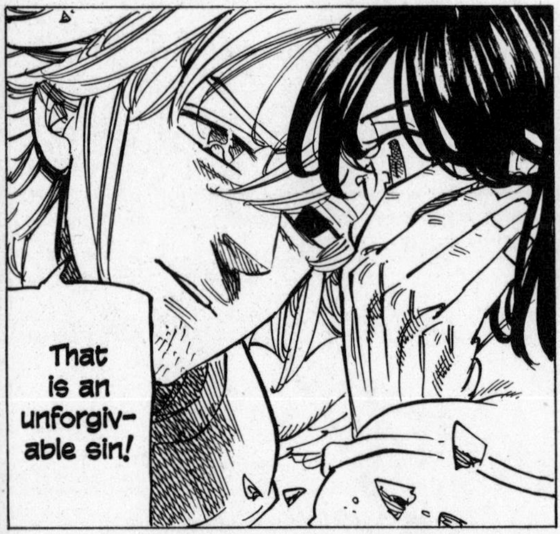
That is an unforgiv-able sin!

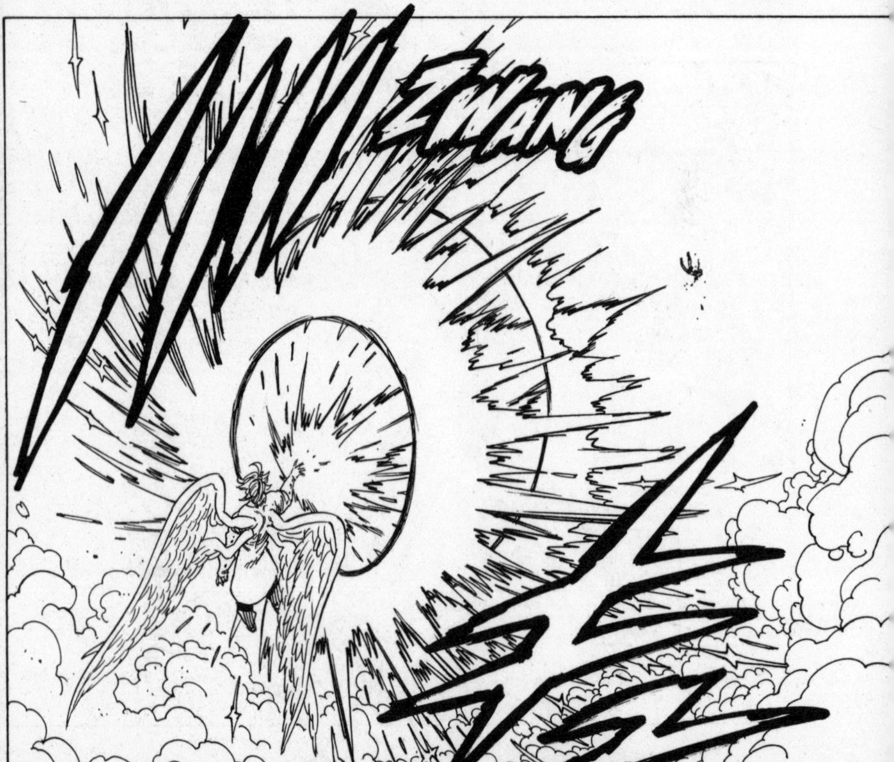
ZWANG

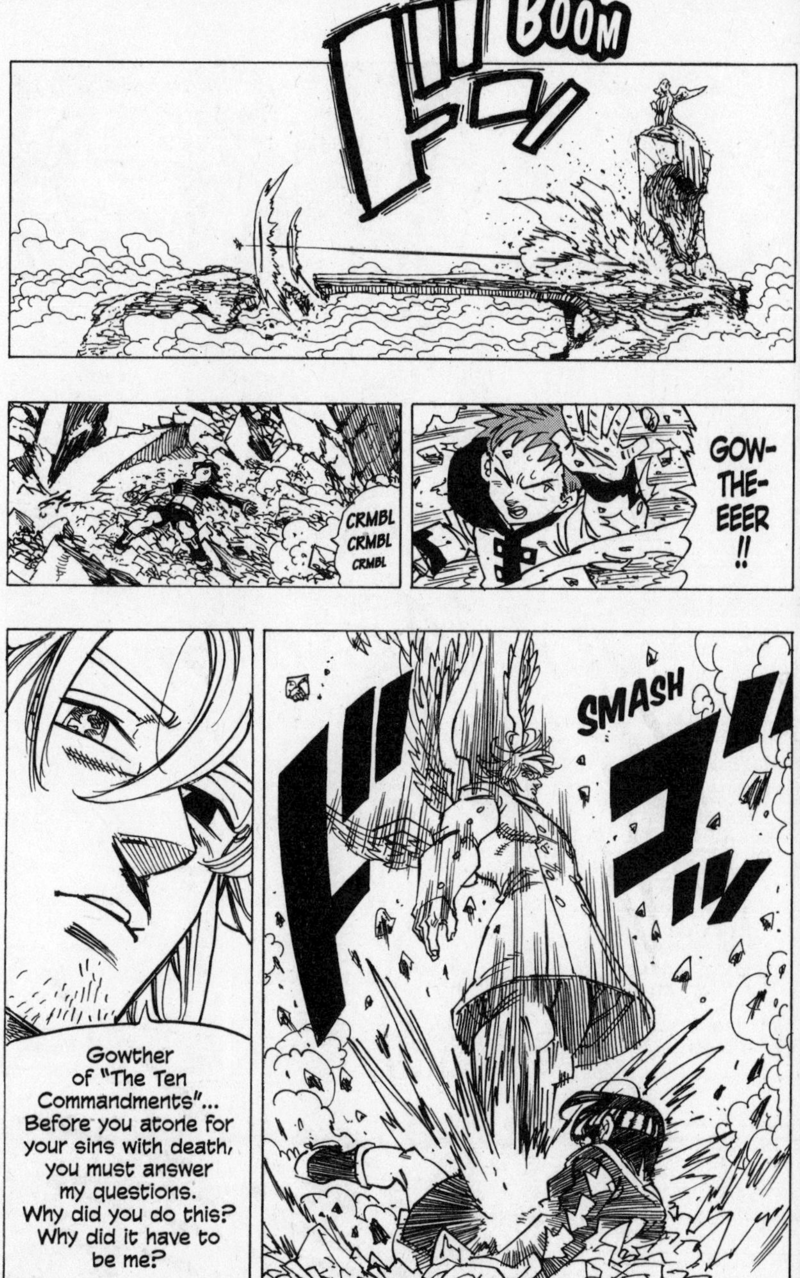
BOOM
GOW-THE-EEER!!
CRMBL CRMBL CRMBL
SMASH
Gowther of "The Ten Commandments"... Before you atone for your sins with death, you must answer my questions. Why did you do this? Why did it have to be me?

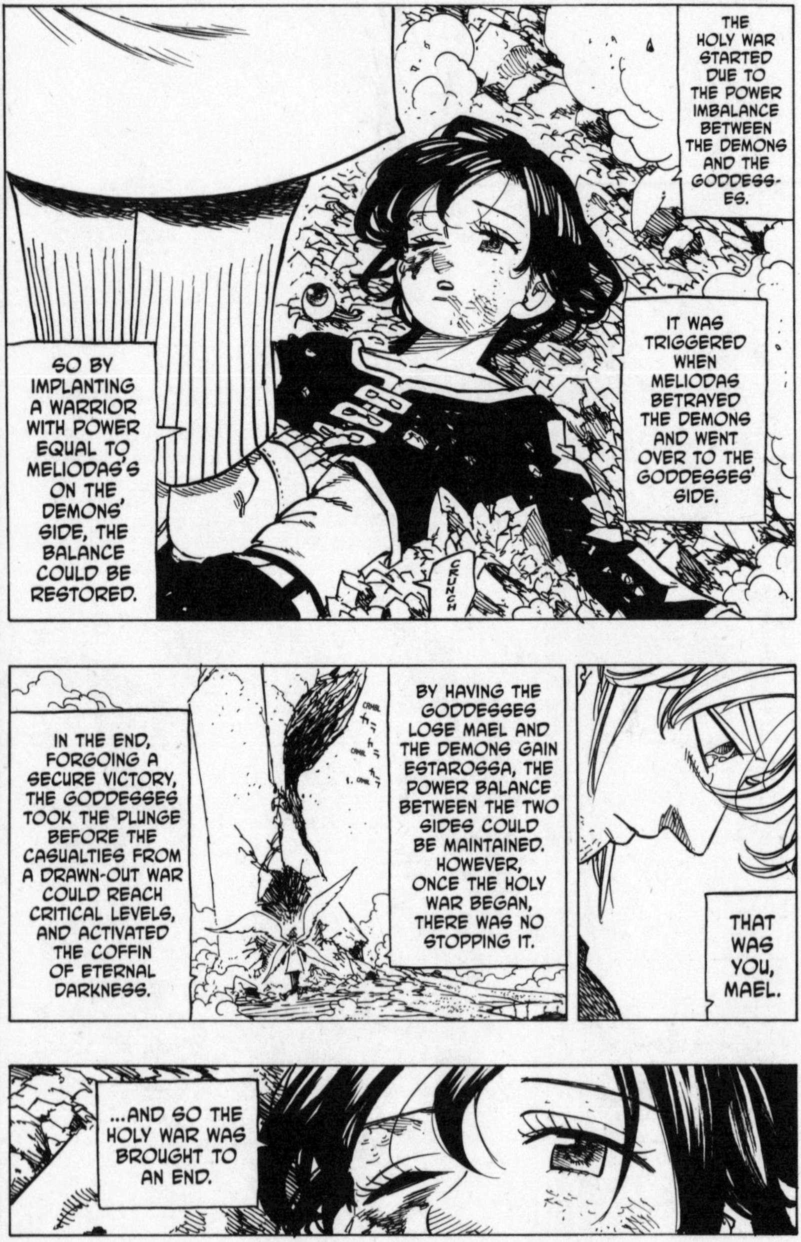
THE HOLY WAR STARTED DUE TO THE POWER IMBALANCE BETWEEN THE DEMONS AND THE GODDESSES.
IT WAS TRIGGERED WHEN MELIODAS BETRAYED THE DEMONS AND WENT OVER TO THE GODDESSES' SIDE.
SO BY IMPLANTING A WARRIOR WITH POWER EQUAL TO MELIODAS'S ON THE DEMONS' SIDE, THE BALANCE COULD BE RESTORED.
CRUNCH
THAT WAS YOU, MAEL.
BY HAVING THE GODDESSES LOSE MAEL AND THE DEMONS GAIN ESTAROSSA, THE POWER BALANCE BETWEEN THE TWO SIDES COULD BE MAINTAINED. HOWEVER, ONCE THE HOLY WAR BEGAN, THERE WAS NO STOPPING IT.
IN THE END, FORGOING A SECURE VICTORY, THE GODDESSES TOOK THE PLUNGE BEFORE THE CASUALTIES FROM A DRAWN-OUT WAR COULD REACH CRITICAL LEVELS, AND ACTIVATED THE COFFIN OF ETERNAL DARKNESS.
...AND SO THE HOLY WAR WAS BROUGHT TO AN END.

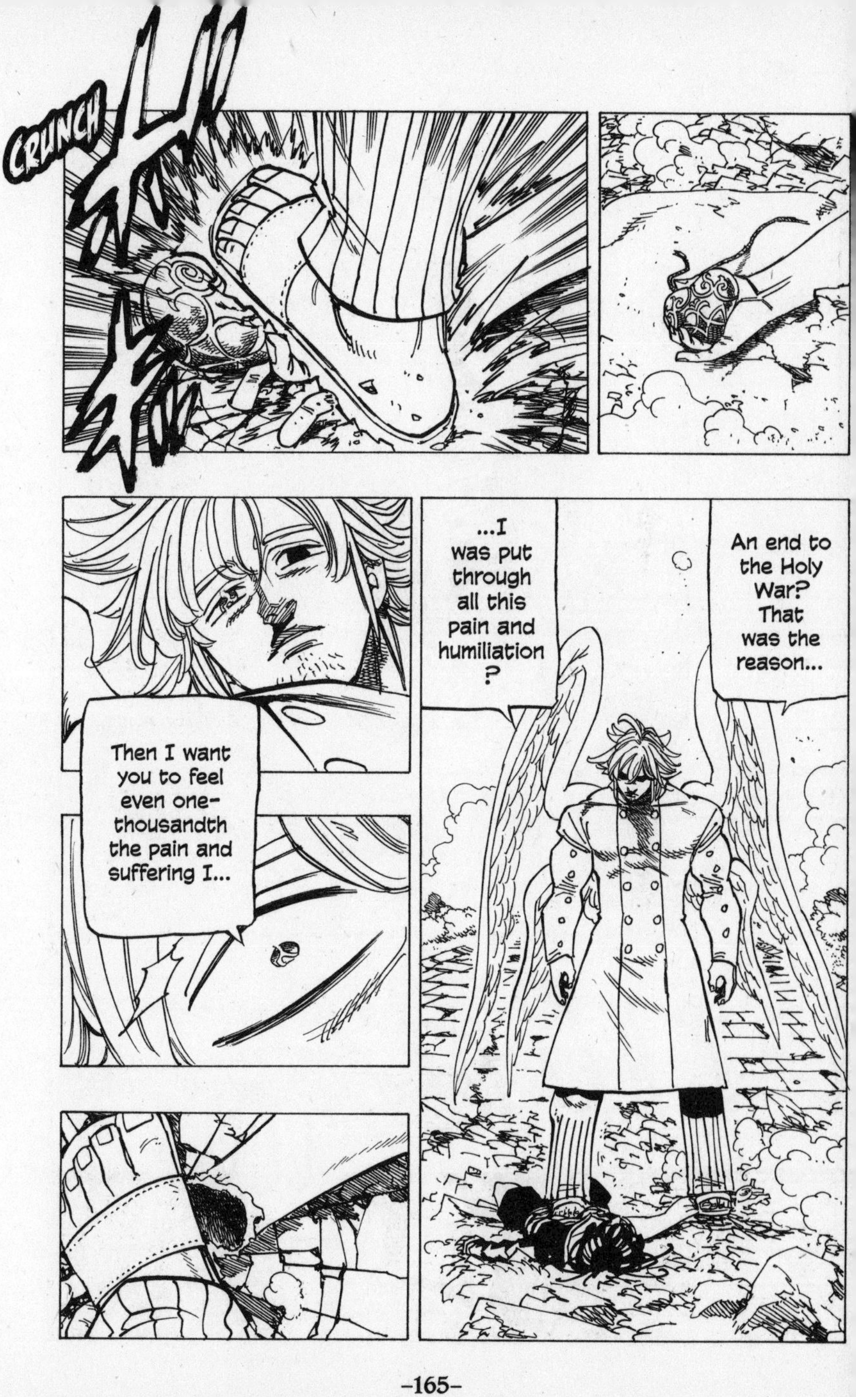
CRUNCH
An end to the Holy War? That was the reason...
...I was put through all this pain and humiliation?
Then I want you to feel even one-thousandth the pain and suffering I...

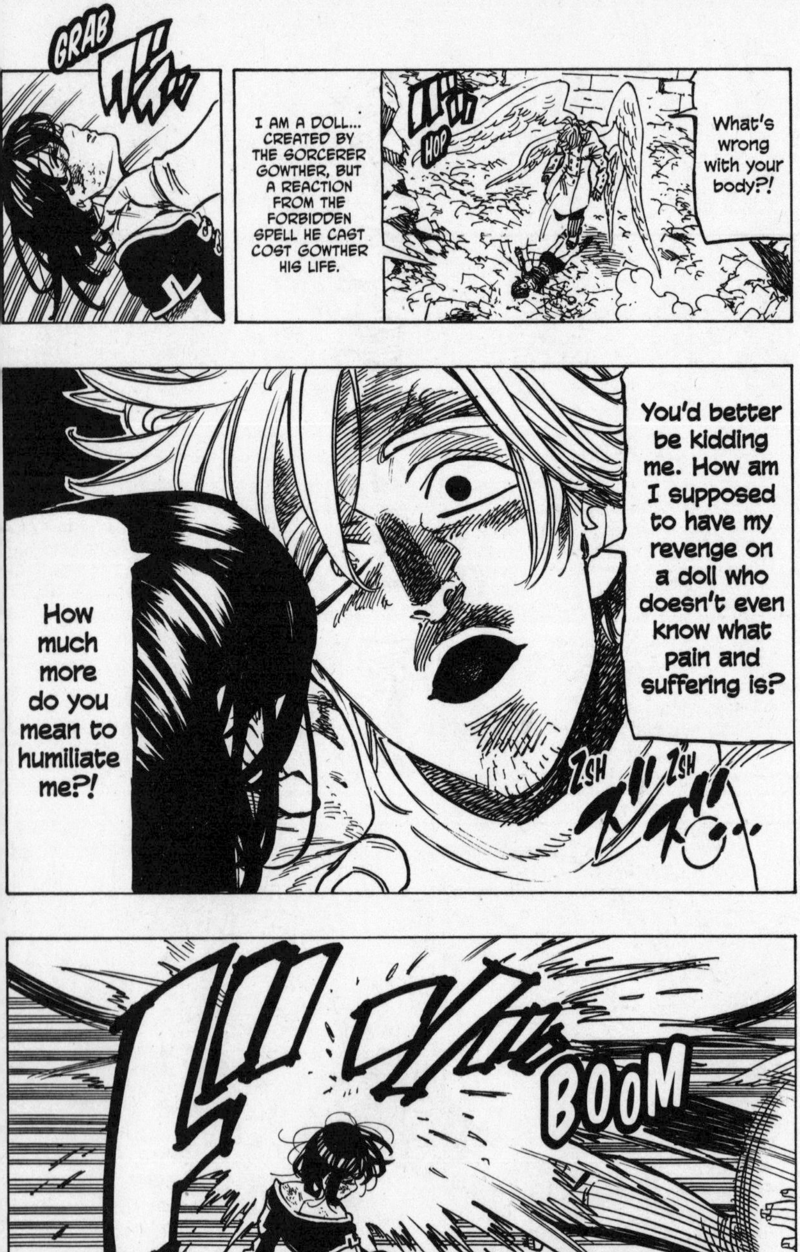
What's wrong with your body?!
HOP
I AM A DOLL... CREATED BY THE SORCERER GOWTHER, BUT A REACTION FROM THE FORBIDDEN SPELL HE CAST COST GOWTHER HIS LIFE.
GRAB
You'd better be kidding me. How am I supposed to have my revenge on a doll who doesn't even know what pain and suffering is?
How much more do you mean to humiliate me?!
Z'SH
Z'SH
BOOM

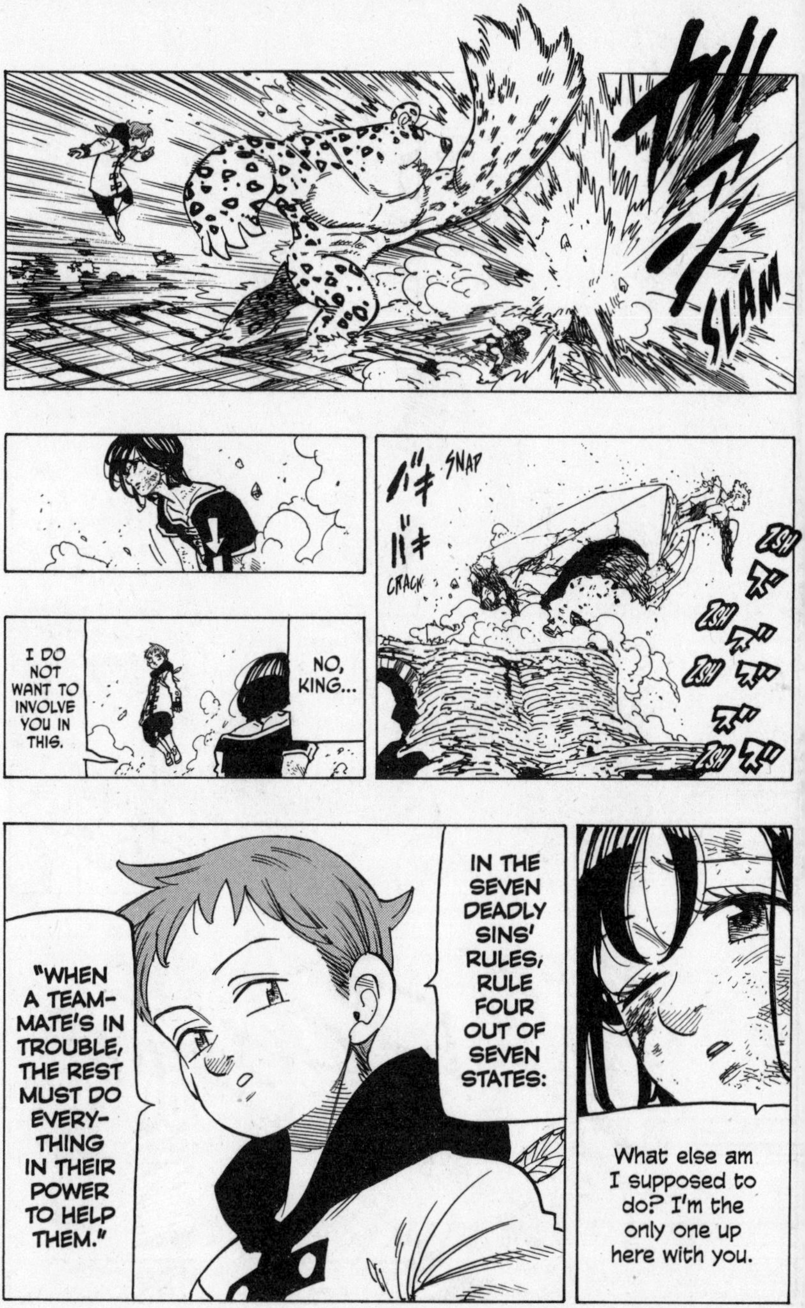
SLAM
バキ
SNAP
バキ
CRACK
ZSH
ズ
ZSH
ズ
ZSH
ズ
ズ
ZSH
ズ
NO, KING...
I DO NOT WANT TO INVOLVE YOU IN THIS.
What else am I supposed to do? I'm the only one up here with you.
IN THE SEVEN DEADLY SINS' RULES, RULE FOUR OUT OF SEVEN STATES:
"WHEN A TEAM-MATE'S IN TROUBLE, THE REST MUST DO EVERY-THING IN THEIR POWER TO HELP THEM."

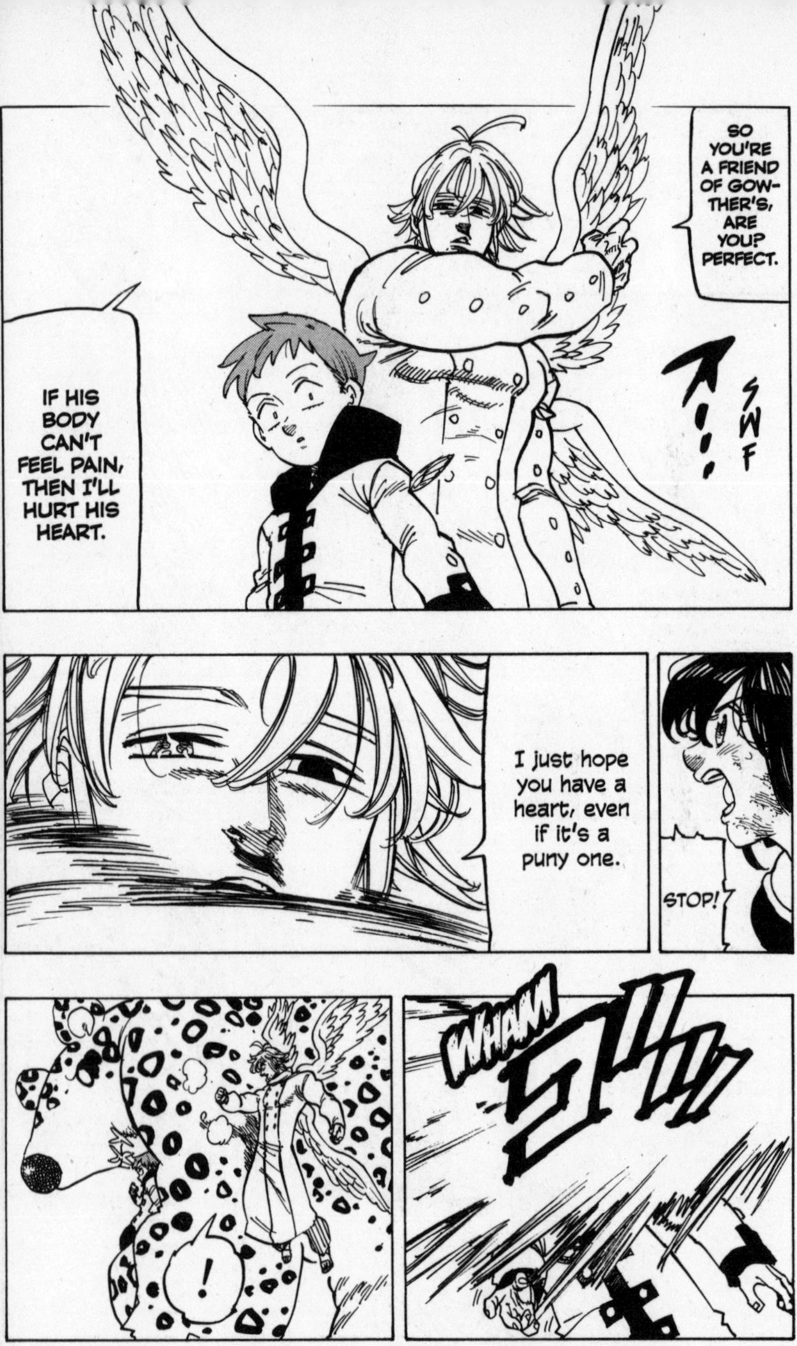
SO YOU'RE A FRIEND OF GOW-THER'S, ARE YOU? PERFECT.
SWF
IF HIS BODY CAN'T FEEL PAIN, THEN I'LL HURT HIS HEART.
STOP!
I just hope you have a heart, even if it's a puny one.
WHAM
!

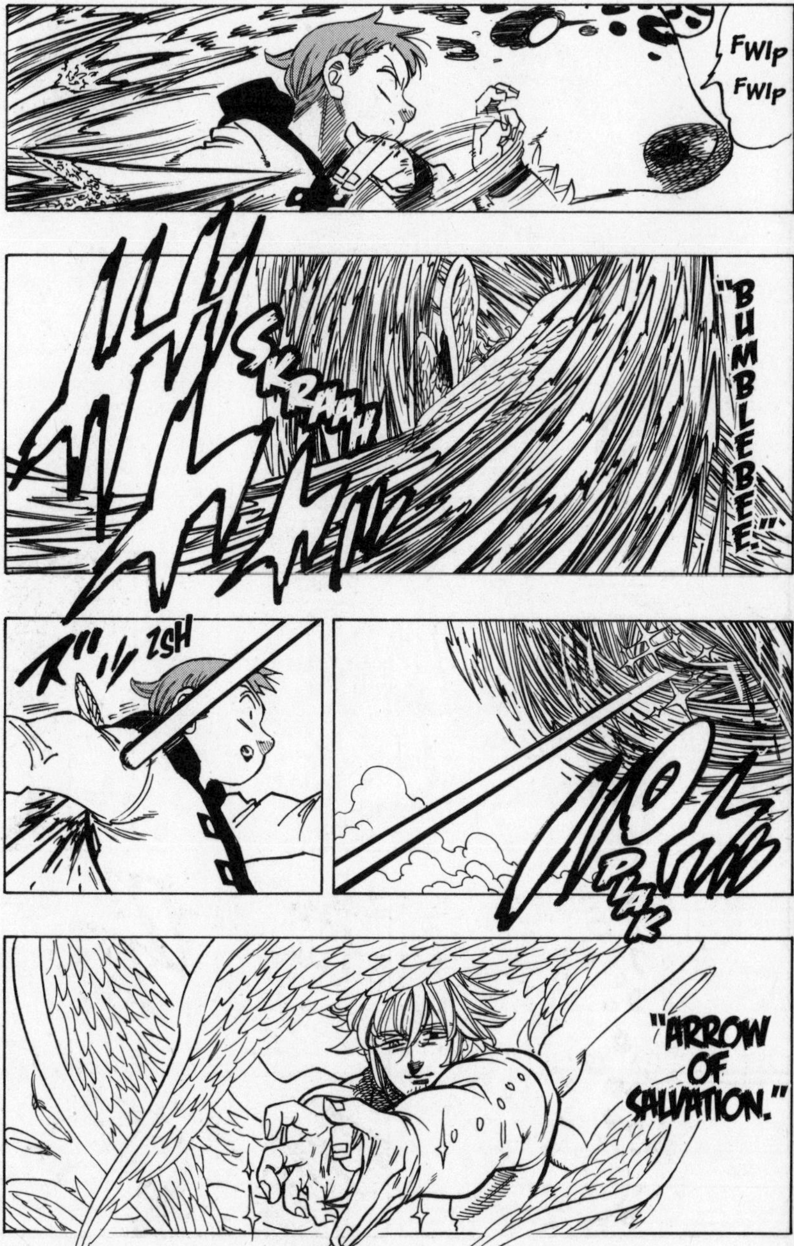
FWIP
FWIP
"BUMBLEBEE."
SKRAAAH
PLAK
ZSH
"ARROW OF SALVATION."

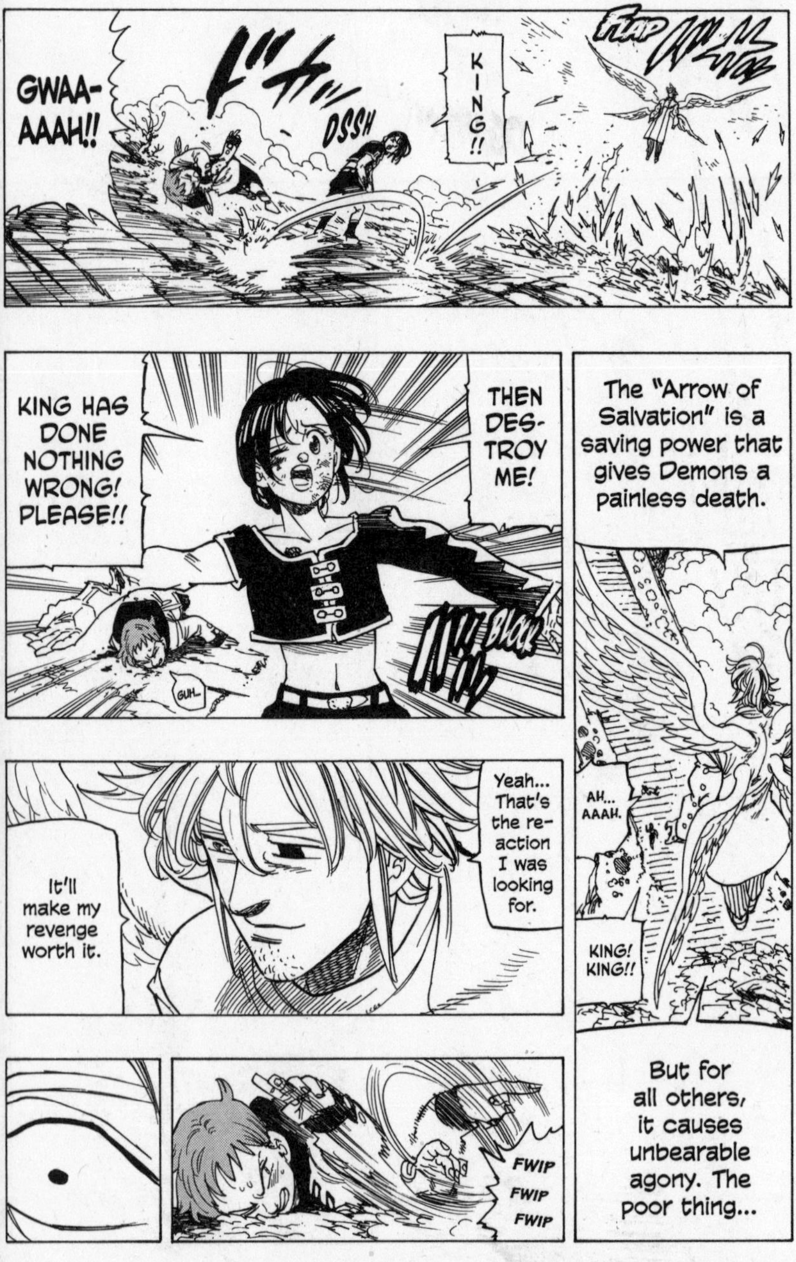
FLAP
KING!!
DSSH
GWAA-AAAH!!
The "Arrow of Salvation" is a saving power that gives Demons a painless death.
AH... AAAH.
KING! KING!!
But for all others, it causes unbearable agony. The poor thing...
THEN DES-TROY ME!
KING HAS DONE NOTHING WRONG! PLEASE!!
BLOCK
GUH...
Yeah... That's the re-action I was looking for.
It'll make my revenge worth it.
FWIP
FWIP
FWIP

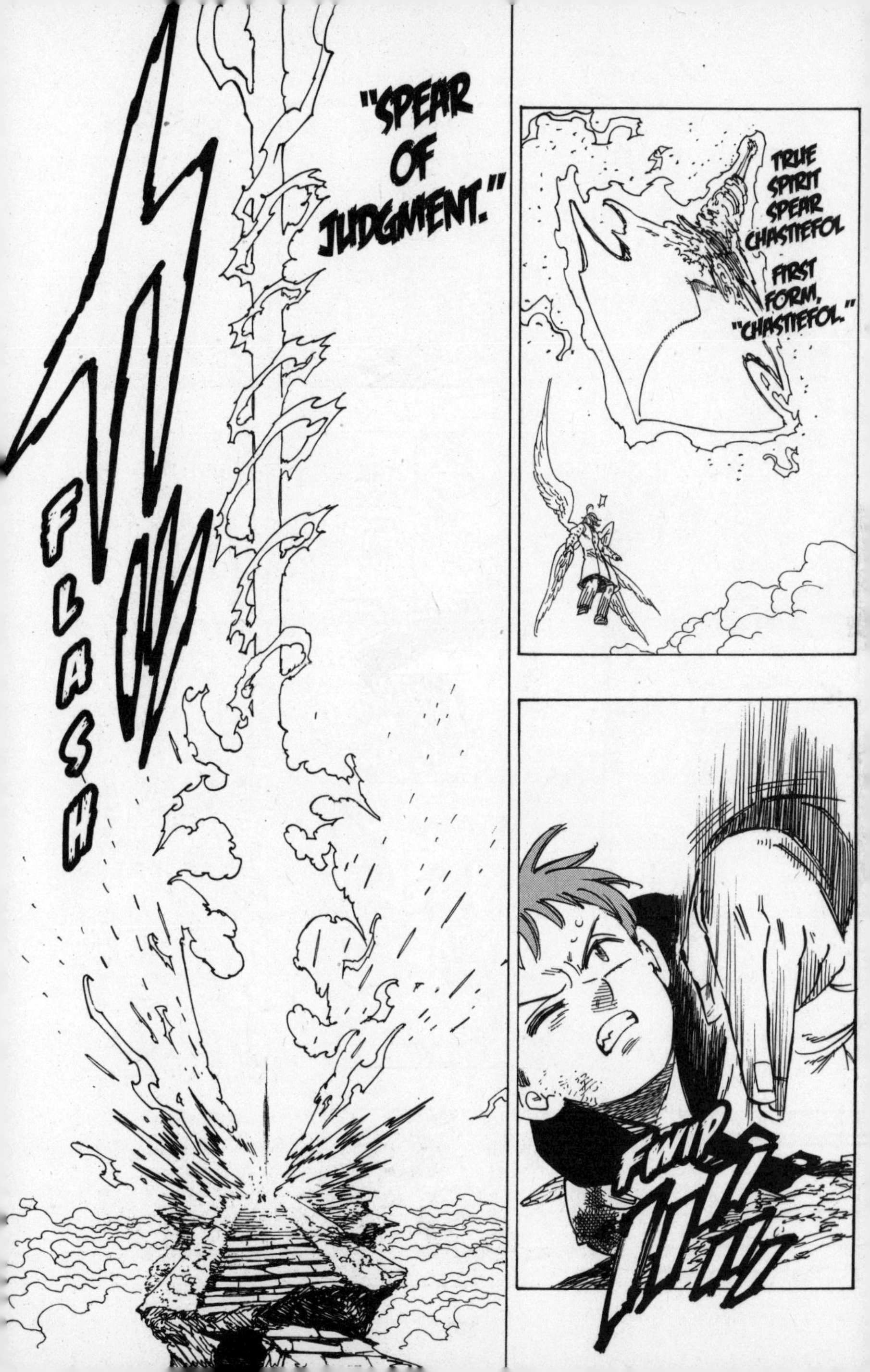
TRUE SPIRIT SPEAR CHASTIEFOL
FIRST FORM, "CHASTIEFOL."
FWIP
"SPEAR OF JUDGMENT."
FLASH

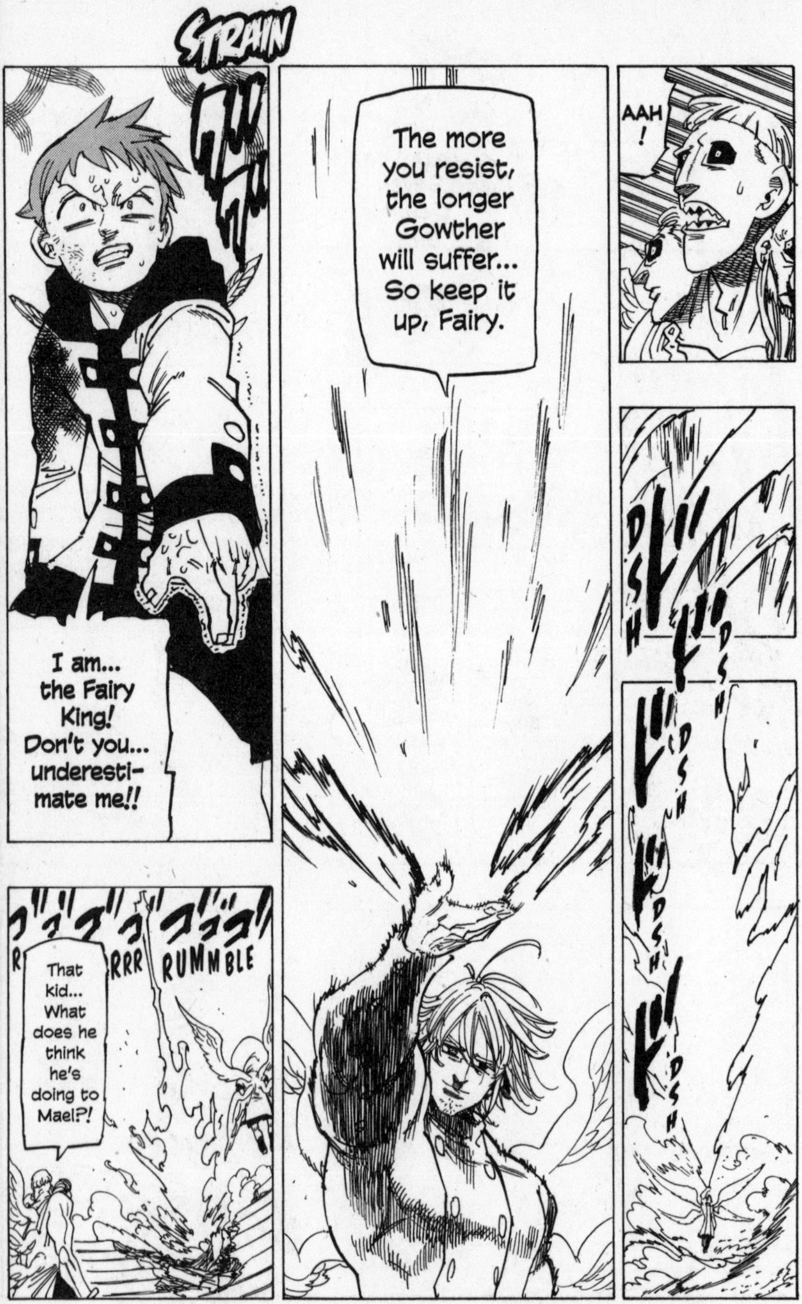
AAH!
DSH
DSH
DSH
DSH
DSH
DSH
The more you resist, the longer Gowther will suffer... So keep it up, Fairy.
STRAIN
I am... the Fairy King! Don't you... underesti-mate me!!
RRR RRR RUMMBLE
That kid... What does he think he's doing to Mael?!

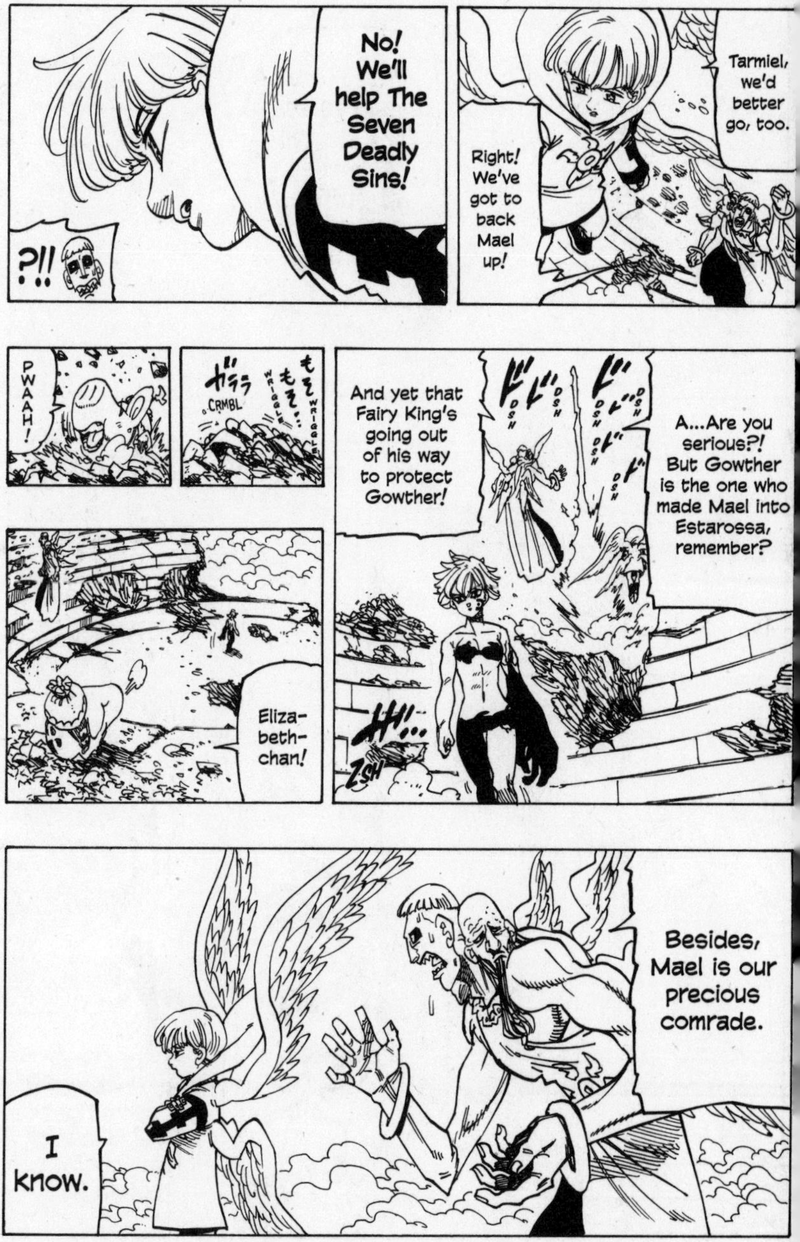
Tarmiel, we'd better go, too.
Right! We've got to back Mael up!
No! We'll help The Seven Deadly Sins!
?!!
A...Are you serious?! But Gowther is the one who made Mael into Estarossa, remember?
And yet that Fairy King's going out of his way to protect Gowther!
DSH DSH DSH DSH DSH DSH
ZSH
WRIGGLE WRIGGLE
CRMBL
PWAAH!
Eliza-beth-chan!
Besides, Mael is our precious comrade.
I know.

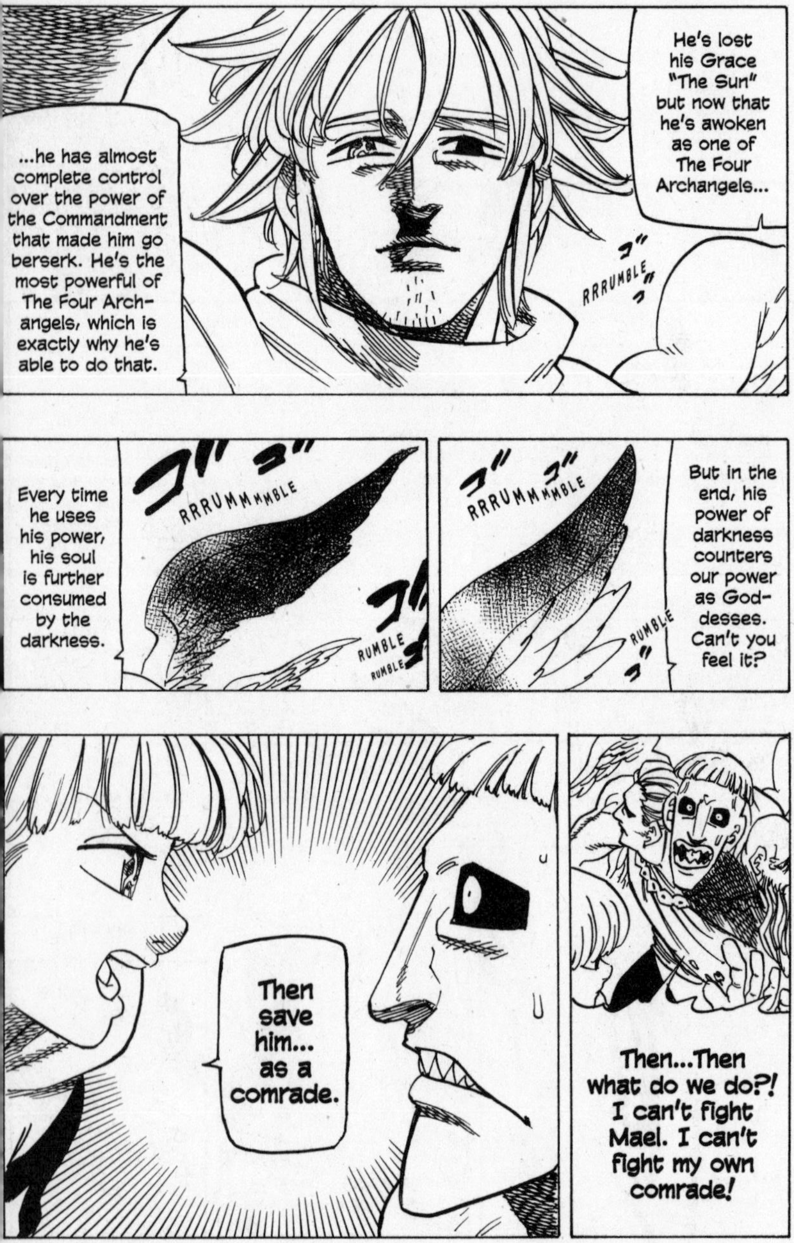
He's lost his Grace "The Sun" but now that he's awoken as one of The Four Archangels...
...he has almost complete control over the power of the Commandment that made him go berserk. He's the most powerful of The Four Arch-angels, which is exactly why he's able to do that.
RRRUMBLE
But in the end, his power of darkness counters our power as God-desses. Can't you feel it?
RRRUMMMMMBLE
RUMBLE
Every time he uses his power, his soul is further consumed by the darkness.
RRRUMMMMMBLE
RUMBLE
RUMBLE
Then...Then what do we do?! I can't fight Mael. I can't fight my own comrade!
Then save him... as a comrade.

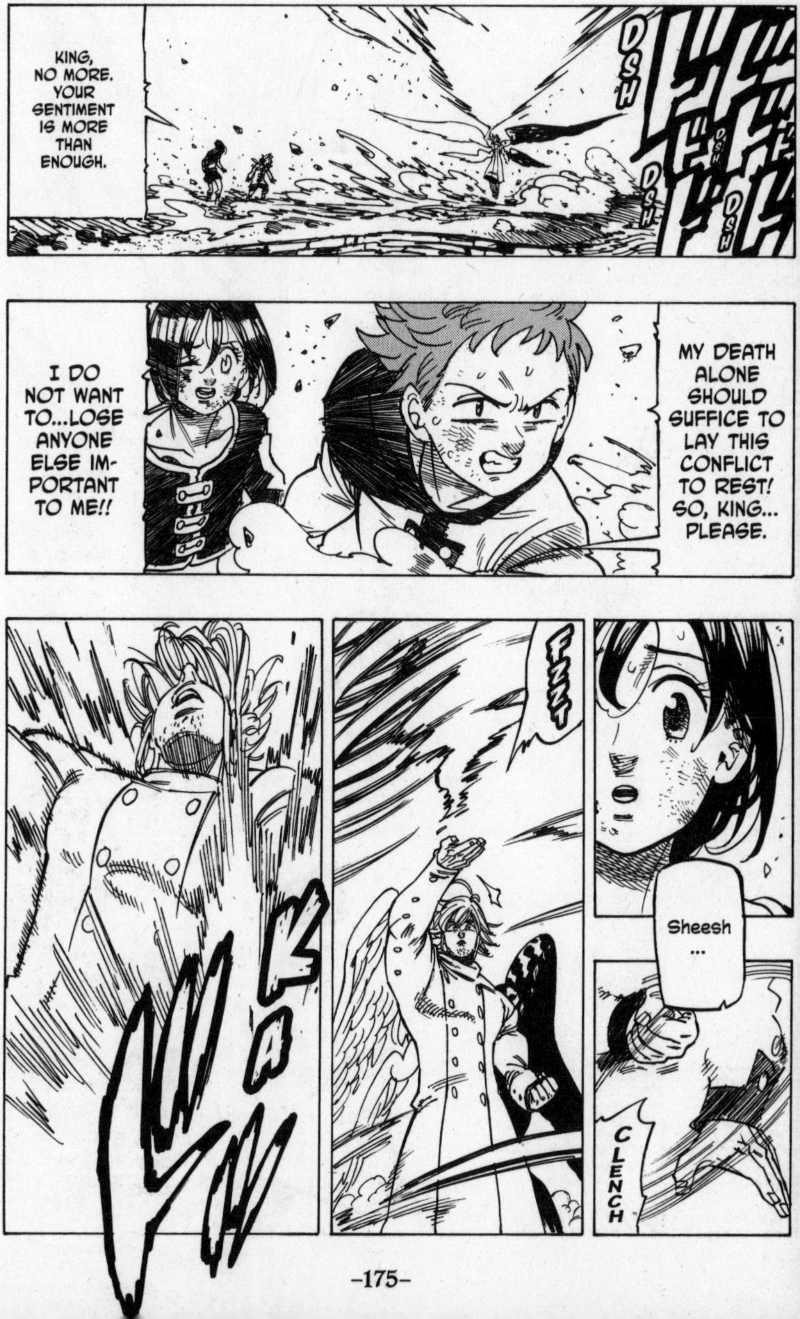
DSH
DSH
DSH
DSH
KING, NO MORE. YOUR SENTIMENT IS MORE THAN ENOUGH.
MY DEATH ALONE SHOULD SUFFICE TO LAY THIS CONFLICT TO REST! SO, KING... PLEASE.
I DO NOT WANT TO...LOSE ANYONE ELSE IMPORTANT TO ME!!
Sheesh...
CLENCH
FZZT

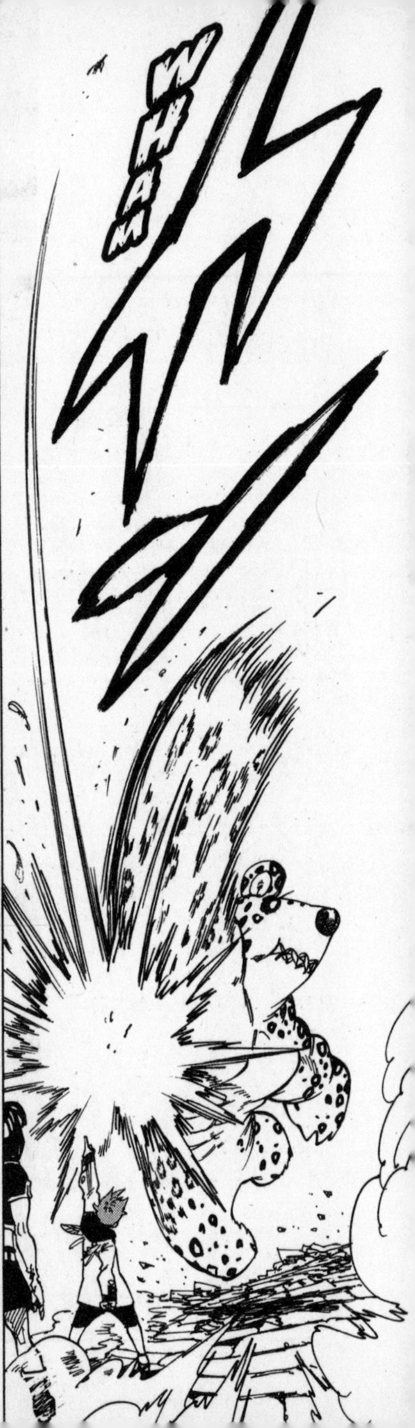
WHAM

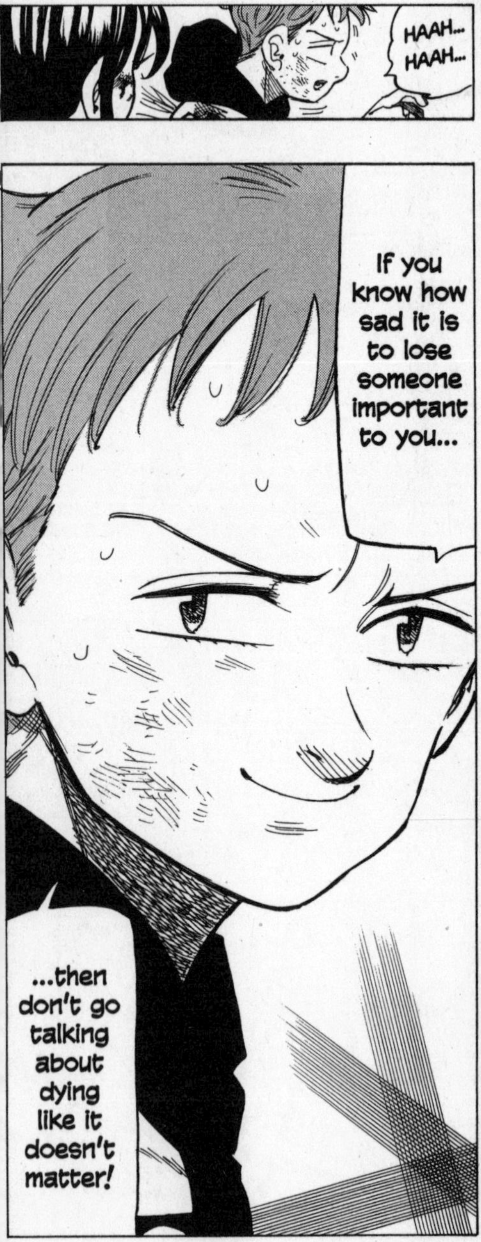
HAAH... HAAH...
If you know how sad it is to lose someone important to you...
...then don't go talking about dying like it doesn't matter!

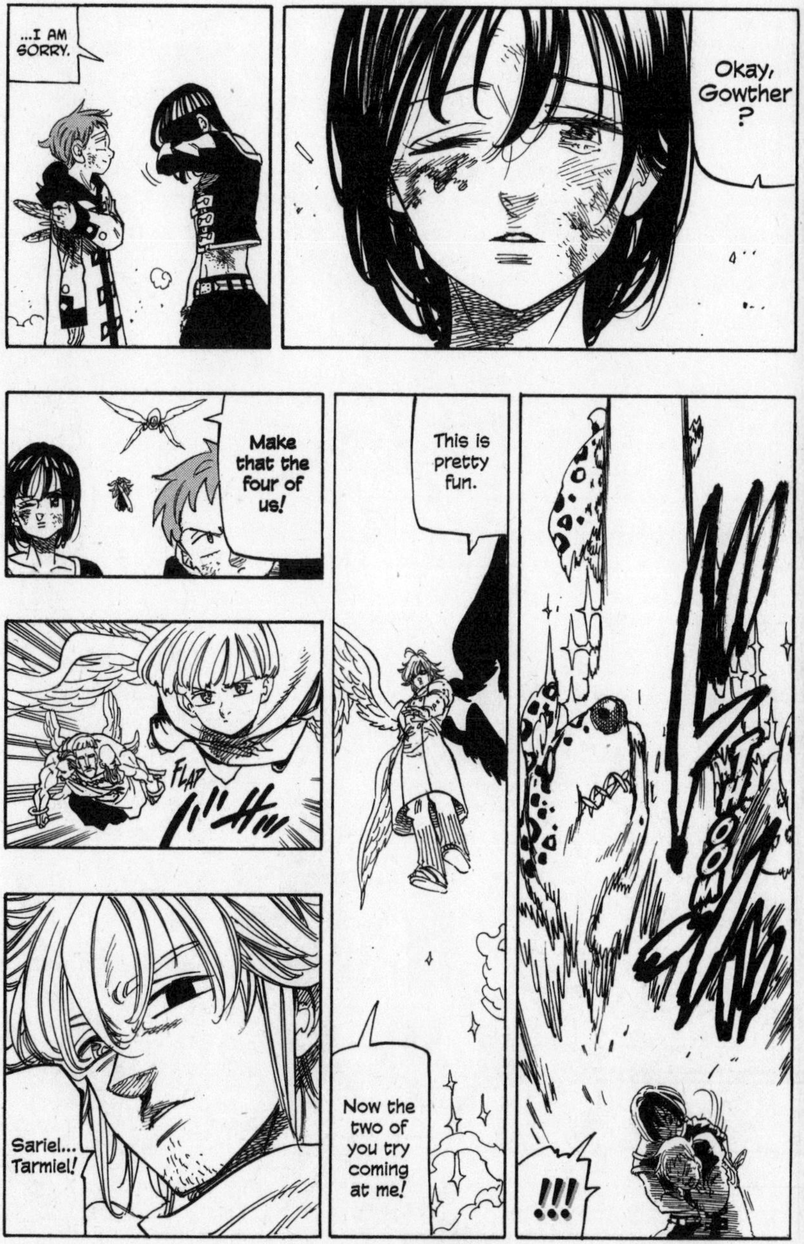

Okay, Gowther?
...I AM SORRY.
!!!
This is pretty fun.
Now the two of you try coming at me!
Make that the four of us!
FLAP
Sariel... Tarmiel!

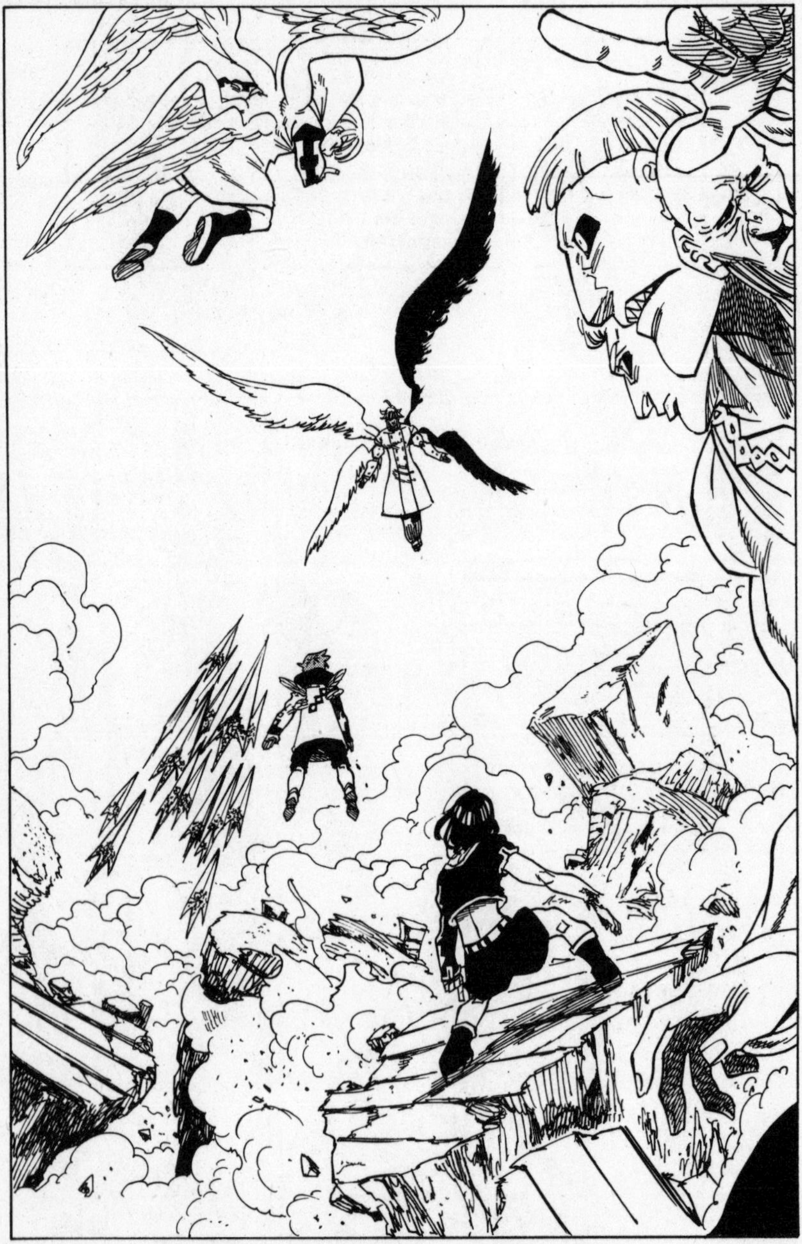

To Be Continued in Volume 34...

The Creatures of Purgatory

These are typical beasts of Purgatory that Meliodas explained to Ban. There's the dog(?) creature that Ban kills and uses to make his and Meliodas's clothing and weapons. Also featured are various initial designs for Hawk's older brother, Wild. For the record, Hawk and Wild are "pig-like-boar-like" Purgatory creatures. By no means are they pigs or boars. Cath is there in the lower right-hand corner because... that's right: He's also a creature of Purgatory.

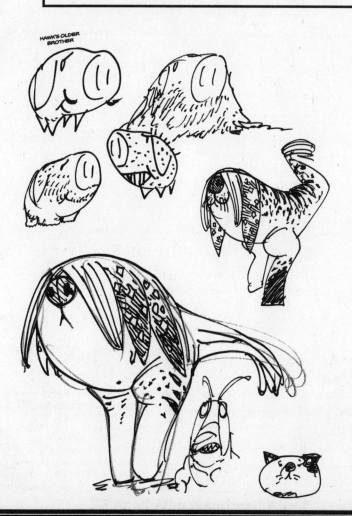

HAWK'S OLDER BROTHER

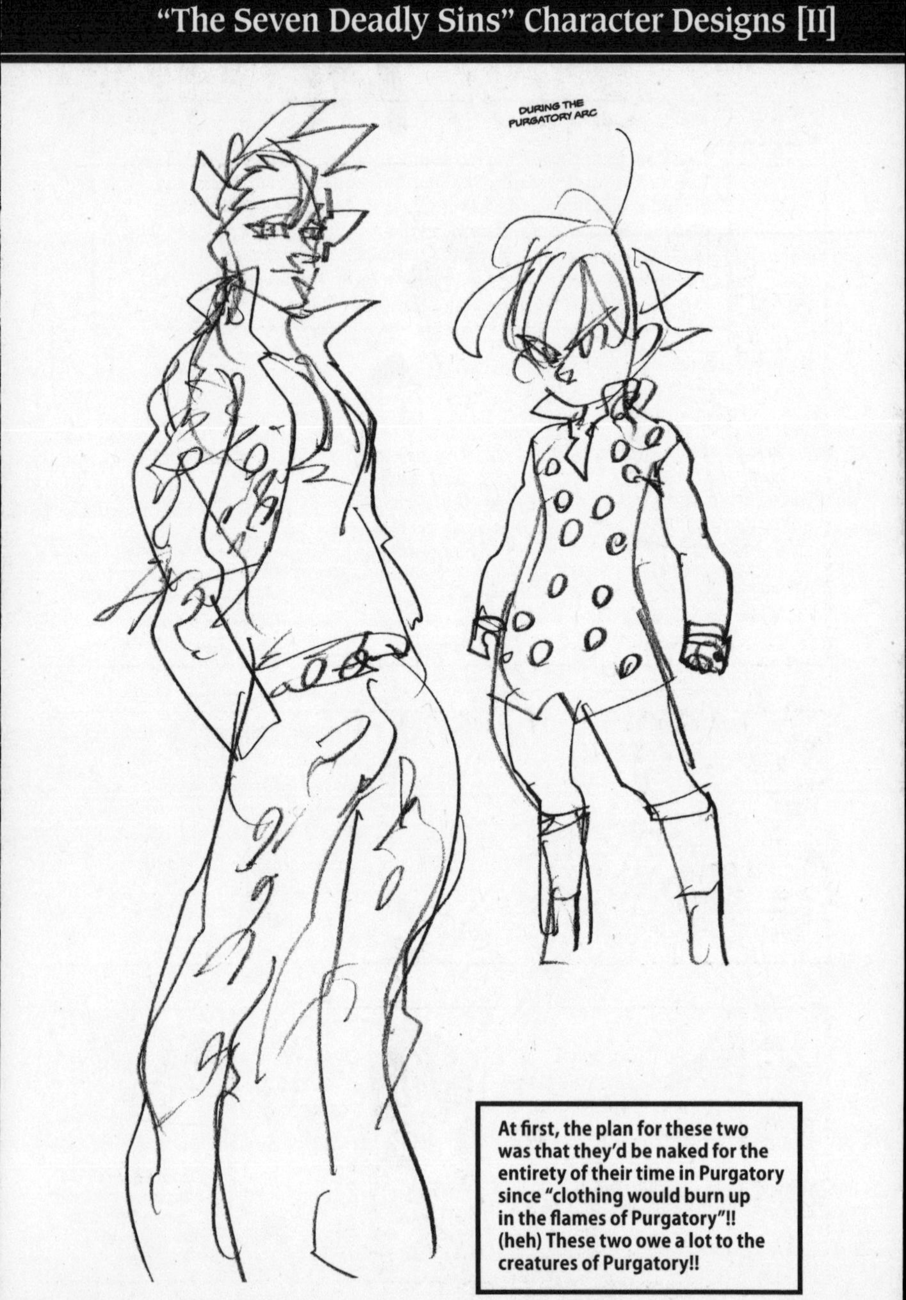
DURING THE PURGATORY ARC

At first, the plan for these two was that they'd be naked for the entirety of their time in Purgatory since "clothing would burn up in the flames of Purgatory"!! (heh) These two owe a lot to the creatures of Purgatory!!

A Special Essay for the Release of the The Seven Deadly Sins Movie

88% FICTION

Cast of Characters

Nakaba

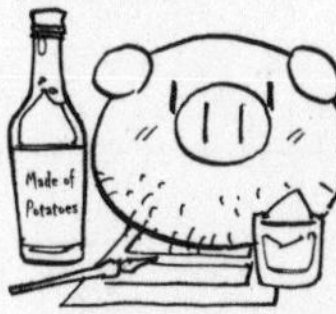
Made of Potatoes

A pig who turns into a worn-out washcloth every week while drawing manga. ...Which is to say, he's a manga artist. But it's sweet-potato shochu that keeps his body and soul afloat!!

Toshi

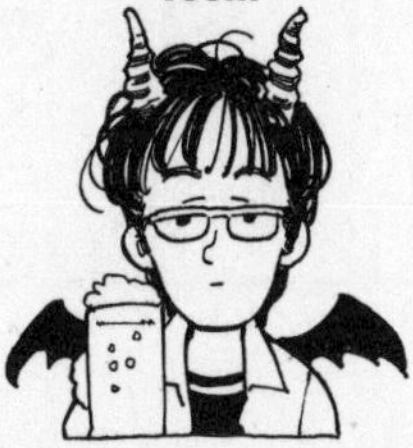

With his tendency to make unreasonable requests with a stoic expression on his face, he's the young editor feared as a Demon Lord by Y'moto. Nakaba Suzuki's chief editor. A beer drinker.

Y'moto

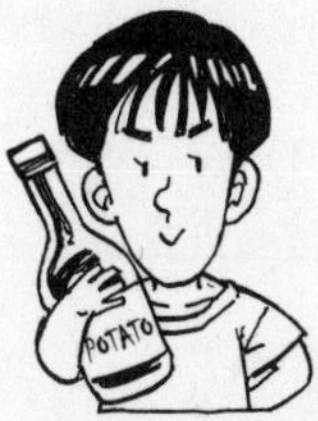
POTATO

An optimistic and naïve editor who only drinks sweet-potato shochu. Still hasn't been influenced by the darker side of the chief...or at least, he hopes not to be. He's Nakaba Suzuki's sub-editor.

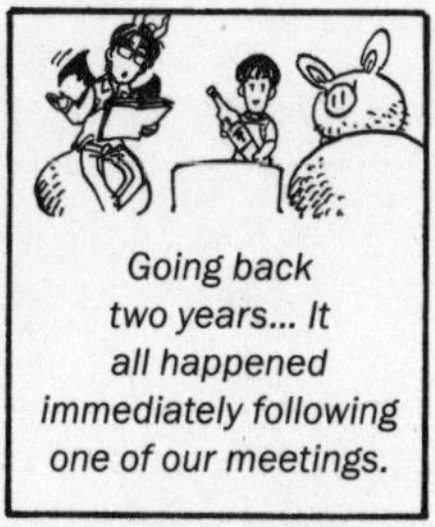
Going back two years... It all happened immediately following one of our meetings.

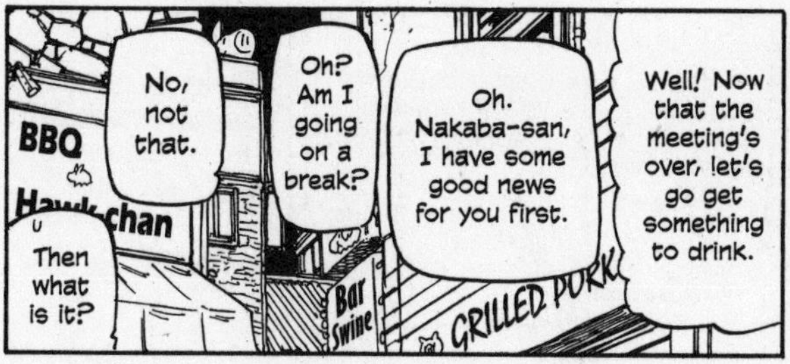
Well! Now that the meeting's over, let's go get something to drink.
Oh. Nakaba-san, I have some good news for you first.
Oh? Am I going on a break?
No, not that.
Then what is it?
BBQ Hawk-chan
Bar Swine
GRILLED PORK

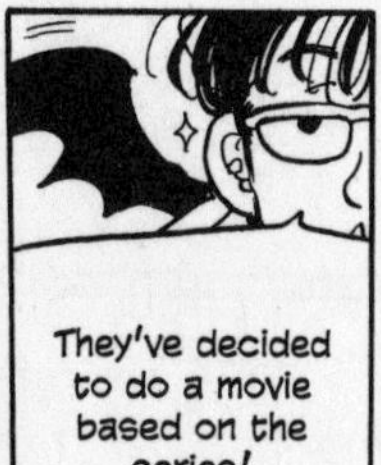
They've decided to do a movie based on the series!

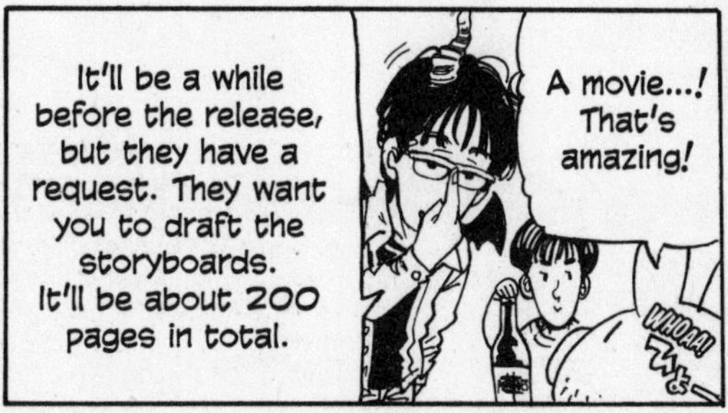
A movie...! That's amazing!
WHOA!
It'll be a while before the release, but they have a request. They want you to draft the storyboards. It'll be about 200 pages in total.

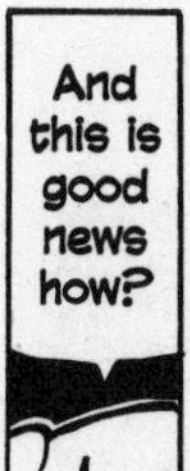
And this is good news how?

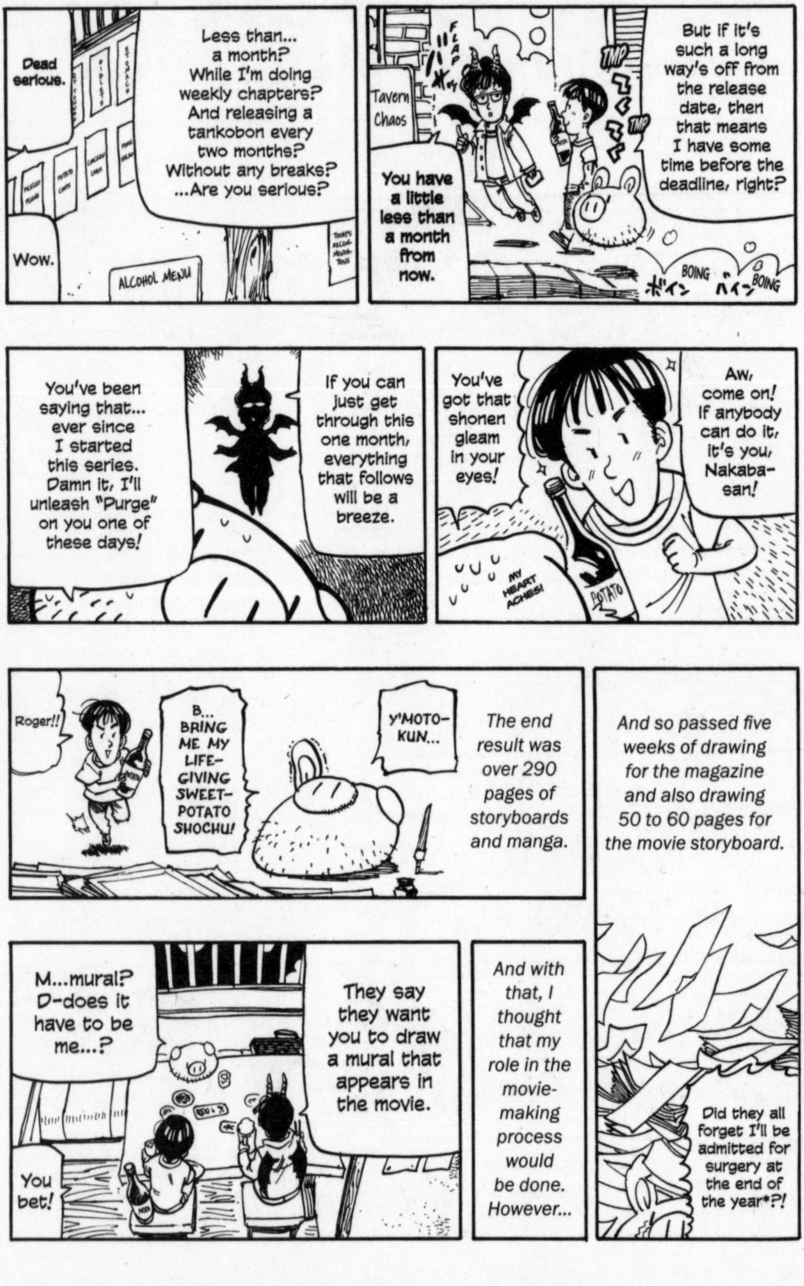
But if it's such a long way's off from the release date, then that means I have some time before the deadline, right?
TMP
TMP
FLAP
Tavern Chaos
You have a little less than a month from now.
BOING
BOING
Less than... a month? While I'm doing weekly chapters? And releasing a tankobon every two months? Without any breaks? ...Are you serious?
Dead serious.
Wow.
ALCOHOL MENU
Aw, come on! If anybody can do it, it's you, Nakaba-san!
You've got that shonen gleam in your eyes!
MY HEART ACHES!
POTATO
If you can just get through this one month, everything that follows will be a breeze.
You've been saying that... ever since I started this series. Damn it, I'll unleash "Purge" on you one of these days!
And so passed five weeks of drawing for the magazine and also drawing 50 to 60 pages for the movie storyboard.
Did they all forget I'll be admitted for surgery at the end of the year*?!
The end result was over 290 pages of storyboards and manga.
Y'MOTO-KUN...
B... BRING ME MY LIFE-GIVING SWEET-POTATO SHOCHU!
Roger!!
And with that, I thought that my role in the movie-making process would be done. However...
They say they want you to draw a mural that appears in the movie.
M...mural? D-does it have to be me...?
You bet!

* This was at the end of 2016. Now I'm all better!

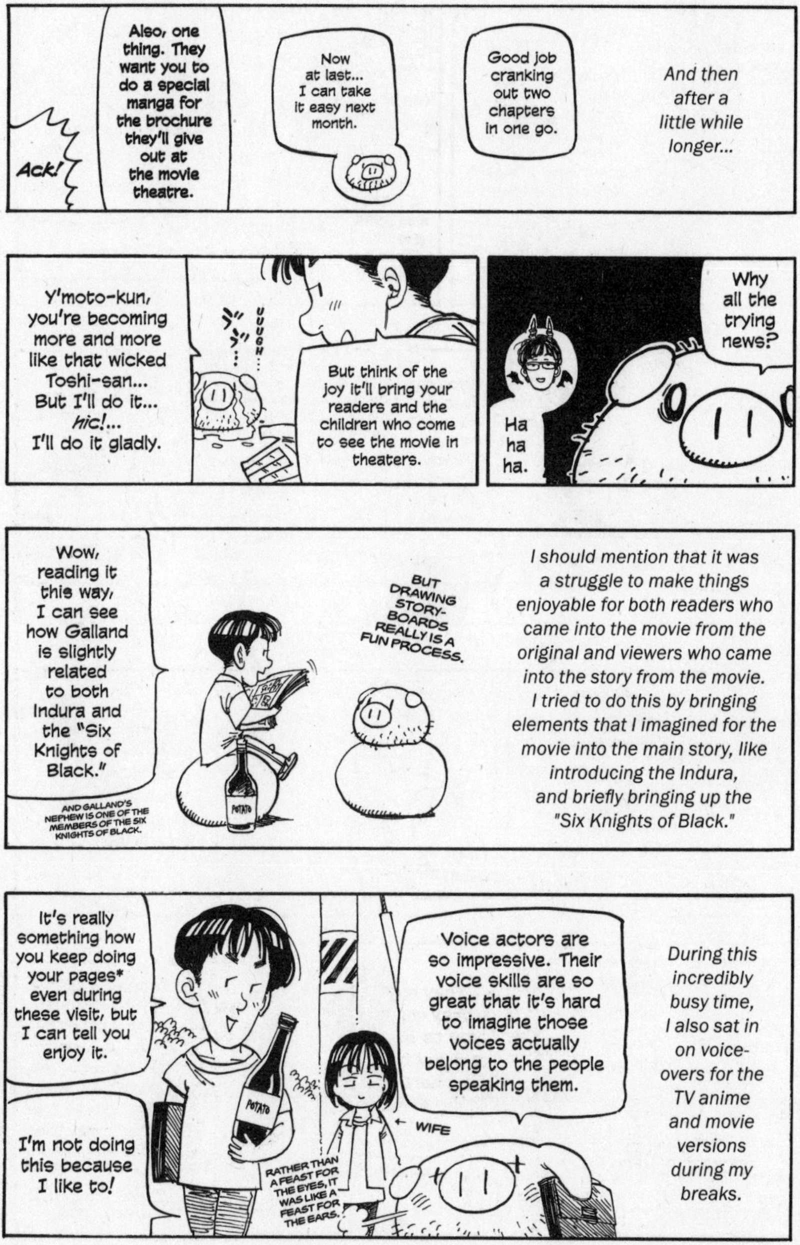
And then after a little while longer...
Good job cranking out two chapters in one go.
Now at last... I can take it easy next month.
Also, one thing. They want you to do a special manga for the brochure they'll give out at the movie theatre.
Ack!
Why all the trying news?
Ha ha ha.
But think of the joy it'll bring your readers and the children who come to see the movie in theaters.
UUUGH...
Y'moto-kun, you're becoming more and more like that wicked Toshi-san... But I'll do it... *hic!*... I'll do it gladly.
I should mention that it was a struggle to make things enjoyable for both readers who came into the movie from the original and viewers who came into the story from the movie. I tried to do this by bringing elements that I imagined for the movie into the main story, like introducing the Indura, and briefly bringing up the "Six Knights of Black."
BUT DRAWING STORY-BOARDS REALLY IS A FUN PROCESS.
POTATO
Wow, reading it this way, I can see how Galland is slightly related to both Indura and the "Six Knights of Black."
AND GALLAND'S NEPHEW IS ONE OF THE MEMBERS OF THE SIX KNIGHTS OF BLACK.
During this incredibly busy time, I also sat in on voice-overs for the TV anime and movie versions during my breaks.
Voice actors are so impressive. Their voice skills are so great that it's hard to imagine those voices actually belong to the people speaking them.
WIFE
RATHER THAN A FEAST FOR THE EYES, IT WAS LIKE A FEAST FOR THE EARS.
It's really something how you keep doing your pages* even during these visit, but I can tell you enjoy it.
POTATO
I'm not doing this because I like to!

* I would be drawing even in the studio. Otherwise, I'd be late!

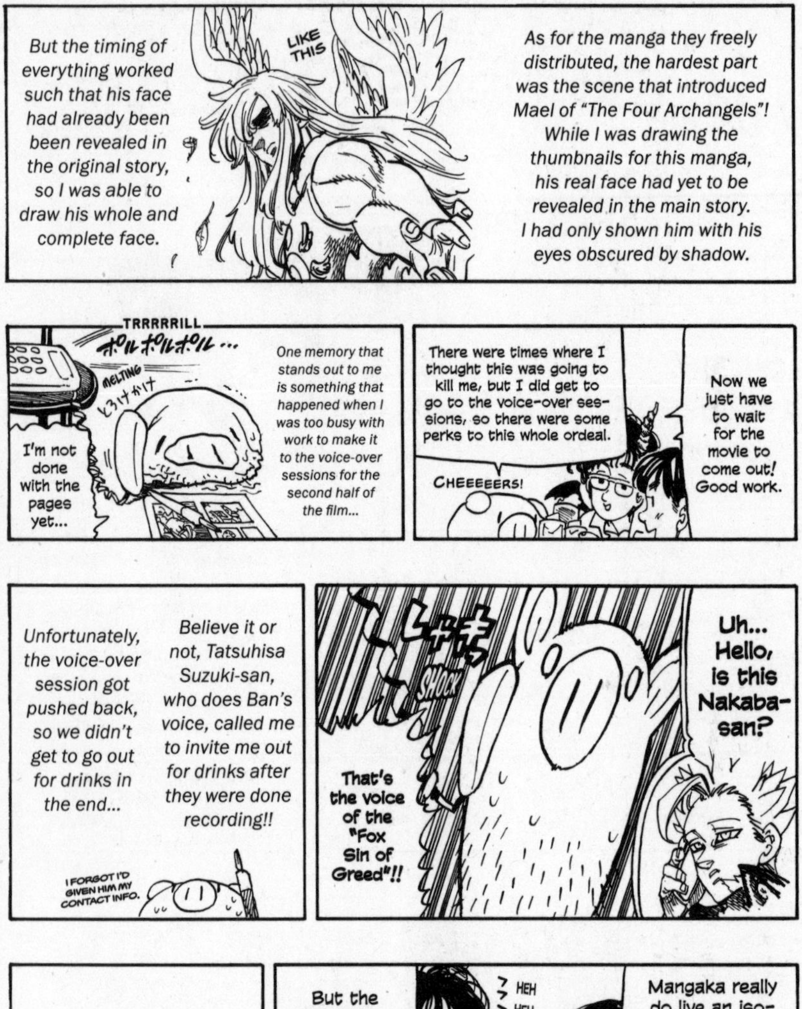
As for the manga they freely distributed, the hardest part was the scene that introduced Mael of "The Four Archangels"! While I was drawing the thumbnails for this manga, his real face had yet to be revealed in the main story. I had only shown him with his eyes obscured by shadow.
LIKE THIS
But the timing of everything worked such that his face had already been been revealed in the original story, so I was able to draw his whole and complete face.
Now we just have to wait for the movie to come out! Good work.
There were times where I thought this was going to kill me, but I did get to go to the voice-over sessions, so there were some perks to this whole ordeal.
CHEEEEERS!
One memory that stands out to me is something that happened when I was too busy with work to make it to the voice-over sessions for the second half of the film...
TRRRRRILL
ポルポルポル…
MELTING
とろけかけ
I'm not done with the pages yet...
Uh... Hello, is this Nakaba-san?
SHOCK
That's the voice of the "Fox Sin of Greed"!!
Believe it or not, Tatsuhisa Suzuki-san, who does Ban's voice, called me to invite me out for drinks after they were done recording!!
Unfortunately, the voice-over session got pushed back, so we didn't get to go out for drinks in the end...
I FORGOT I'D GIVEN HIM MY CONTACT INFO.
Mangaka really do live an isolated existence, so the opportunity to go out and drink with voice actors and others who live in a different world can be a really stimulating experience.
HEH HEH HEH
But the truth is that you're usually too shy to talk to people unless you drink, Nakaba-san.
And so (?), I hope you will enjoy "The Seven Deadly Sins The Movie"!! I can't wait to go see it myself as a regular moviegoer!!

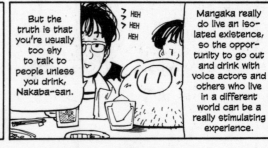

THE END

"THE SEVEN DEADLY SINS" ILLUSTRATION CORNER

"THE DRAWING KNIGHTHOOD" SPACE

Be sure to include your name and address on your postcard!

M = H = E = D = B = K = G = Mer = Esc = El = J =

SPECIAL PRIZE

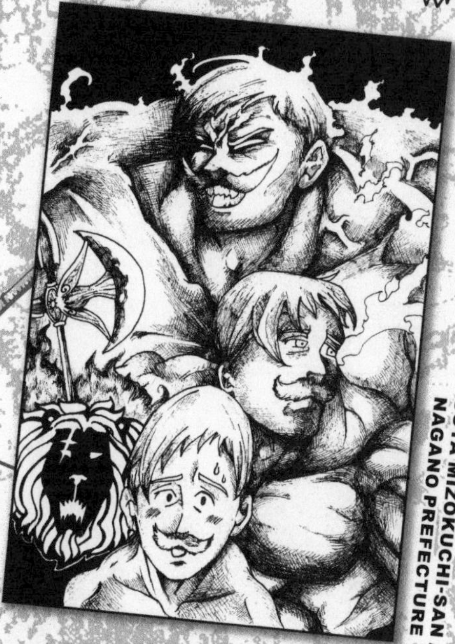

SOTA MIZOKUCHI-SAN / NAGANO PREFECTURE

"I am THE strongest and—the one and only!"

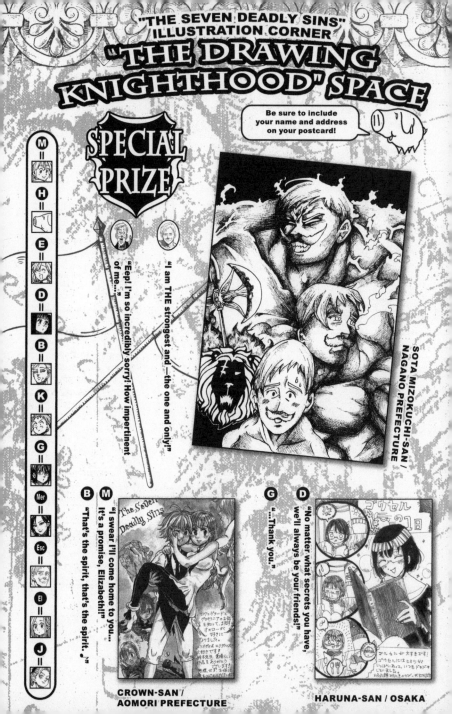

"Eep! I'm so incredibly sorry! How impertinent of me..."

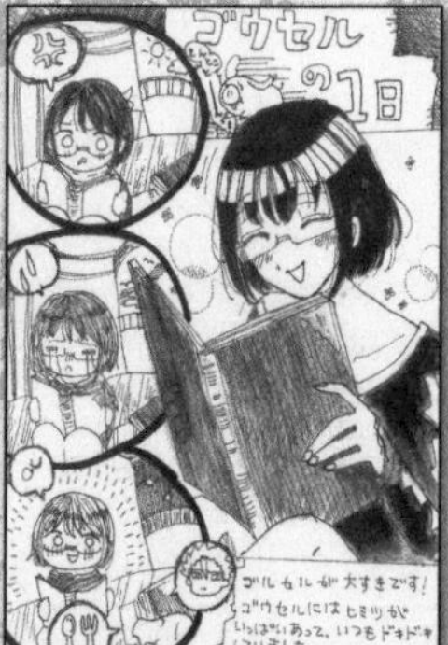

HARUNA-SAN / OSAKA

D "No matter what secrets you have, we'll always be your friends!"

G "...Thank you."

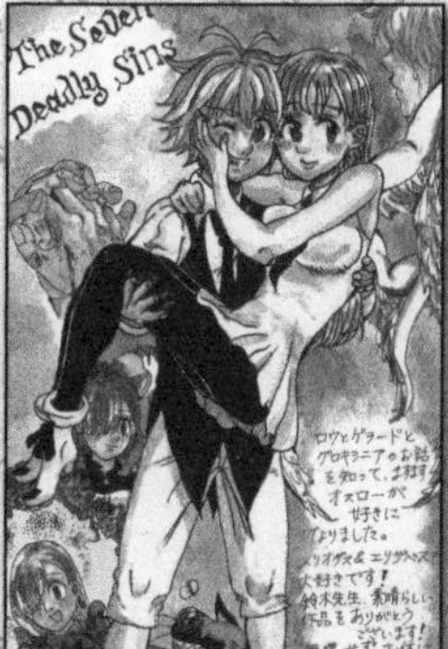
The Seven Deadly Sins

CROWN-SAN / AOMORI PREFECTURE

M "I swear I'll come home to you... It's a promise, Elizabeth!!"

B "That's the spirit, that's the spirit. ♪"

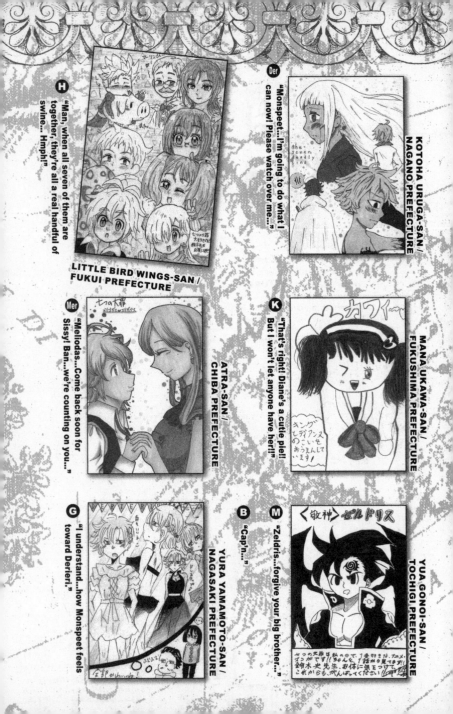

KOTOHA URUGA-SAN / NAGANO PREFECTURE

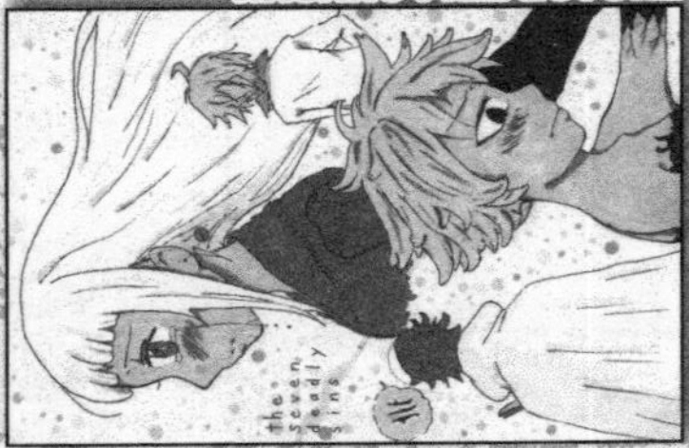
the seven deadly sins

Der "Monspeet...I'm going to do what I can now! Please watch over me..."

MANA UKAWA-SAN / FUKUSHIMA PREFECTURE

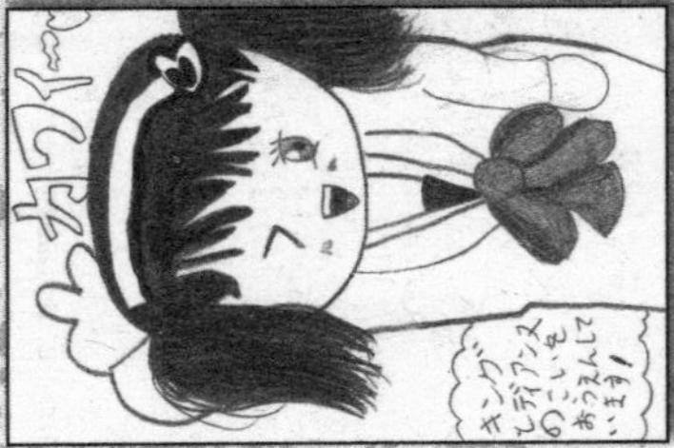

K "That's right! Diane's a cutie pie!! But I won't let anyone have her!!"

YUA GONOI-SAN / TOCHIGI PREFECTURE

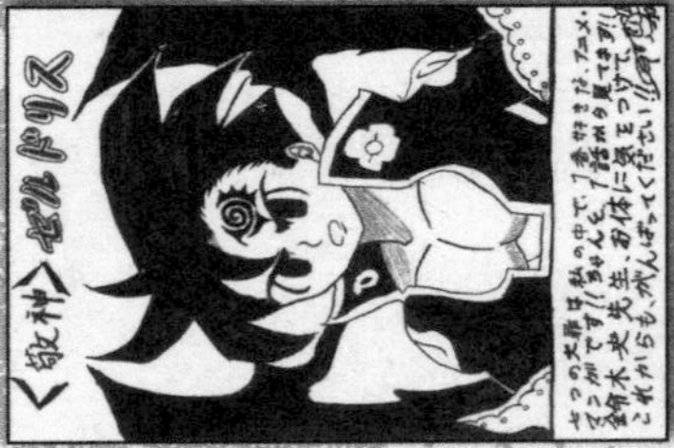

M "Zeldris...forgive your big brother..."

B "Cap'n..."

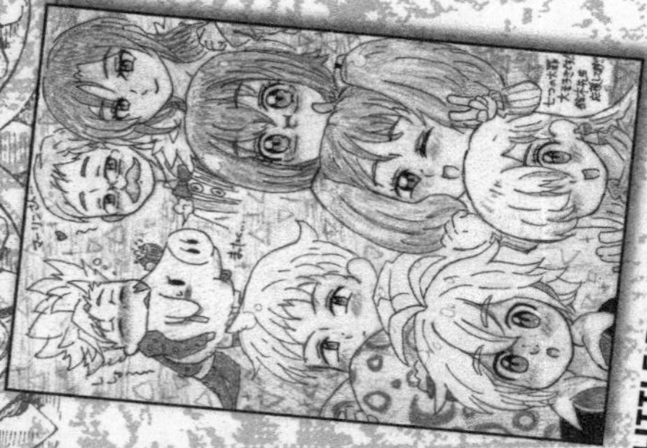

LITTLE BIRD WINGS-SAN / FUKUI PREFECTURE

H "Man, when all seven of them are together, they're all a real handful of swine... Hmph!"

ATRA-SAN / CHIBA PREFECTURE

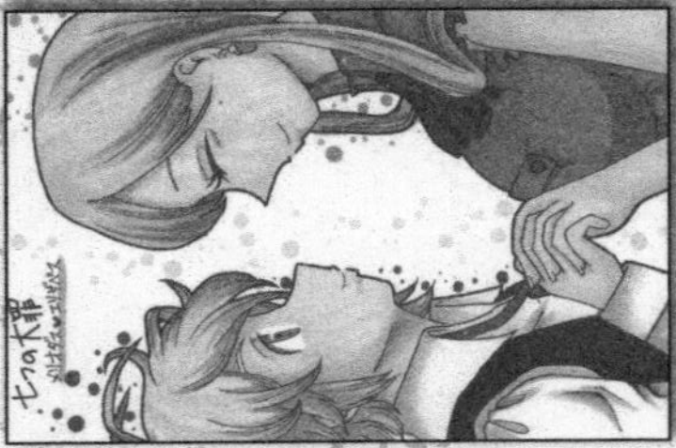

Mer "Meliodas...Come back soon for Sissy! Ban...we're counting on you..."

YURA YAMAMOTO-SAN / NAGASAKI PREFECTURE

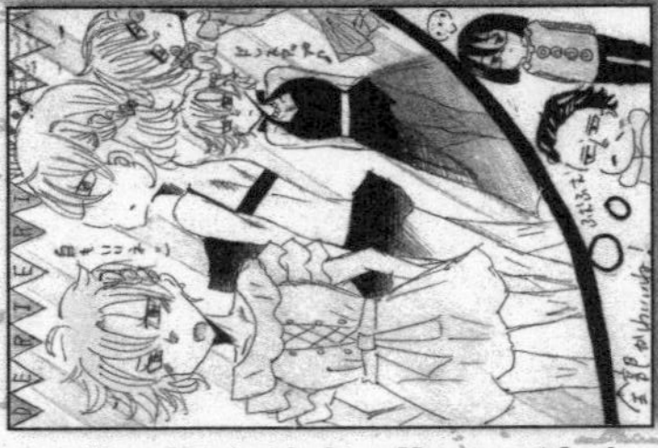

G "I understand...how Monspeet feels toward Derieri."

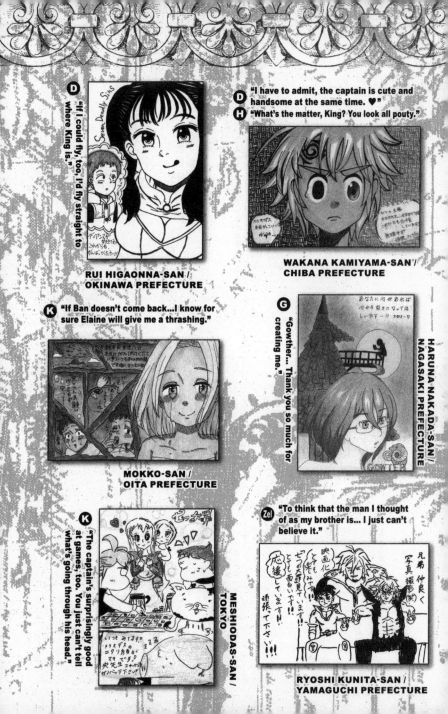

D "If I could fly, too, I'd fly straight to where King is."

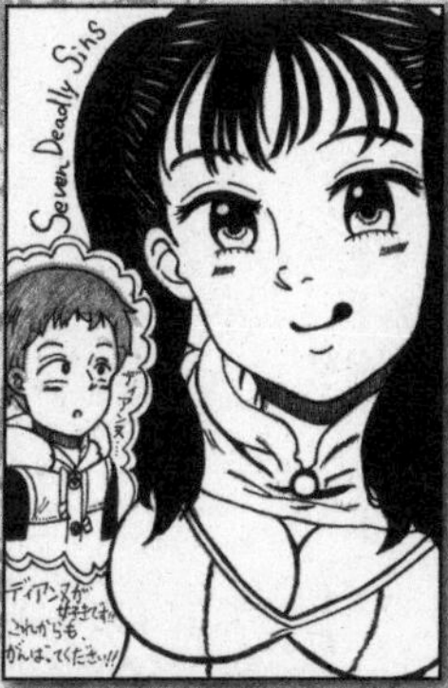
Seven Deadly Sins

RUI HIGAONNA-SAN /
OKINAWA PREFECTURE

D "I have to admit, the captain is cute and handsome at the same time. ♥"

H "What's the matter, King? You look all pouty."

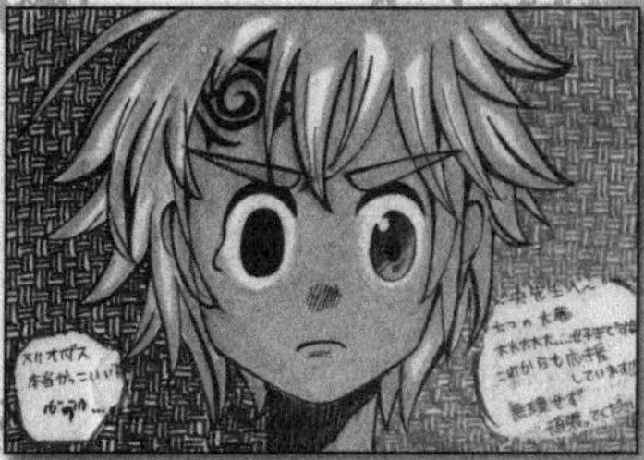

WAKANA KAMIYAMA-SAN /
CHIBA PREFECTURE

K "If Ban doesn't come back...I know for sure Elaine will give me a thrashing."

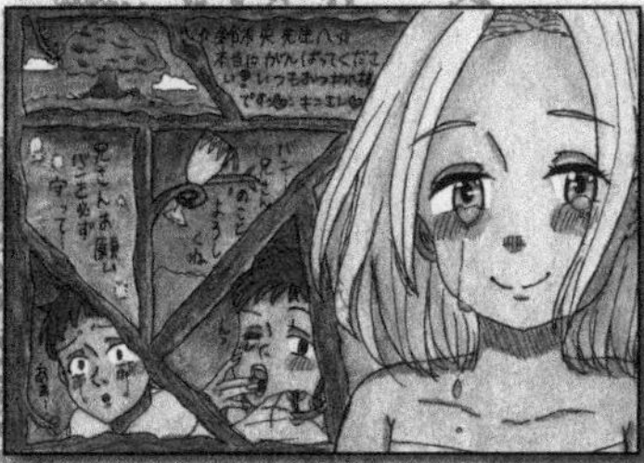

MOKKO-SAN /
OITA PREFECTURE

G "Gowther... Thank you so much for creating me."

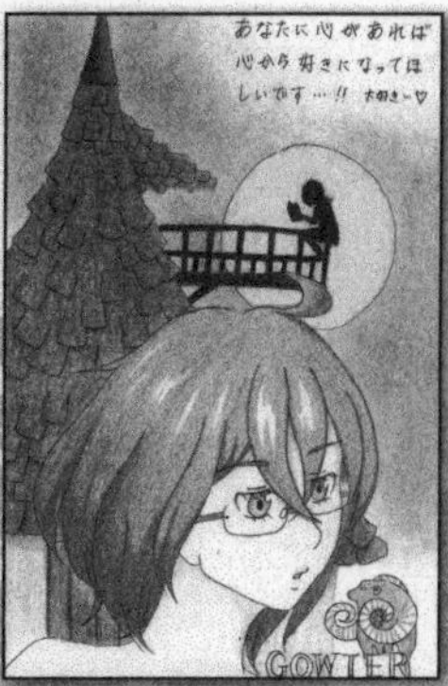
GOWTER

HARUNA NAKADA-SAN /
NAGASAKI PREFECTURE

K "The captain's surprisingly good at games, too. You just can't tell what's going through his head."

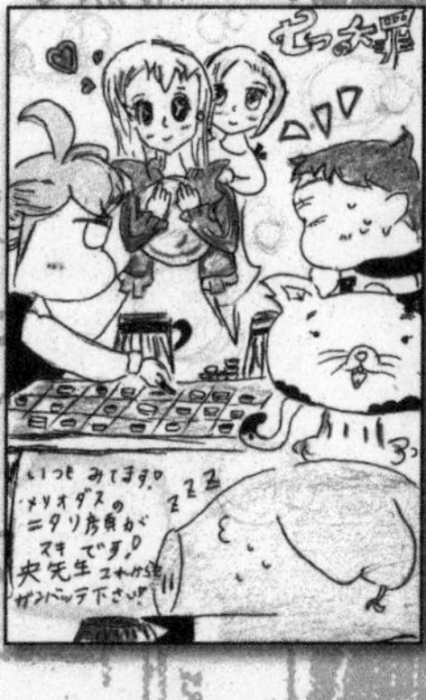

MESHIODAS-SAN /
TOKYO

Zel "To think that the man I thought of as my brother is... I just can't believe it."

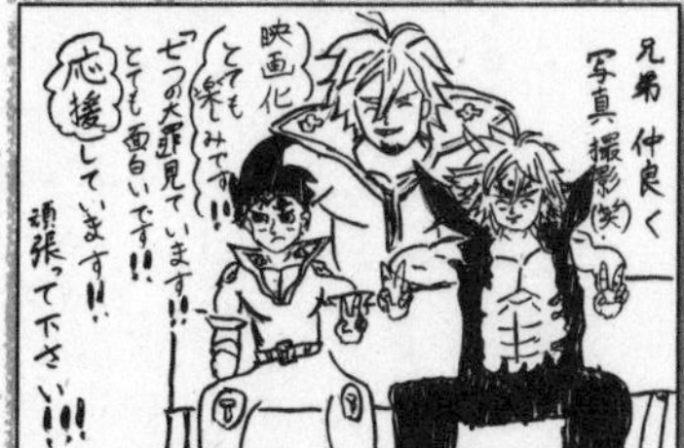
応援しています!!
頑張って下さい!!!

RYOSHI KUNITA-SAN /
YAMAGUCHI PREFECTURE

MAI SAZAKI-SAN / FUKUSHIMA PREFECTURE

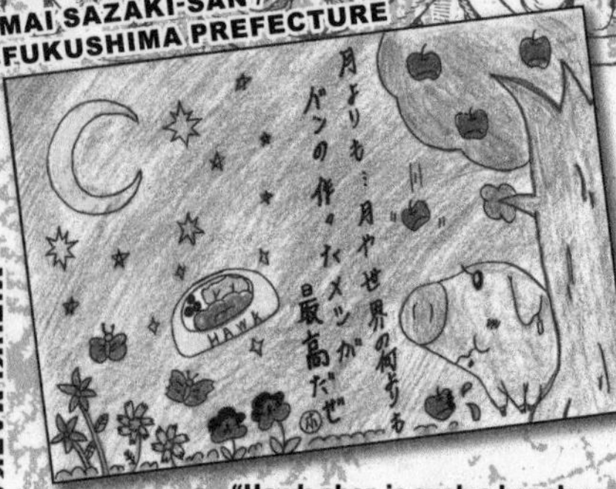
月よりも…月や世界の何よりも
バンの作ったメシが
最高だぜ
HAWK

E "Hawk-chan is such a hopeless romantic!"

D "Yeah, but I don't know about the subject of that poem..."

MIZUKI MAEKAWA-SAN / IBARAKI PREFECTURE

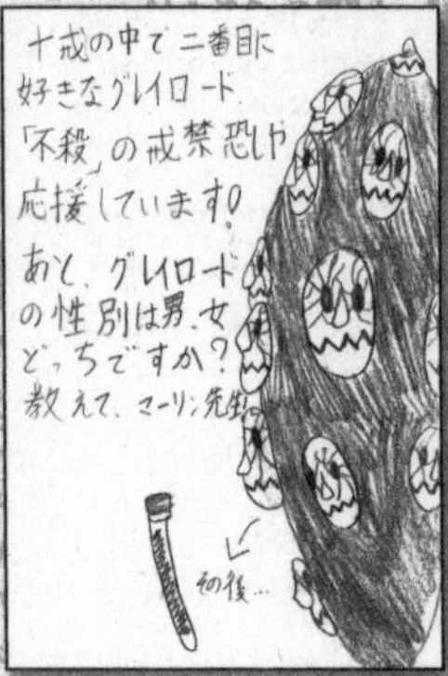
十戒の中で二番目に
好きなグレイロード
「不殺」の戒禁恐いけど
応援しています!
あと、グレイロード
の性別は男、女
どっちですか?
教えて、マーリン先生!
その後…

H "So, which is your favorite swine of 'The Ten Commandments'?"

Mer "For the record, Gray Road is a she."

YO HOSHIZUKI-SAN / SAGA PREFECTURE

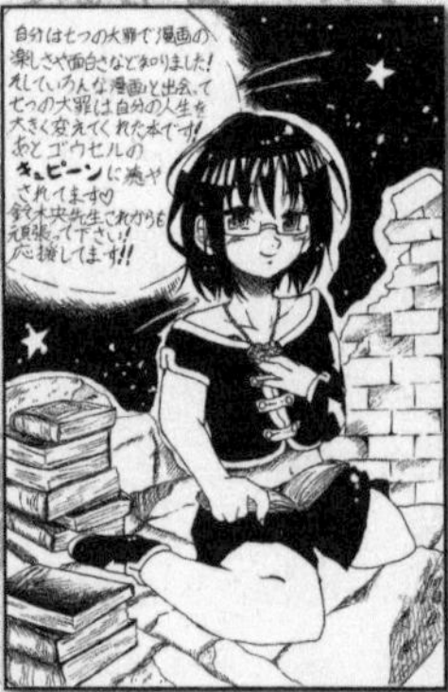
自分は七つの大罪で漫画の
楽しさや面白さなど知りました!
そしていろんな漫画と出会って
七つの大罪は自分の人生を
大きく変えてくれた本です!
あとゴウセルの
キュピーンに癒や
されてます♡
鈴木央先生これからも
頑張って下さい!
応援してます!!

G "Shwiiing. ☆"

Esc "Huh? Wh...What happened?"

G "That's supposed to heal you..."

Wild "Mild!! Wait for meeee! Arooooo!"

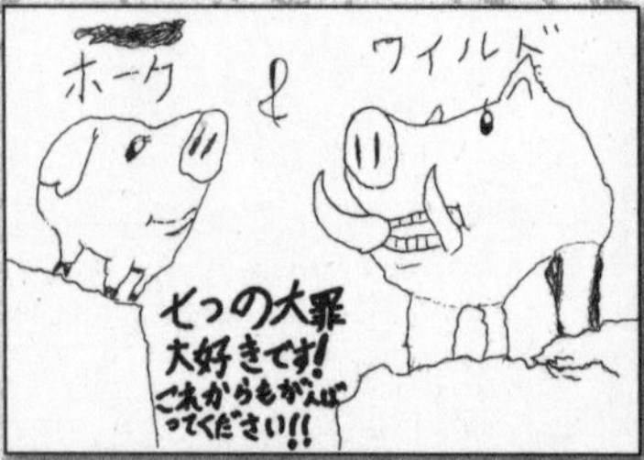
ホーク
&
ワイルド
七つの大罪
大好きです!
これからもがんばってください!!

MUSHROOM CHANNEL-SAN / SHIZUOKA PREFECTURE

H "I'm also a star on the big screen! Go and see me!"

K "What's the 'big screen'?"

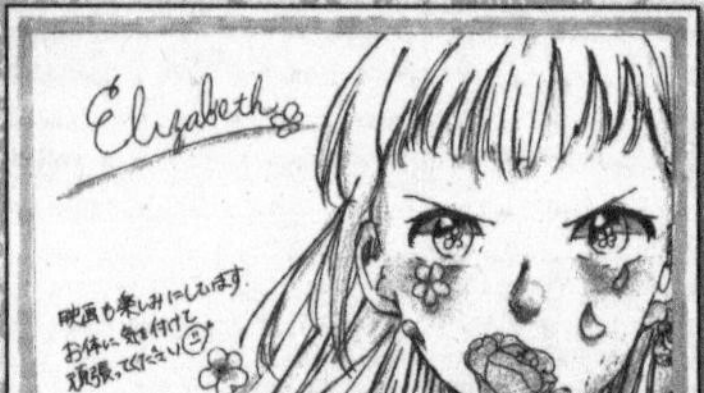
Elizabeth
映画も楽しみにしています。
お体に気を付けて
頑張ってください

PINO-SAN / HYOGO PREFECTURE

HINATA TAKASHIRA-SAN / SHIGA PREFECTURE

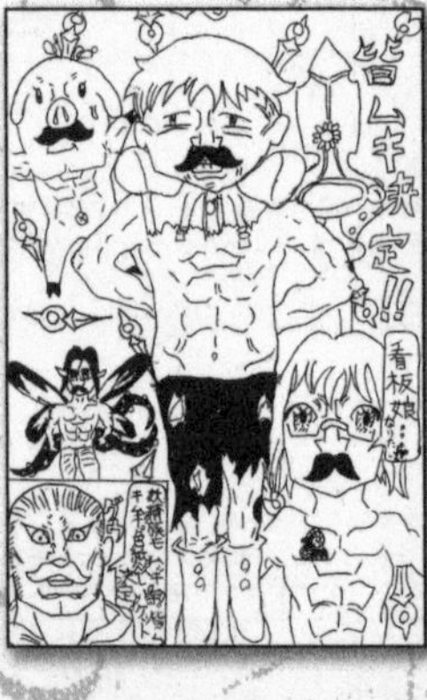
皆ムキ決定!!

K "Gyaaah! It's a nightmare!!"

G "That is correct, King. This is 'Nightmare Teller'! Shwiiing."

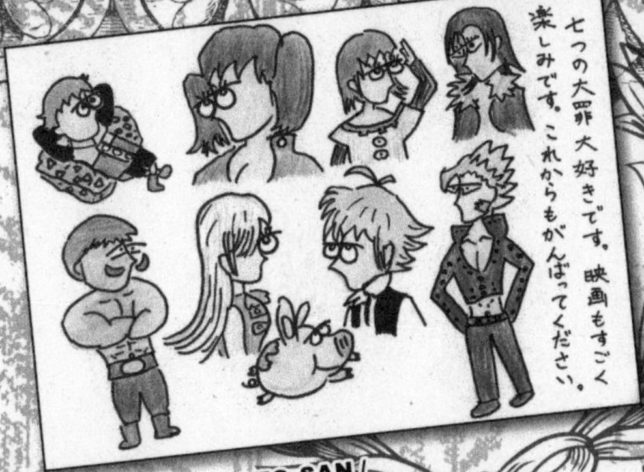
七つの大罪大好きです。映画もすごく楽しみです。これからもがんばってください。

SASUKE AKIMOTO-SAN / HOKKAIDO

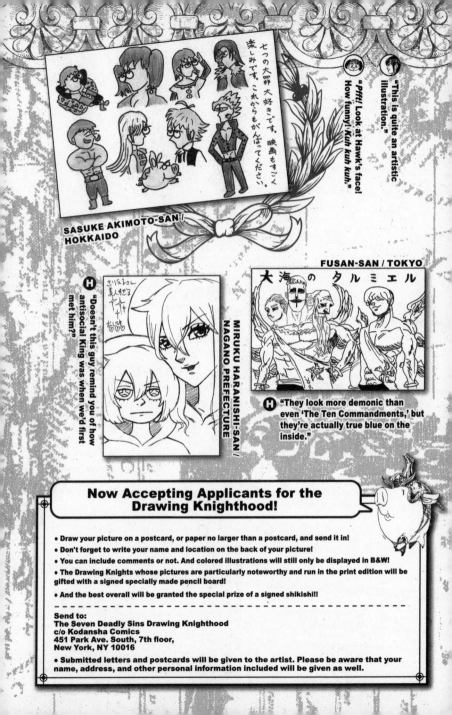

"This is quite an artistic illustration."

"*Pfft!* Look at Hawk's face! How funny! *Kuh kuh kuh.*"

FUSAN-SAN / TOKYO

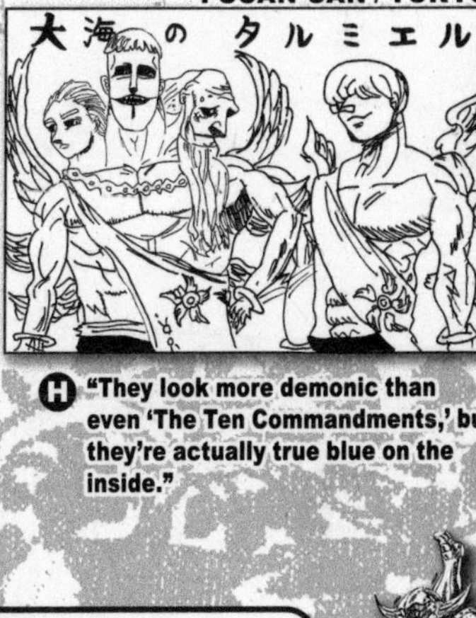
大海のタルミエル

"They look more demonic than even 'The Ten Commandments,' but they're actually true blue on the inside."

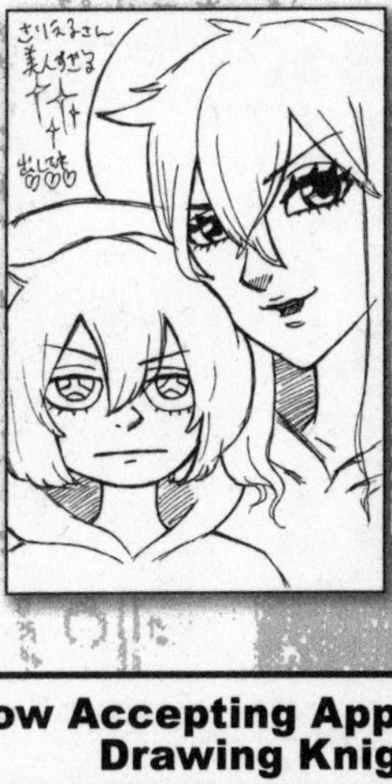

MIRUKU HARANISHI-SAN / NAGANO PREFECTURE

"Doesn't this guy remind you of how antisocial King was when we'd first met him?"

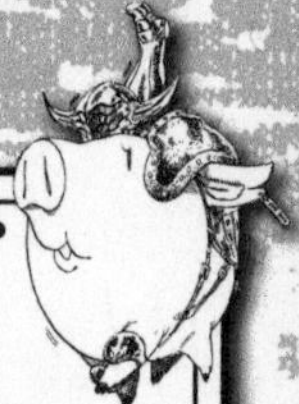

Now Accepting Applicants for the Drawing Knighthood!

- Draw your picture on a postcard, or paper no larger than a postcard, and send it in!
- Don't forget to write your name and location on the back of your picture!
- You can include comments or not. And colored illustrations will still only be displayed in B&W!
- The Drawing Knights whose pictures are particularly noteworthy and run in the print edition will be gifted with a signed specially made pencil board!
- And the best overall will be granted the special prize of a signed shikishi!

Send to:
The Seven Deadly Sins Drawing Knighthood
c/o Kodansha Comics
451 Park Ave. South, 7th floor,
New York, NY 10016

- Submitted letters and postcards will be given to the artist. Please be aware that your name, address, and other personal information included will be given as well.

A new series from the creator of *Soul Eater*, the megahit manga and anime seen on Toonami!

"Fun and lively... a great start!"
-Adventures in Poor Taste

FIRE FORCE

By Atsushi Ohkubo

The city of Tokyo is plagued by a deadly phenomenon: spontaneous human combustion! Luckily, a special team is there to quench the inferno: The Fire Force! The fire soldiers at Special Fire Cathedral 8 are about to get a unique addition. Enter Shinra, a boy who possesses the power to run at the speed of a rocket, leaving behind the famous "devil's footprints" (and destroying his shoes in the process). Can Shinra and his colleagues discover the source of this strange epidemic before the city burns to ashes?